MW00649470

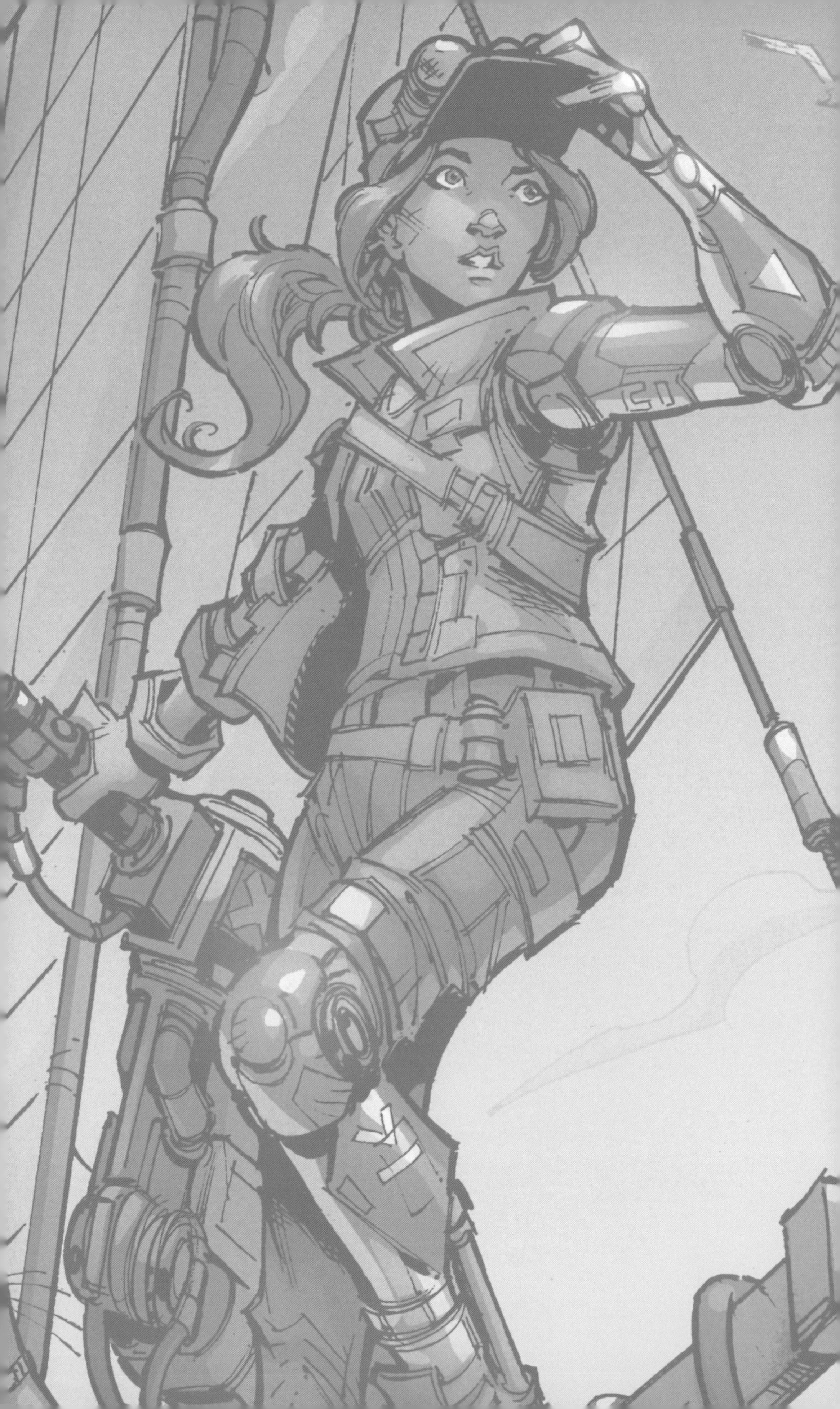

maybe Someday

edited by
Eric Palicki,
Matt Miner &
Tyler Chin-Tanner

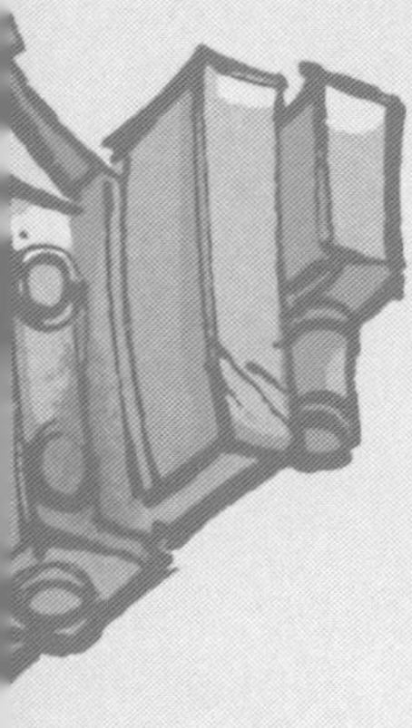

cover illustration
line art:
Max Dunbar

color art:
Espen Grundetjern

logo and
cover design:
Tim Daniel

interior design:
Pete Carlsson

A Wave Blue World

Tyler Chin-Tanner: Co-Publisher
Wendy Chin-Tanner: Co-Publisher
Justin Zimmerman: Director of Operations and Media
Pete Carlsson: Production Designer
Erin Beasley: Sales Manager
Jesse Post: Book Publicist
Hazel Newlevant: Social Media Coordinator

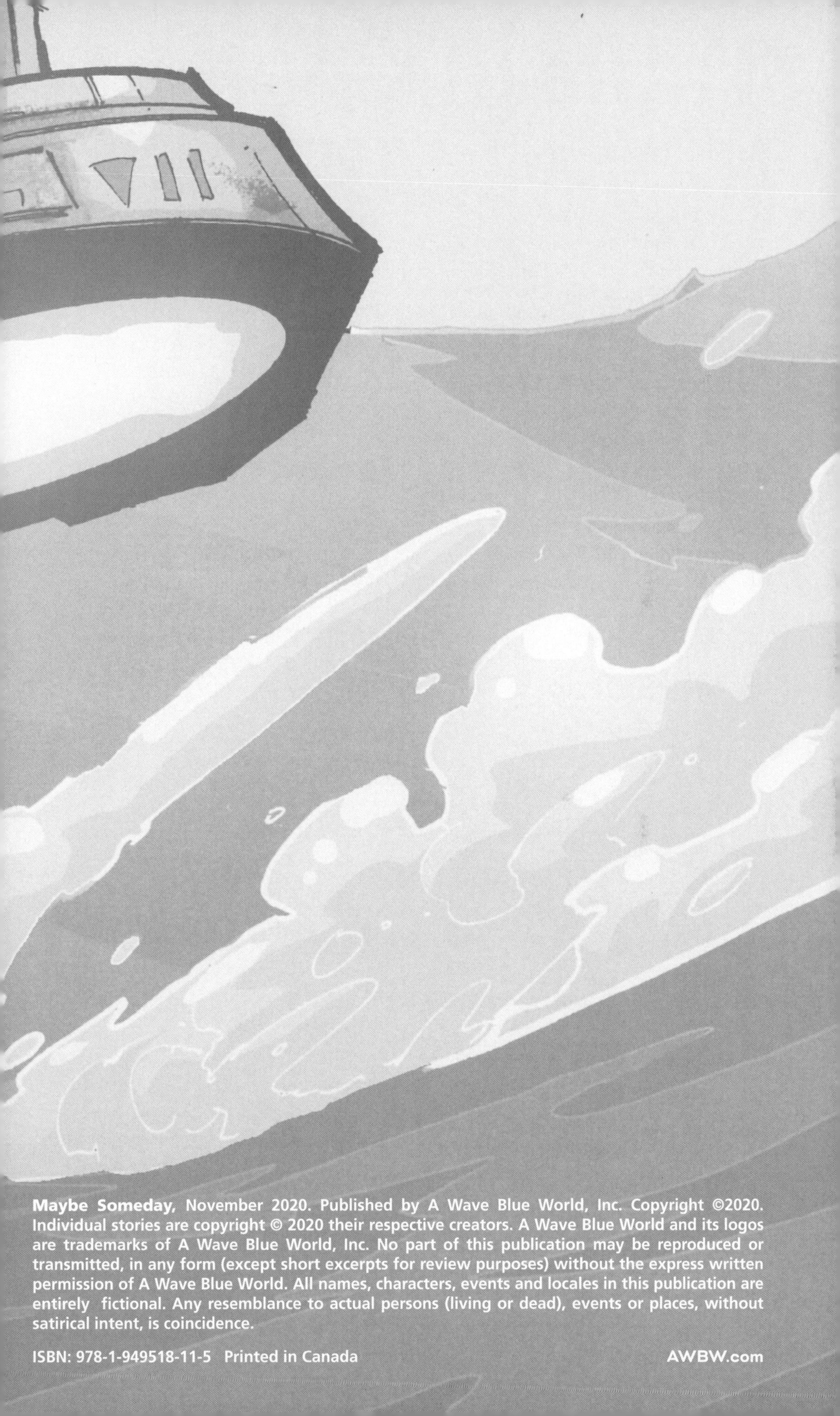

ISBN: 978-1-949518-11-5 Printed in Canada

AWBW.com

Table of Contents

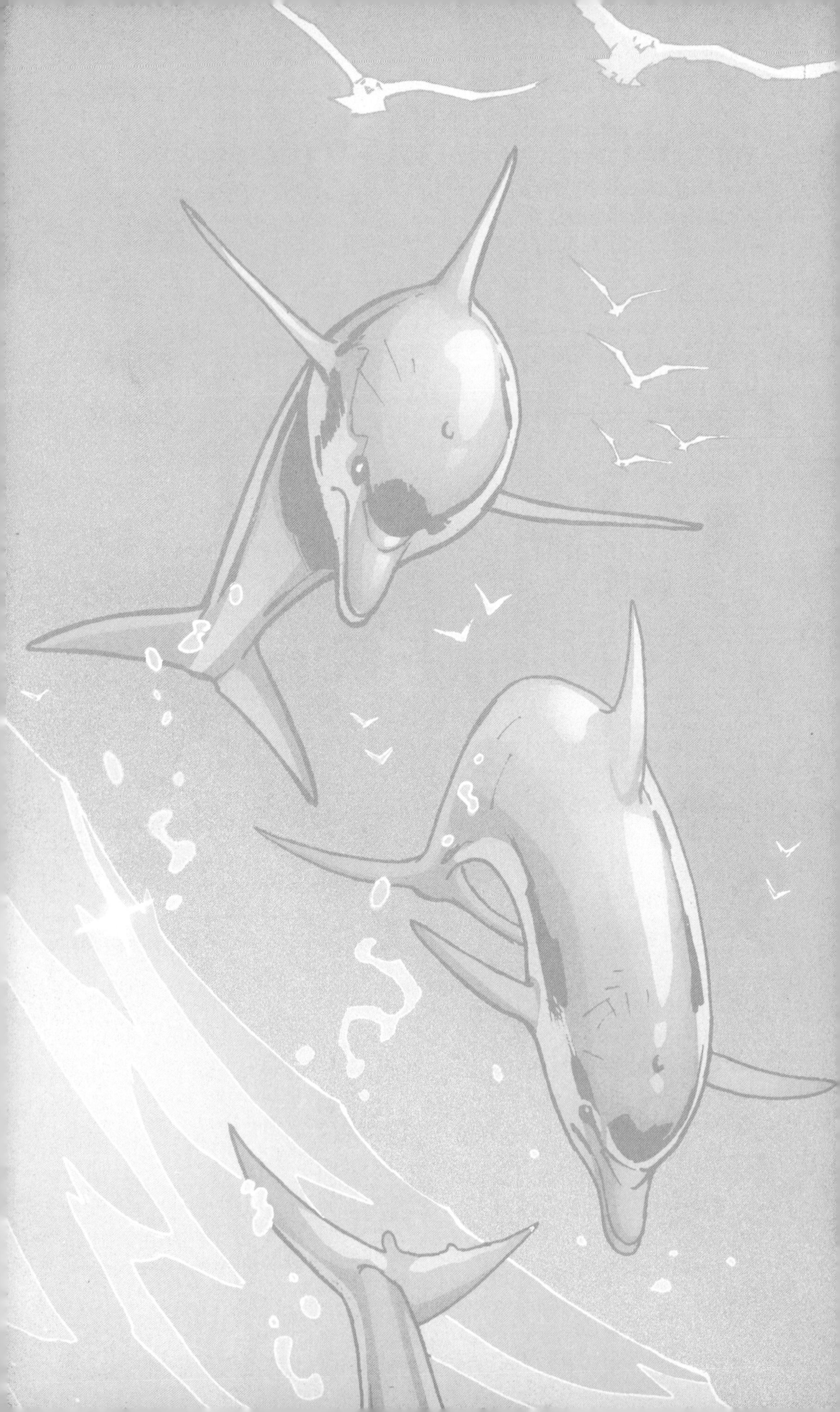

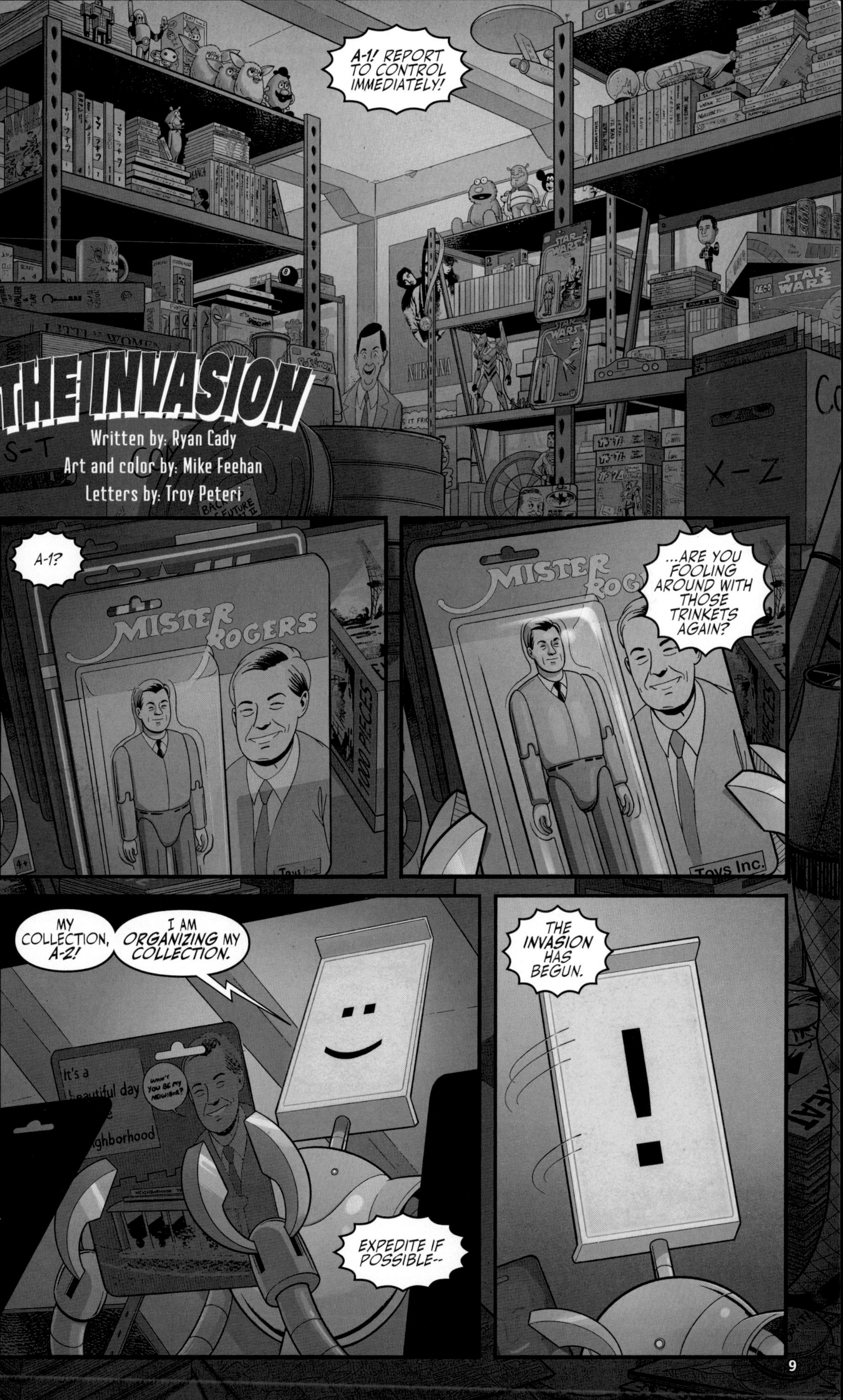
A-1! REPORT TO CONTROL IMMEDIATELY!
THE INVASION
Written by: Ryan Cady
Art and color by: Mike Feehan
Letters by: Troy Peteri
A-1?
MISTER ROGERS
...ARE YOU FOOLING AROUND WITH THOSE TRINKETS AGAIN?
Toys Inc.
MY COLLECTION, A-2!
I AM ORGANIZING MY COLLECTION.
EXPEDITE IF POSSIBLE--
THE INVASION HAS BEGUN.

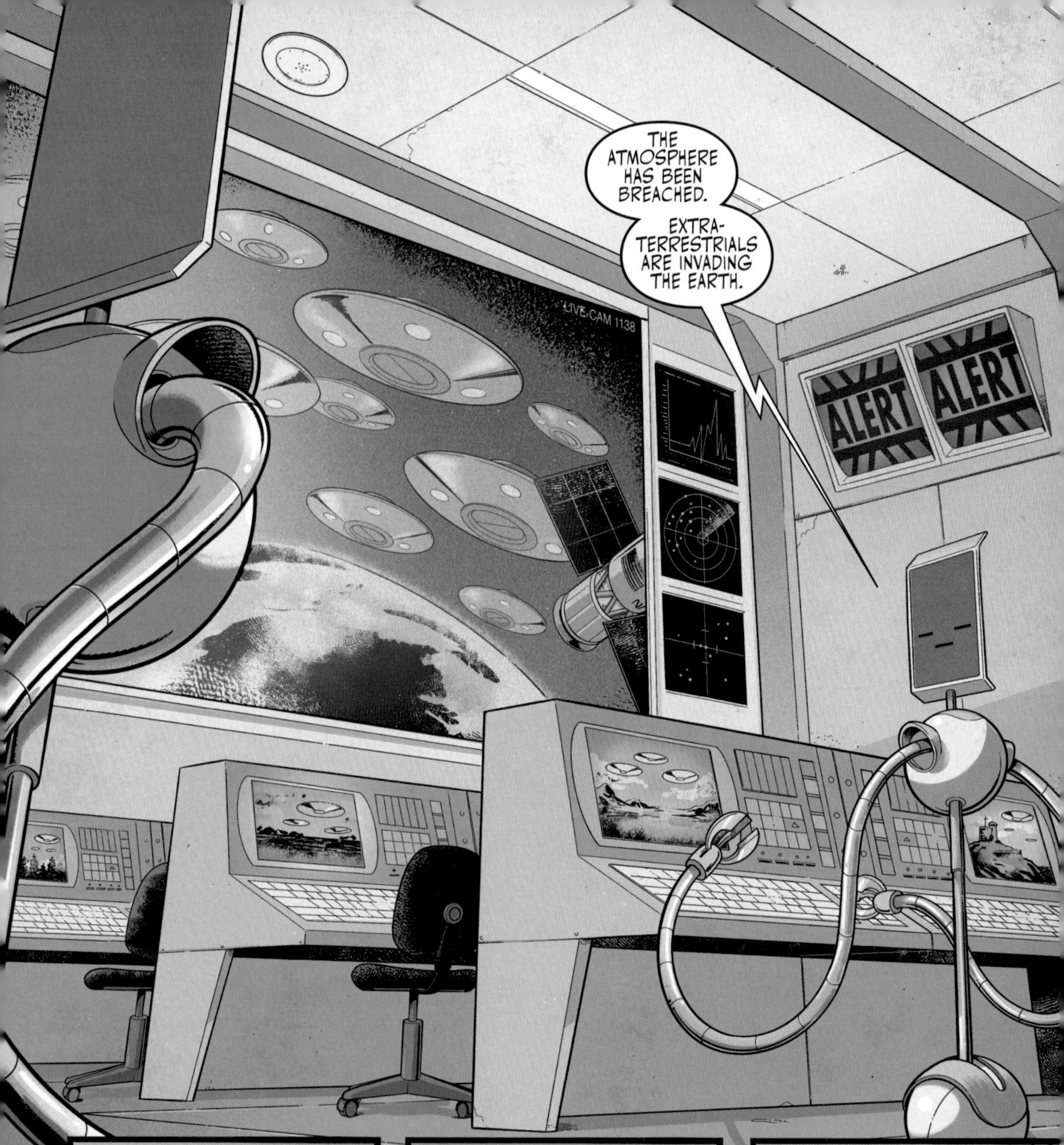
THE ATMOSPHERE HAS BEEN BREACHED.
EXTRA-TERRESTRIALS ARE INVADING THE EARTH.
LIVE-CAM 1138
ALERT
ALERT

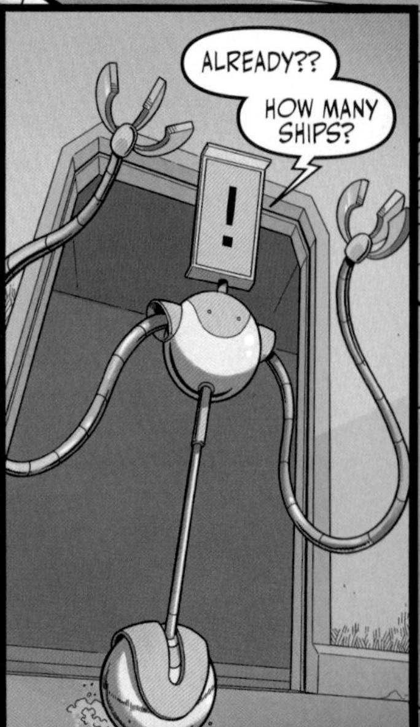
ALREADY??
HOW MANY SHIPS?
!

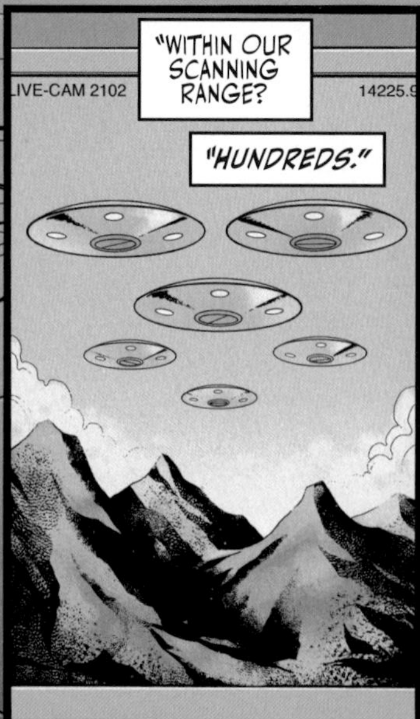
"WITHIN OUR SCANNING RANGE?
"HUNDREDS."
LIVE-CAM 2102

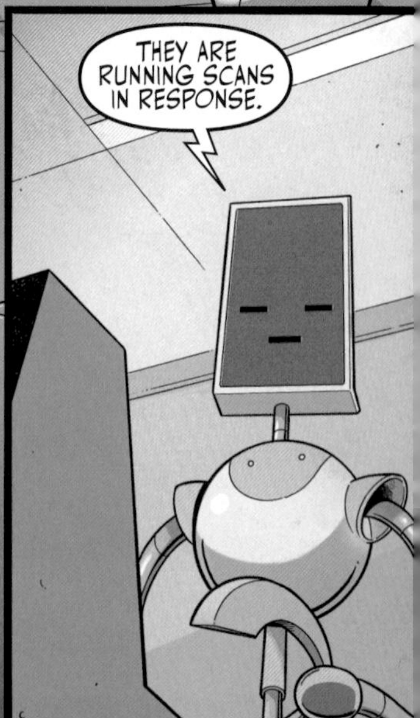
THEY ARE RUNNING SCANS IN RESPONSE.

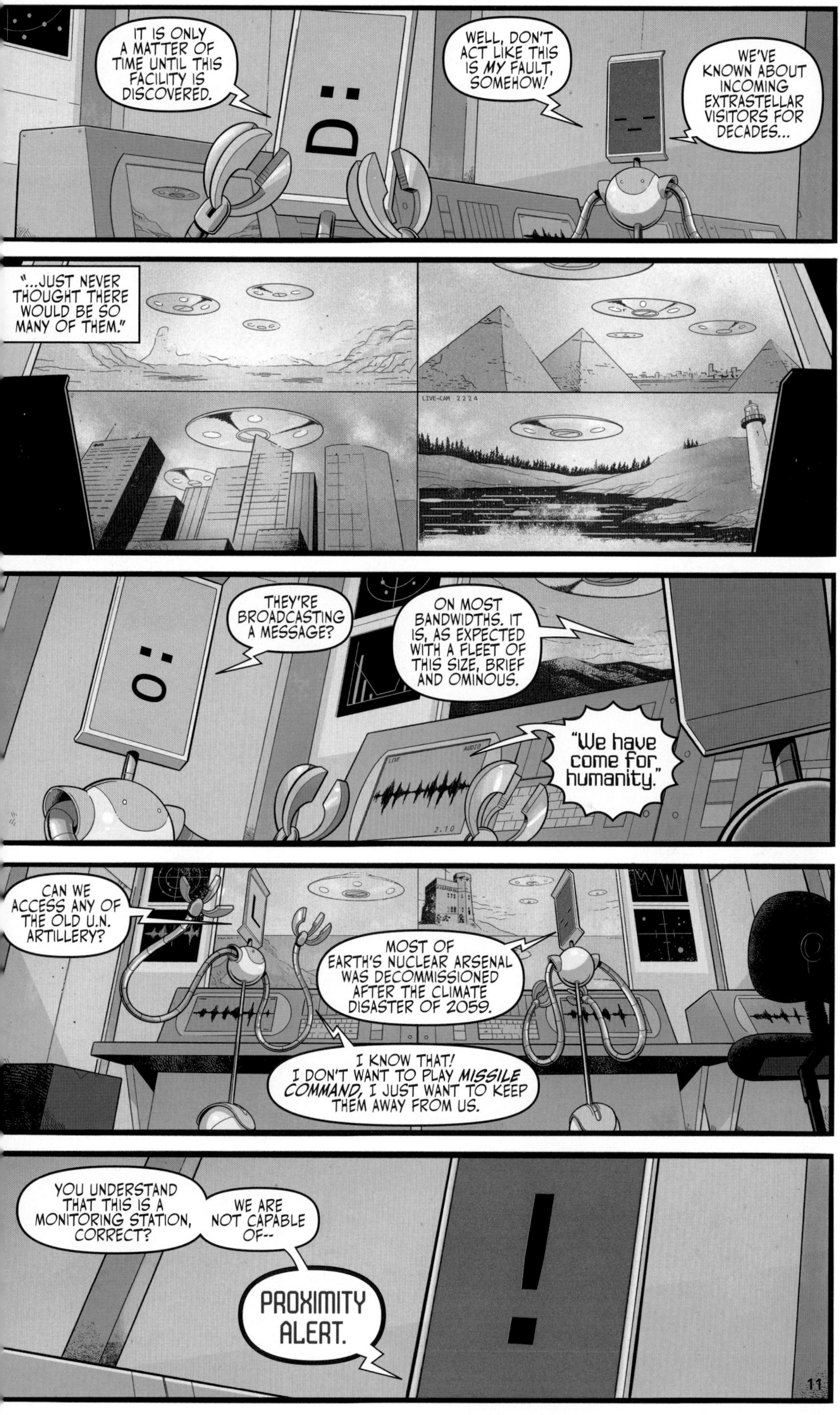
IT IS ONLY A MATTER OF TIME UNTIL THIS FACILITY IS DISCOVERED.
WELL, DON'T ACT LIKE THIS IS *MY* FAULT, SOMEHOW!
WE'VE KNOWN ABOUT INCOMING EXTRASTELLAR VISITORS FOR DECADES...
"...JUST NEVER THOUGHT THERE WOULD BE SO MANY OF THEM."
LIVE-CAM 2224
THEY'RE BROADCASTING A MESSAGE?
ON MOST BANDWIDTHS. IT IS, AS EXPECTED WITH A FLEET OF THIS SIZE, BRIEF AND OMINOUS.
"We have come for humanity."
CAN WE ACCESS ANY OF THE OLD U.N. ARTILLERY?
MOST OF EARTH'S NUCLEAR ARSENAL WAS DECOMMISSIONED AFTER THE CLIMATE DISASTER OF 2059.
I KNOW THAT! I DON'T WANT TO PLAY *MISSILE COMMAND,* I JUST WANT TO KEEP THEM AWAY FROM US.
YOU UNDERSTAND THAT THIS IS A MONITORING STATION, CORRECT?
WE ARE NOT CAPABLE OF--
PROXIMITY ALERT.
!

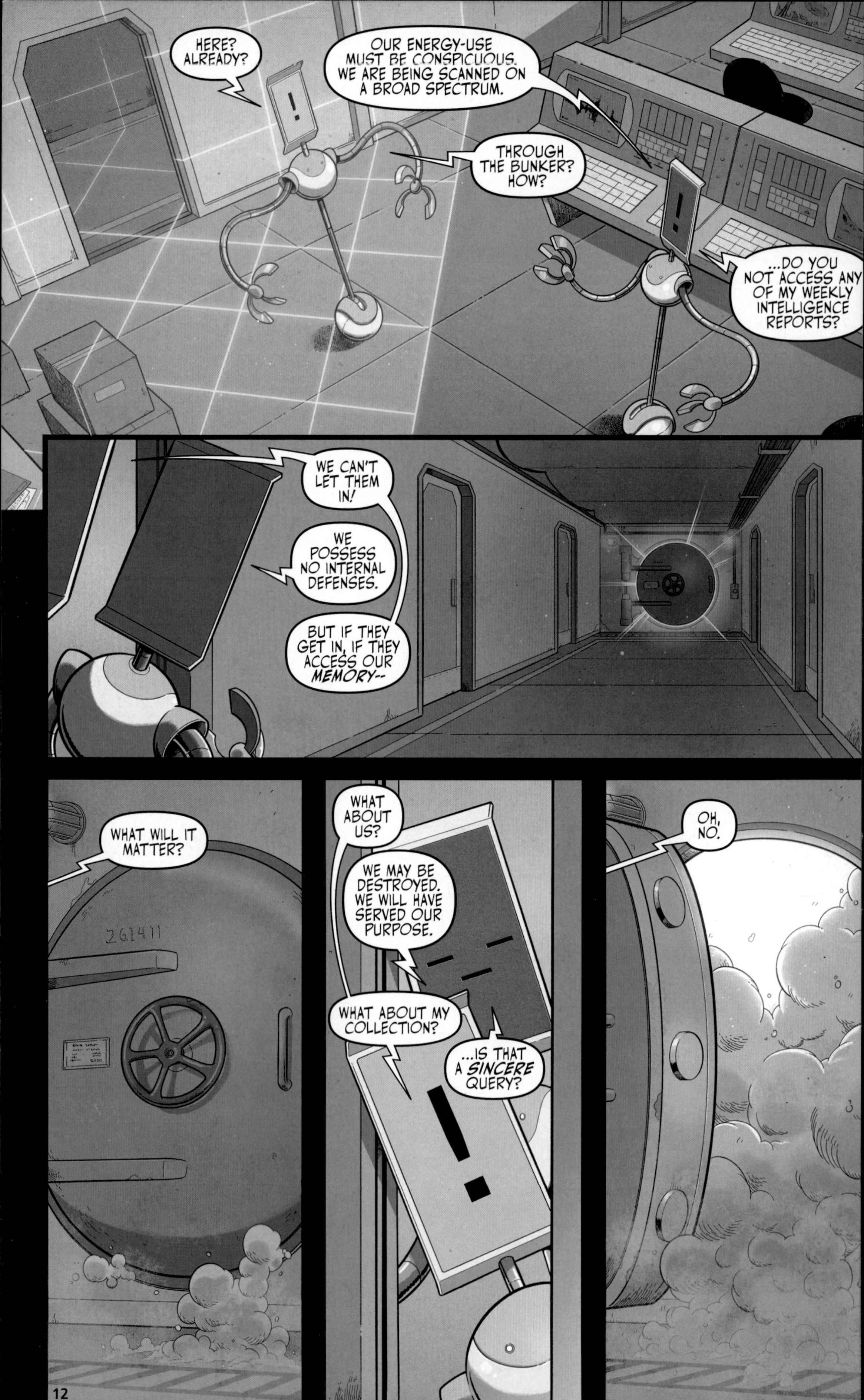
HERE? ALREADY?
OUR ENERGY-USE MUST BE CONSPICUOUS. WE ARE BEING SCANNED ON A BROAD SPECTRUM.
THROUGH THE BUNKER? HOW?
...DO YOU NOT ACCESS ANY OF MY WEEKLY INTELLIGENCE REPORTS?
WE CAN'T LET THEM IN!
WE POSSESS NO INTERNAL DEFENSES.
BUT IF THEY GET IN, IF THEY ACCESS OUR *MEMORY*--
WHAT WILL IT MATTER?
WHAT ABOUT US?
WE MAY BE DESTROYED. WE WILL HAVE SERVED OUR PURPOSE.
WHAT ABOUT MY COLLECTION?
...IS THAT A *SINCERE* QUERY?
OH, NO.

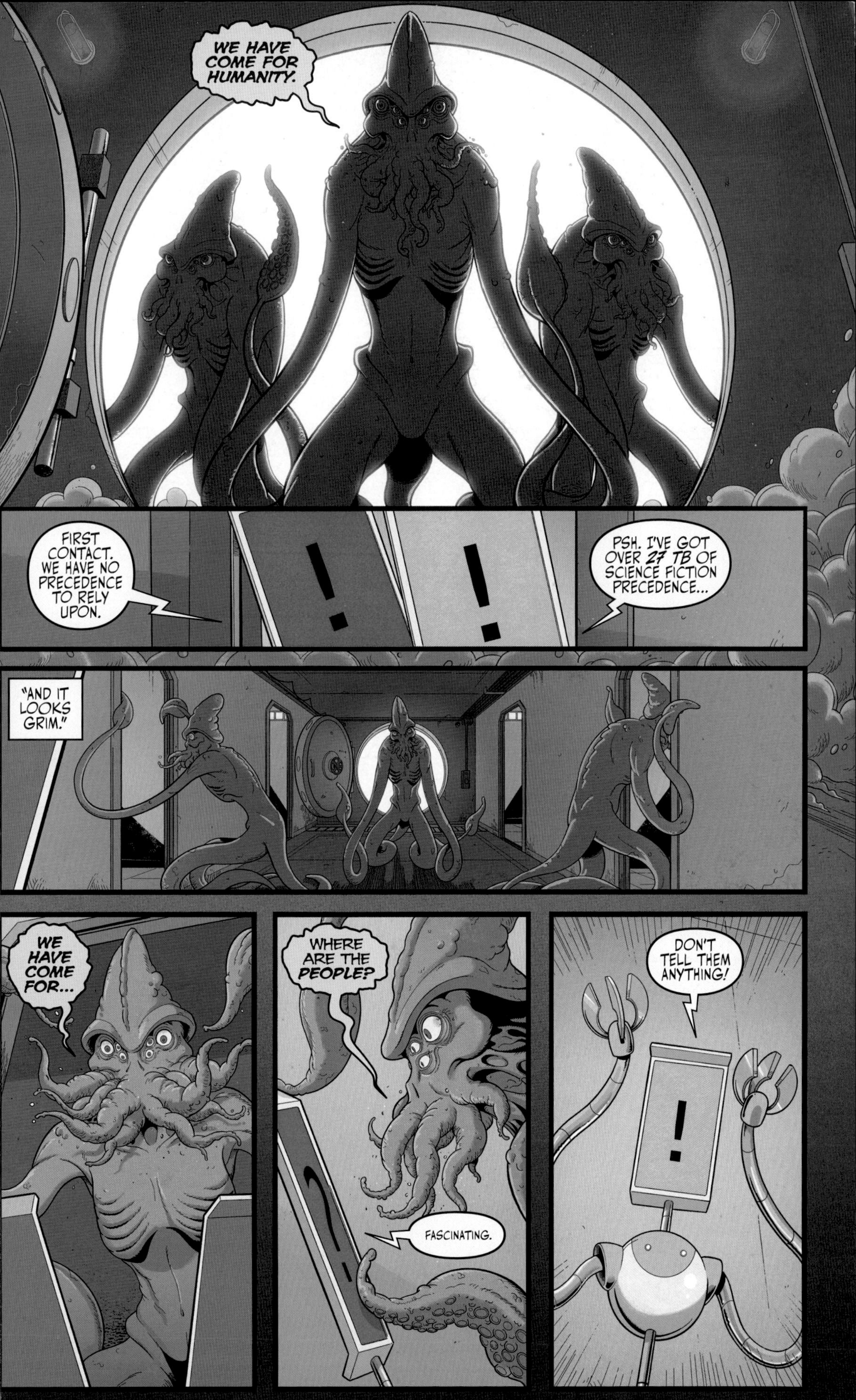
WE HAVE COME FOR HUMANITY.
FIRST CONTACT. WE HAVE NO PRECEDENCE TO RELY UPON.
!
!
PSH. I'VE GOT OVER 27 TB OF SCIENCE FICTION PRECEDENCE...
"AND IT LOOKS GRIM."
WE HAVE COME FOR...
WHERE ARE THE PEOPLE?
FASCINATING.
?
DON'T TELL THEM ANYTHING!
!

HUMANS RULED THIS PLANET FOR ALMOST 900 MILLENNIA--
BUT IN THE PAST CENTURY, THE EARTH BECAME IRRADIATED, BARREN, AND UNSUPPORTIVE OF LIFE.
o_o
THERE ARE NO MORE PEOPLE HERE.
ONLY WHAT THEY *LEFT BEHIND.*
SO DESTROY US IF YOU MUST, BUT YOU'LL NEVER...
WAIT, ARE YOU... *CRYING?*
WE ARE TOO LATE.

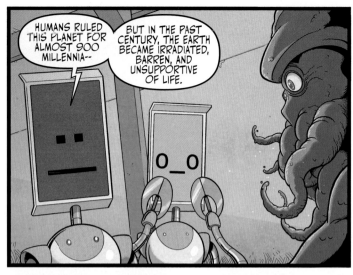

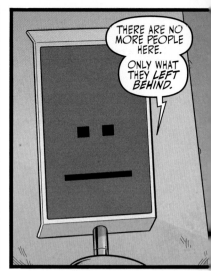

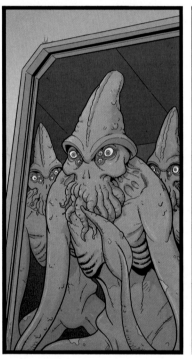

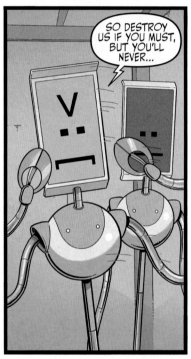

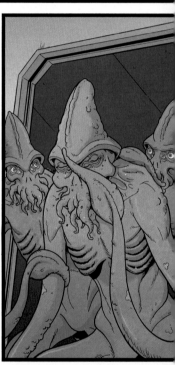

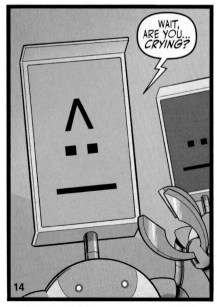

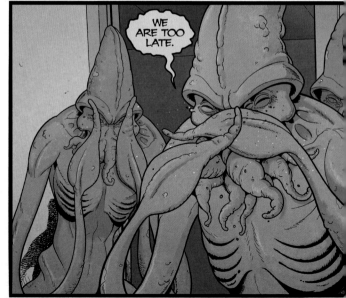

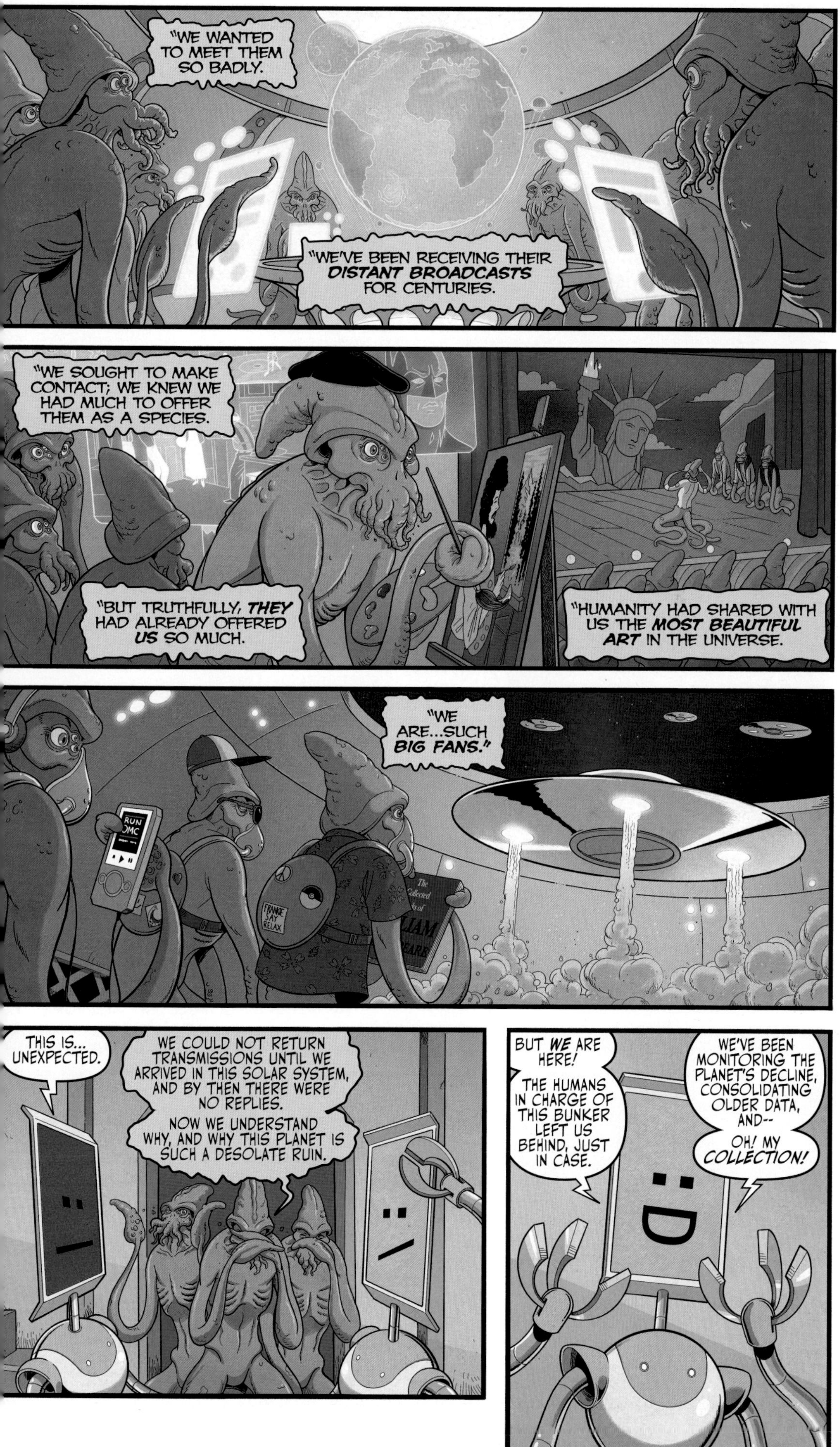
"WE WANTED TO MEET THEM SO BADLY.
"WE'VE BEEN RECEIVING THEIR DISTANT BROADCASTS FOR CENTURIES.
"WE SOUGHT TO MAKE CONTACT; WE KNEW WE HAD MUCH TO OFFER THEM AS A SPECIES.
"BUT TRUTHFULLY, THEY HAD ALREADY OFFERED US SO MUCH.
"HUMANITY HAD SHARED WITH US THE MOST BEAUTIFUL ART IN THE UNIVERSE.
"WE ARE...SUCH BIG FANS."
RUN DMC
FRANKIE SAY RELAX
THIS IS... UNEXPECTED.
WE COULD NOT RETURN TRANSMISSIONS UNTIL WE ARRIVED IN THIS SOLAR SYSTEM, AND BY THEN THERE WERE NO REPLIES.
NOW WE UNDERSTAND WHY, AND WHY THIS PLANET IS SUCH A DESOLATE RUIN.
BUT WE ARE HERE!
THE HUMANS IN CHARGE OF THIS BUNKER LEFT US BEHIND, JUST IN CASE.
WE'VE BEEN MONITORING THE PLANET'S DECLINE, CONSOLIDATING OLDER DATA, AND--
OH! MY COLLECTION!

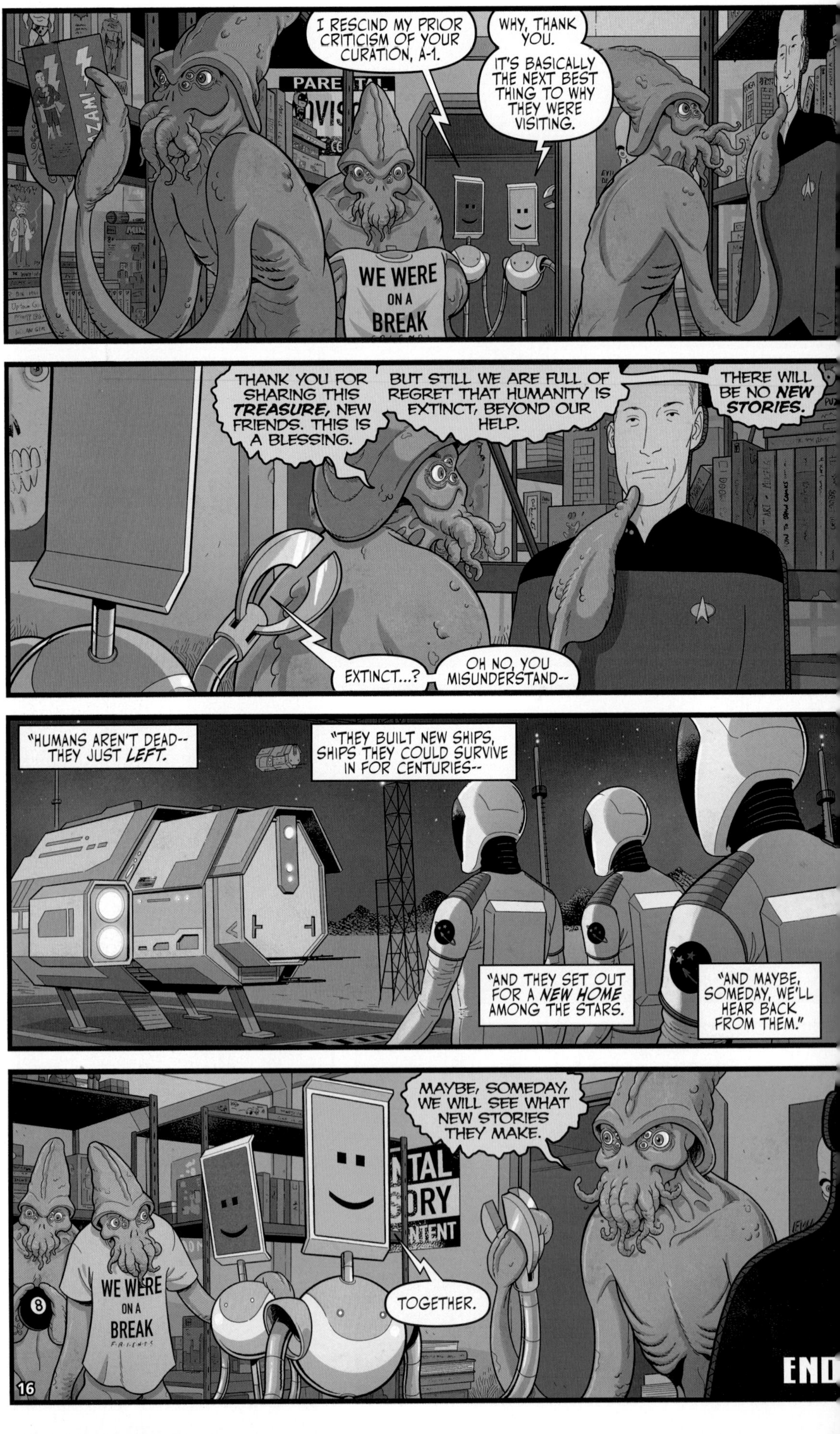

I RESCIND MY PRIOR CRITICISM OF YOUR CURATION, A-1.
WHY, THANK YOU.
IT'S BASICALLY THE NEXT BEST THING TO WHY THEY WERE VISITING.
WE WERE ON A BREAK
THANK YOU FOR SHARING THIS *TREASURE,* NEW FRIENDS. THIS IS A BLESSING.
BUT STILL WE ARE FULL OF REGRET THAT HUMANITY IS EXTINCT, BEYOND OUR HELP.
THERE WILL BE NO *NEW STORIES.*
EXTINCT...?
OH NO, YOU MISUNDERSTAND--
"HUMANS AREN'T DEAD-- THEY JUST *LEFT.*
"THEY BUILT NEW SHIPS, SHIPS THEY COULD SURVIVE IN FOR CENTURIES--
"AND THEY SET OUT FOR A *NEW HOME* AMONG THE STARS.
"AND MAYBE, SOMEDAY, WE'LL HEAR BACK FROM THEM."
MAYBE, SOMEDAY, WE WILL SEE WHAT NEW STORIES THEY MAKE.
TOGETHER.
WE WERE ON A BREAK
F·R·I·E·N·D·S
END

DRIFTERS

WRITTEN BY:
CURT PIRES & ROCKWELL WHITE
LINEART BY:
VALENTINE DE LANDRO
COLORS BY:
OLIVER MERTZ
LETTERS BY:
MATT KROTZER

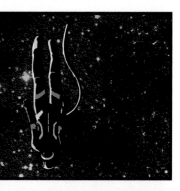

MY NAME IS SYLVIA ORTEGA...

...AND THIS...

...THIS IS MY STORY.

THIS IS HOW I DIE.

MARS. HIGGS COLONY. EST. 2079.
POPULATION= 1.2 MILLION.

FIREHOUSE. ATMOSPHERIC MONITORING
STATION. POPULATION= 7.

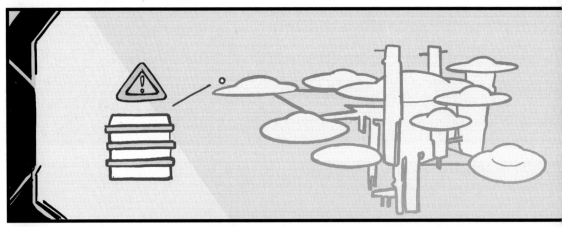

I SINK THIS ONE, YOU TAKE MY NEXT RUN. DEAL?

YOU SINK THIS ONE, I'LL COVER YOU FOR THE NEXT **WEEK.**

ALERT! ALERT!
KEY COMPONENT FAILURE IMMINENT.

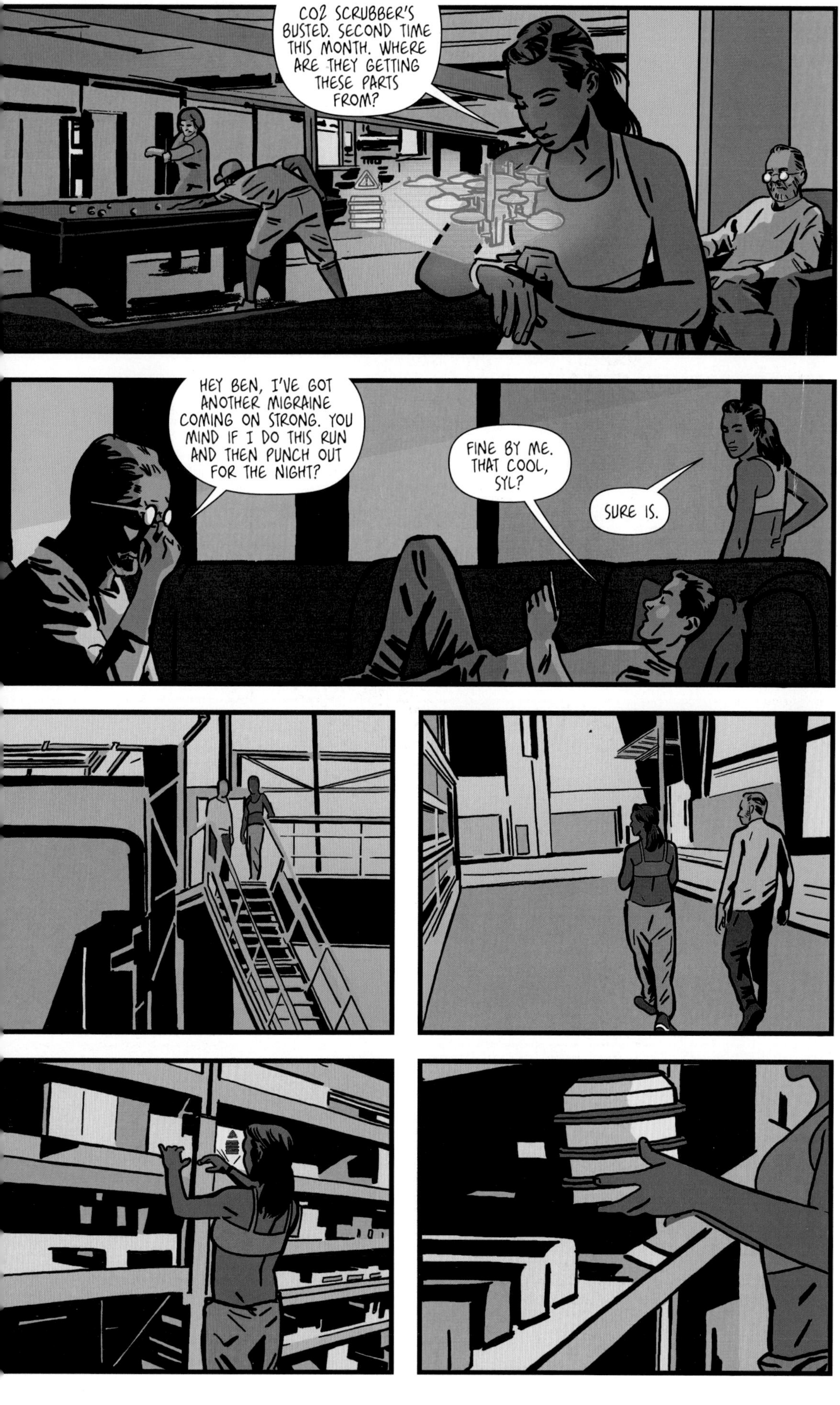
CO2 SCRUBBER'S BUSTED. SECOND TIME THIS MONTH. WHERE ARE THEY GETTING THESE PARTS FROM?
HEY BEN, I'VE GOT ANOTHER MIGRAINE COMING ON STRONG. YOU MIND IF I DO THIS RUN AND THEN PUNCH OUT FOR THE NIGHT?
FINE BY ME. THAT COOL, SYL?
SURE IS.

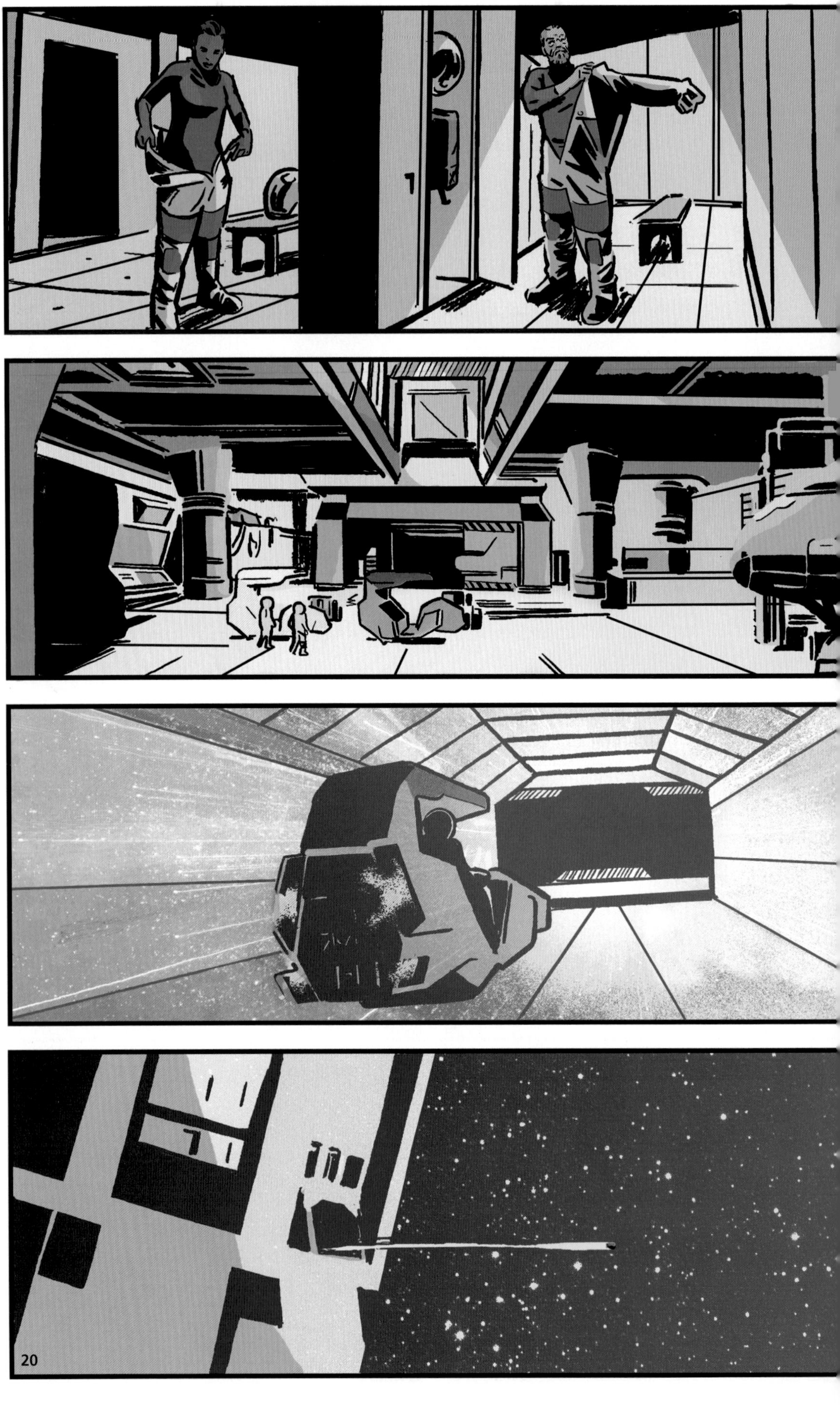

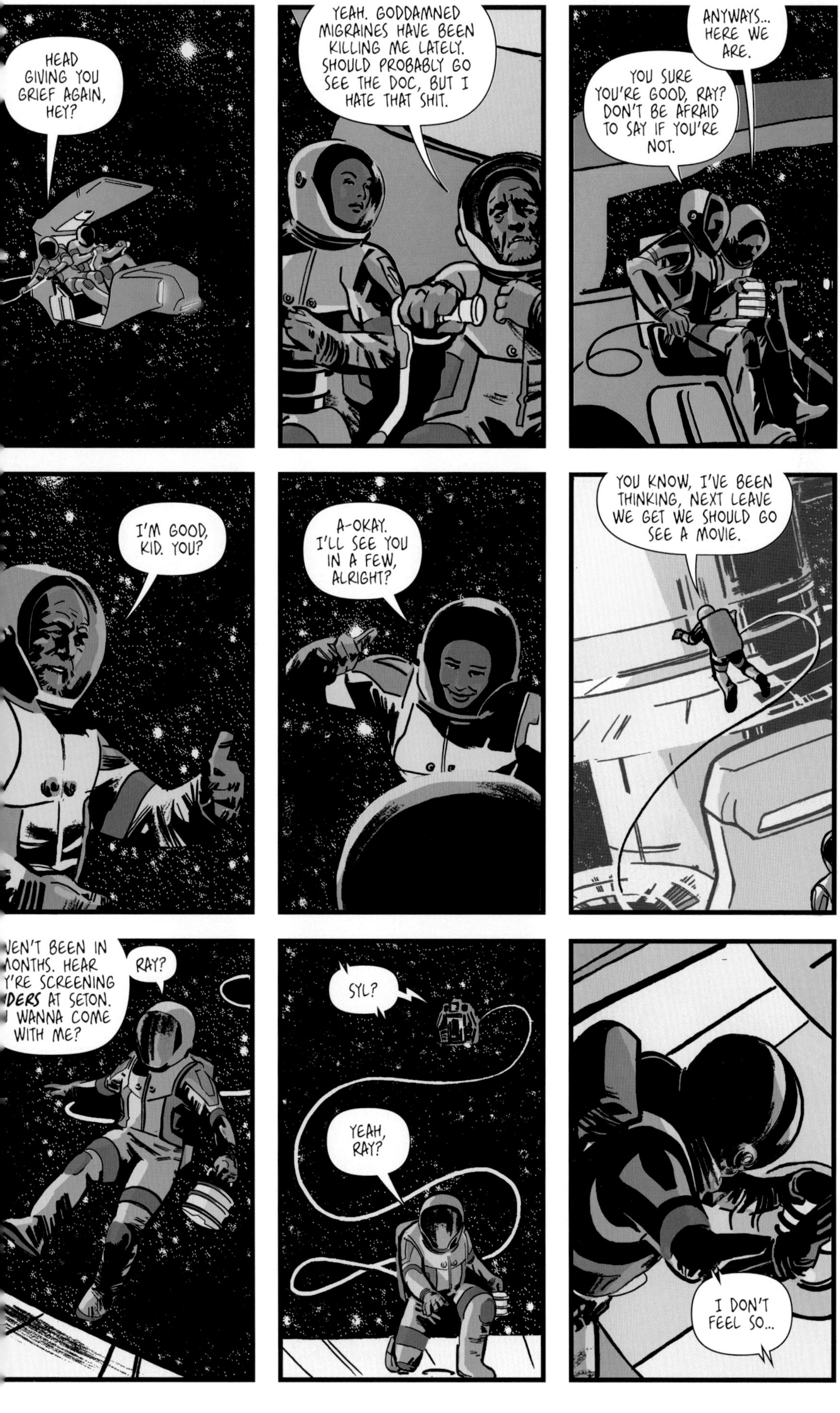
HEAD GIVING YOU GRIEF AGAIN, HEY?
YEAH. GODDAMNED MIGRAINES HAVE BEEN KILLING ME LATELY. SHOULD PROBABLY GO SEE THE DOC, BUT I HATE THAT SHIT.
ANYWAYS... HERE WE ARE.
YOU SURE YOU'RE GOOD, RAY? DON'T BE AFRAID TO SAY IF YOU'RE NOT.
I'M GOOD, KID. YOU?
A-OKAY. I'LL SEE YOU IN A FEW, ALRIGHT?
YOU KNOW, I'VE BEEN THINKING, NEXT LEAVE WE GET WE SHOULD GO SEE A MOVIE.
VEN'T BEEN IN MONTHS. HEAR Y'RE SCREENING DERS AT SETON. WANNA COME WITH ME?
RAY?
SYL?
YEAH, RAY?
I DON'T FEEL SO...

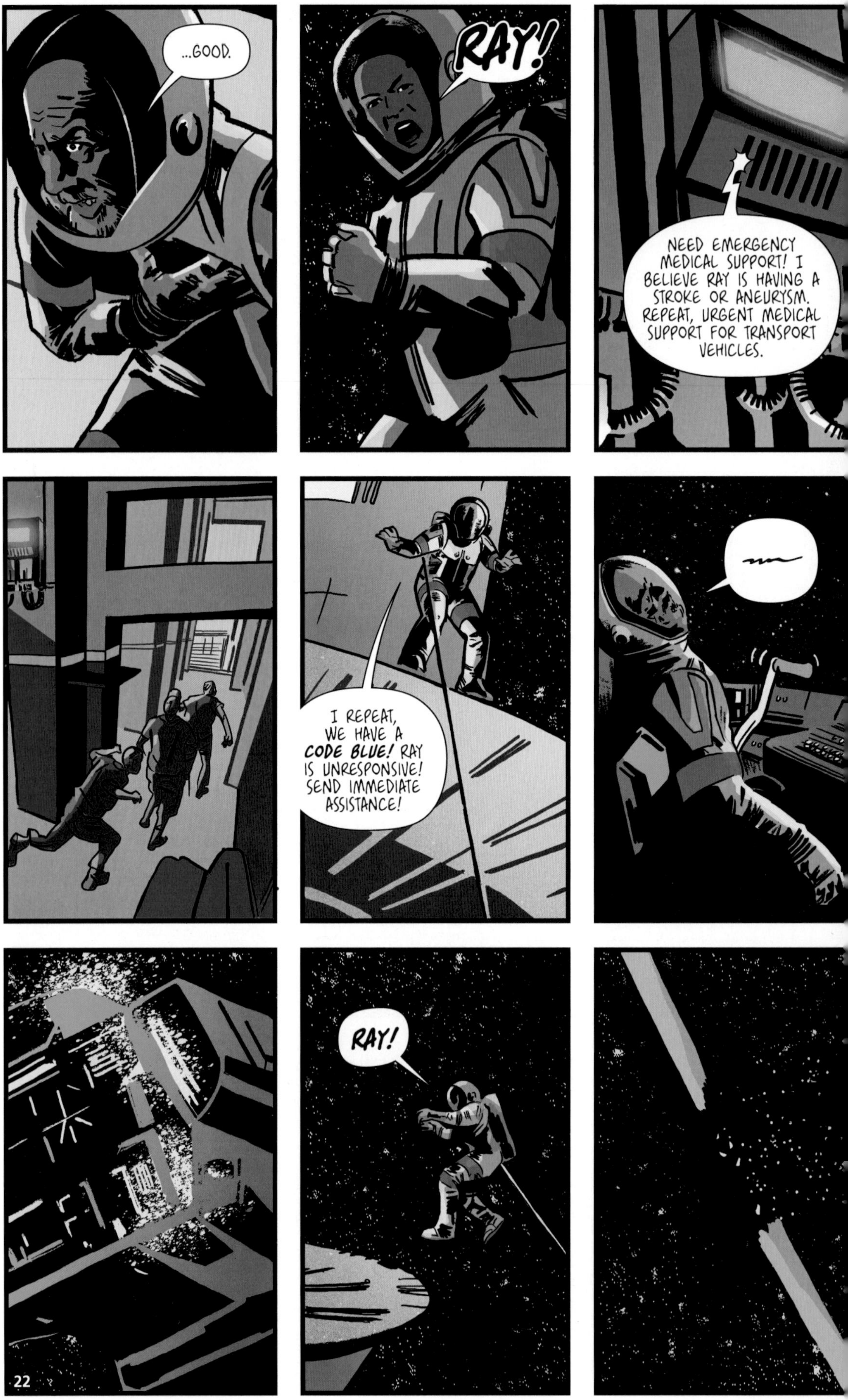
...GOOD.
RAY!
NEED EMERGENCY MEDICAL SUPPORT! I BELIEVE RAY IS HAVING A STROKE OR ANEURYSM. REPEAT, URGENT MEDICAL SUPPORT FOR TRANSPORT VEHICLES.
I REPEAT, WE HAVE A **CODE BLUE!** RAY IS UNRESPONSIVE! SEND IMMEDIATE ASSISTANCE!
RAY!

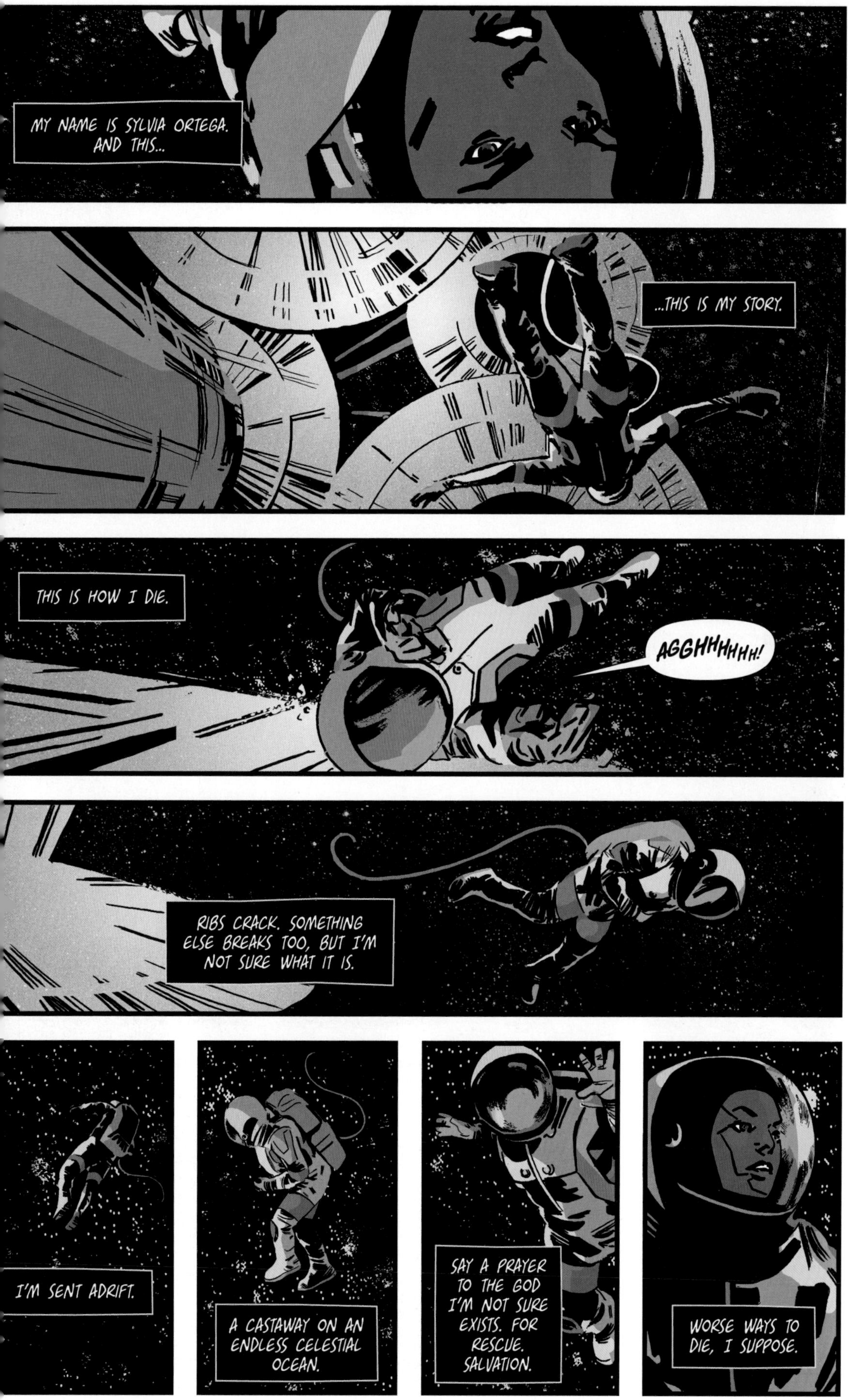
MY NAME IS SYLVIA ORTEGA. AND THIS...
...THIS IS MY STORY.
THIS IS HOW I DIE.
AGGHHHHHH!
RIBS CRACK. SOMETHING ELSE BREAKS TOO, BUT I'M NOT SURE WHAT IT IS.
I'M SENT ADRIFT.
A CASTAWAY ON AN ENDLESS CELESTIAL OCEAN.
SAY A PRAYER TO THE GOD I'M NOT SURE EXISTS. FOR RESCUE. SALVATION.
WORSE WAYS TO DIE, I SUPPOSE.

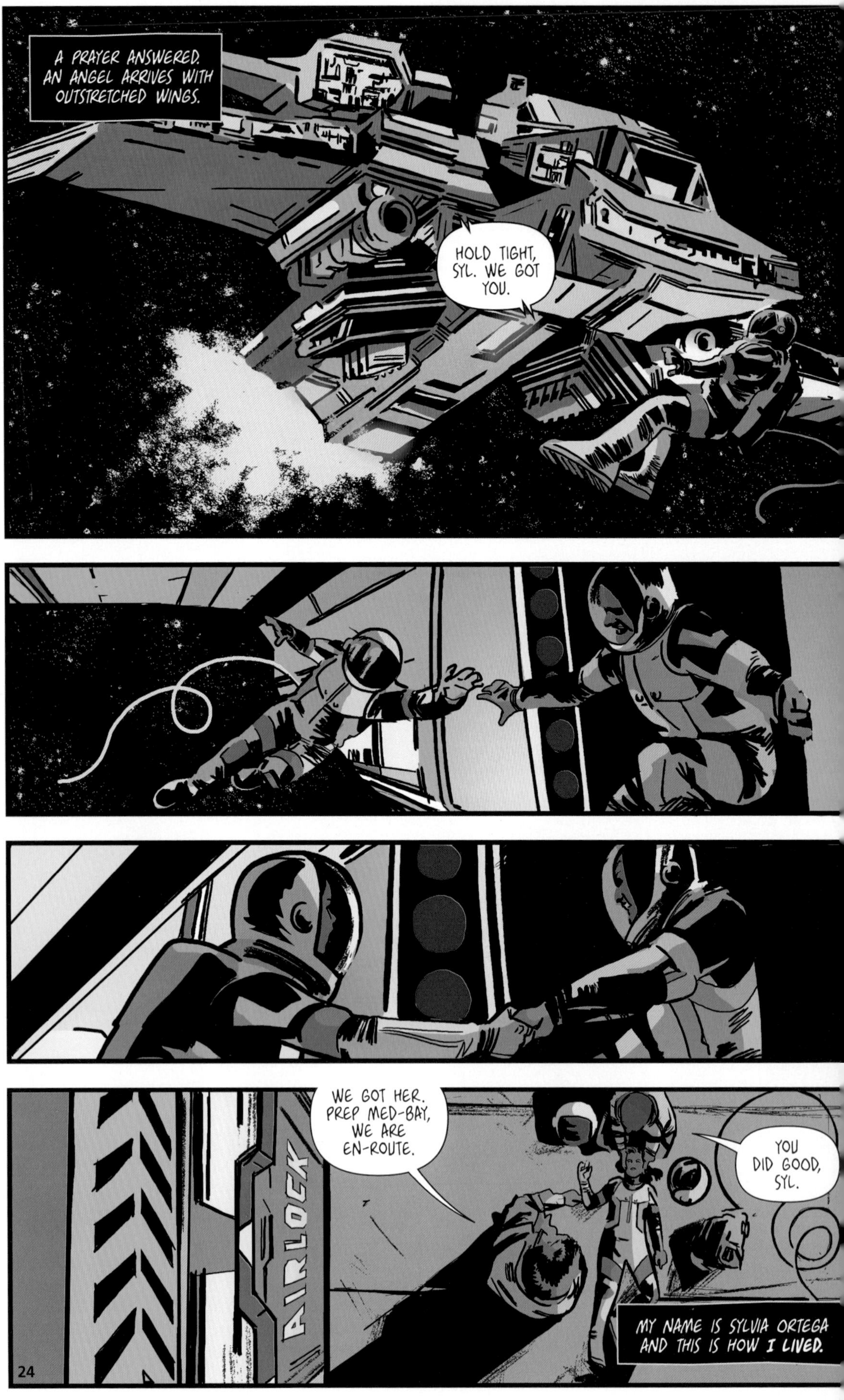
A PRAYER ANSWERED. AN ANGEL ARRIVES WITH OUTSTRETCHED WINGS.
HOLD TIGHT, SYL. WE GOT YOU.
AIRLOCK
WE GOT HER. PREP MED-BAY, WE ARE EN-ROUTE.
YOU DID GOOD, SYL.
MY NAME IS SYLVIA ORTEGA AND THIS IS HOW **I LIVED.**

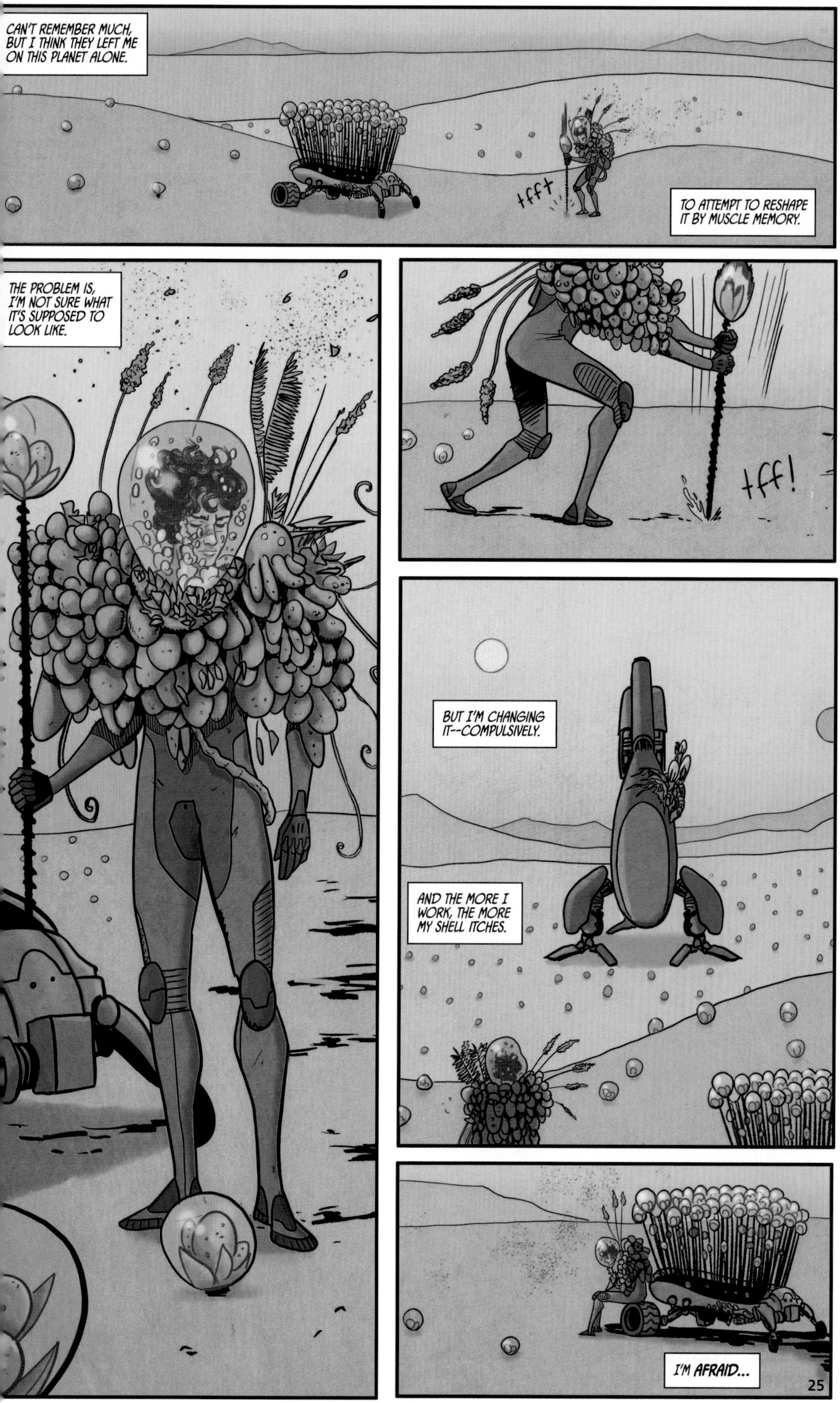
CAN'T REMEMBER MUCH, BUT I THINK THEY LEFT ME ON THIS PLANET ALONE.
tfft
TO ATTEMPT TO RESHAPE IT BY MUSCLE MEMORY.
THE PROBLEM IS, I'M NOT SURE WHAT IT'S SUPPOSED TO LOOK LIKE.
tff!
BUT I'M CHANGING IT--COMPULSIVELY.
AND THE MORE I WORK, THE MORE MY SHELL ITCHES.
I'M AFRAID...

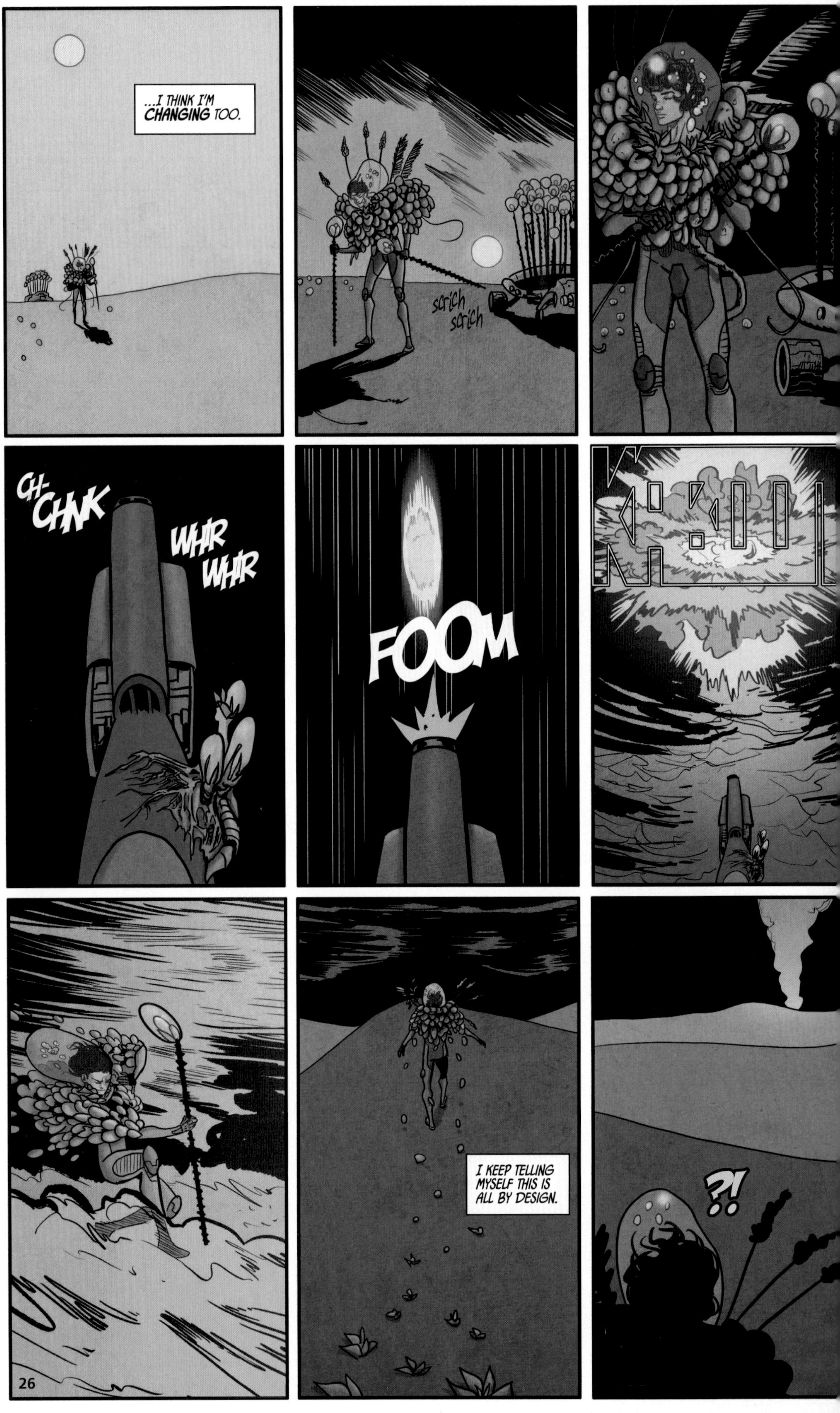

...I THINK I'M CHANGING TOO.
scrich scrich
CH-CHNK
WHR WHR
FOOM
I KEEP TELLING MYSELF THIS IS ALL BY DESIGN.
?!

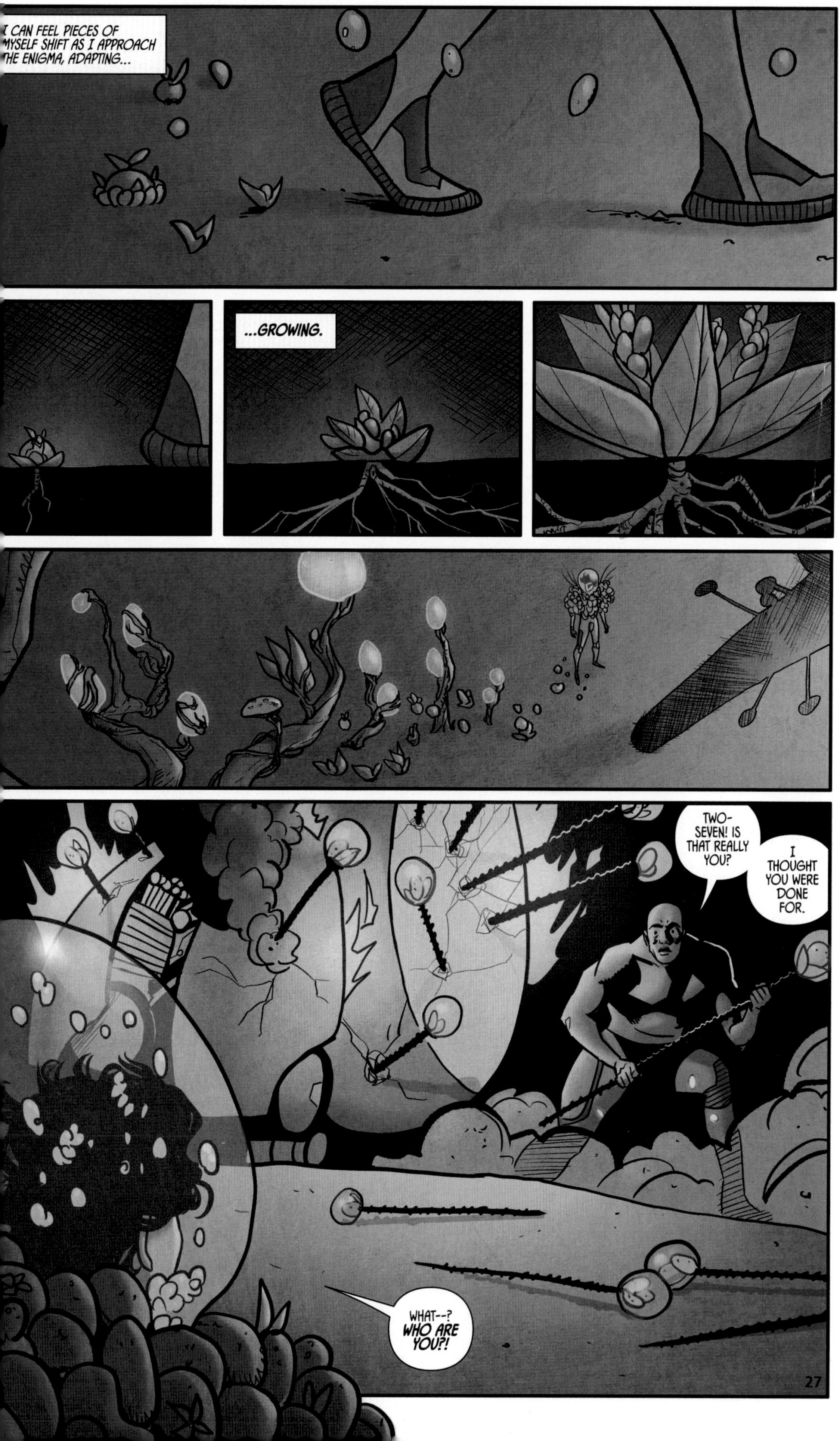
I CAN FEEL PIECES OF MYSELF SHIFT AS I APPROACH THE ENIGMA, ADAPTING...
...GROWING.
TWO-SEVEN! IS THAT REALLY YOU?
I THOUGHT YOU WERE DONE FOR.
WHAT--? WHO ARE YOU?!

YIKES, THAT'S BAD, YOU MUST NOT REMEMBER MUCH...
HOW ABOUT YOU TAKE YOUR HELMET OFF?
CAN I TRUST YOU?
YES--I PROMISE.
GASP
WHAT HAPPENED TO YOU?
HERE... TAKE MY HAND.
"WE WERE BORN FULL OF DREAMS."

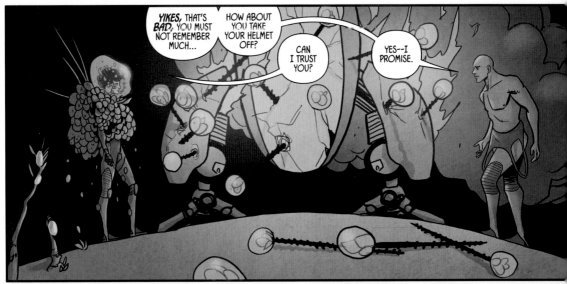

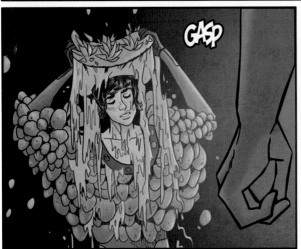

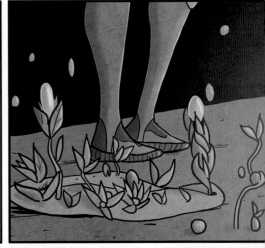

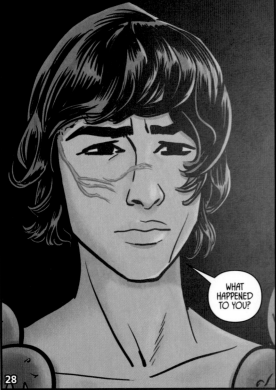

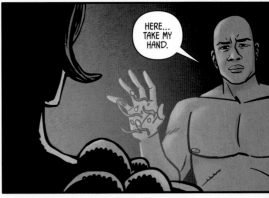

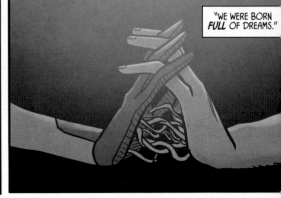

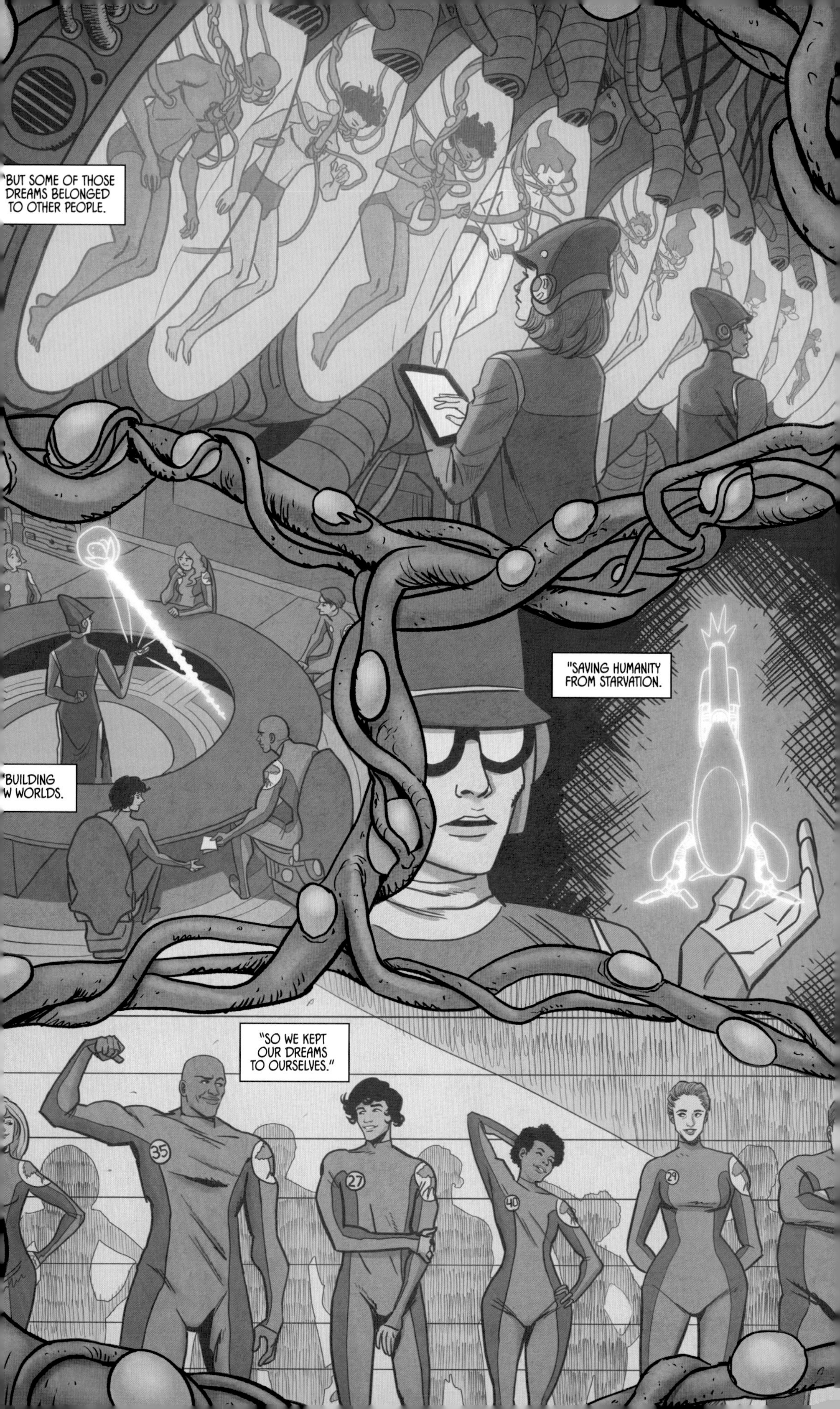
"BUT SOME OF THOSE DREAMS BELONGED TO OTHER PEOPLE.
"BUILDING
W WORLDS.
"SAVING HUMANITY FROM STARVATION.
"SO WE KEPT OUR DREAMS TO OURSELVES."
35
27
40
29

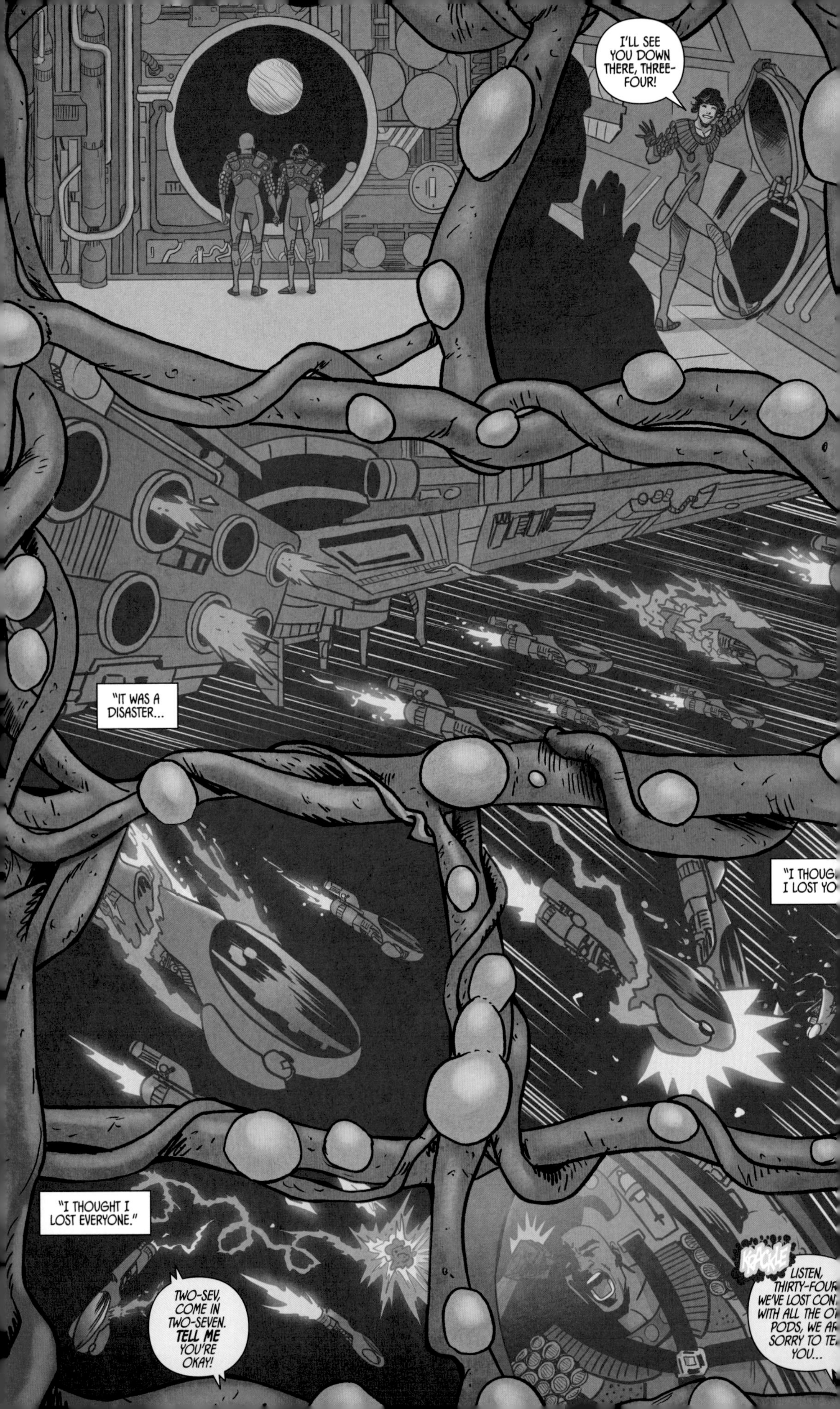
I'LL SEE YOU DOWN THERE, THREE-FOUR!
"IT WAS A DISASTER...
"I THOUG... I LOST YO...
"I THOUGHT I LOST EVERYONE."
TWO-SEV, COME IN TWO-SEVEN. **TELL ME** YOU'RE OKAY!
KRACKLE
LISTEN, THIRTY-FOUR... WE'VE LOST CON... WITH ALL THE O... PODS, WE AR... SORRY TO TE... YOU...

OH.

LOSING YOU AND THE OTHERS CHANGED ME, AND WHEN BLOOM CORP. SAID THEY WEREN'T SENDING A RECOVERY TEAM...

...I KINDA SNAPPED.

KRAKKKOOM

IT'S GOING TO BE OKAY.

NO, IT'S NOT...WE NEED TO ACTIVATE AT LEAST TWO PODS BEFORE THIS STORM ENDS OR THE ATMOSPHERE WON'T LAST...

IF ONLY I HADN'T GIVEN UP--

JUST SHUT UP AND *TRUST* ME!

WHA--

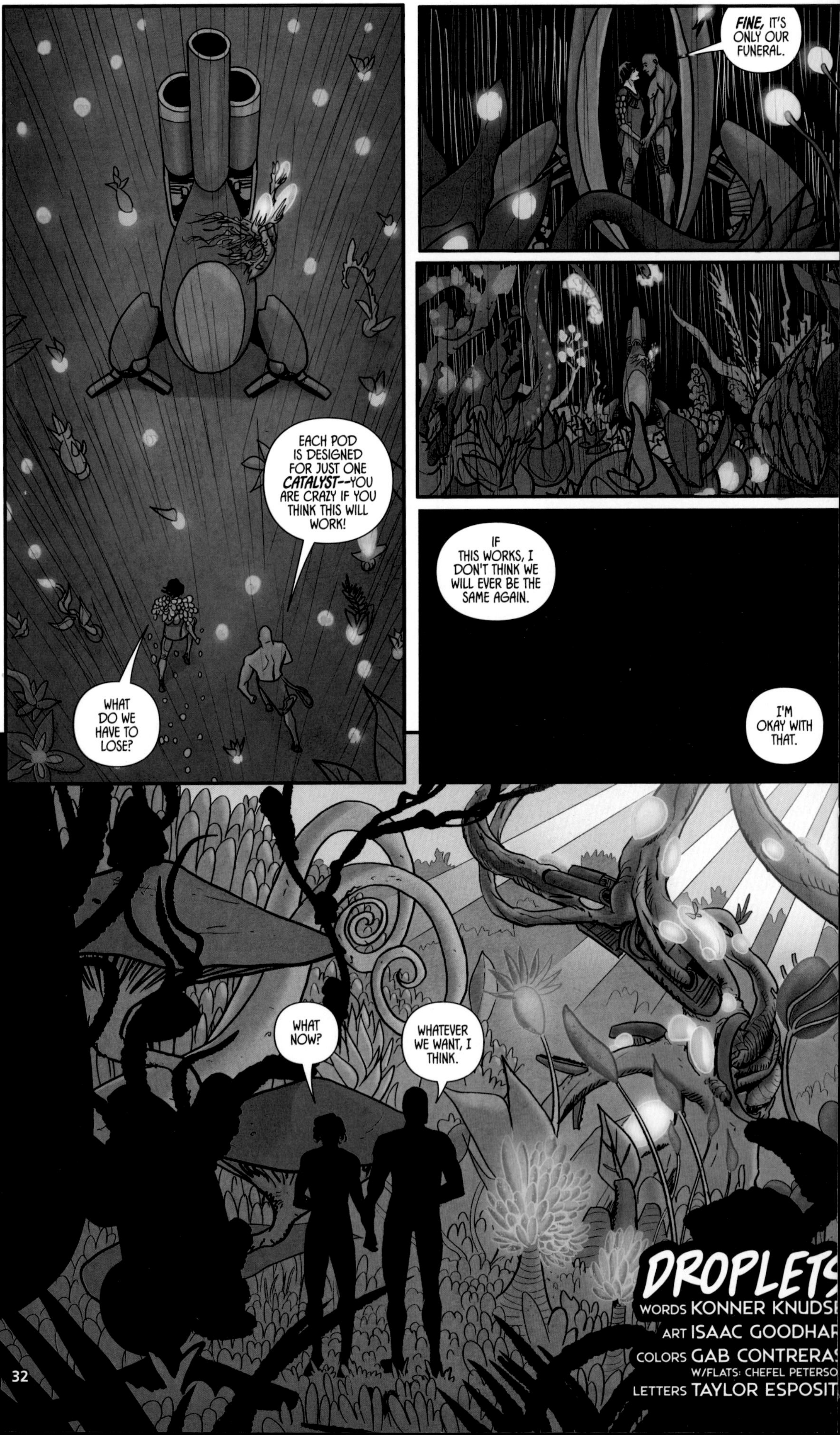
EACH POD IS DESIGNED FOR JUST ONE ***CATALYST***--YOU ARE CRAZY IF YOU THINK THIS WILL WORK!
WHAT DO WE HAVE TO LOSE?
FINE, IT'S ONLY OUR FUNERAL.
IF THIS WORKS, I DON'T THINK WE WILL EVER BE THE SAME AGAIN.
I'M OKAY WITH THAT.
WHAT NOW?
WHATEVER WE WANT, I THINK.
DROPLET
WORDS KONNER KNUDS
ART ISAAC GOODHA
COLORS GAB CONTRERA
W/FLATS: CHEFEL PETERSO
LETTERS TAYLOR ESPOSIT

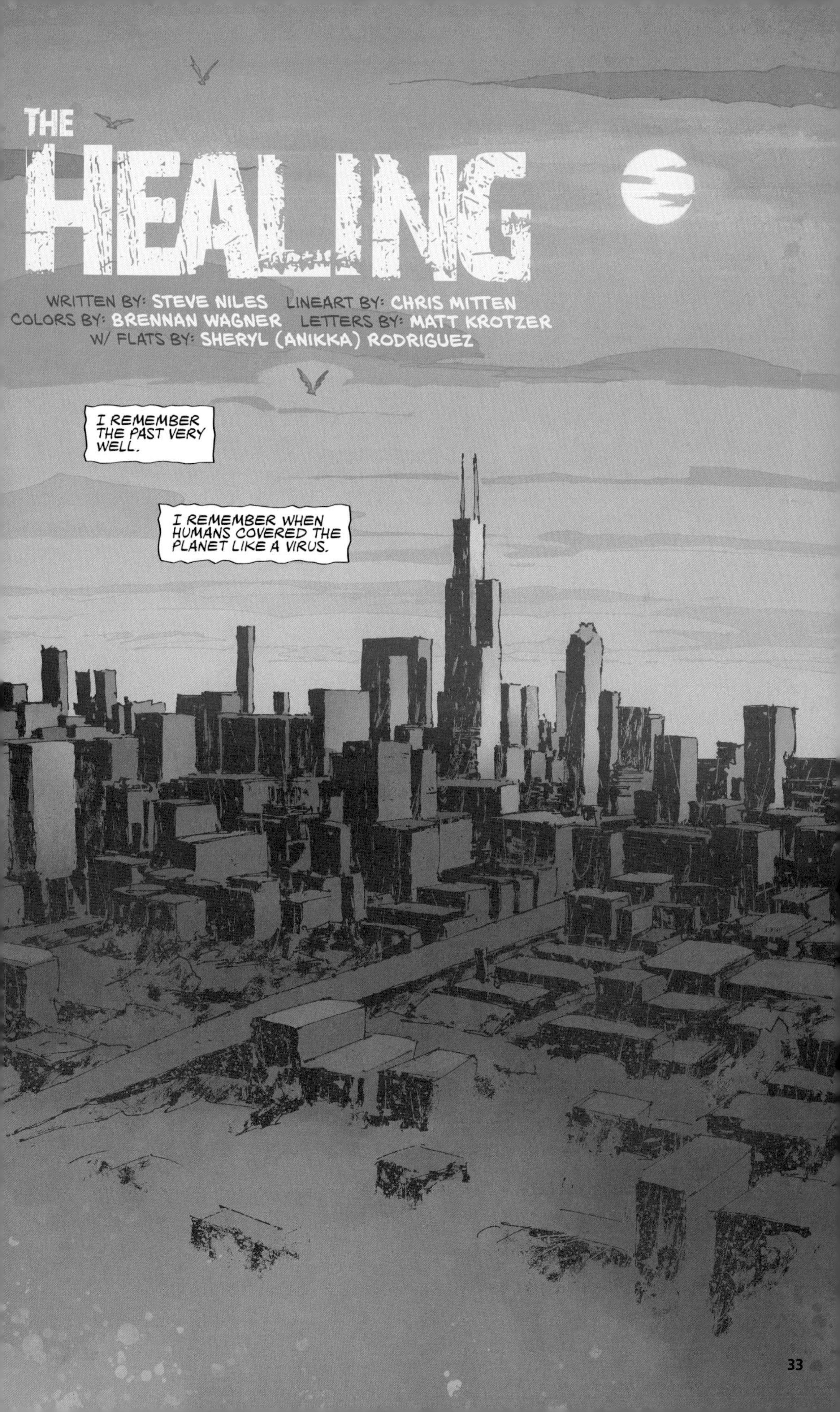
THE HEALING
WRITTEN BY: STEVE NILES LINEART BY: CHRIS MITTEN
COLORS BY: BRENNAN WAGNER LETTERS BY: MATT KROTZER
W/ FLATS BY: SHERYL (ANIKKA) RODRIGUEZ
I REMEMBER THE PAST VERY WELL.
I REMEMBER WHEN HUMANS COVERED THE PLANET LIKE A VIRUS.

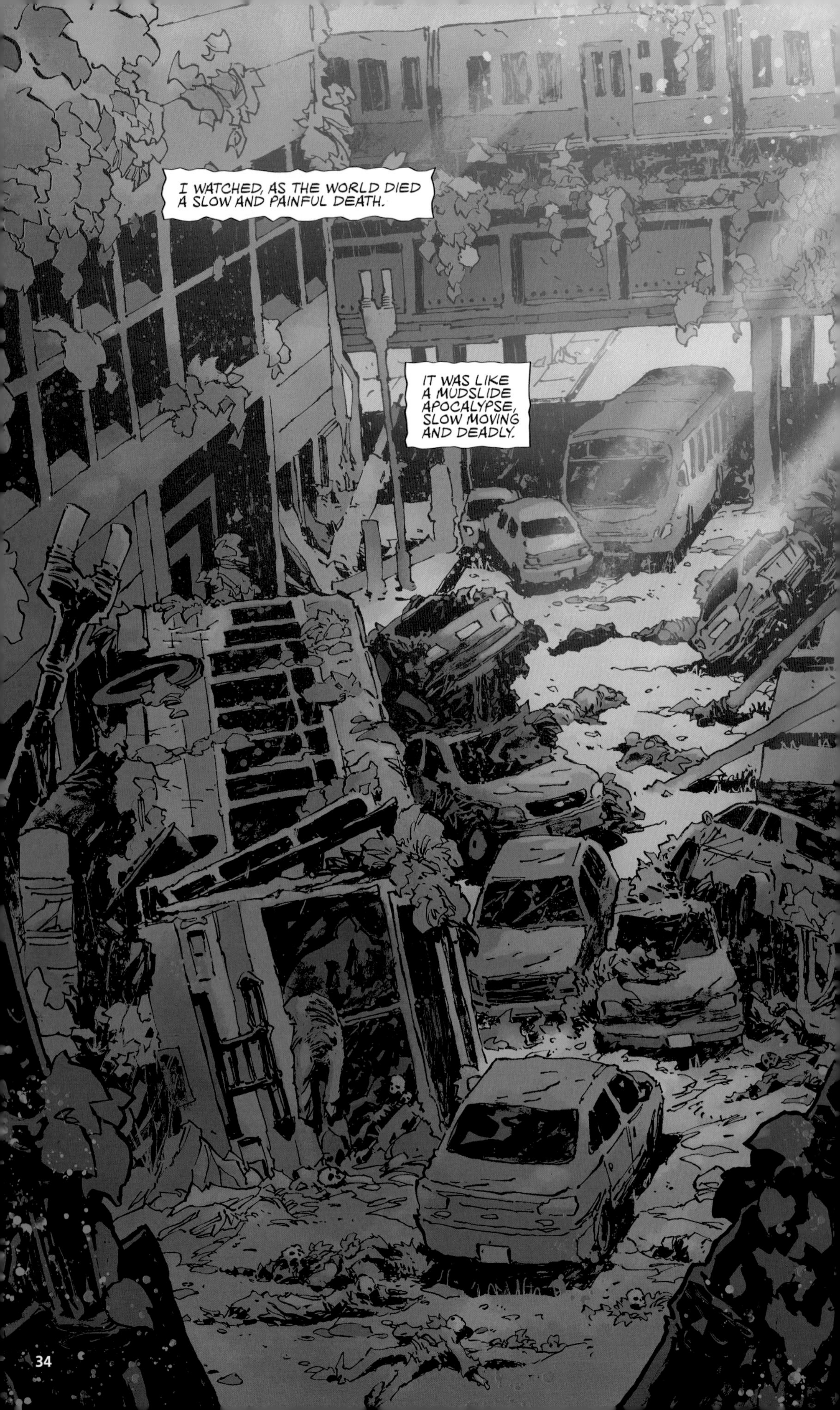
I WATCHED, AS THE WORLD DIED A SLOW AND PAINFUL DEATH.
IT WAS LIKE A MUDSLIDE APOCALYPSE, SLOW MOVING AND DEADLY.

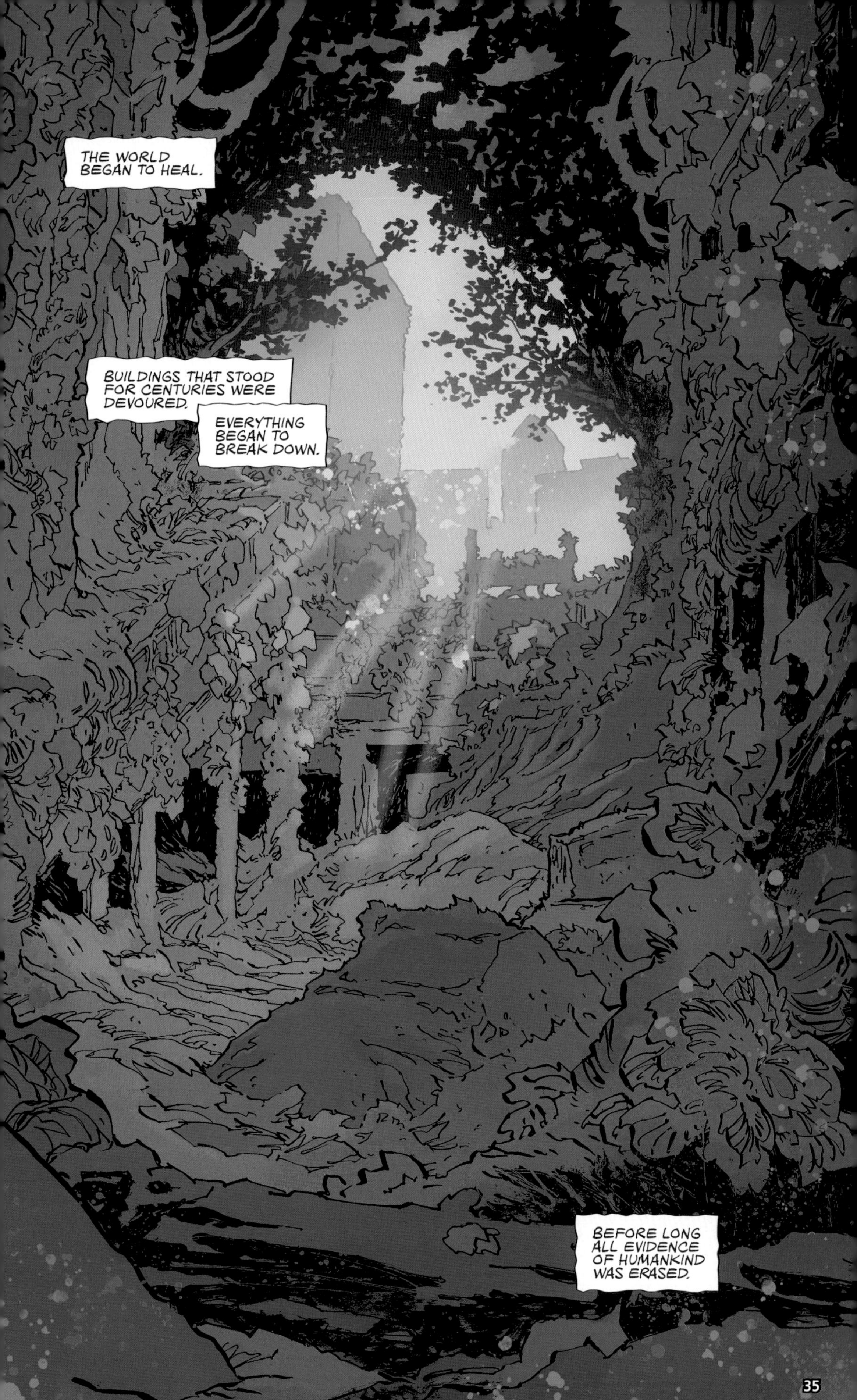
THE WORLD BEGAN TO HEAL.
BUILDINGS THAT STOOD FOR CENTURIES WERE DEVOURED.
EVERYTHING BEGAN TO BREAK DOWN.
BEFORE LONG ALL EVIDENCE OF HUMANKIND WAS ERASED.

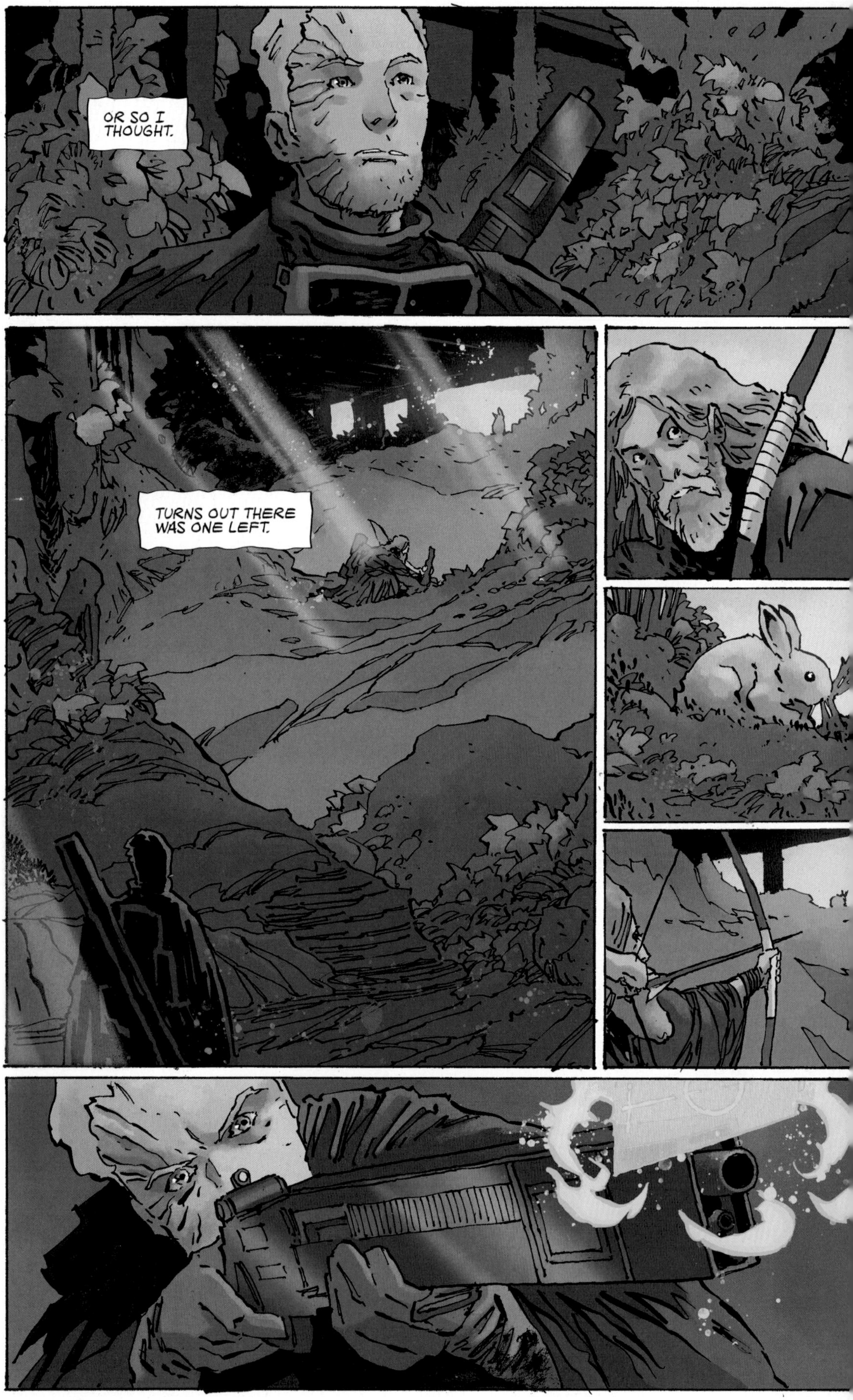
OR SO I THOUGHT.
TURNS OUT THERE WAS ONE LEFT.

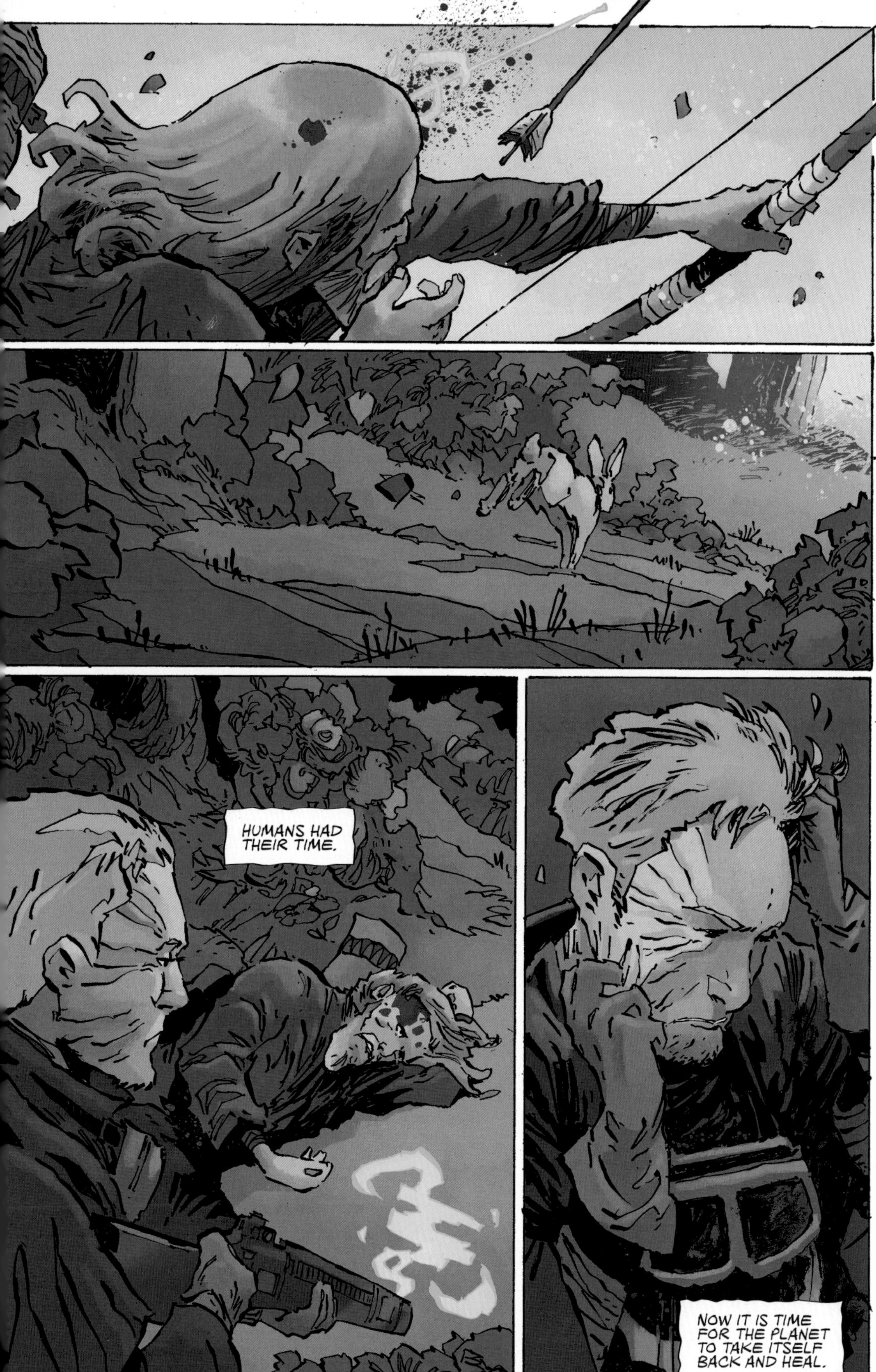
HUMANS HAD THEIR TIME.
NOW IT IS TIME FOR THE PLANET TO TAKE ITSELF BACK AND HEAL.

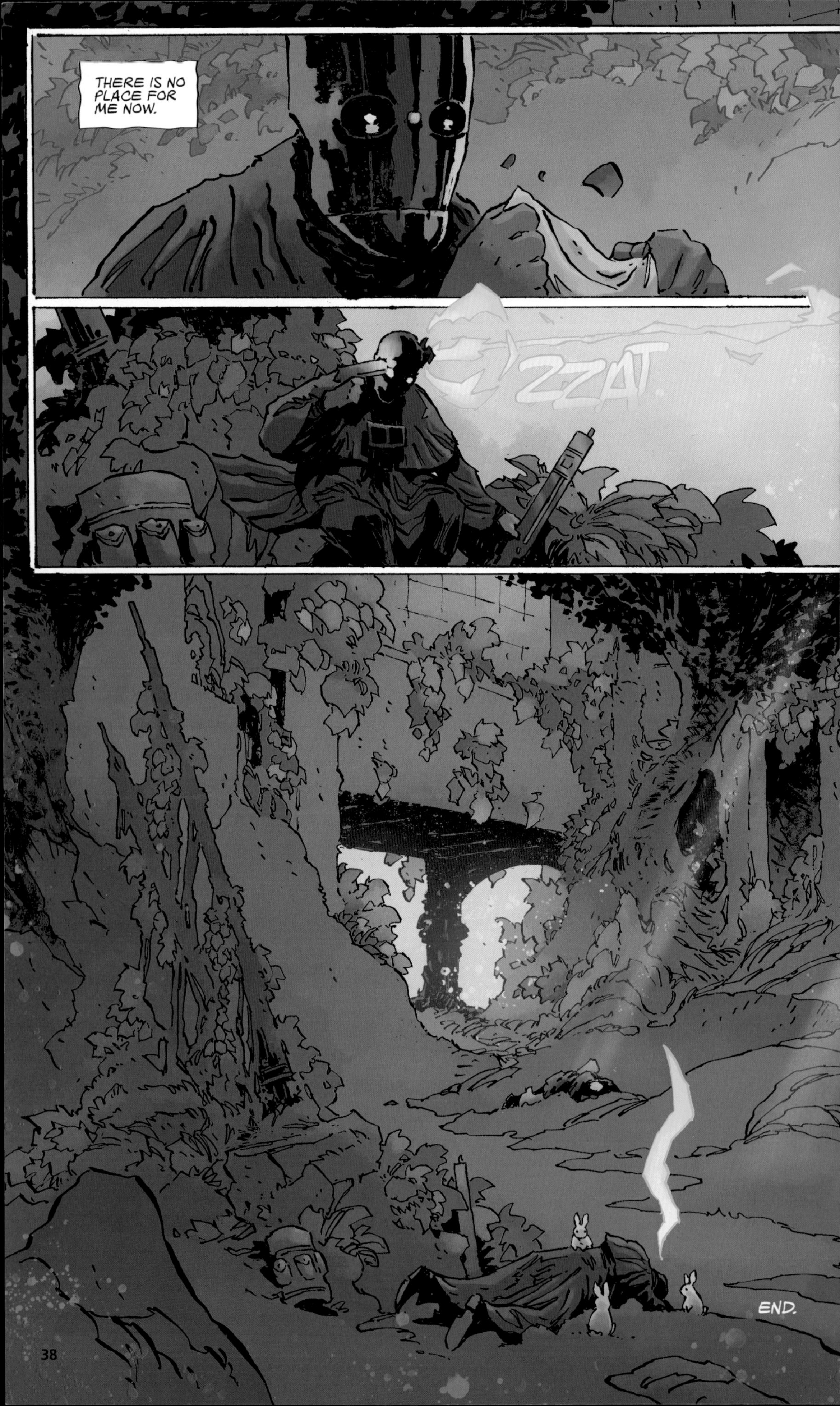
THERE IS NO PLACE FOR ME NOW.
ZZAT
END.

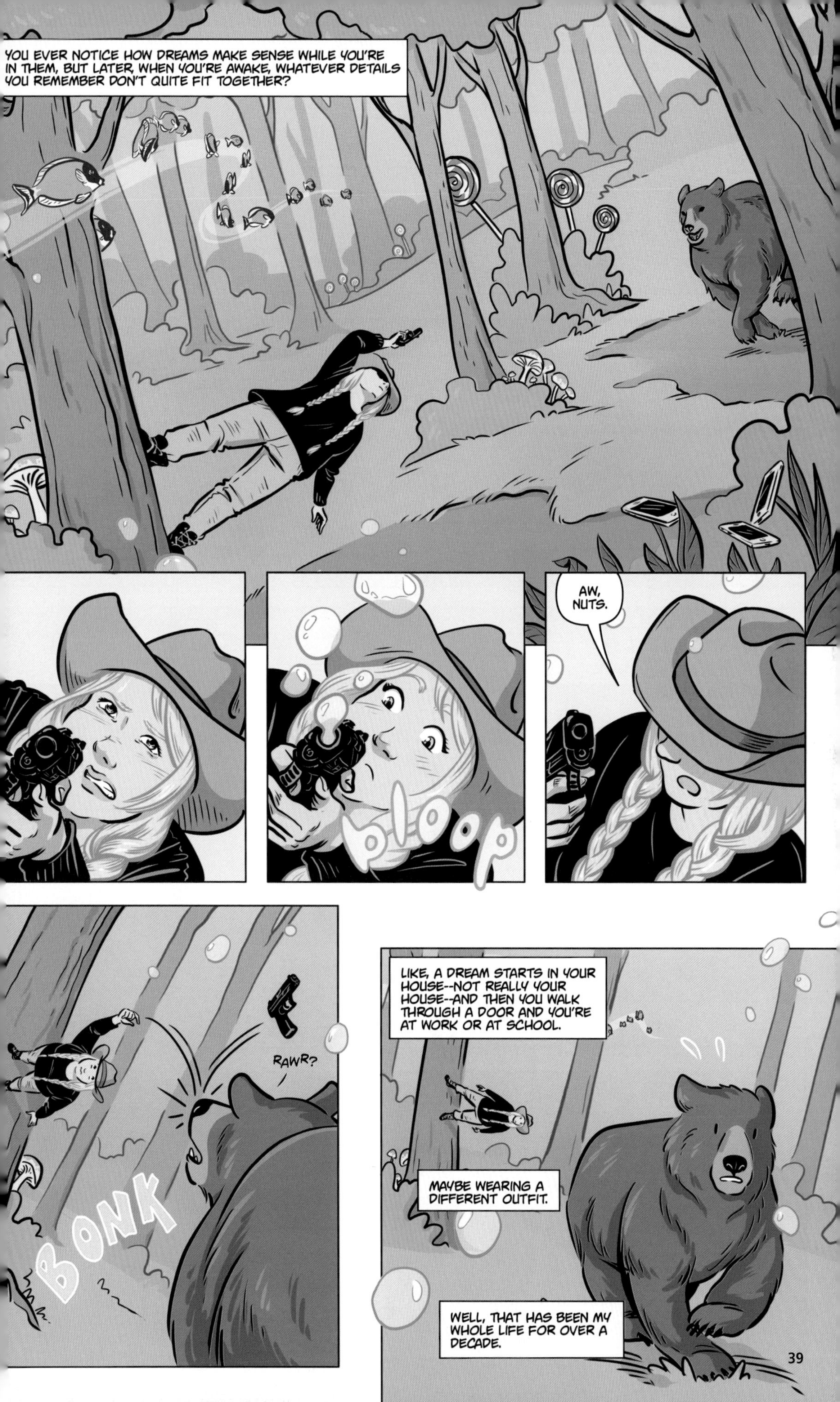

YOU EVER NOTICE HOW DREAMS MAKE SENSE WHILE YOU'RE IN THEM, BUT LATER, WHEN YOU'RE AWAKE, WHATEVER DETAILS YOU REMEMBER DON'T QUITE FIT TOGETHER?
PLOOP
AW, NUTS.
RAWR?
BONK
LIKE, A DREAM STARTS IN YOUR HOUSE--NOT REALLY YOUR HOUSE--AND THEN YOU WALK THROUGH A DOOR AND YOU'RE AT WORK OR AT SCHOOL.
MAYBE WEARING A DIFFERENT OUTFIT.
WELL, THAT HAS BEEN MY WHOLE LIFE FOR OVER A DECADE.

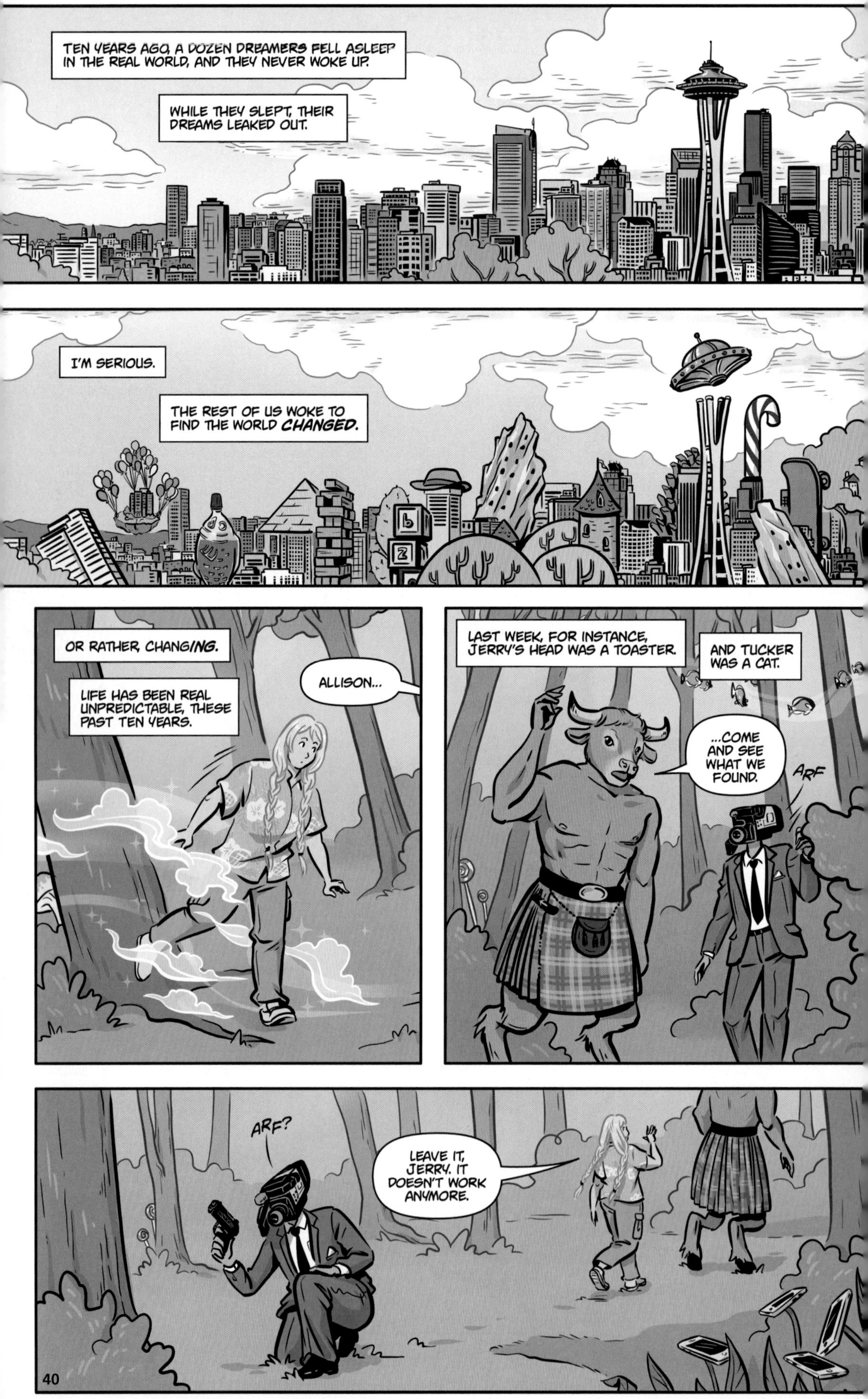
TEN YEARS AGO, A DOZEN DREAMERS FELL ASLEEP IN THE REAL WORLD, AND THEY NEVER WOKE UP.
WHILE THEY SLEPT, THEIR DREAMS LEAKED OUT.
I'M SERIOUS.
THE REST OF US WOKE TO FIND THE WORLD *CHANGED*.
OR RATHER, CHANG*ING*.
LIFE HAS BEEN REAL UNPREDICTABLE, THESE PAST TEN YEARS.
ALLISON...
LAST WEEK, FOR INSTANCE, JERRY'S HEAD WAS A TOASTER.
AND TUCKER WAS A CAT.
...COME AND SEE WHAT WE FOUND.
ARF
ARF?
LEAVE IT, JERRY. IT DOESN'T WORK ANYMORE.

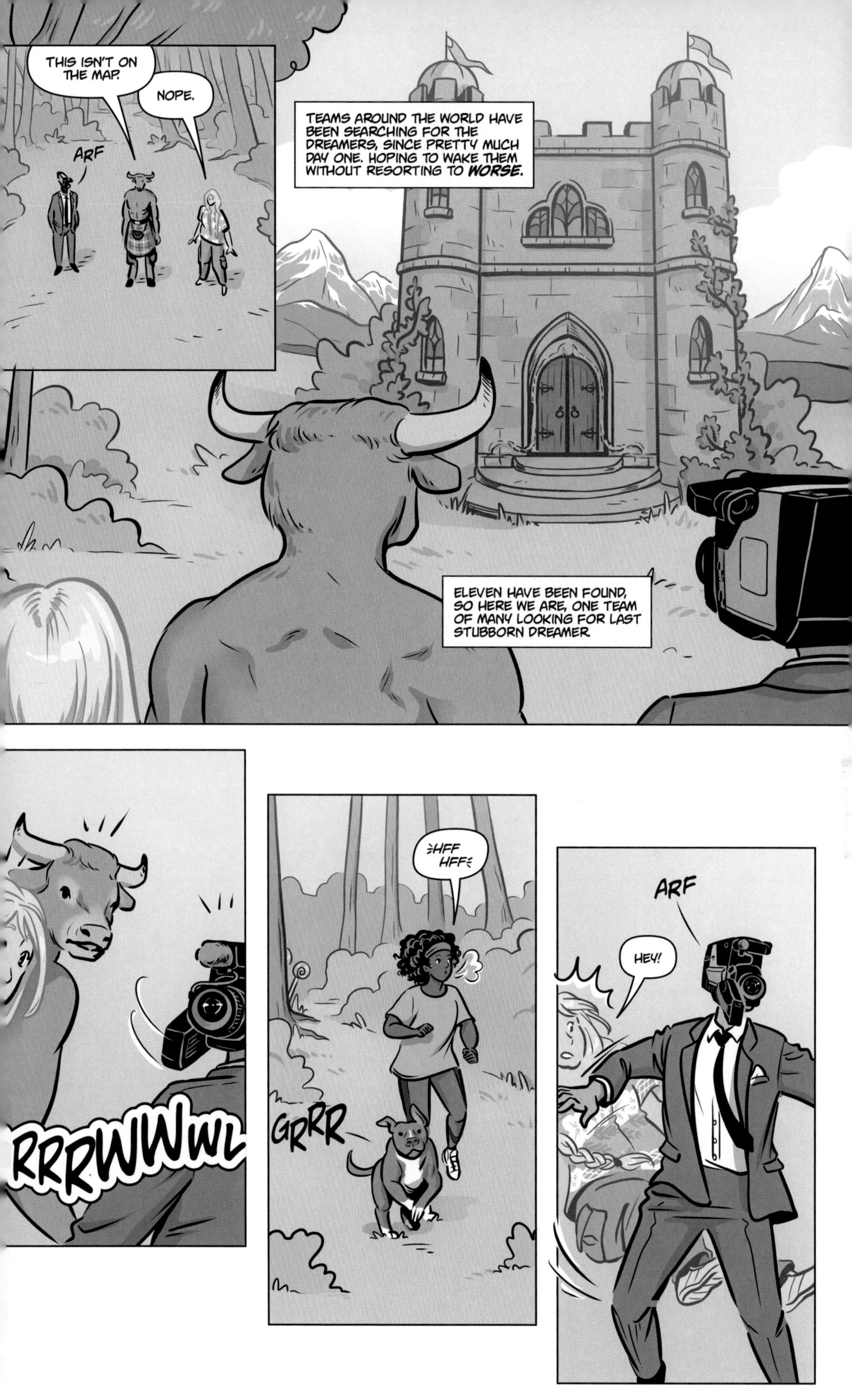
THIS ISN'T ON THE MAP.
NOPE.
ARF
TEAMS AROUND THE WORLD HAVE BEEN SEARCHING FOR THE DREAMERS, SINCE PRETTY MUCH DAY ONE. HOPING TO WAKE THEM WITHOUT RESORTING TO ***WORSE.***
ELEVEN HAVE BEEN FOUND, SO HERE WE ARE, ONE TEAM OF MANY LOOKING FOR LAST STUBBORN DREAMER.
RRRWWWL
HFF HFF
GRRR
ARF
HEY!

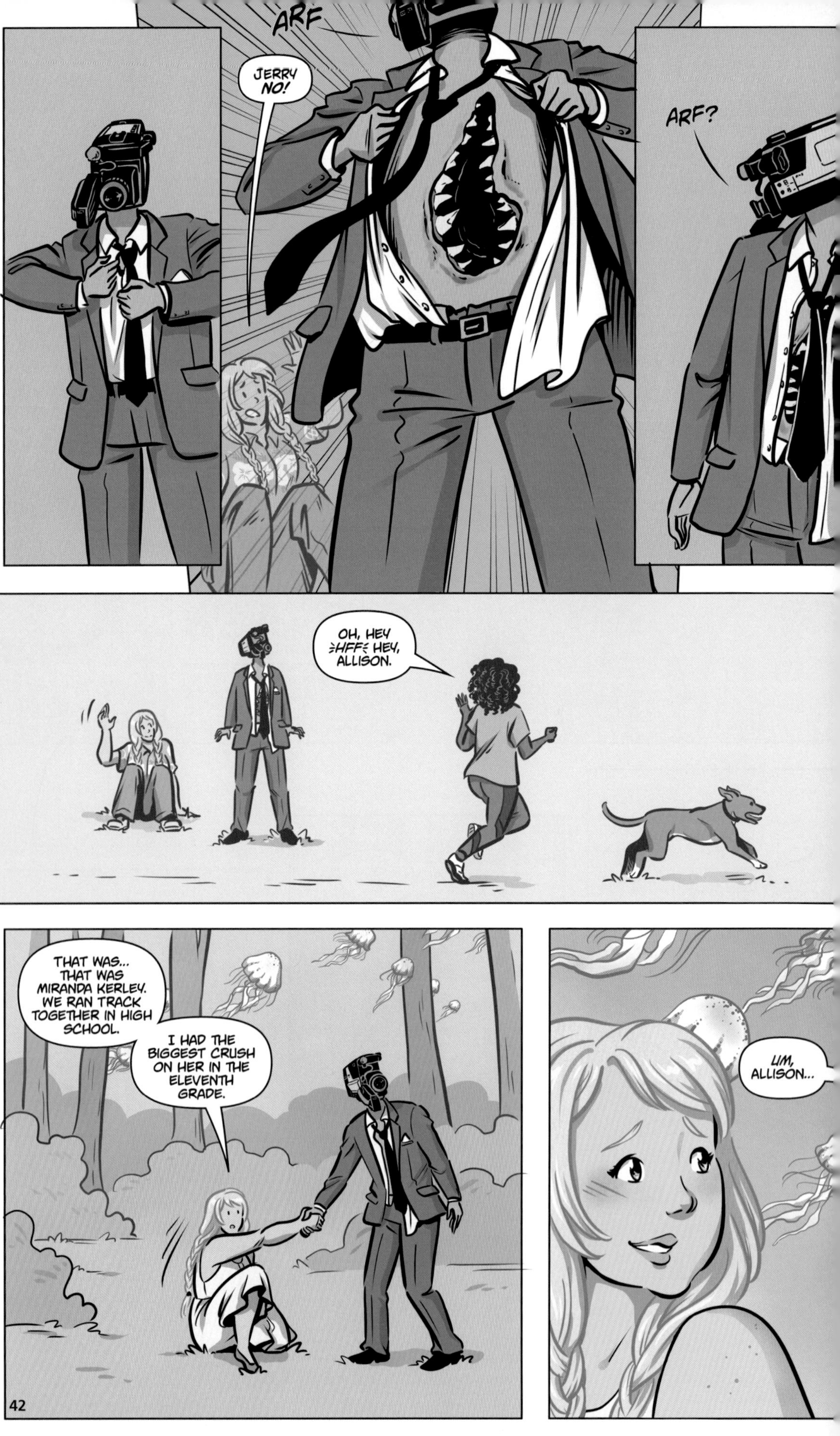
ARF
JERRY NO!
ARF?
OH, HEY HFF HEY, ALLISON.
THAT WAS... THAT WAS MIRANDA KERLEY. WE RAN TRACK TOGETHER IN HIGH SCHOOL.
I HAD THE BIGGEST CRUSH ON HER IN THE ELEVENTH GRADE.
UM, ALLISON...

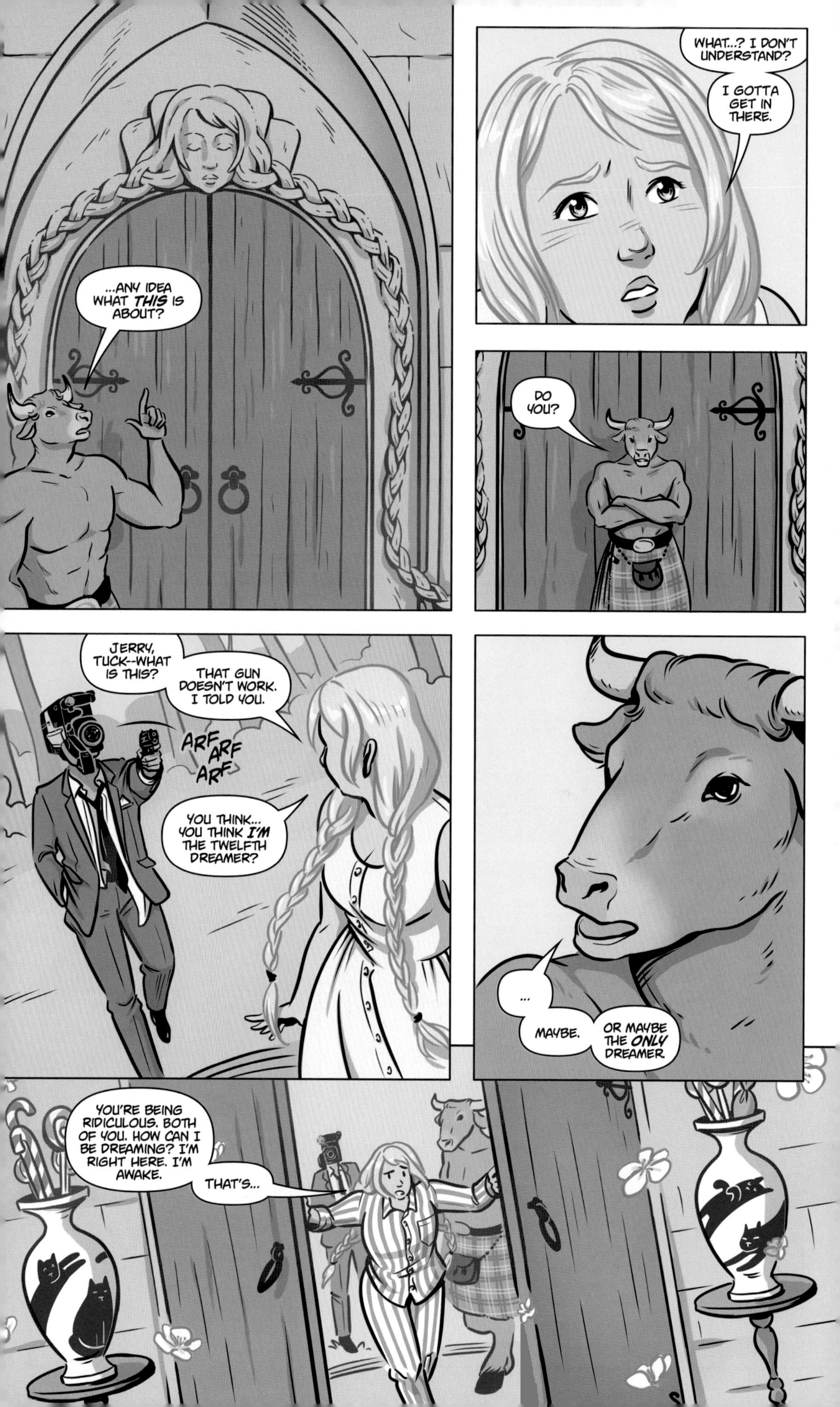
...ANY IDEA WHAT *THIS* IS ABOUT?
WHAT...? I DON'T UNDERSTAND?
I GOTTA GET IN THERE.
DO YOU?
JERRY, TUCK--WHAT IS THIS?
THAT GUN DOESN'T WORK. I TOLD YOU.
ARF ARF ARF
YOU THINK... YOU THINK *I'M* THE TWELFTH DREAMER?
...
MAYBE.
OR MAYBE THE *ONLY* DREAMER.
YOU'RE BEING RIDICULOUS. BOTH OF YOU. HOW CAN I BE DREAMING? I'M RIGHT HERE. I'M AWAKE.
THAT'S...

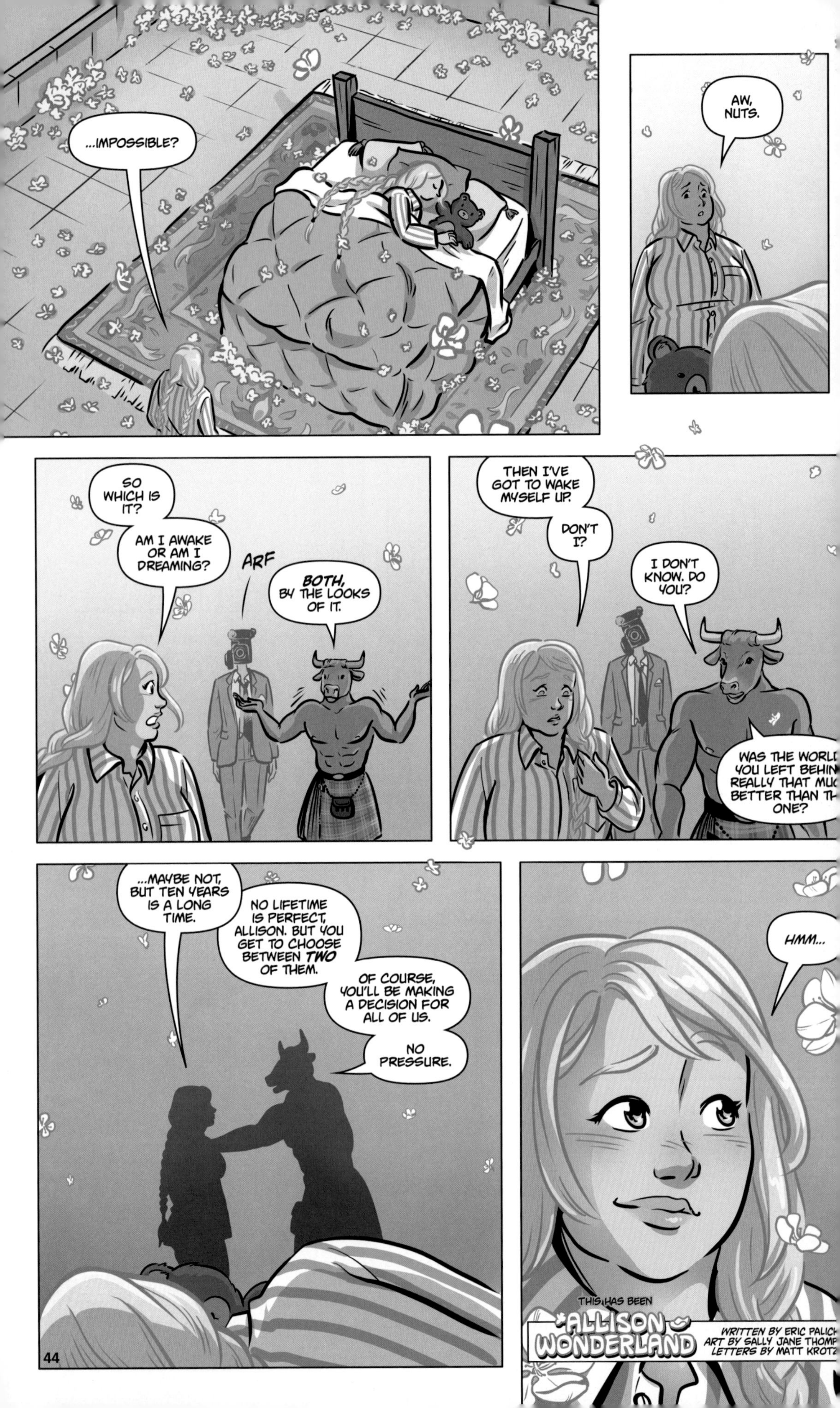

...IMPOSSIBLE?
AW, NUTS.
SO WHICH IS IT?
AM I AWAKE OR AM I DREAMING?
ARF
BOTH, BY THE LOOKS OF IT.
THEN I'VE GOT TO WAKE MYSELF UP.
DON'T I?
I DON'T KNOW. DO YOU?
WAS THE WORLD YOU LEFT BEHIN REALLY THAT MUC BETTER THAN TH ONE?
...MAYBE NOT, BUT TEN YEARS IS A LONG TIME.
NO LIFETIME IS PERFECT, ALLISON. BUT YOU GET TO CHOOSE BETWEEN *TWO* OF THEM.
OF COURSE, YOU'LL BE MAKING A DECISION FOR ALL OF US.
NO PRESSURE.
HMM...
THIS HAS BEEN
ALLISON WONDERLAND
WRITTEN BY ERIC PALICH
ART BY SALLY JANE THOMP
LETTERS BY MATT KROTZ

HEY BUDDY! I'M HOME! DON'T WORRY, EVERYTHING'S *STILL AWFUL.*

...EMPTY.

YOU HAVE IT GOOD, VICTOR. YOU DON'T HAVE TO WORRY ABOUT THE WEIGHT OF THE WORLD.

05:32 PM

BUT IT MAKES ME THINK, WHY HAVEN'T I MADE THE LEAP YET?

KSSHH

BECAUSE--

YOU'RE BETTER THAN THAT, NATHAN.

Support Animals

WRITTEN by Jono DIENER • LINE ART by Sebastian PIRIZ
COLORS by Shaun STRUBLE • LETTERS by Jim CAMPBELL

45

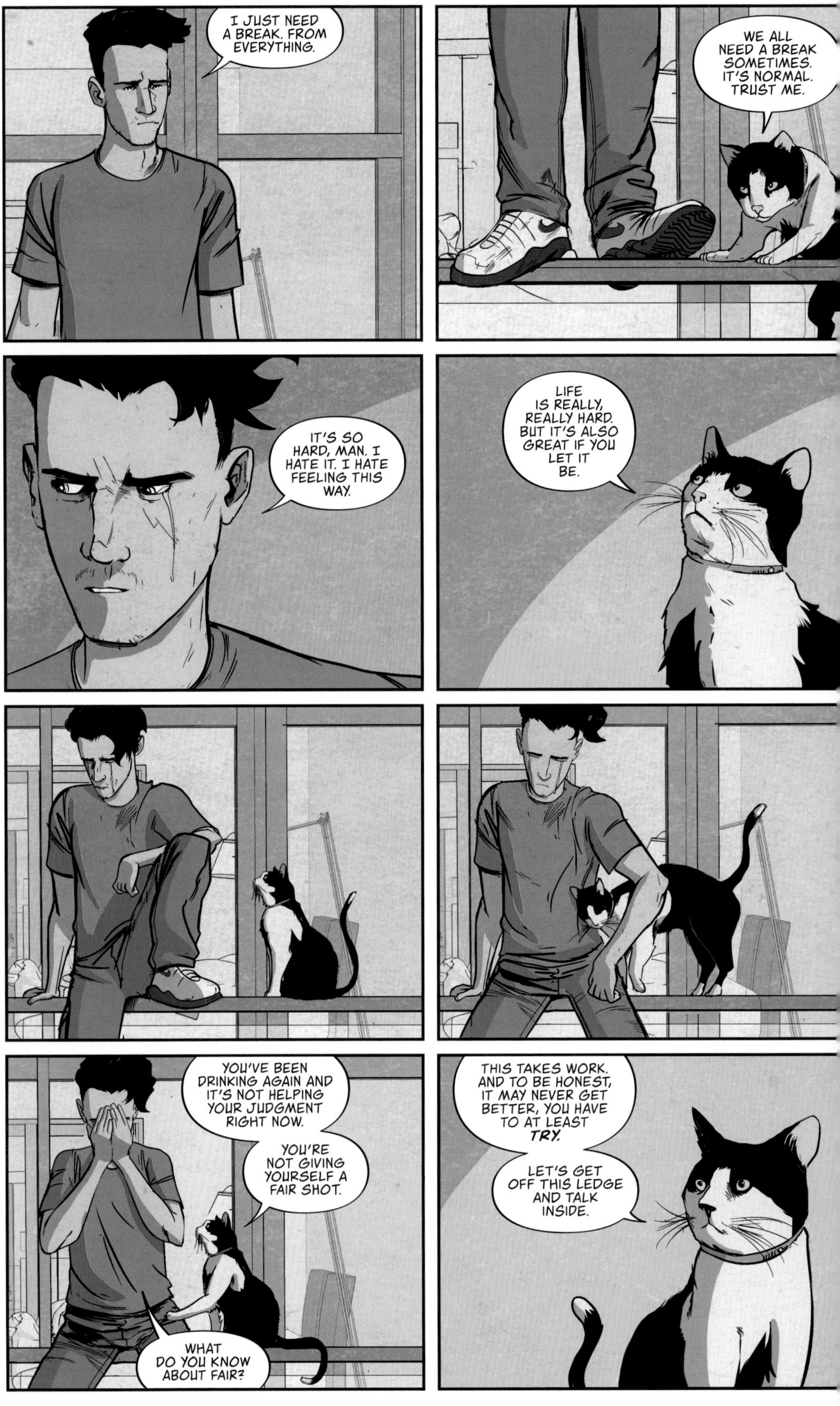
I JUST NEED A BREAK. FROM EVERYTHING.
WE ALL NEED A BREAK SOMETIMES. IT'S NORMAL. TRUST ME.
IT'S SO HARD, MAN. I HATE IT. I HATE FEELING THIS WAY.
LIFE IS REALLY, REALLY HARD. BUT IT'S ALSO GREAT IF YOU LET IT BE.
YOU'VE BEEN DRINKING AGAIN AND IT'S NOT HELPING YOUR JUDGMENT RIGHT NOW.
YOU'RE NOT GIVING YOURSELF A FAIR SHOT.
WHAT DO YOU KNOW ABOUT FAIR?
THIS TAKES WORK. AND TO BE HONEST, IT MAY NEVER GET BETTER, YOU HAVE TO AT LEAST ***TRY.***
LET'S GET OFF THIS LEDGE AND TALK INSIDE.

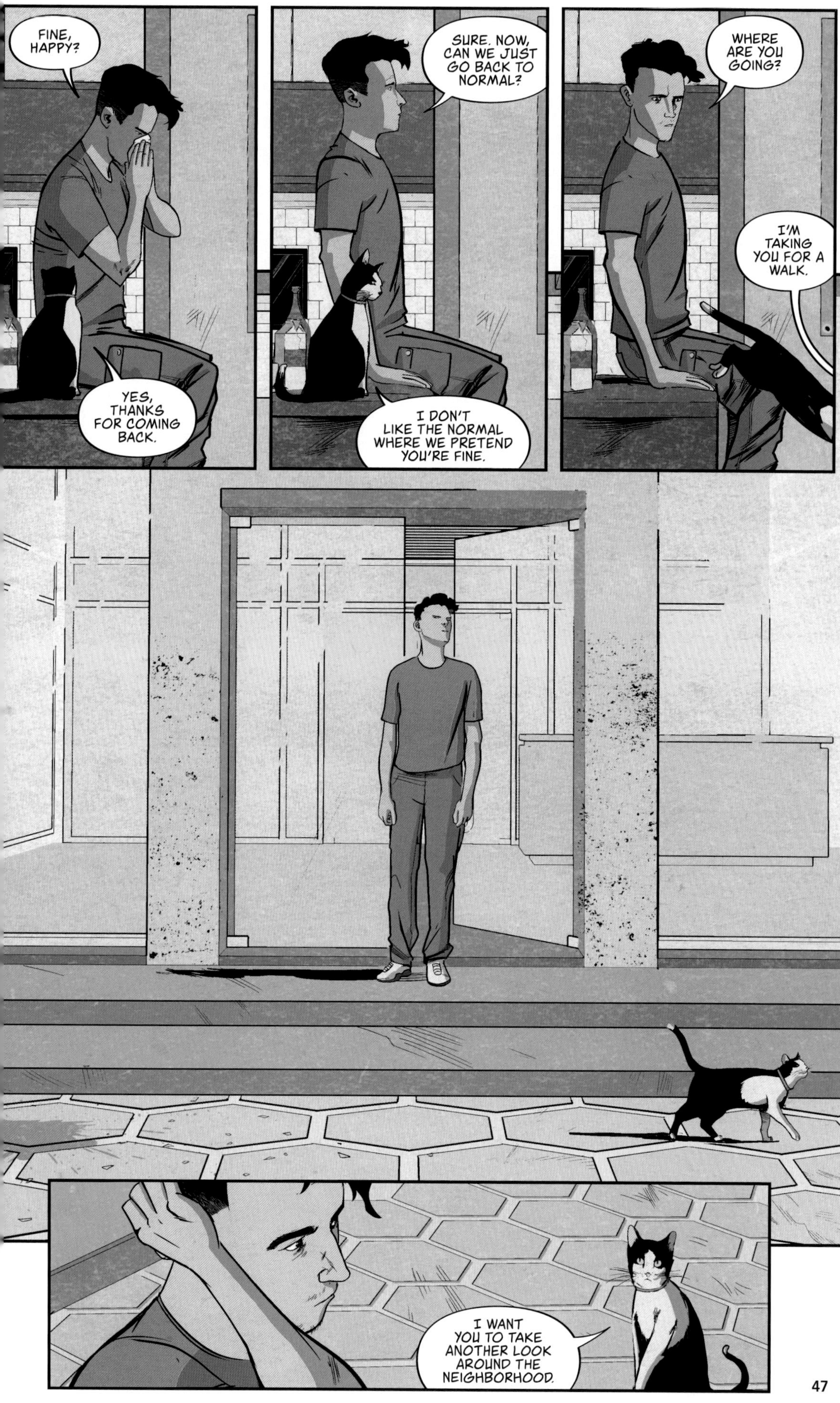
FINE, HAPPY?
YES, THANKS FOR COMING BACK.
SURE. NOW, CAN WE JUST GO BACK TO NORMAL?
I DON'T LIKE THE NORMAL WHERE WE PRETEND YOU'RE FINE.
WHERE ARE YOU GOING?
I'M TAKING YOU FOR A WALK.
I WANT YOU TO TAKE ANOTHER LOOK AROUND THE NEIGHBORHOOD.

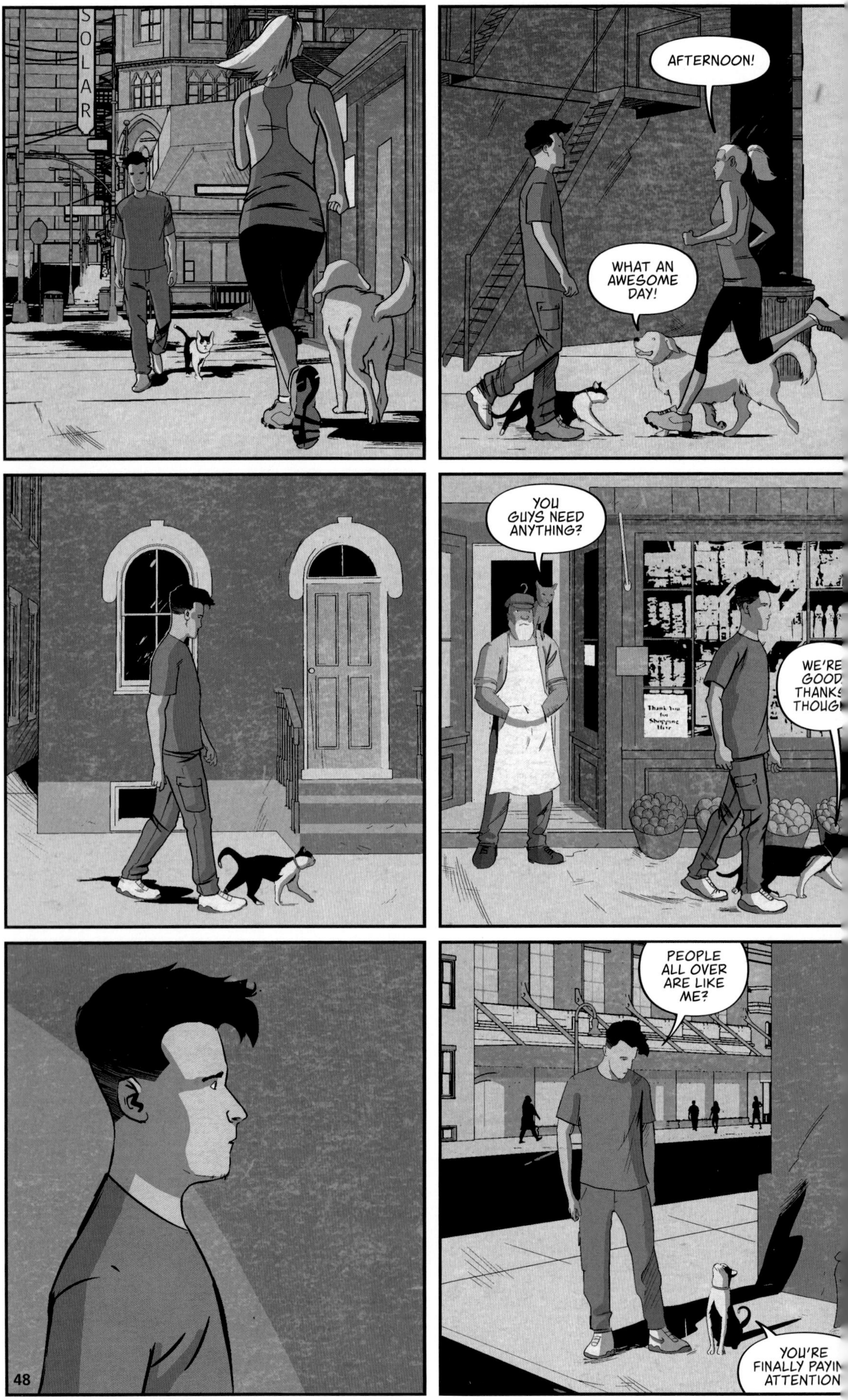
SOLAR
AFTERNOON!
WHAT AN AWESOME DAY!
YOU GUYS NEED ANYTHING?
Thank You for Shopping Here
WE'RE GOOD THANKS THOUG
PEOPLE ALL OVER ARE LIKE ME?
YOU'RE FINALLY PAYIN ATTENTION

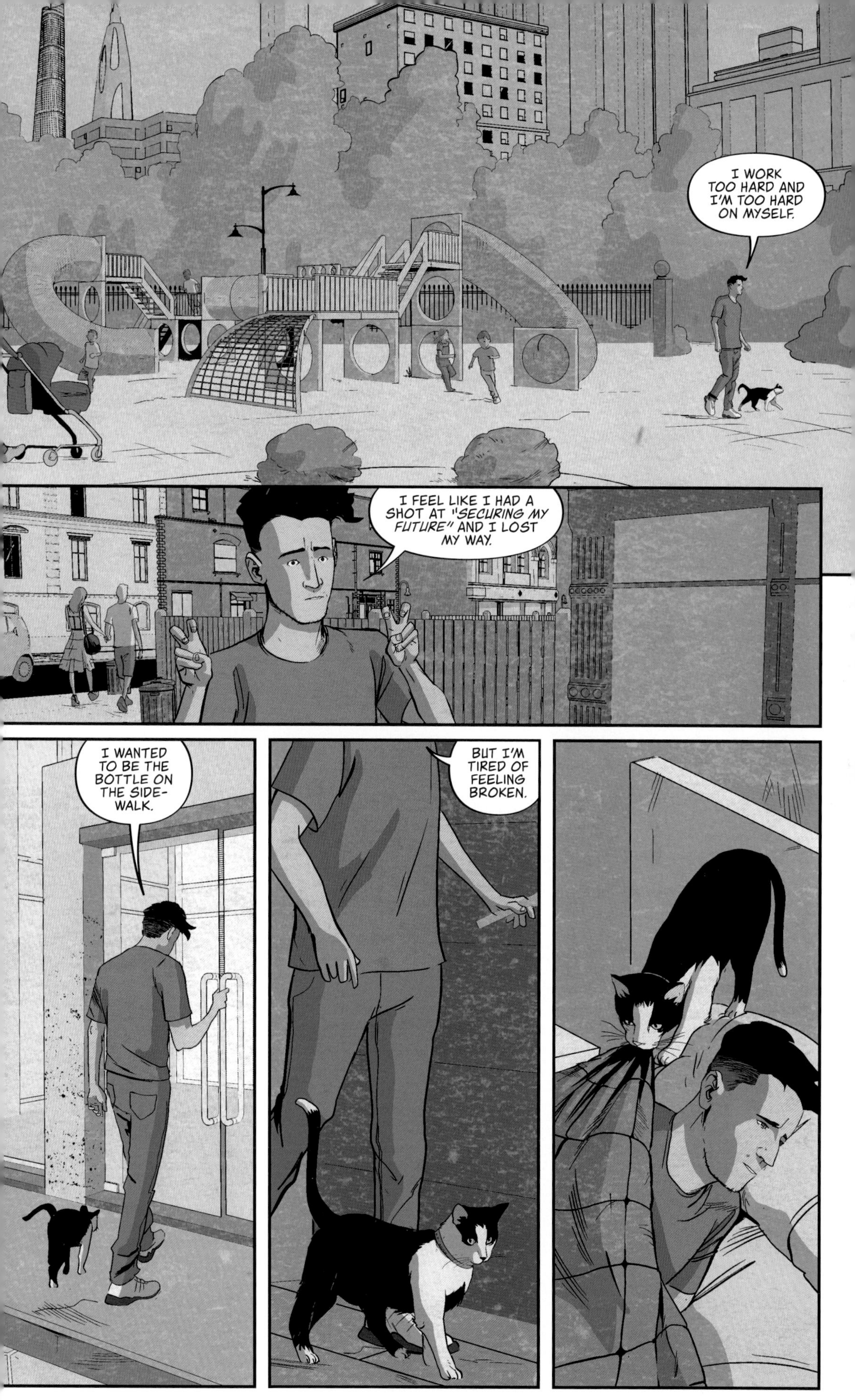
I WORK TOO HARD AND I'M TOO HARD ON MYSELF.
I FEEL LIKE I HAD A SHOT AT "SECURING MY FUTURE" AND I LOST MY WAY.
I WANTED TO BE THE BOTTLE ON THE SIDE-WALK.
BUT I'M TIRED OF FEELING BROKEN.

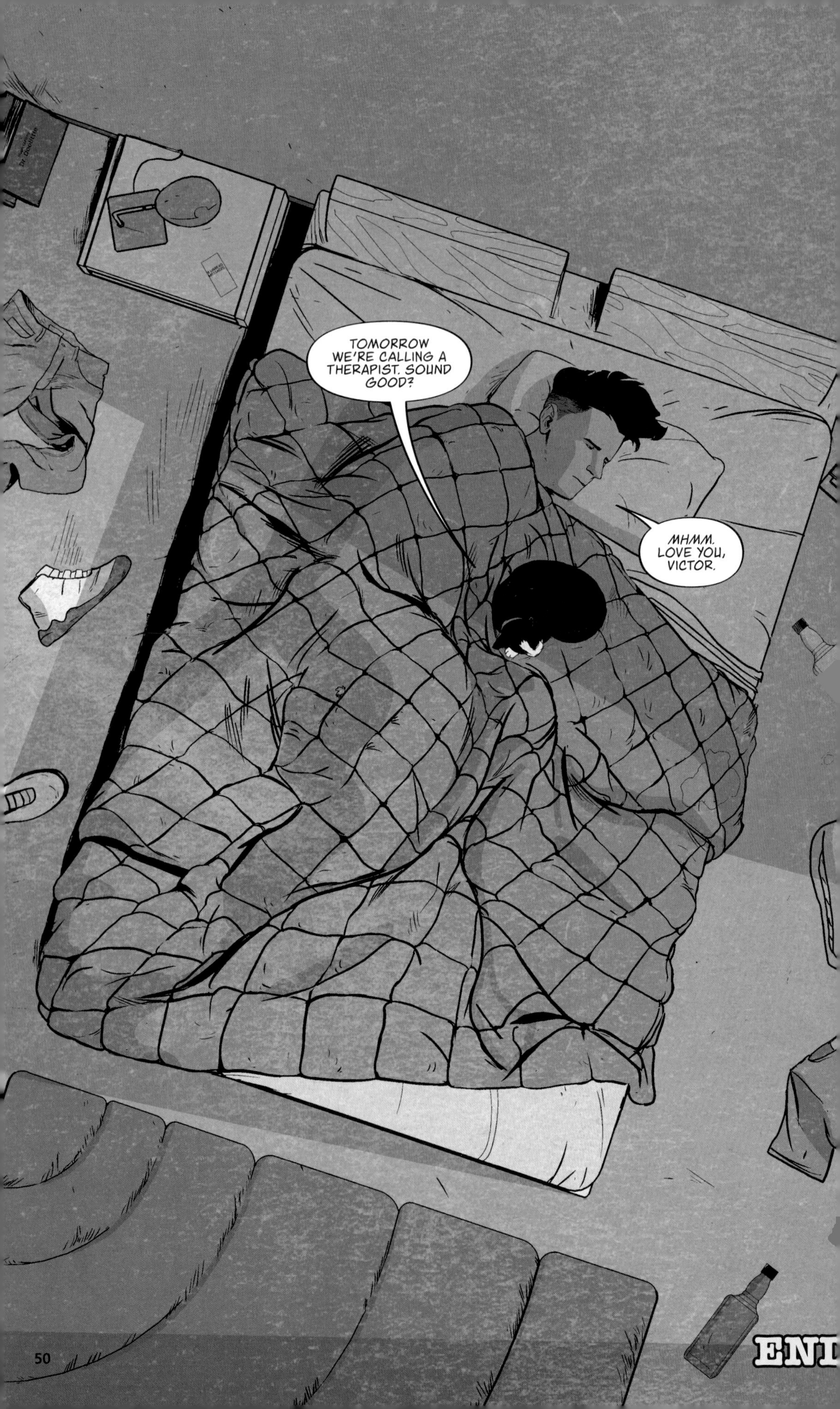
TOMORROW WE'RE CALLING A THERAPIST. SOUND GOOD?
MHMM. LOVE YOU, VICTOR.
END

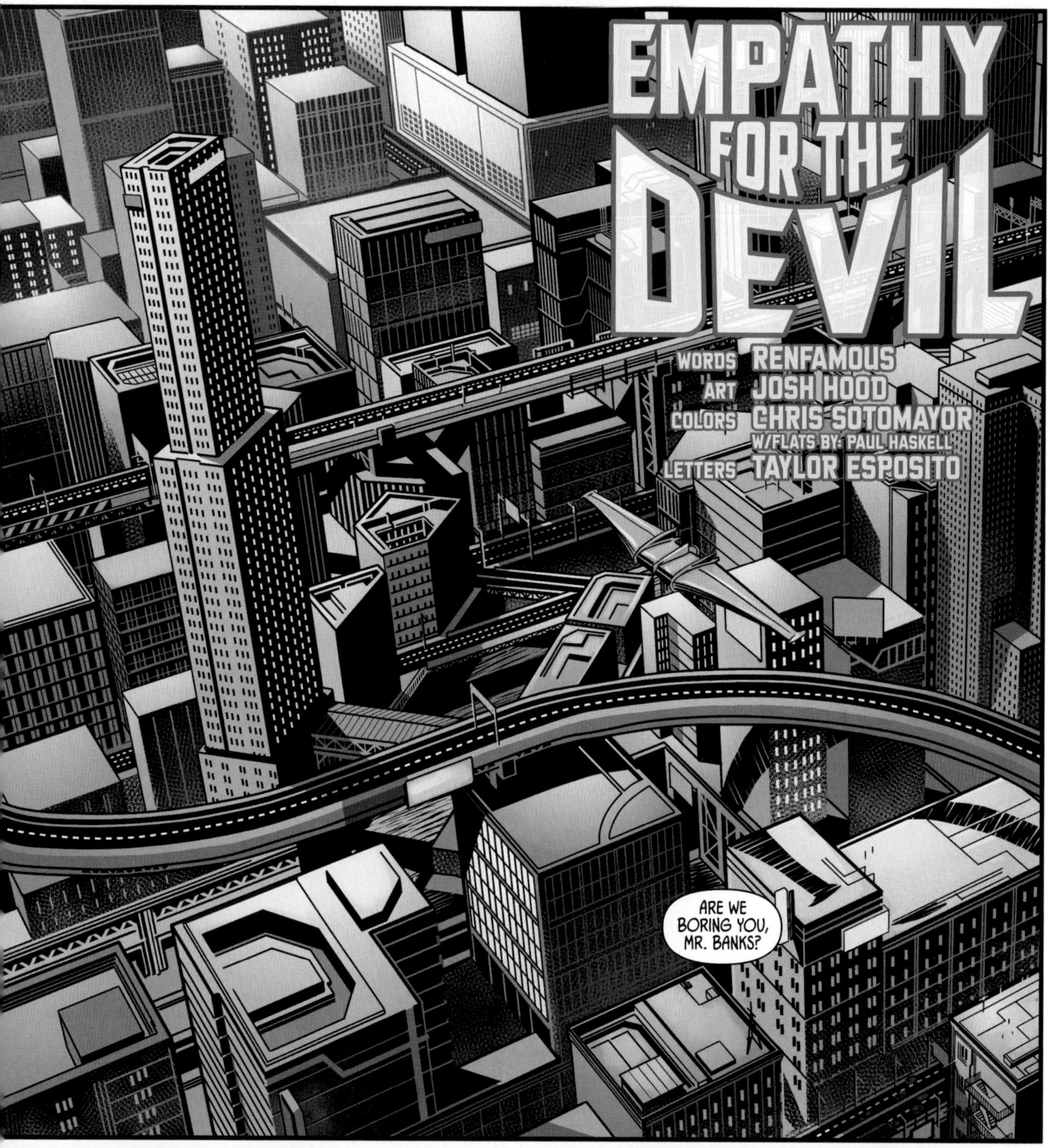
EMPATHY FOR THE DEVIL
WORDS RENFAMOUS
ART JOSH HOOD
COLORS CHRIS SOTOMAYOR
W/FLATS BY: PAUL HASKELL
LETTERS TAYLOR ESPOSITO
ARE WE BORING YOU, MR. BANKS?
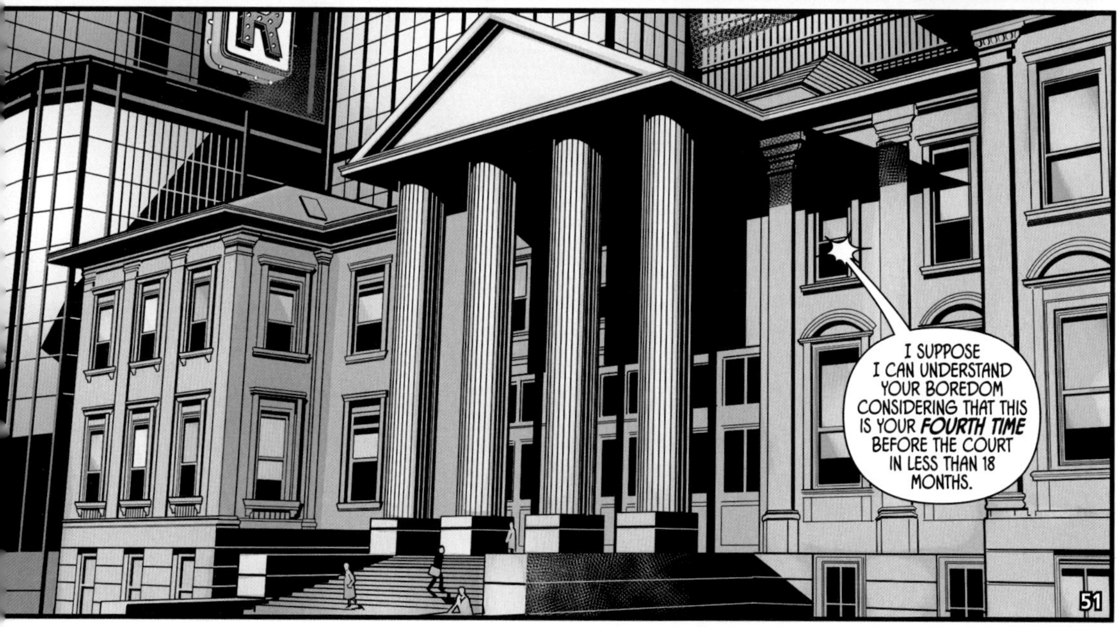
I SUPPOSE I CAN UNDERSTAND YOUR BOREDOM CONSIDERING THAT THIS IS YOUR ***FOURTH TIME*** BEFORE THE COURT IN LESS THAN 18 MONTHS.

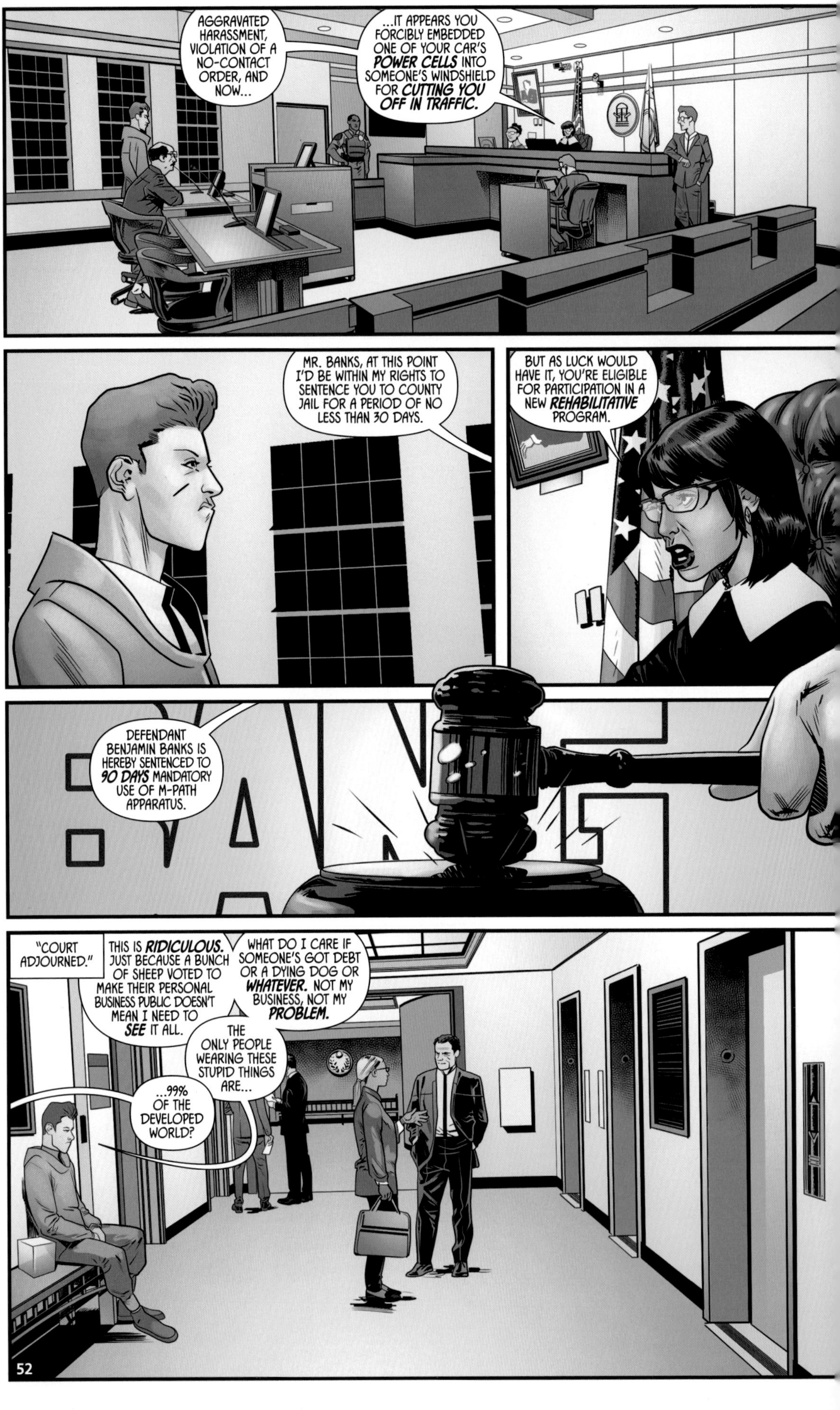
AGGRAVATED HARASSMENT, VIOLATION OF A NO-CONTACT ORDER, AND NOW...
...IT APPEARS YOU FORCIBLY EMBEDDED ONE OF YOUR CAR'S POWER CELLS INTO SOMEONE'S WINDSHIELD FOR CUTTING YOU OFF IN TRAFFIC.
MR. BANKS, AT THIS POINT I'D BE WITHIN MY RIGHTS TO SENTENCE YOU TO COUNTY JAIL FOR A PERIOD OF NO LESS THAN 30 DAYS.
BUT AS LUCK WOULD HAVE IT, YOU'RE ELIGIBLE FOR PARTICIPATION IN A NEW REHABILITATIVE PROGRAM.
DEFENDANT BENJAMIN BANKS IS HEREBY SENTENCED TO 90 DAYS MANDATORY USE OF M-PATH APPARATUS.
"COURT ADJOURNED."
THIS IS RIDICULOUS. JUST BECAUSE A BUNCH OF SHEEP VOTED TO MAKE THEIR PERSONAL BUSINESS PUBLIC DOESN'T MEAN I NEED TO SEE IT ALL.
WHAT DO I CARE IF SOMEONE'S GOT DEBT OR A DYING DOG OR WHATEVER. NOT MY BUSINESS, NOT MY PROBLEM.
THE ONLY PEOPLE WEARING THESE STUPID THINGS ARE...
...99% OF THE DEVELOPED WORLD?

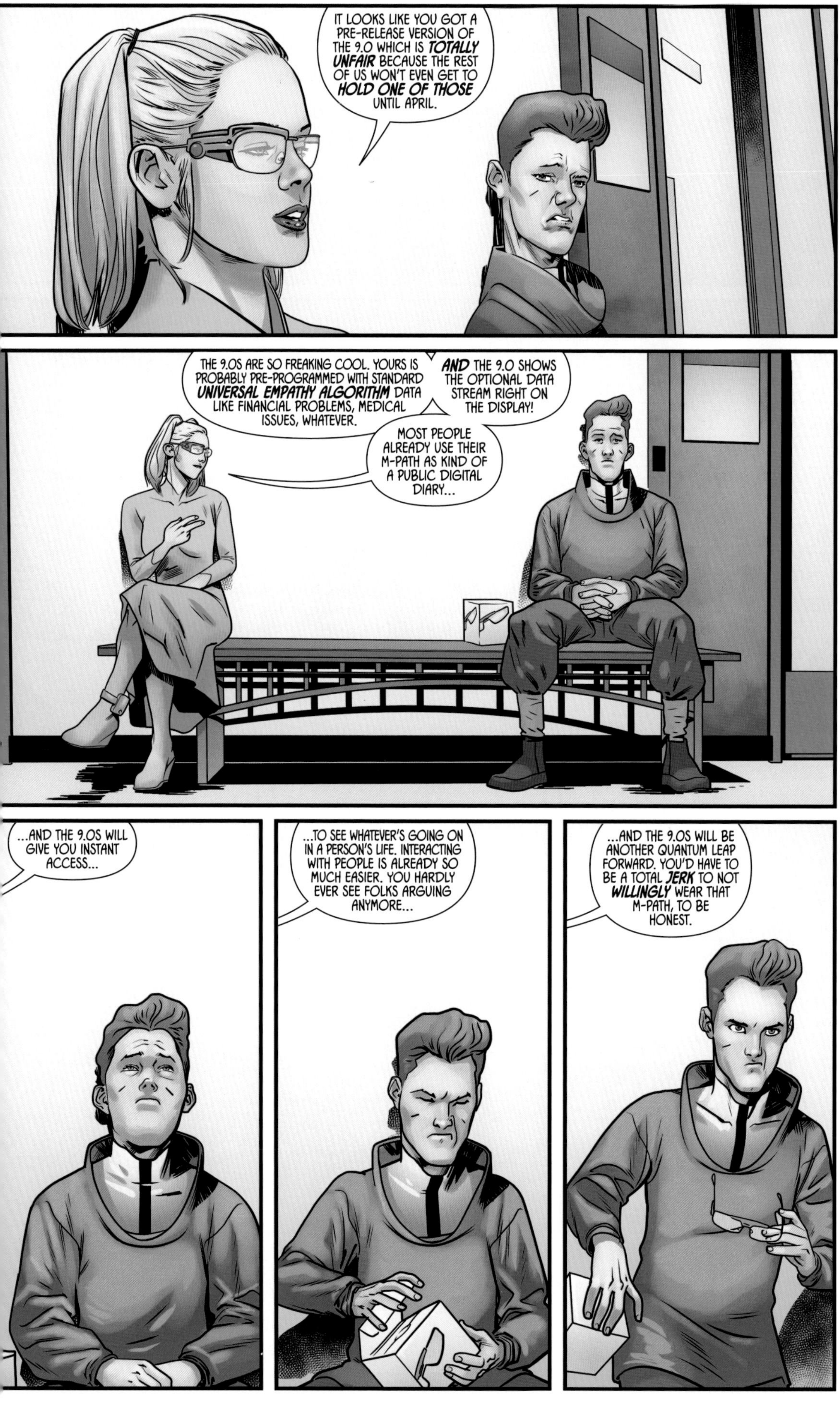
IT LOOKS LIKE YOU GOT A PRE-RELEASE VERSION OF THE 9.0 WHICH IS TOTALLY UNFAIR BECAUSE THE REST OF US WON'T EVEN GET TO HOLD ONE OF THOSE UNTIL APRIL.
THE 9.0S ARE SO FREAKING COOL. YOURS IS PROBABLY PRE-PROGRAMMED WITH STANDARD UNIVERSAL EMPATHY ALGORITHM DATA LIKE FINANCIAL PROBLEMS, MEDICAL ISSUES, WHATEVER.
AND THE 9.0 SHOWS THE OPTIONAL DATA STREAM RIGHT ON THE DISPLAY!
MOST PEOPLE ALREADY USE THEIR M-PATH AS KIND OF A PUBLIC DIGITAL DIARY...
...AND THE 9.0S WILL GIVE YOU INSTANT ACCESS...
...TO SEE WHATEVER'S GOING ON IN A PERSON'S LIFE. INTERACTING WITH PEOPLE IS ALREADY SO MUCH EASIER. YOU HARDLY EVER SEE FOLKS ARGUING ANYMORE...
...AND THE 9.0S WILL BE ANOTHER QUANTUM LEAP FORWARD. YOU'D HAVE TO BE A TOTAL JERK TO NOT WILLINGLY WEAR THAT M-PATH, TO BE HONEST.

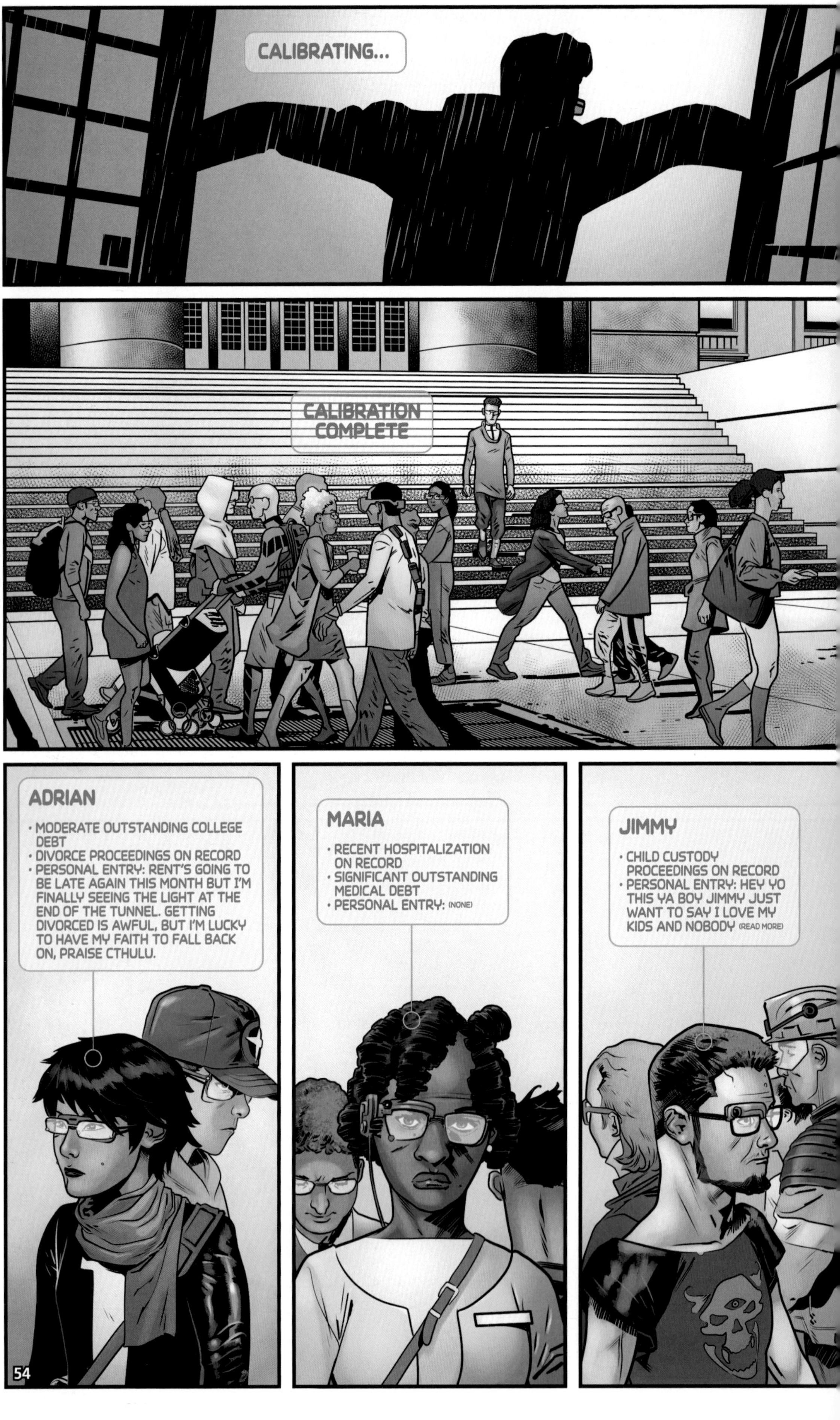
CALIBRATING...
CALIBRATION COMPLETE
ADRIAN
• MODERATE OUTSTANDING COLLEGE DEBT
• DIVORCE PROCEEDINGS ON RECORD
• PERSONAL ENTRY: RENT'S GOING TO BE LATE AGAIN THIS MONTH BUT I'M FINALLY SEEING THE LIGHT AT THE END OF THE TUNNEL. GETTING DIVORCED IS AWFUL, BUT I'M LUCKY TO HAVE MY FAITH TO FALL BACK ON, PRAISE CTHULU.
MARIA
• RECENT HOSPITALIZATION ON RECORD
• SIGNIFICANT OUTSTANDING MEDICAL DEBT
• PERSONAL ENTRY: (NONE)
JIMMY
• CHILD CUSTODY PROCEEDINGS ON RECORD
• PERSONAL ENTRY: HEY YO THIS YA BOY JIMMY JUST WANT TO SAY I LOVE MY KIDS AND NOBODY (READ MORE)

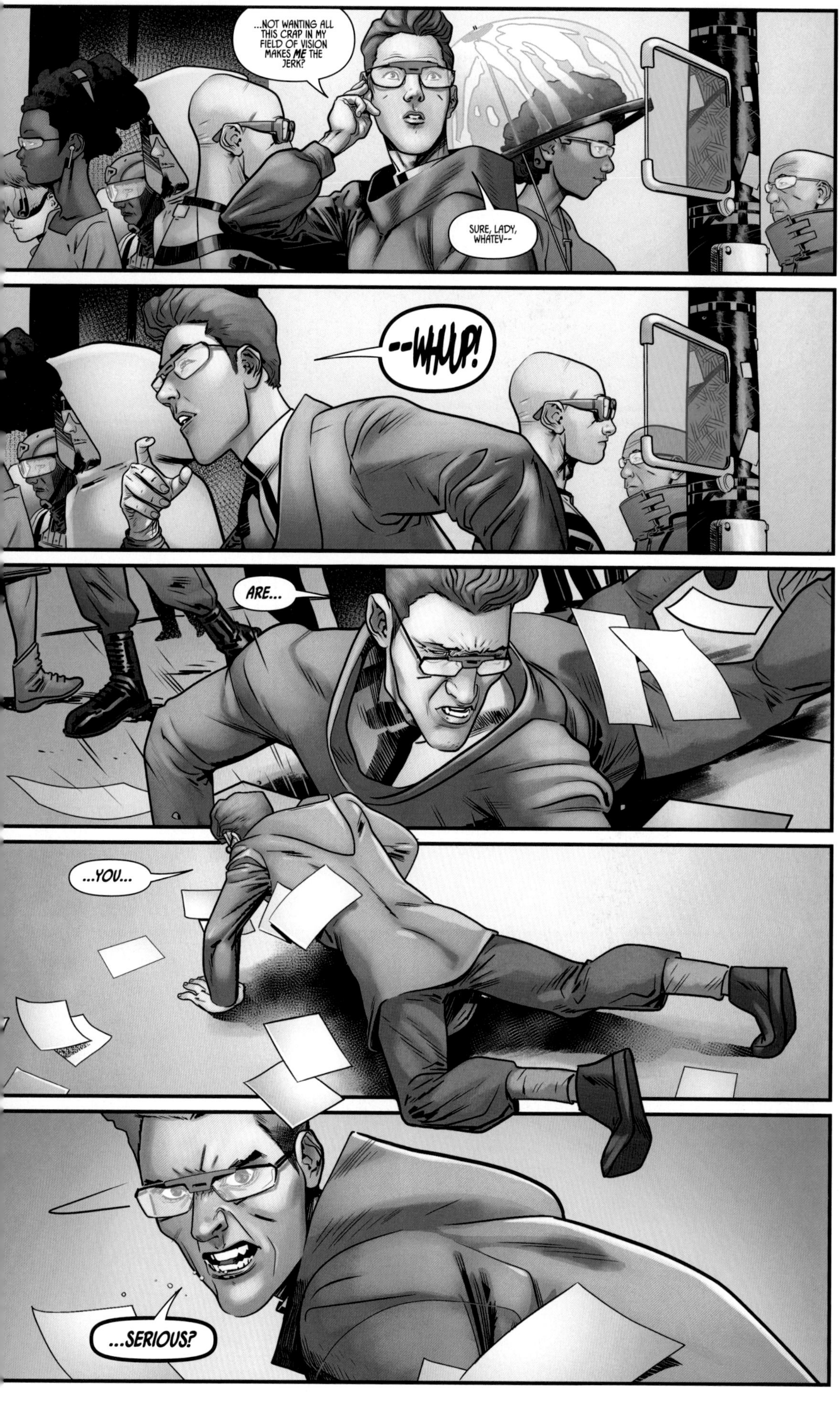
...NOT WANTING ALL THIS CRAP IN MY FIELD OF VISION MAKES *ME* THE JERK?
SURE, LADY, WHATEV--
--WHUP!
ARE...
...YOU...
...SERIOUS?

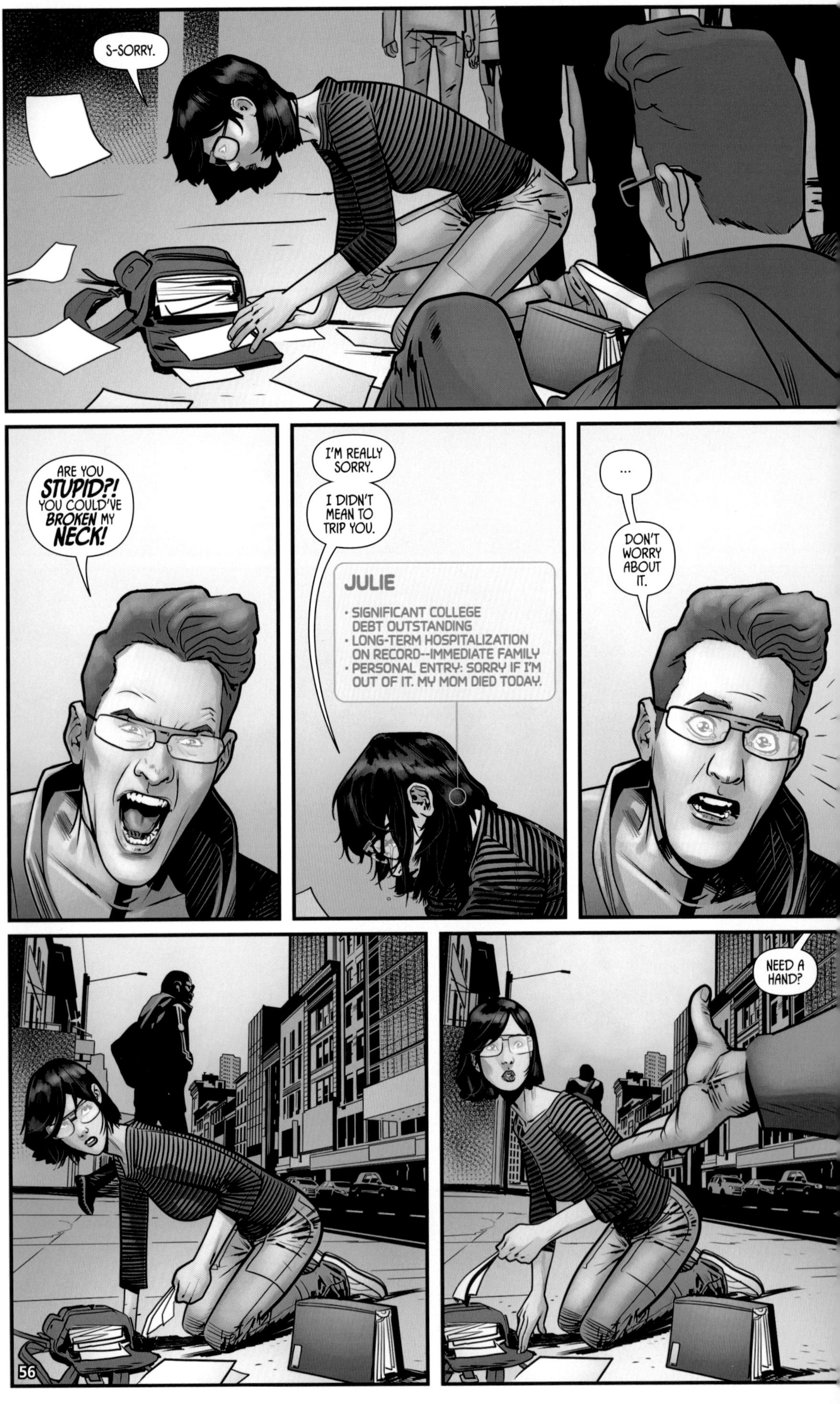
S-SORRY.
ARE YOU STUPID?! YOU COULD'VE BROKEN MY NECK!
I'M REALLY SORRY.
I DIDN'T MEAN TO TRIP YOU.
JULIE
• SIGNIFICANT COLLEGE DEBT OUTSTANDING
• LONG-TERM HOSPITALIZATION ON RECORD--IMMEDIATE FAMILY
• PERSONAL ENTRY: SORRY IF I'M OUT OF IT. MY MOM DIED TODAY.
...
DON'T WORRY ABOUT IT.
NEED A HAND?

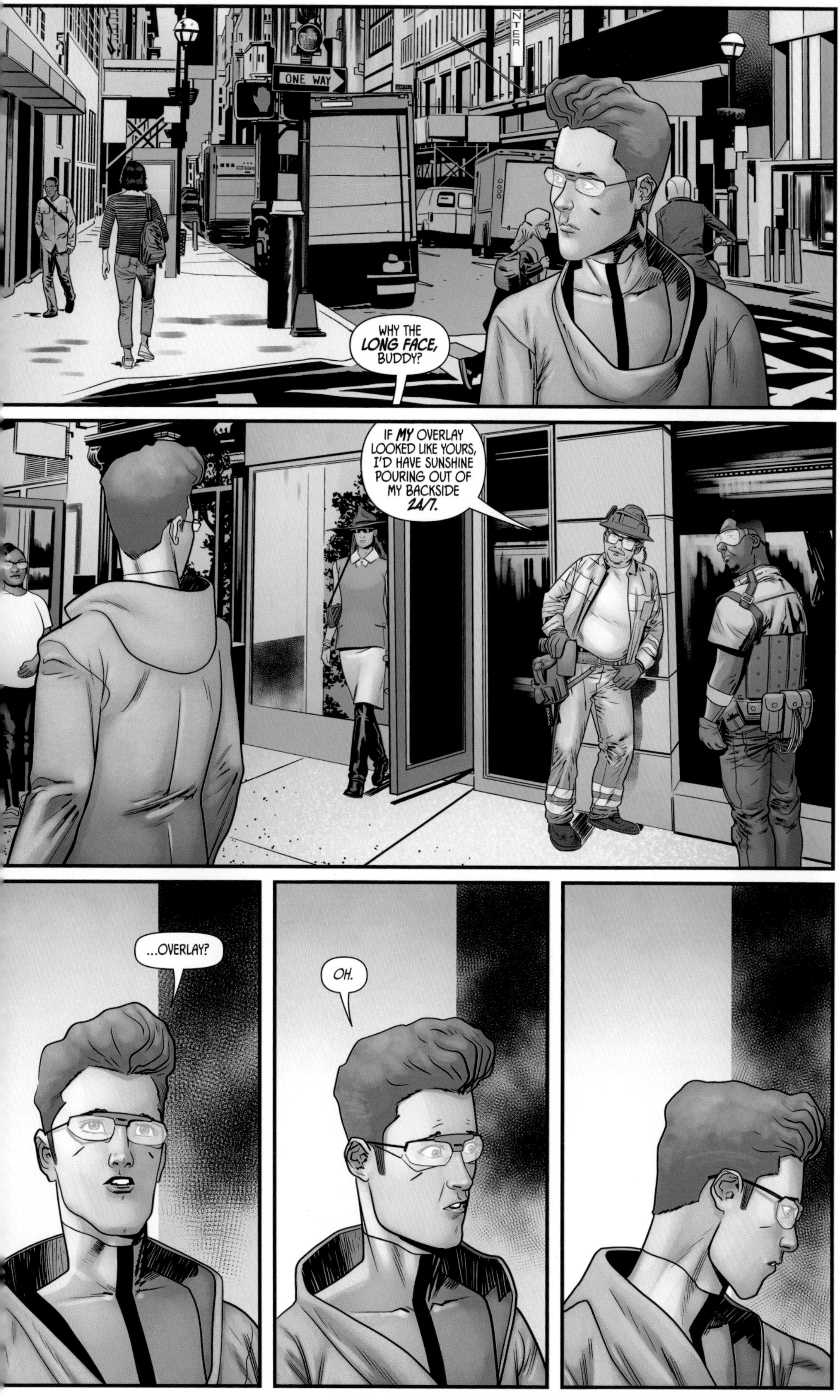
ONE WAY
WHY THE LONG FACE, BUDDY?
IF MY OVERLAY LOOKED LIKE YOURS, I'D HAVE SUNSHINE POURING OUT OF MY BACKSIDE 24/7.
...OVERLAY?
OH.

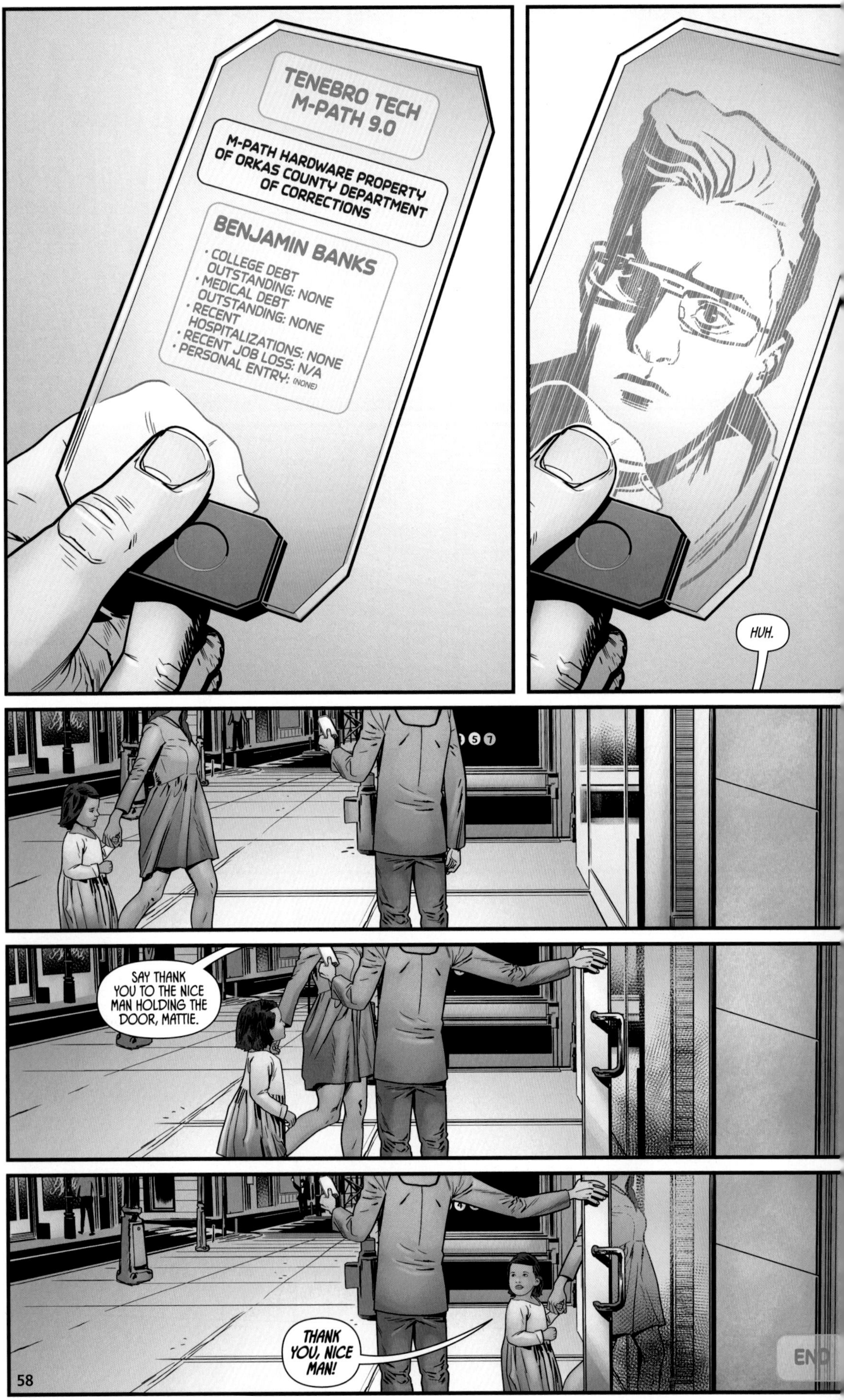
TENEBRO TECH M-PATH 9.0
M-PATH HARDWARE PROPERTY OF ORKAS COUNTY DEPARTMENT OF CORRECTIONS
BENJAMIN BANKS
• COLLEGE DEBT OUTSTANDING: NONE
• MEDICAL DEBT OUTSTANDING: NONE
• RECENT HOSPITALIZATIONS: NONE
• RECENT JOB LOSS: N/A
• PERSONAL ENTRY: (NONE)
HUH.
SAY THANK YOU TO THE NICE MAN HOLDING THE DOOR, MATTIE.
THANK YOU, NICE MAN!
END

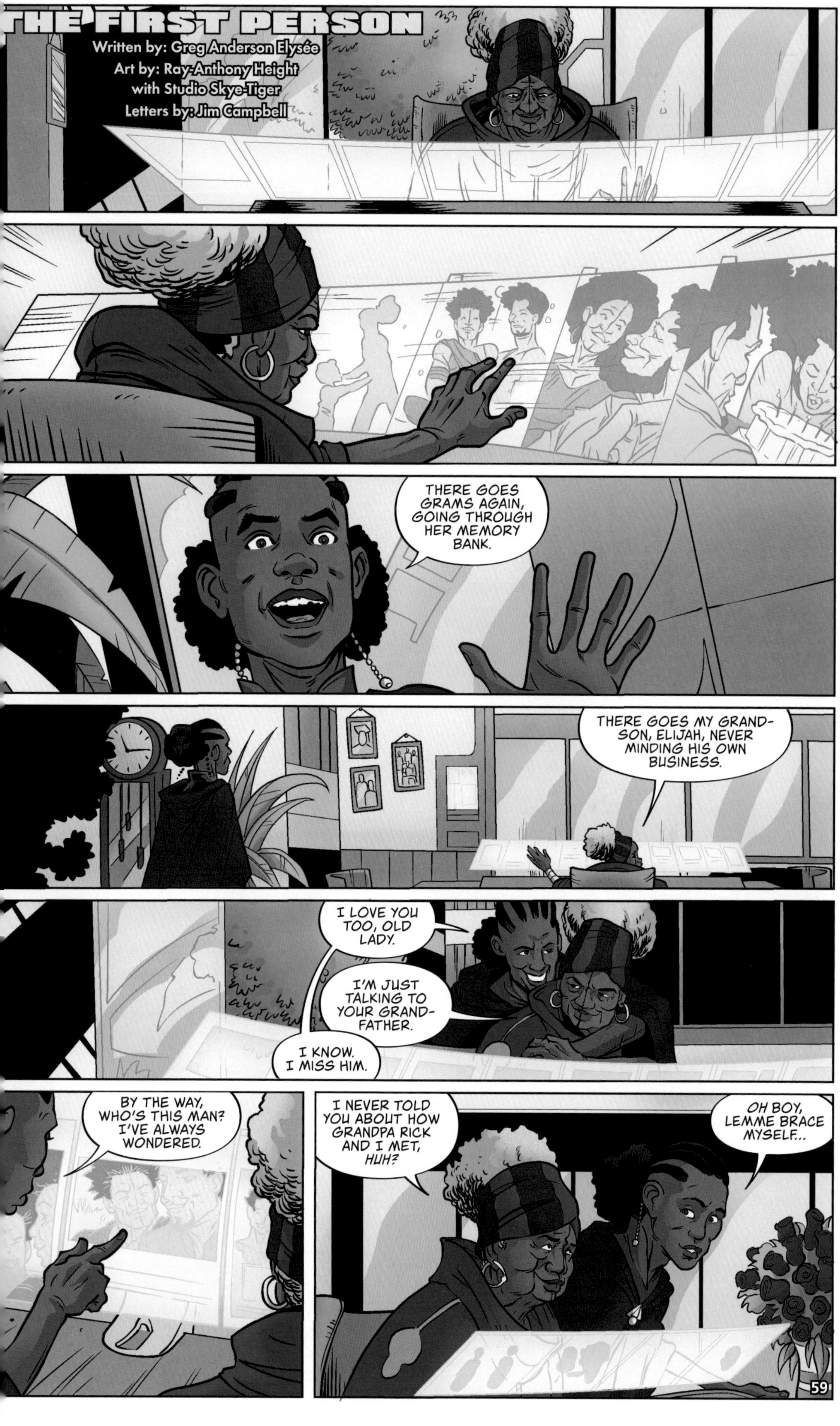
THE FIRST PERSON
Written by: Greg Anderson Elysée
Art by: Ray-Anthony Height
with Studio Skye-Tiger
Letters by: Jim Campbell
THERE GOES GRAMS AGAIN, GOING THROUGH HER MEMORY BANK.
THERE GOES MY GRANDSON, ELIJAH, NEVER MINDING HIS OWN BUSINESS.
I LOVE YOU TOO, OLD LADY.
I'M JUST TALKING TO YOUR GRANDFATHER.
I KNOW. I MISS HIM.
BY THE WAY, WHO'S THIS MAN? I'VE ALWAYS WONDERED.
I NEVER TOLD YOU ABOUT HOW GRANDPA RICK AND I MET, *HUH?*
OH BOY, LEMME BRACE MYSELF...

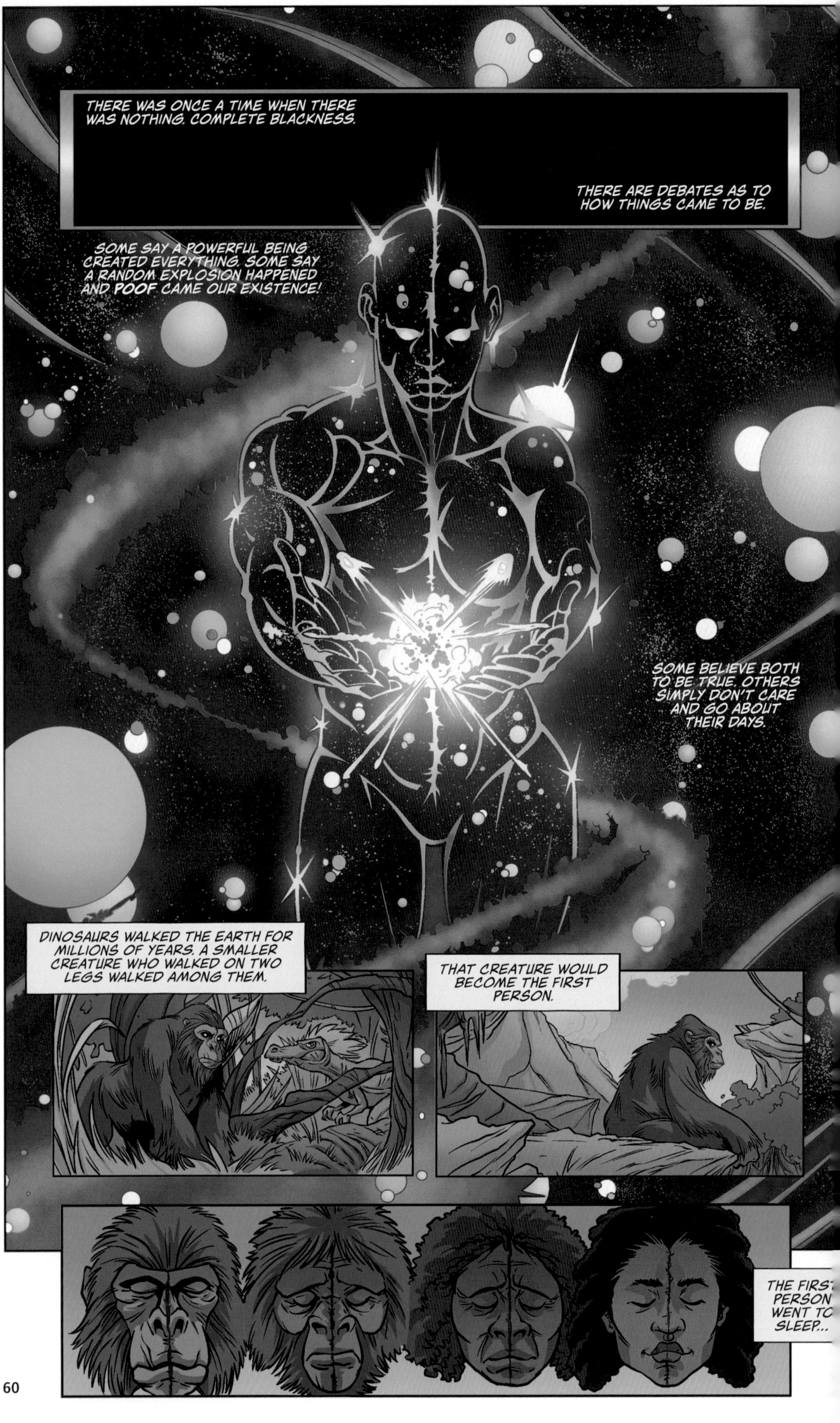
THERE WAS ONCE A TIME WHEN THERE WAS NOTHING. COMPLETE BLACKNESS.
THERE ARE DEBATES AS TO HOW THINGS CAME TO BE.
SOME SAY A POWERFUL BEING CREATED EVERYTHING. SOME SAY A RANDOM EXPLOSION HAPPENED AND POOF CAME OUR EXISTENCE!
SOME BELIEVE BOTH TO BE TRUE. OTHERS SIMPLY DON'T CARE AND GO ABOUT THEIR DAYS.
DINOSAURS WALKED THE EARTH FOR MILLIONS OF YEARS. A SMALLER CREATURE WHO WALKED ON TWO LEGS WALKED AMONG THEM.
THAT CREATURE WOULD BECOME THE FIRST PERSON.
THE FIRST PERSON WENT TO SLEEP...

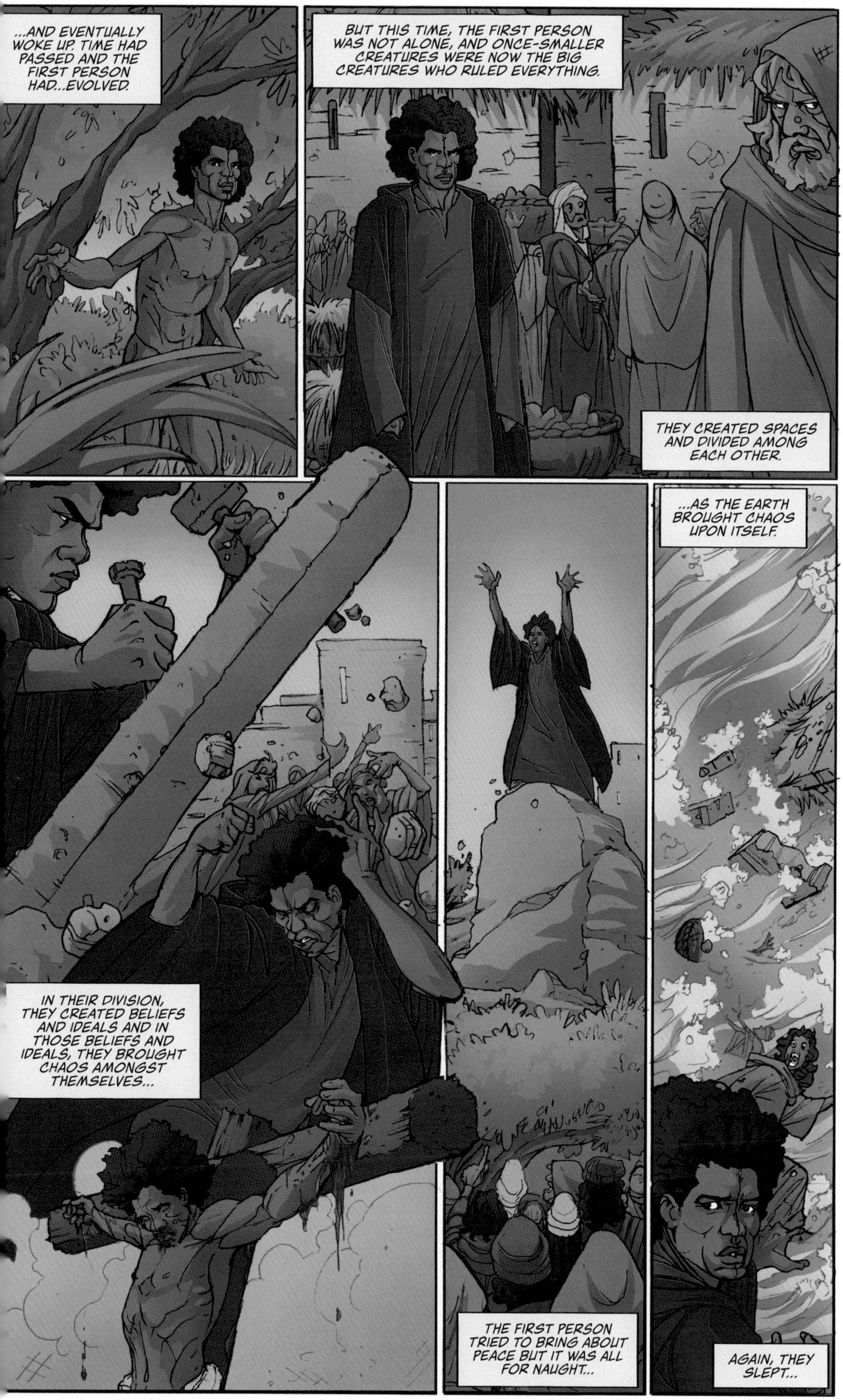
...AND EVENTUALLY WOKE UP. TIME HAD PASSED AND THE FIRST PERSON HAD...EVOLVED.
BUT THIS TIME, THE FIRST PERSON WAS NOT ALONE, AND ONCE-SMALLER CREATURES WERE NOW THE BIG CREATURES WHO RULED EVERYTHING.
THEY CREATED SPACES AND DIVIDED AMONG EACH OTHER.
IN THEIR DIVISION, THEY CREATED BELIEFS AND IDEALS AND IN THOSE BELIEFS AND IDEALS, THEY BROUGHT CHAOS AMONGST THEMSELVES...
THE FIRST PERSON TRIED TO BRING ABOUT PEACE BUT IT WAS ALL FOR NAUGHT...
...AS THE EARTH BROUGHT CHAOS UPON ITSELF.
AGAIN, THEY SLEPT...

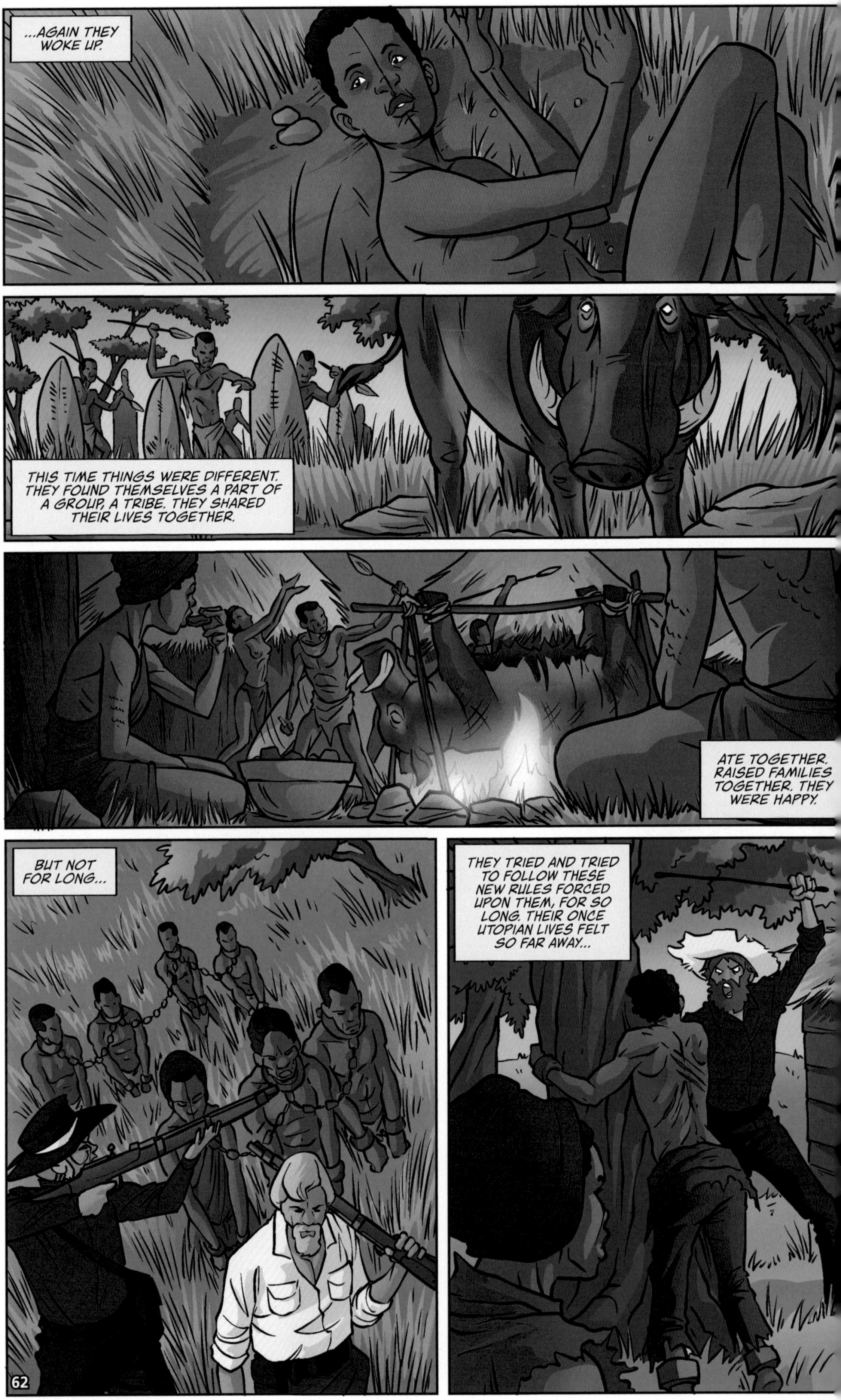
...AGAIN THEY WOKE UP.
THIS TIME THINGS WERE DIFFERENT. THEY FOUND THEMSELVES A PART OF A GROUP, A TRIBE. THEY SHARED THEIR LIVES TOGETHER.
ATE TOGETHER. RAISED FAMILIES TOGETHER. THEY WERE HAPPY.
BUT NOT FOR LONG...
THEY TRIED AND TRIED TO FOLLOW THESE NEW RULES FORCED UPON THEM, FOR SO LONG. THEIR ONCE UTOPIAN LIVES FELT SO FAR AWAY...

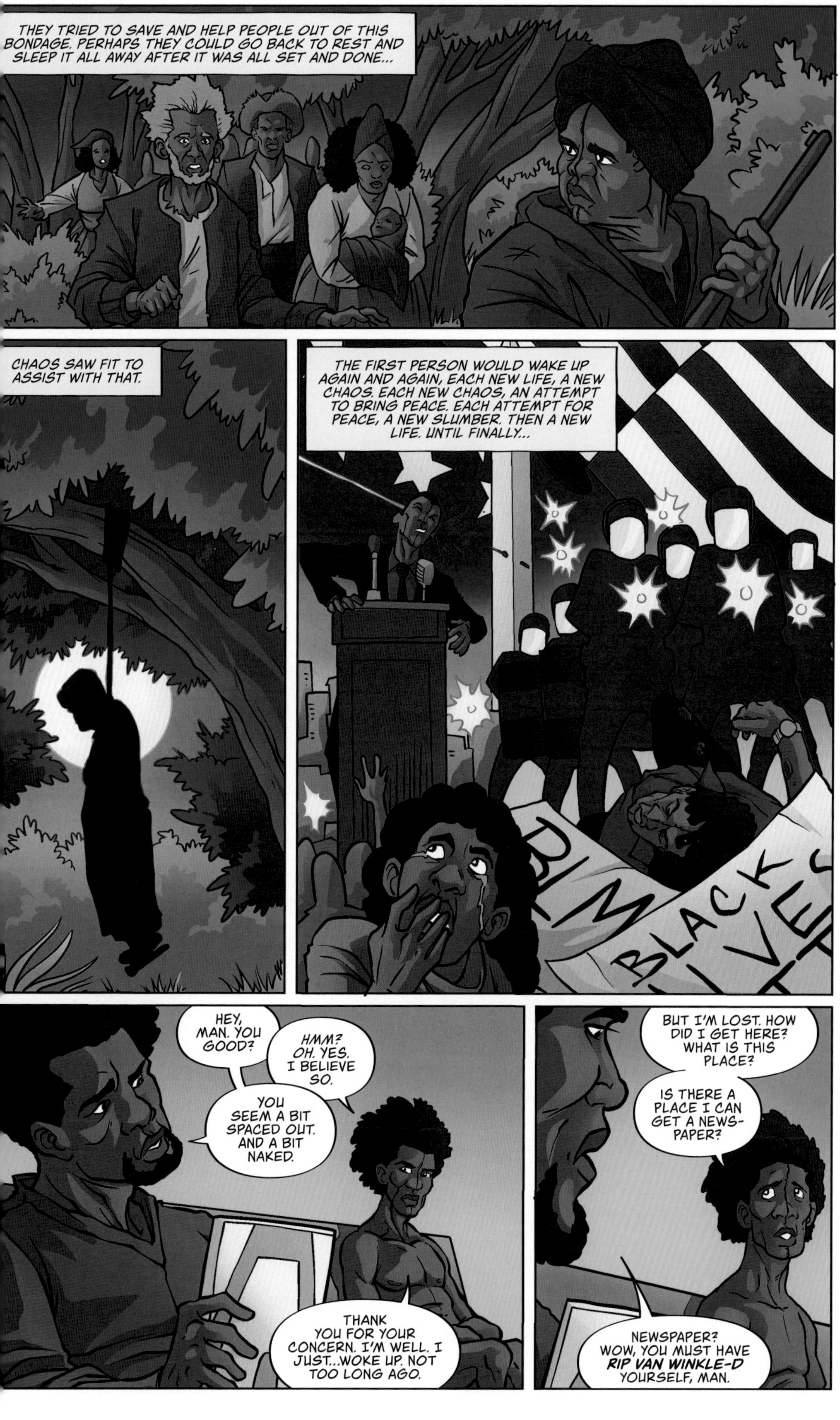
THEY TRIED TO SAVE AND HELP PEOPLE OUT OF THIS BONDAGE. PERHAPS THEY COULD GO BACK TO REST AND SLEEP IT ALL AWAY AFTER IT WAS ALL SET AND DONE...
CHAOS SAW FIT TO ASSIST WITH THAT.
THE FIRST PERSON WOULD WAKE UP AGAIN AND AGAIN, EACH NEW LIFE, A NEW CHAOS. EACH NEW CHAOS, AN ATTEMPT TO BRING PEACE. EACH ATTEMPT FOR PEACE, A NEW SLUMBER. THEN A NEW LIFE. UNTIL FINALLY...
BLACK
HEY, MAN. YOU GOOD?
HMM? OH. YES. I BELIEVE SO.
YOU SEEM A BIT SPACED OUT. AND A BIT NAKED.
THANK YOU FOR YOUR CONCERN. I'M WELL. I JUST...WOKE UP. NOT TOO LONG AGO.
BUT I'M LOST. HOW DID I GET HERE? WHAT IS THIS PLACE?
IS THERE A PLACE I CAN GET A NEWSPAPER?
NEWSPAPER? WOW, YOU MUST HAVE ***RIP VAN WINKLE-D*** YOURSELF, MAN.

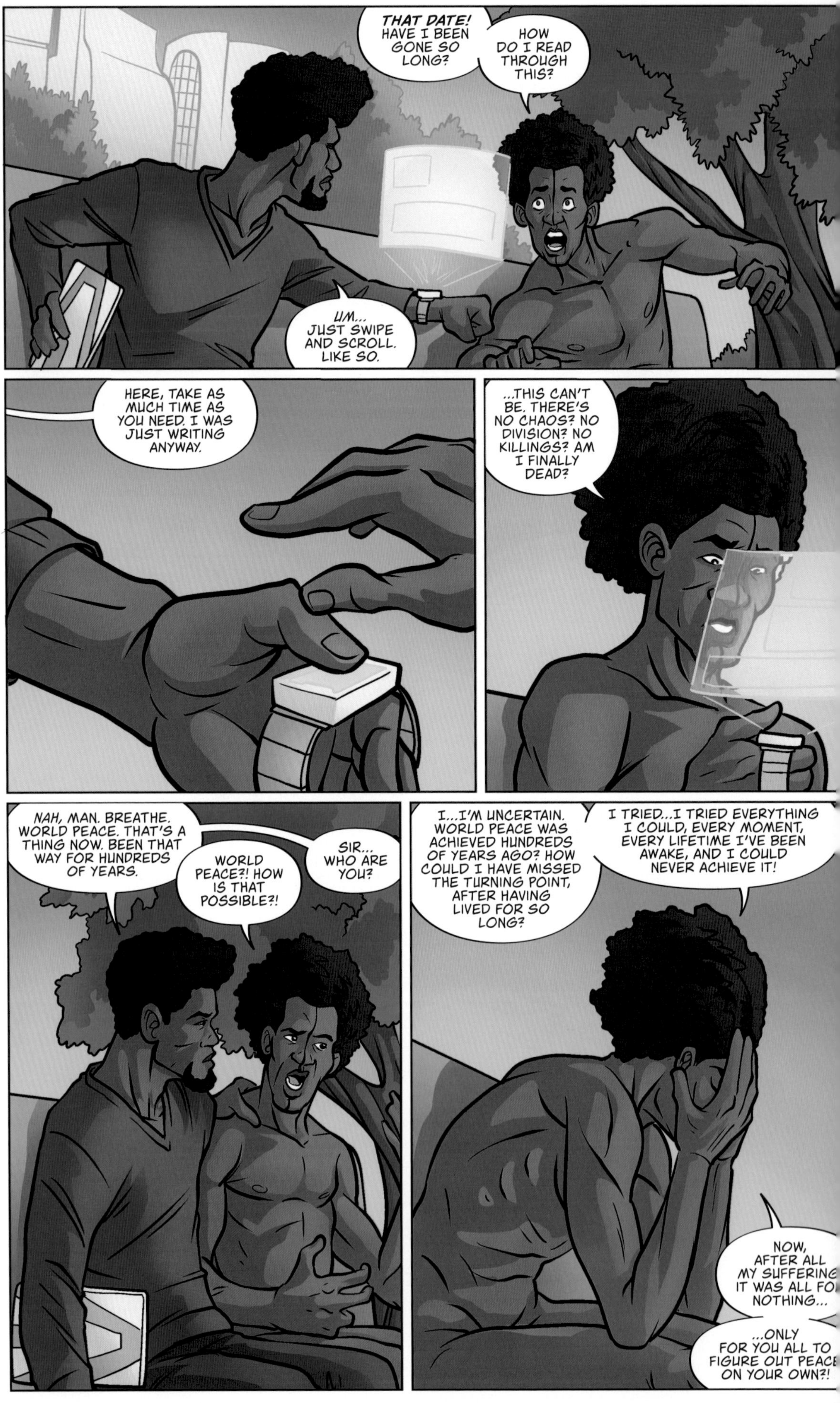
THAT DATE! HAVE I BEEN GONE SO LONG?
HOW DO I READ THROUGH THIS?
UM... JUST SWIPE AND SCROLL. LIKE SO.
HERE, TAKE AS MUCH TIME AS YOU NEED. I WAS JUST WRITING ANYWAY.
...THIS CAN'T BE. THERE'S NO CHAOS? NO DIVISION? NO KILLINGS? AM I FINALLY DEAD?
NAH, MAN. BREATHE. WORLD PEACE. THAT'S A THING NOW. BEEN THAT WAY FOR HUNDREDS OF YEARS.
WORLD PEACE?! HOW IS THAT POSSIBLE?!
SIR... WHO ARE YOU?
I...I'M UNCERTAIN. WORLD PEACE WAS ACHIEVED HUNDREDS OF YEARS AGO? HOW COULD I HAVE MISSED THE TURNING POINT, AFTER HAVING LIVED FOR SO LONG?
I TRIED...I TRIED EVERYTHING I COULD, EVERY MOMENT, EVERY LIFETIME I'VE BEEN AWAKE, AND I COULD NEVER ACHIEVE IT!
NOW, AFTER ALL MY SUFFERING IT WAS ALL FO NOTHING...
...ONLY FOR YOU ALL TO FIGURE OUT PEACE ON YOUR OWN?!

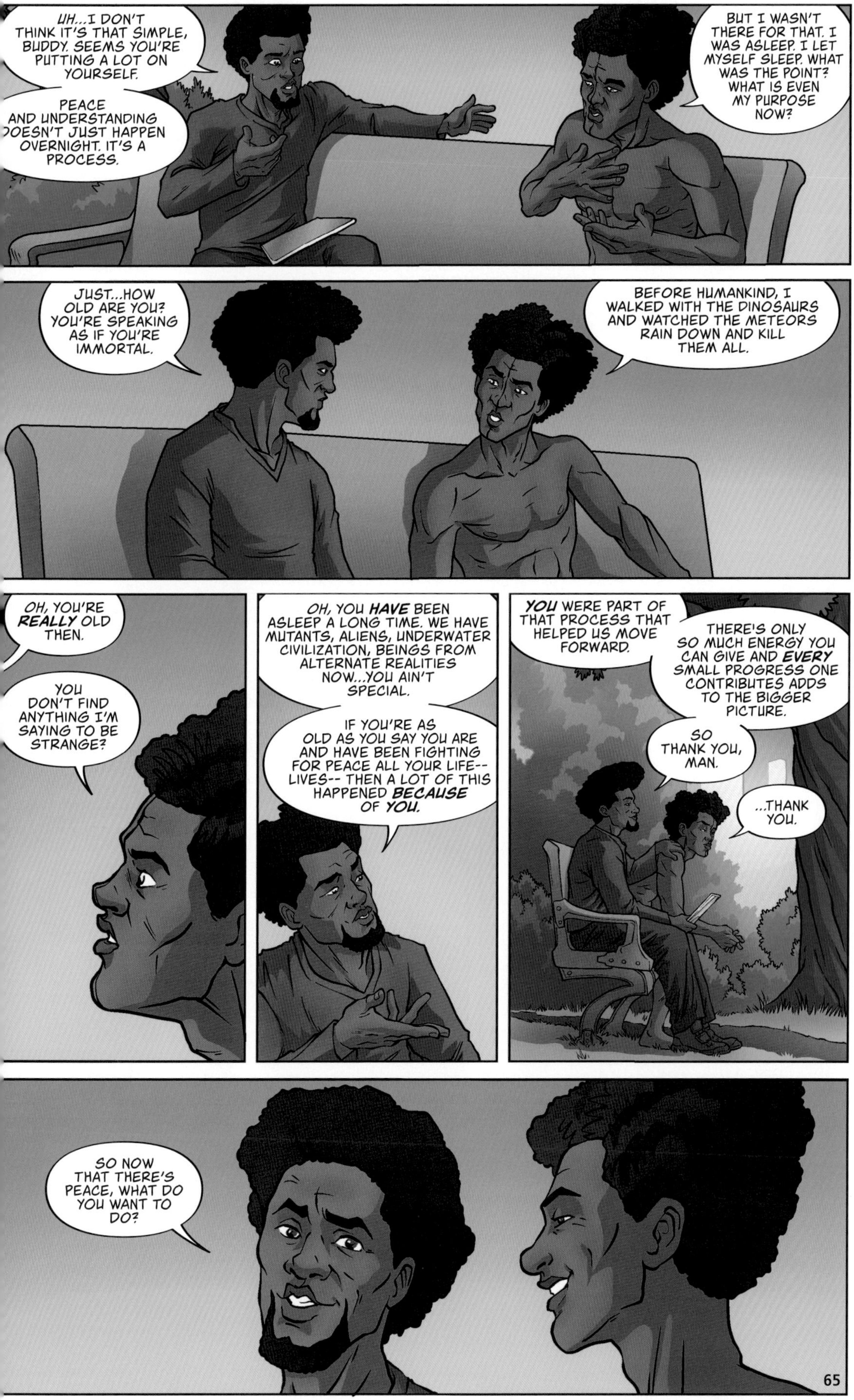
UH...I DON'T THINK IT'S THAT SIMPLE, BUDDY. SEEMS YOU'RE PUTTING A LOT ON YOURSELF.
PEACE AND UNDERSTANDING DOESN'T JUST HAPPEN OVERNIGHT. IT'S A PROCESS.
BUT I WASN'T THERE FOR THAT. I WAS ASLEEP. I LET MYSELF SLEEP. WHAT WAS THE POINT? WHAT IS EVEN MY PURPOSE NOW?
JUST...HOW OLD ARE YOU? YOU'RE SPEAKING AS IF YOU'RE IMMORTAL.
BEFORE HUMANKIND, I WALKED WITH THE DINOSAURS AND WATCHED THE METEORS RAIN DOWN AND KILL THEM ALL.
OH, YOU'RE **REALLY** OLD THEN.
YOU DON'T FIND ANYTHING I'M SAYING TO BE STRANGE?
OH, YOU **HAVE** BEEN ASLEEP A LONG TIME. WE HAVE MUTANTS, ALIENS, UNDERWATER CIVILIZATION, BEINGS FROM ALTERNATE REALITIES NOW...YOU AIN'T SPECIAL.
IF YOU'RE AS OLD AS YOU SAY YOU ARE AND HAVE BEEN FIGHTING FOR PEACE ALL YOUR LIFE--LIVES-- THEN A LOT OF THIS HAPPENED **BECAUSE** OF **YOU.**
YOU WERE PART OF THAT PROCESS THAT HELPED US MOVE FORWARD.
THERE'S ONLY SO MUCH ENERGY YOU CAN GIVE AND **EVERY** SMALL PROGRESS ONE CONTRIBUTES ADDS TO THE BIGGER PICTURE.
SO THANK YOU, MAN.
...THANK YOU.
SO NOW THAT THERE'S PEACE, WHAT DO YOU WANT TO DO?

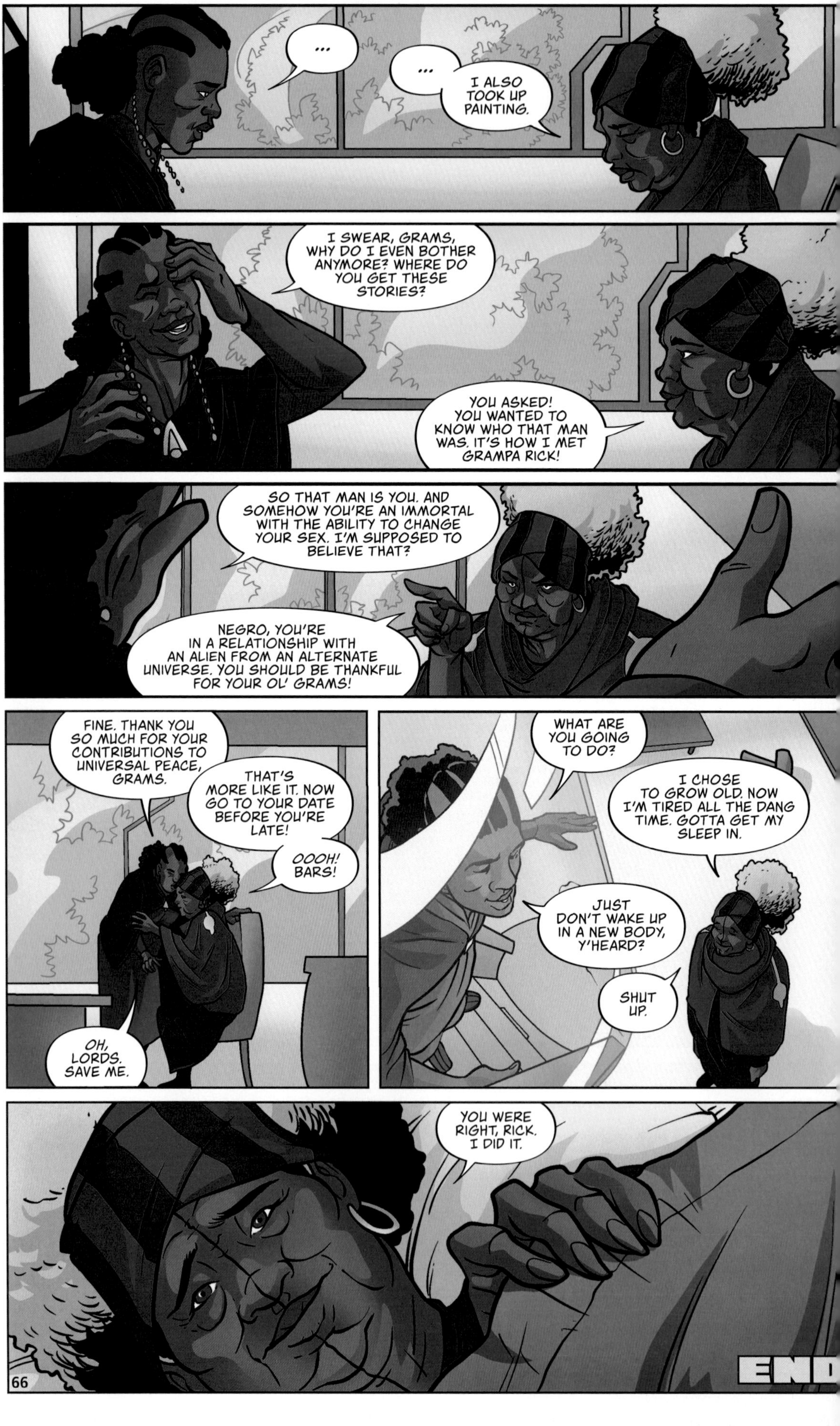
...
...
I ALSO TOOK UP PAINTING.
I SWEAR, GRAMS, WHY DO I EVEN BOTHER ANYMORE? WHERE DO YOU GET THESE STORIES?
YOU ASKED! YOU WANTED TO KNOW WHO THAT MAN WAS. IT'S HOW I MET GRAMPA RICK!
SO THAT MAN IS YOU. AND SOMEHOW YOU'RE AN IMMORTAL WITH THE ABILITY TO CHANGE YOUR SEX. I'M SUPPOSED TO BELIEVE THAT?
NEGRO, YOU'RE IN A RELATIONSHIP WITH AN ALIEN FROM AN ALTERNATE UNIVERSE. YOU SHOULD BE THANKFUL FOR YOUR OL' GRAMS!
FINE. THANK YOU SO MUCH FOR YOUR CONTRIBUTIONS TO UNIVERSAL PEACE, GRAMS.
THAT'S MORE LIKE IT. NOW GO TO YOUR DATE BEFORE YOU'RE LATE!
OOOH! BARS!
OH, LORDS. SAVE ME.
WHAT ARE YOU GOING TO DO?
I CHOSE TO GROW OLD. NOW I'M TIRED ALL THE DANG TIME. GOTTA GET MY SLEEP IN.
JUST DON'T WAKE UP IN A NEW BODY, Y'HEARD?
SHUT UP.
YOU WERE RIGHT, RICK. I DID IT.
END

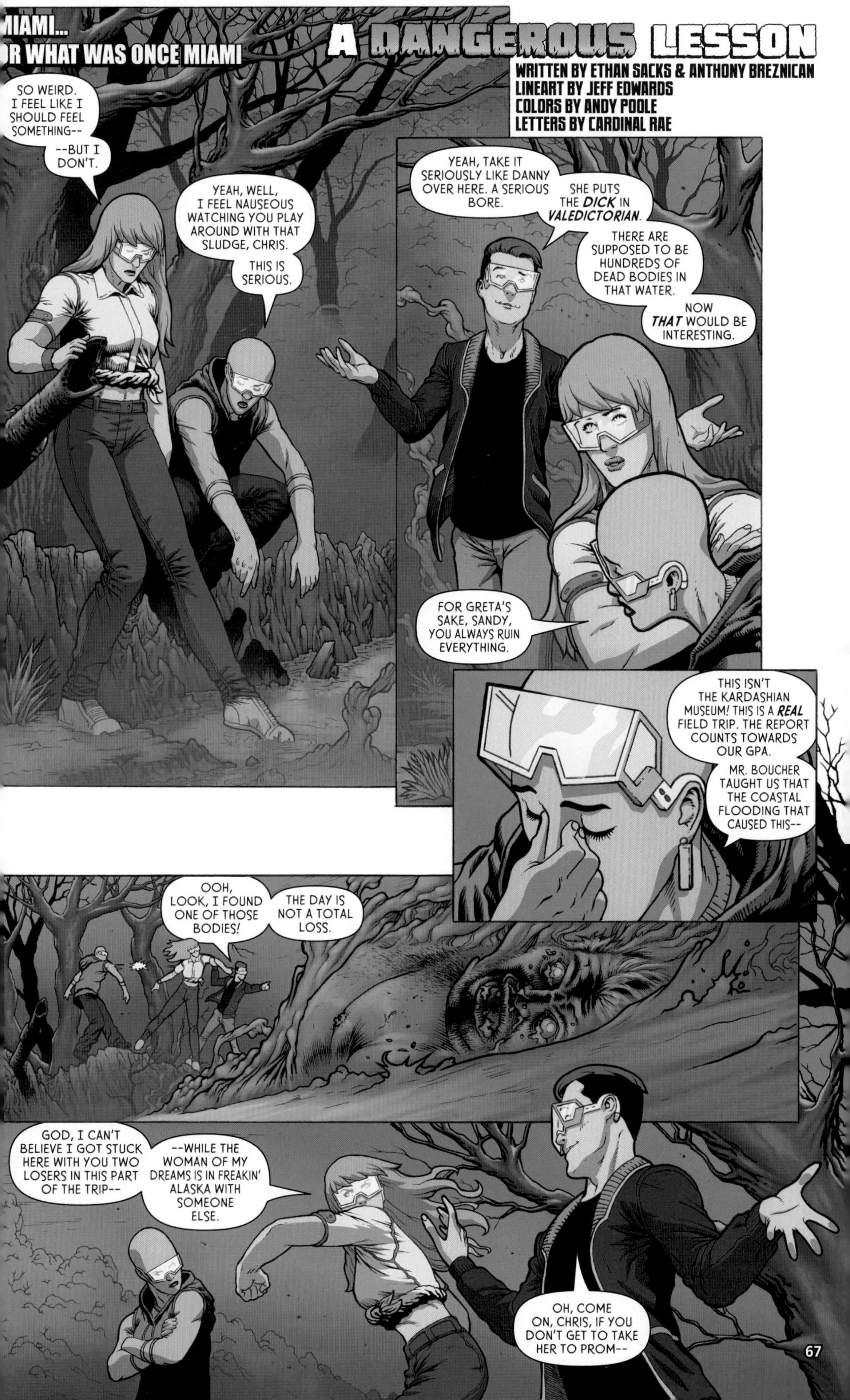
A DANGEROUS LESSON
WRITTEN BY ETHAN SACKS & ANTHONY BREZNICAN
LINEART BY JEFF EDWARDS
COLORS BY ANDY POOLE
LETTERS BY CARDINAL RAE
MIAMI...
R WHAT WAS ONCE MIAMI
SO WEIRD. I FEEL LIKE I SHOULD FEEL SOMETHING--
--BUT I DON'T.
YEAH, WELL, I FEEL NAUSEOUS WATCHING YOU PLAY AROUND WITH THAT SLUDGE, CHRIS.
THIS IS SERIOUS.
YEAH, TAKE IT SERIOUSLY LIKE DANNY OVER HERE. A SERIOUS BORE.
SHE PUTS THE DICK IN VALEDICTORIAN.
THERE ARE SUPPOSED TO BE HUNDREDS OF DEAD BODIES IN THAT WATER.
NOW THAT WOULD BE INTERESTING.
FOR GRETA'S SAKE, SANDY, YOU ALWAYS RUIN EVERYTHING.
THIS ISN'T THE KARDASHIAN MUSEUM! THIS IS A REAL FIELD TRIP. THE REPORT COUNTS TOWARDS OUR GPA.
MR. BOUCHER TAUGHT US THAT THE COASTAL FLOODING THAT CAUSED THIS--
OOH, LOOK, I FOUND ONE OF THOSE BODIES!
THE DAY IS NOT A TOTAL LOSS.
GOD, I CAN'T BELIEVE I GOT STUCK HERE WITH YOU TWO LOSERS IN THIS PART OF THE TRIP--
--WHILE THE WOMAN OF MY DREAMS IS IN FREAKIN' ALASKA WITH SOMEONE ELSE.
OH, COME ON, CHRIS, IF YOU DON'T GET TO TAKE HER TO PROM--

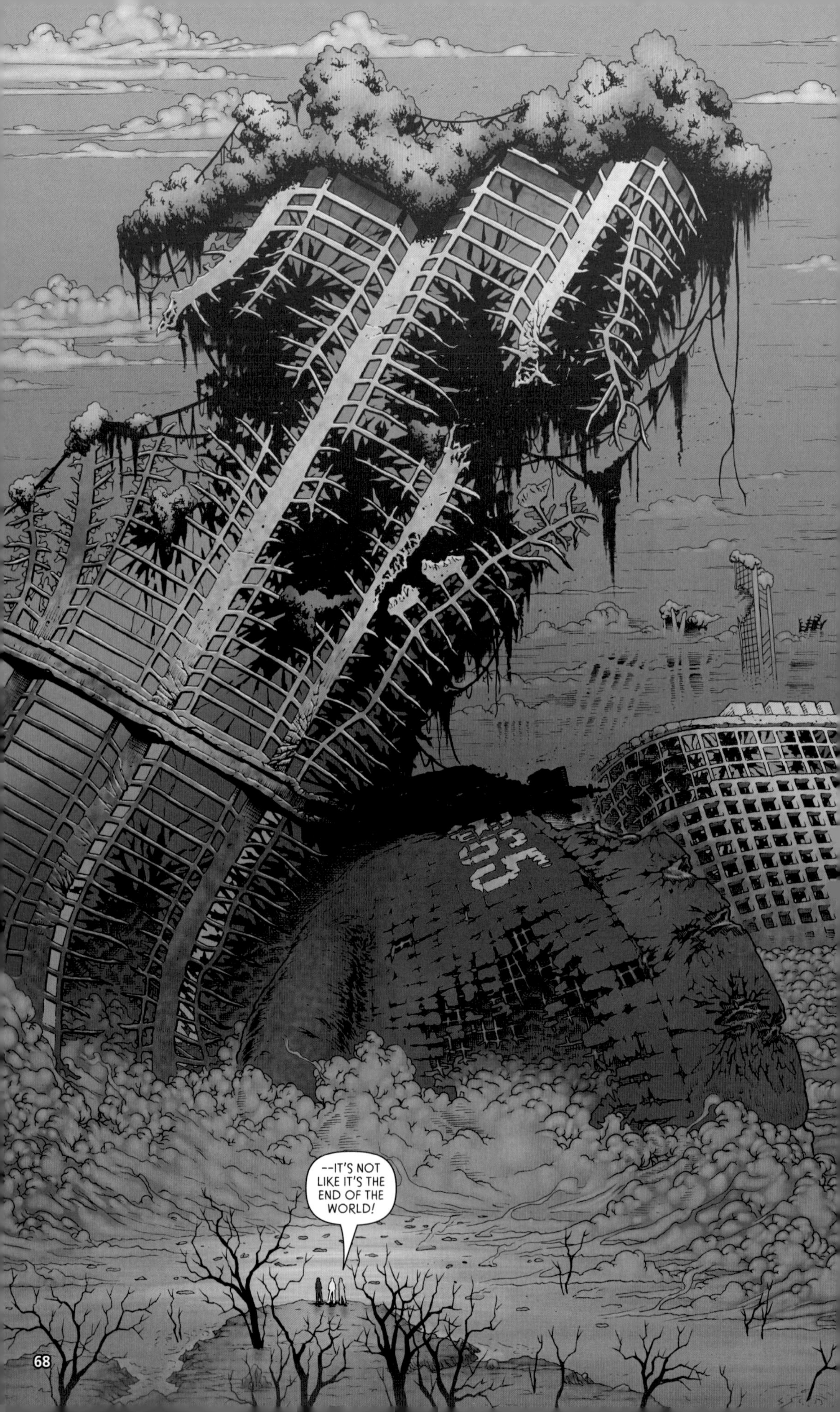
--IT'S NOT LIKE IT'S THE END OF THE WORLD!

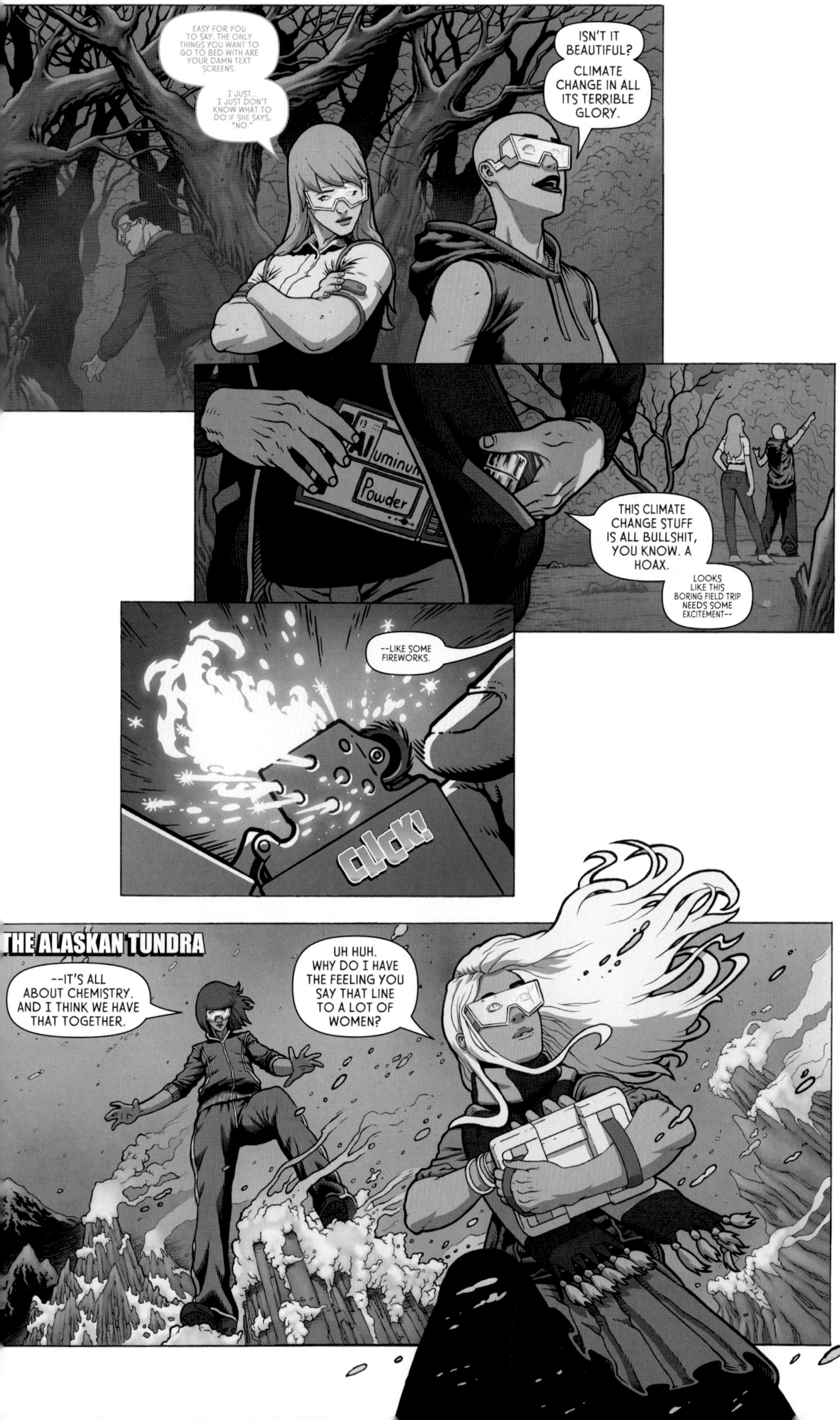

EASY FOR YOU TO SAY. THE ONLY THINGS YOU WANT TO GO TO BED WITH ARE YOUR DAMN TEXT SCREENS.
I JUST... I JUST DON'T KNOW WHAT TO DO IF SHE SAYS, "NO."
ISN'T IT BEAUTIFUL?
CLIMATE CHANGE IN ALL ITS TERRIBLE GLORY.
13 Aluminum Powder
THIS CLIMATE CHANGE STUFF IS ALL BULLSHIT, YOU KNOW. A HOAX.
LOOKS LIKE THIS BORING FIELD TRIP NEEDS SOME EXCITEMENT--
--LIKE SOME FIREWORKS.
CLICK!
THE ALASKAN TUNDRA
--IT'S ALL ABOUT CHEMISTRY. AND I THINK WE HAVE THAT TOGETHER.
UH HUH. WHY DO I HAVE THE FEELING YOU SAY THAT LINE TO A LOT OF WOMEN?

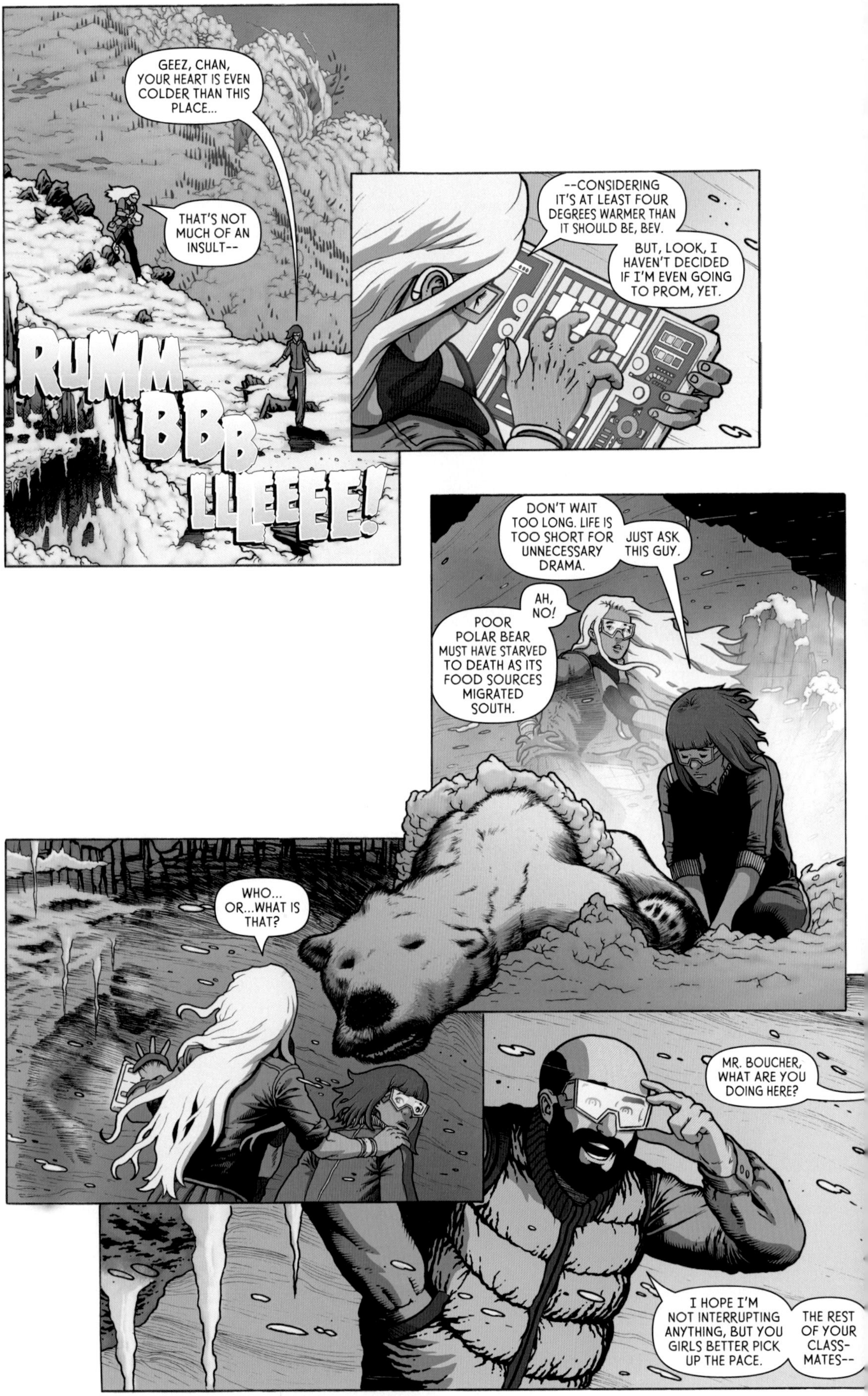
GEEZ, CHAN, YOUR HEART IS EVEN COLDER THAN THIS PLACE...
THAT'S NOT MUCH OF AN INSULT--
RUMM BBB LLEEEE!
--CONSIDERING IT'S AT LEAST FOUR DEGREES WARMER THAN IT SHOULD BE, BEV.
BUT, LOOK, I HAVEN'T DECIDED IF I'M EVEN GOING TO PROM, YET.
DON'T WAIT TOO LONG. LIFE IS TOO SHORT FOR UNNECESSARY DRAMA.
JUST ASK THIS GUY.
AH, NO!
POOR POLAR BEAR MUST HAVE STARVED TO DEATH AS ITS FOOD SOURCES MIGRATED SOUTH.
WHO... OR...WHAT IS THAT?
MR. BOUCHER, WHAT ARE YOU DOING HERE?
I HOPE I'M NOT INTERRUPTING ANYTHING, BUT YOU GIRLS BETTER PICK UP THE PACE.
THE REST OF YOUR CLASS-MATES--

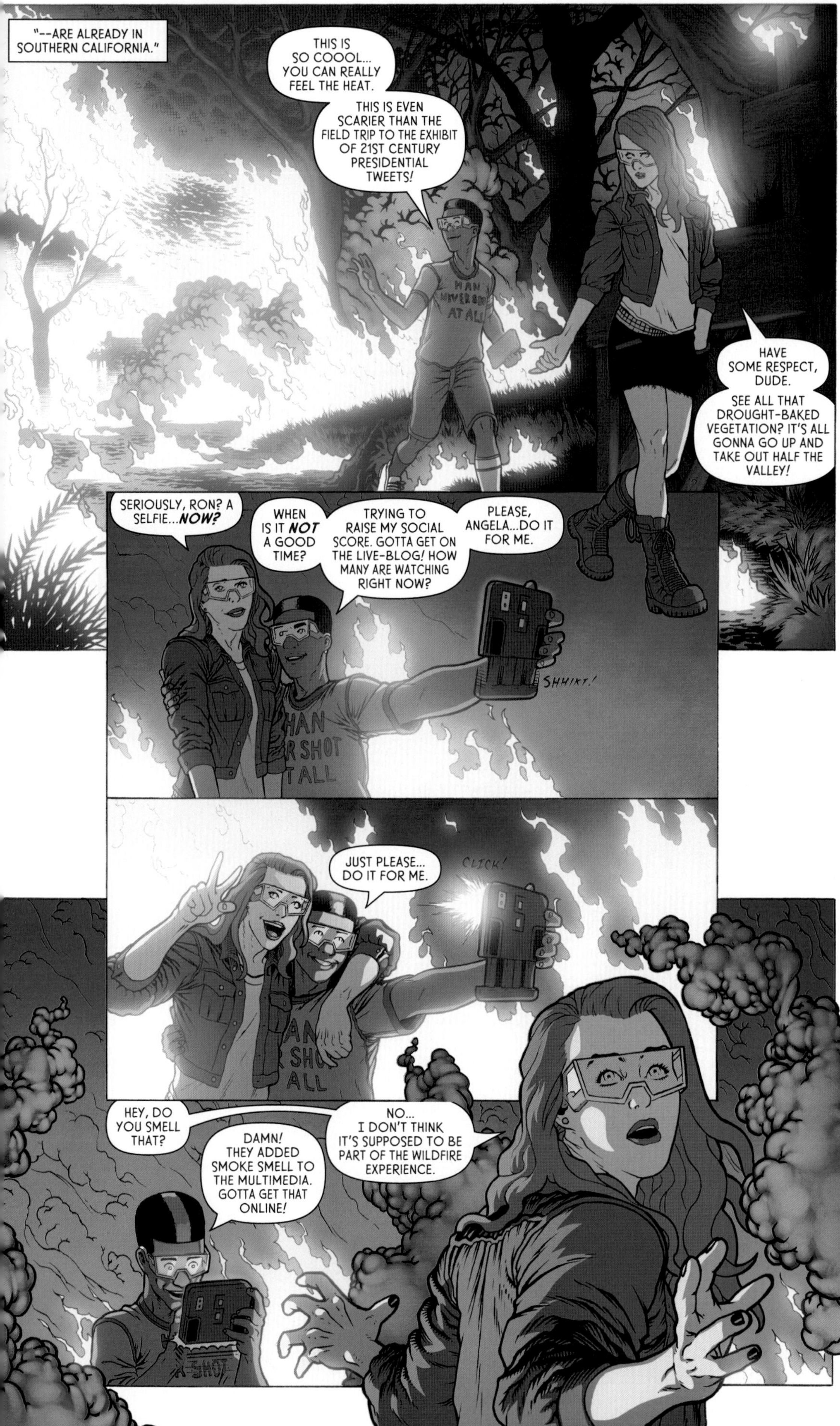
"--ARE ALREADY IN SOUTHERN CALIFORNIA."
THIS IS SO COOOL... YOU CAN REALLY FEEL THE HEAT.
THIS IS EVEN SCARIER THAN THE FIELD TRIP TO THE EXHIBIT OF 21ST CENTURY PRESIDENTIAL TWEETS!
HAVE SOME RESPECT, DUDE.
SEE ALL THAT DROUGHT-BAKED VEGETATION? IT'S ALL GONNA GO UP AND TAKE OUT HALF THE VALLEY!
SERIOUSLY, RON? A SELFIE...**NOW?**
WHEN IS IT **NOT** A GOOD TIME?
TRYING TO RAISE MY SOCIAL SCORE. GOTTA GET ON THE LIVE-BLOG! HOW MANY ARE WATCHING RIGHT NOW?
PLEASE, ANGELA...DO IT FOR ME.
SHHIKT!
JUST PLEASE... DO IT FOR ME.
CLICK!
HEY, DO YOU SMELL THAT?
DAMN! THEY ADDED SMOKE SMELL TO THE MULTIMEDIA. GOTTA GET THAT ONLINE!
NO... I DON'T THINK IT'S SUPPOSED TO BE PART OF THE WILDFIRE EXPERIENCE.

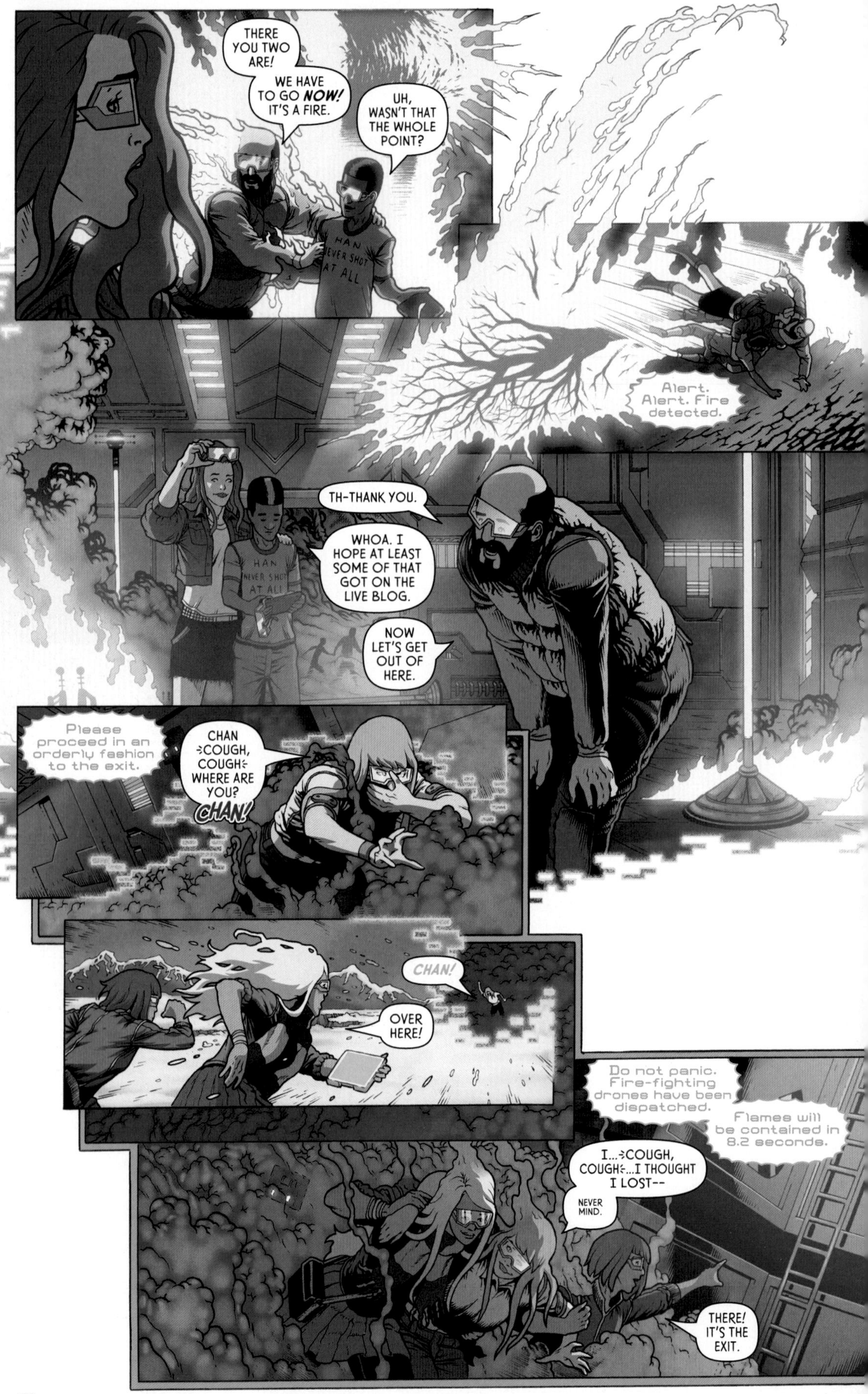
THERE YOU TWO ARE!
WE HAVE TO GO **NOW!** IT'S A FIRE.
UH, WASN'T THAT THE WHOLE POINT?
HAN NEVER SHOT AT ALL
Alert. Alert. Fire detected.
TH-THANK YOU.
WHOA. I HOPE AT LEAST SOME OF THAT GOT ON THE LIVE BLOG.
NOW LET'S GET OUT OF HERE.
Please proceed in an orderly fashion to the exit.
CHAN ⋟COUGH, COUGH⋞ WHERE ARE YOU?
CHAN!
CHAN!
OVER HERE!
Do not panic. Fire-fighting drones have been dispatched.
Flames will be contained in 8.2 seconds.
I...⋟COUGH, COUGH⋞...I THOUGHT I LOST--
NEVER MIND.
THERE! IT'S THE EXIT.

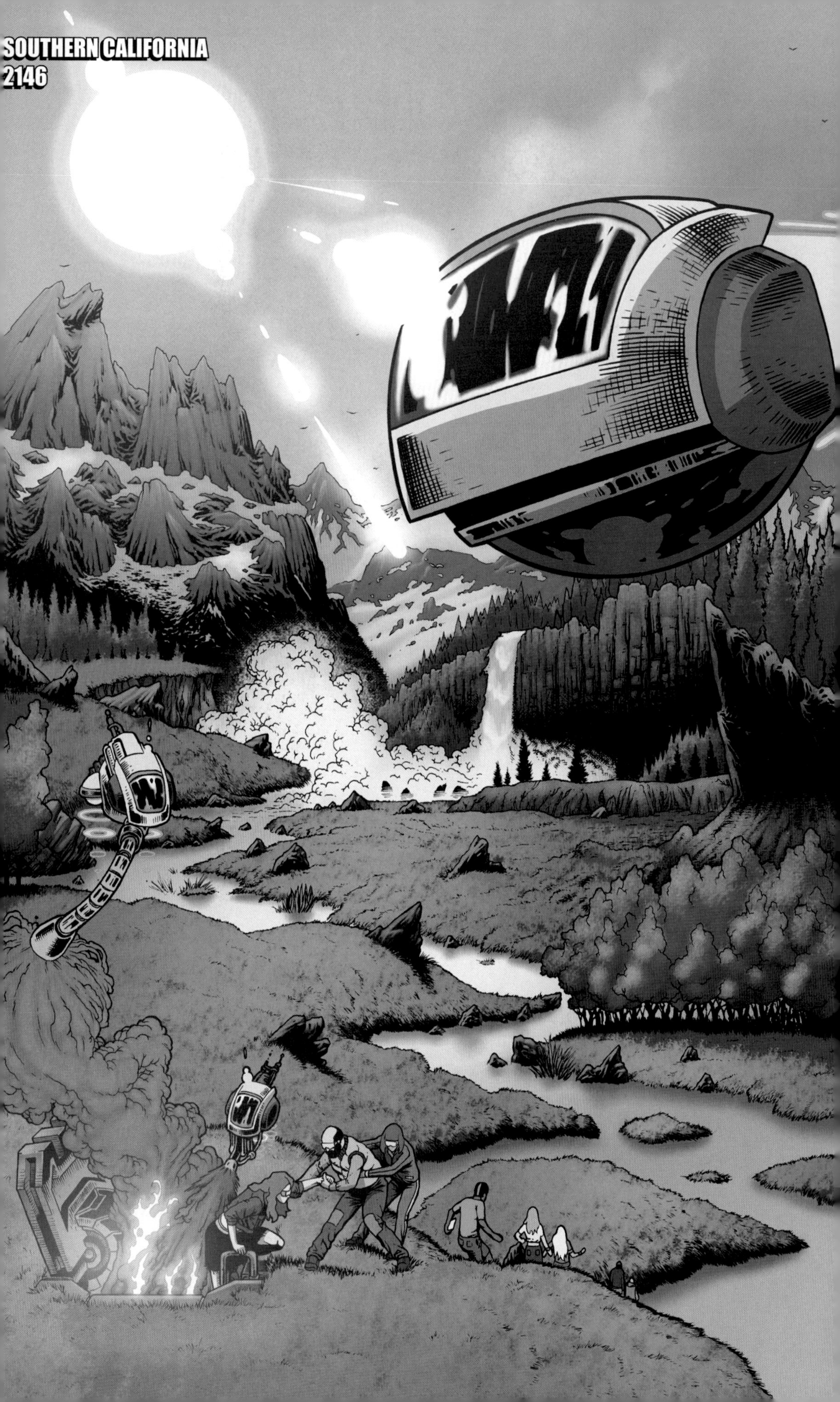
SOUTHERN CALIFORNIA
2146

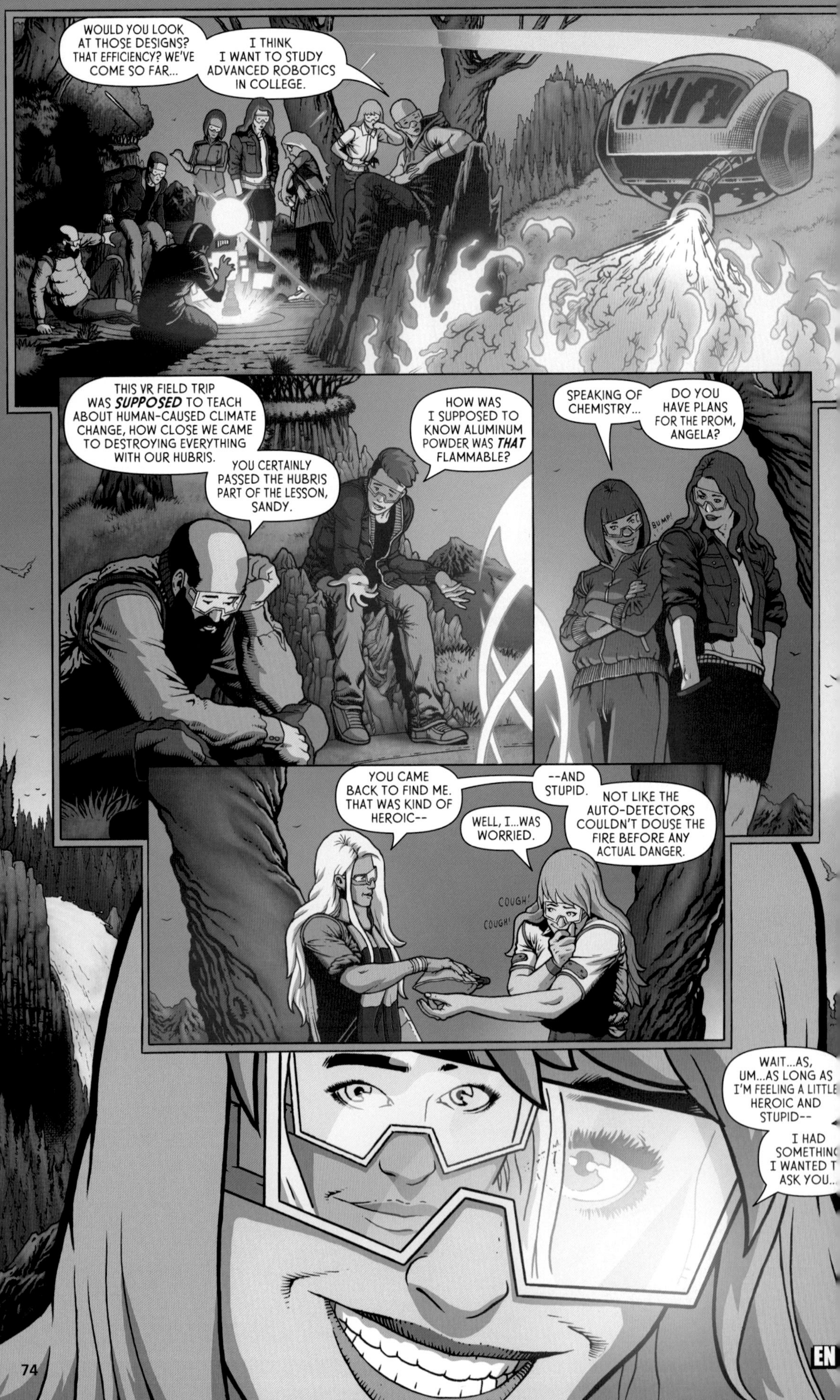
WOULD YOU LOOK AT THOSE DESIGNS? THAT EFFICIENCY? WE'VE COME SO FAR...
I THINK I WANT TO STUDY ADVANCED ROBOTICS IN COLLEGE.
THIS VR FIELD TRIP WAS SUPPOSED TO TEACH ABOUT HUMAN-CAUSED CLIMATE CHANGE, HOW CLOSE WE CAME TO DESTROYING EVERYTHING WITH OUR HUBRIS.
YOU CERTAINLY PASSED THE HUBRIS PART OF THE LESSON, SANDY.
HOW WAS I SUPPOSED TO KNOW ALUMINUM POWDER WAS THAT FLAMMABLE?
SPEAKING OF CHEMISTRY...
DO YOU HAVE PLANS FOR THE PROM, ANGELA?
BUMP!
YOU CAME BACK TO FIND ME. THAT WAS KIND OF HEROIC--
--AND STUPID.
WELL, I...WAS WORRIED.
NOT LIKE THE AUTO-DETECTORS COULDN'T DOUSE THE FIRE BEFORE ANY ACTUAL DANGER.
COUGH!
COUGH!
WAIT...AS, UM...AS LONG AS I'M FEELING A LITTLE HEROIC AND STUPID--
I HAD SOMETHING I WANTED T ASK YOU...
EN

THE FUTURE ISN'T WRITTEN.

SOME PEOPLE WANT IT TO BE.

SOME EVEN **NEED** IT TO BE.

TO MAINTAIN POWER.

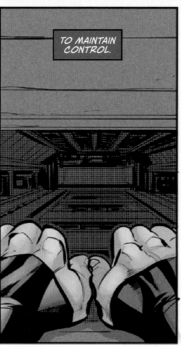

TO MAINTAIN CONTROL.

THEY'RE SCARED. THEY ASSUME IF SOMEONE ELSE **WINS**...

...THEY **LOSE**.

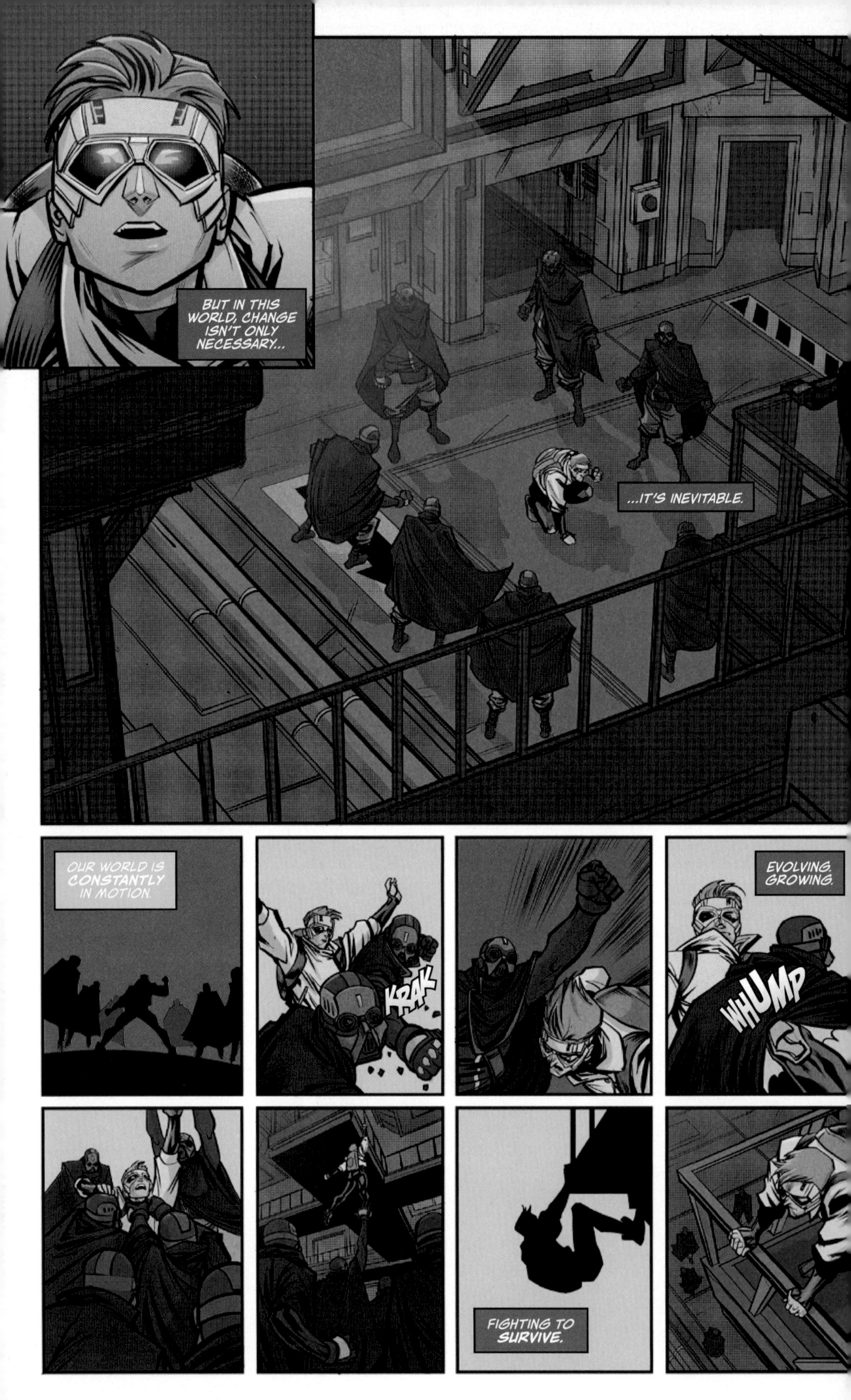
BUT IN THIS WORLD, CHANGE ISN'T ONLY NECESSARY...
...IT'S INEVITABLE.
OUR WORLD IS CONSTANTLY IN MOTION.
KRAK
EVOLVING. GROWING.
WHUMP
FIGHTING TO SURVIVE.

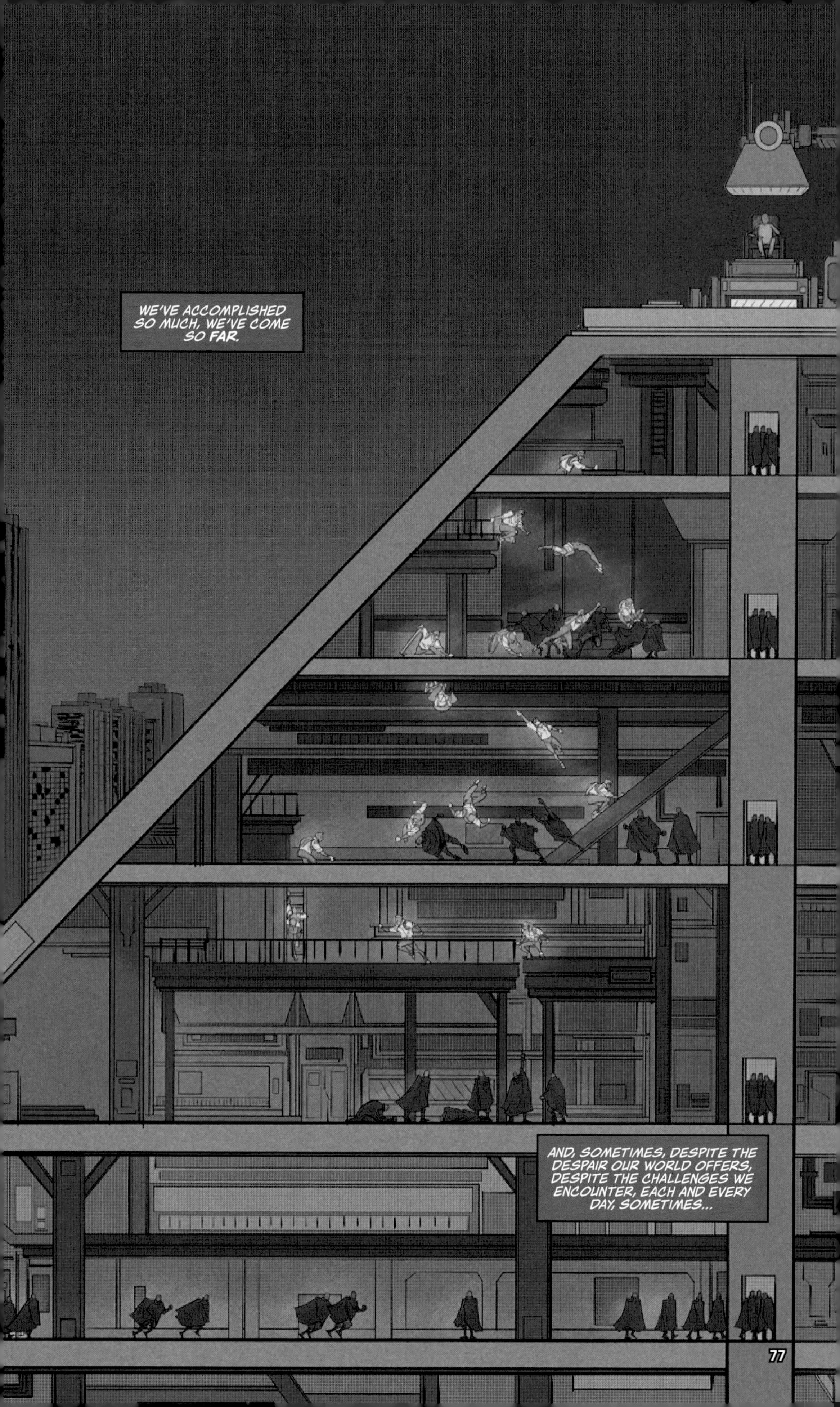
WE'VE ACCOMPLISHED SO MUCH, WE'VE COME SO FAR.
AND, SOMETIMES, DESPITE THE DESPAIR OUR WORLD OFFERS, DESPITE THE CHALLENGES WE ENCOUNTER, EACH AND EVERY DAY, SOMETIMES...

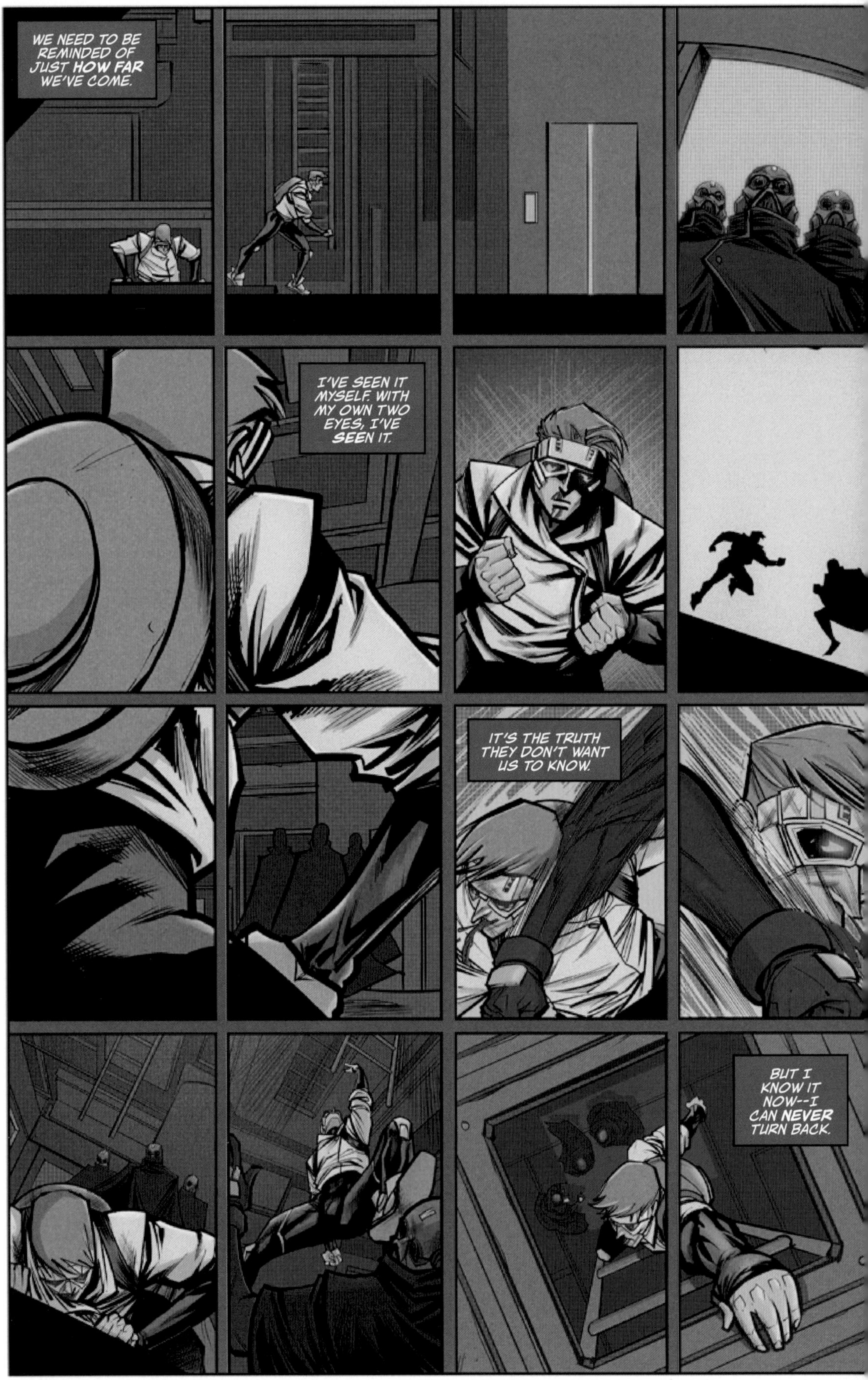
WE NEED TO BE REMINDED OF JUST **HOW FAR** WE'VE COME.
I'VE SEEN IT MYSELF. WITH MY OWN TWO EYES, I'VE **SEEN** IT.
IT'S THE TRUTH THEY DON'T WANT US TO KNOW.
BUT I KNOW IT NOW--I CAN **NEVER** TURN BACK.

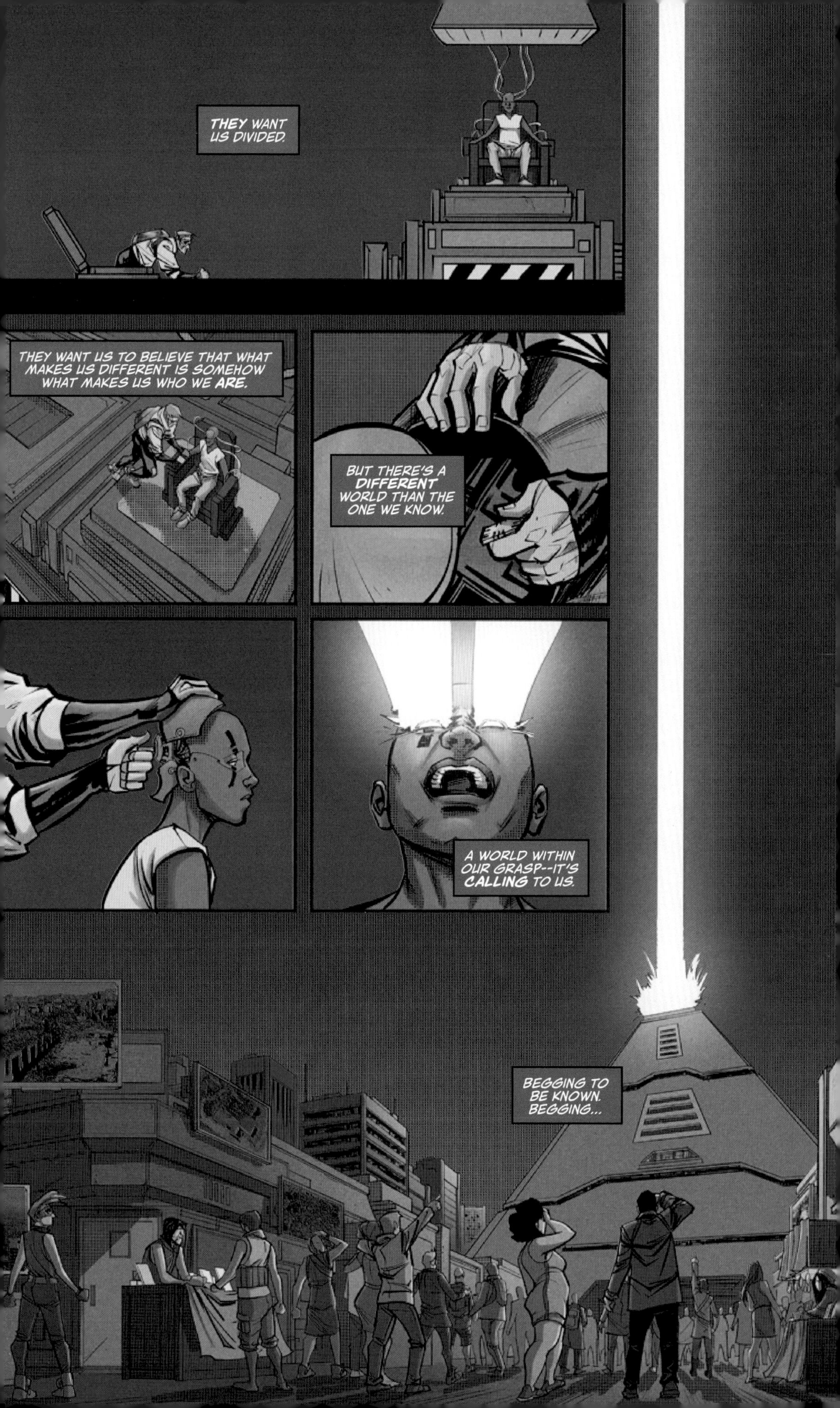
THEY WANT US DIVIDED.
THEY WANT US TO BELIEVE THAT WHAT MAKES US DIFFERENT IS SOMEHOW WHAT MAKES US WHO WE ARE.
BUT THERE'S A DIFFERENT WORLD THAN THE ONE WE KNOW.
A WORLD WITHIN OUR GRASP--IT'S CALLING TO US.
BEGGING TO BE KNOWN. BEGGING...

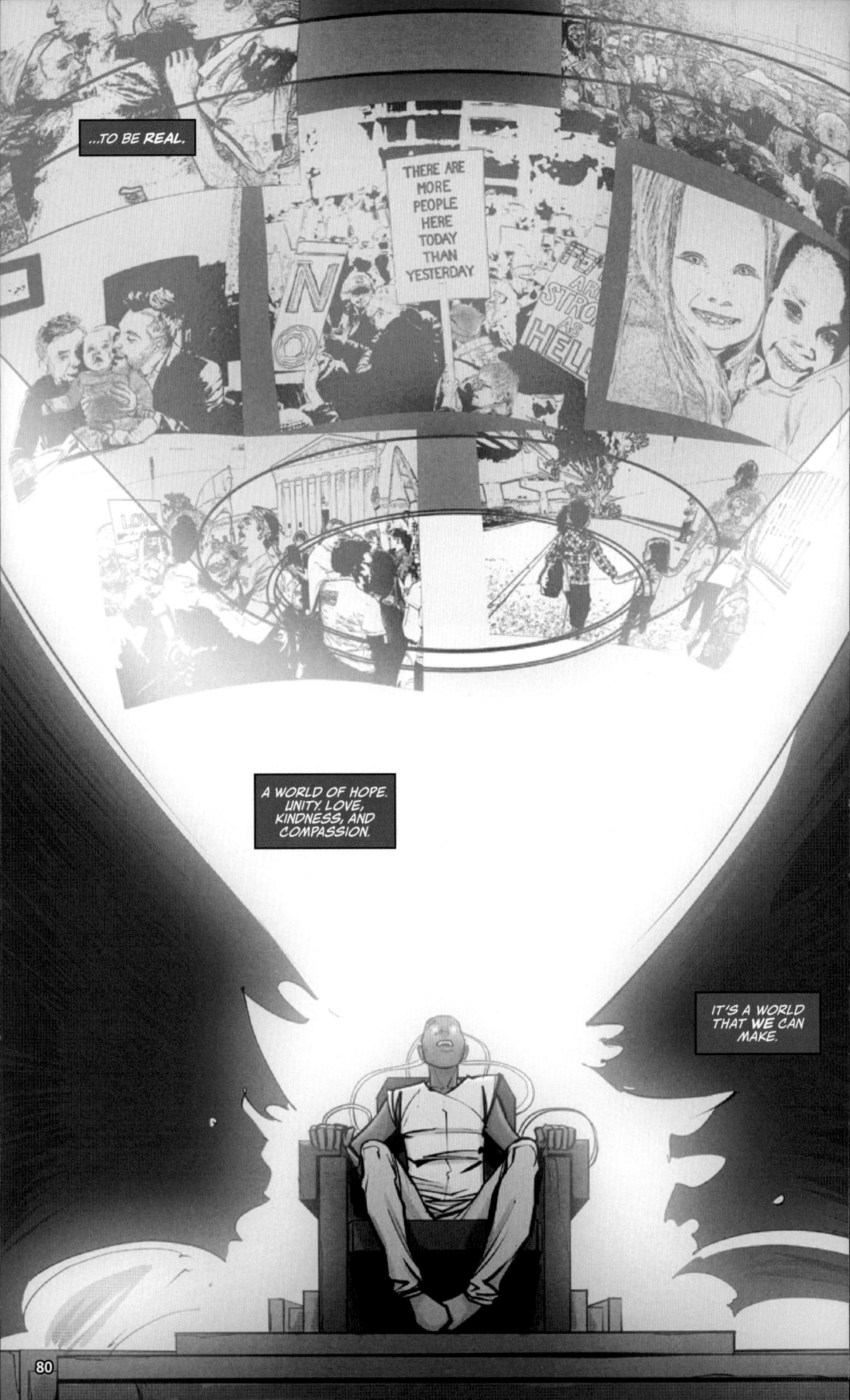
...TO BE REAL.
THERE ARE MORE PEOPLE HERE TODAY THAN YESTERDAY
LOVE
A WORLD OF HOPE. UNITY. LOVE, KINDNESS, AND COMPASSION.
IT'S A WORLD THAT WE CAN MAKE.

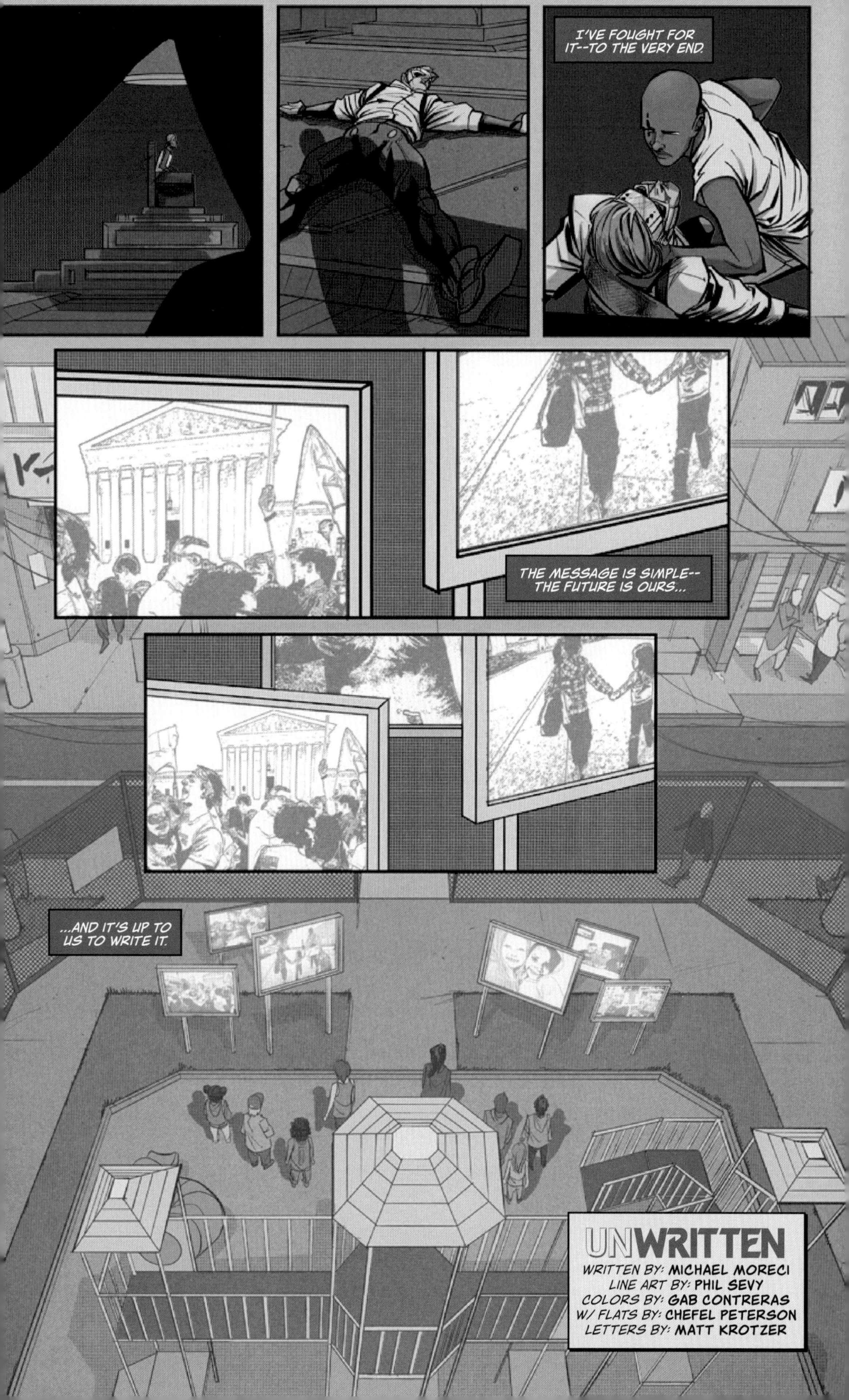
I'VE FOUGHT FOR IT--TO THE VERY END.
THE MESSAGE IS SIMPLE-- THE FUTURE IS OURS...
...AND IT'S UP TO US TO WRITE IT.
UNWRITTEN
WRITTEN BY: MICHAEL MORECI
LINE ART BY: PHIL SEVY
COLORS BY: GAB CONTRERAS
W/ FLATS BY: CHEFEL PETERSON
LETTERS BY: MATT KROTZER

4 THINGS THAT MADE 6103 EXTRA OPWOWSICAL

MELLISHING THE FROOB

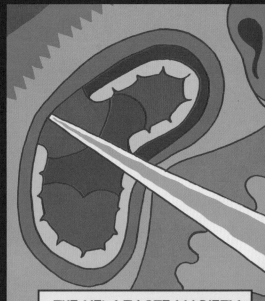

THE NEW TASTE VARIETY OF BALTY'S PEZZOS

MARS BALLS

THE TIME HOLE

MKUPPERMAN

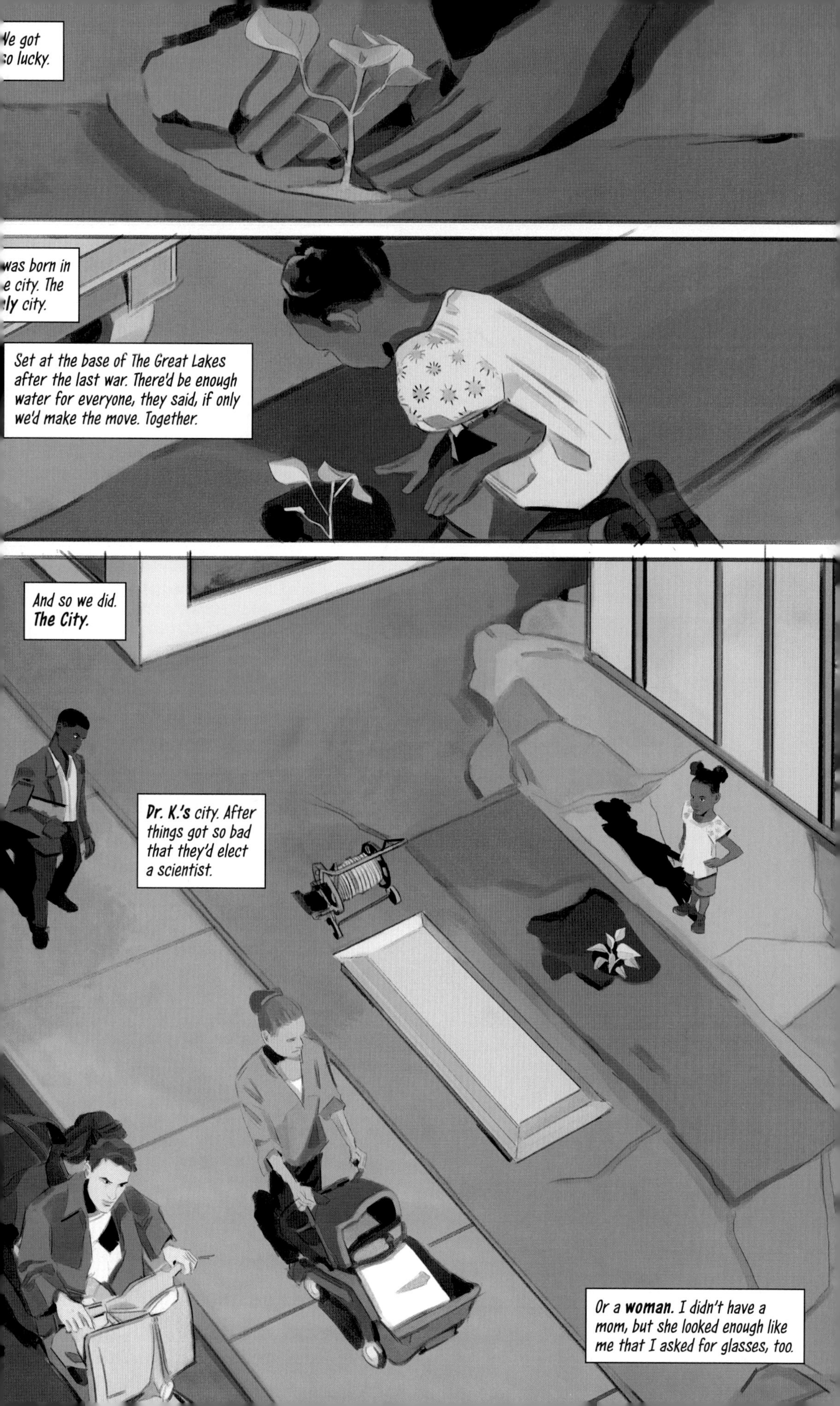

e got o lucky.
was born in e city. The ly city.
Set at the base of The Great Lakes after the last war. There'd be enough water for everyone, they said, if only we'd make the move. Together.
And so we did. **The City.**
Dr. K.'s city. After things got so bad that they'd elect a scientist.
Or a **woman**. I didn't have a mom, but she looked enough like me that I asked for glasses, too.

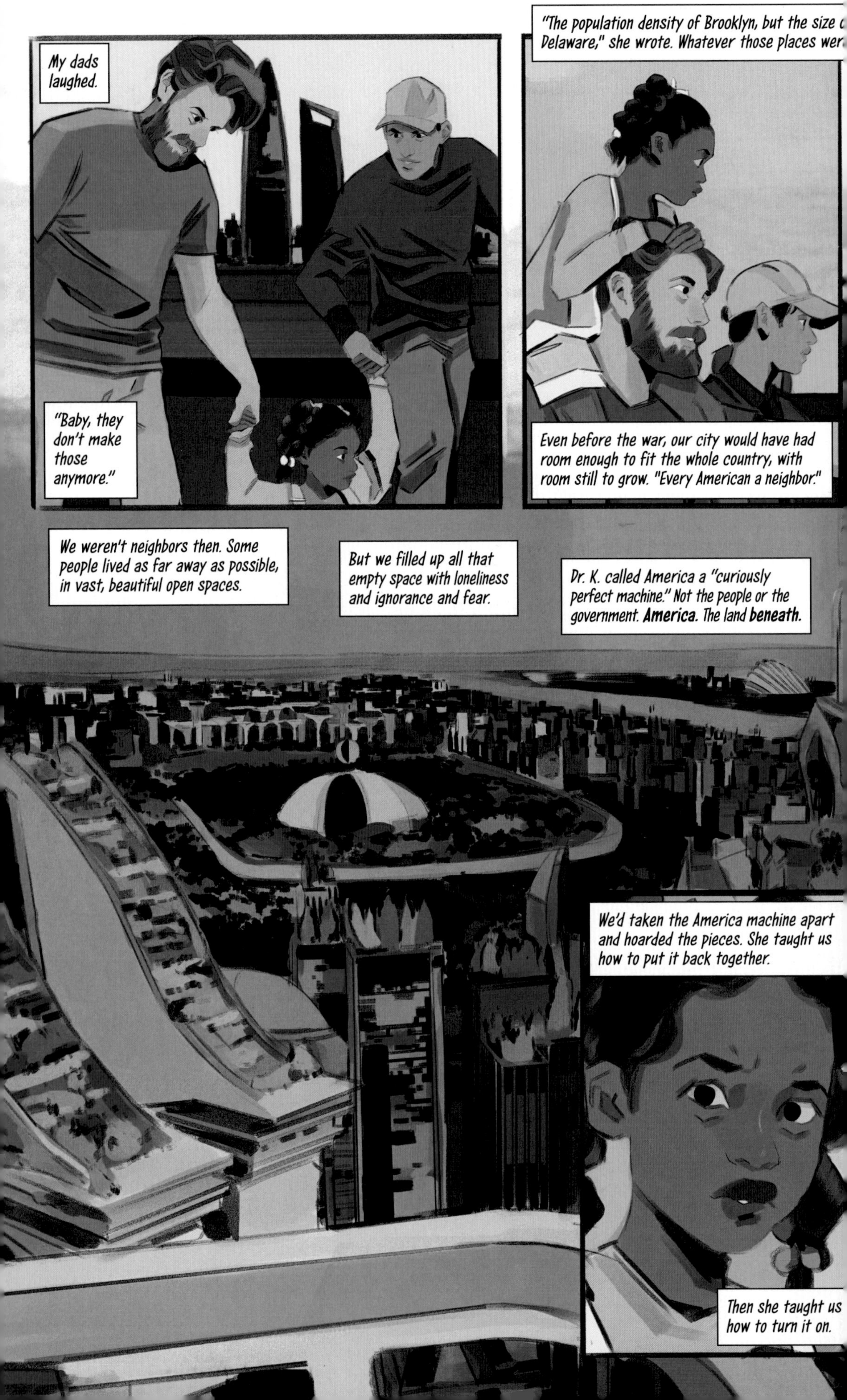
My dads laughed.
"Baby, they don't make those anymore."
"The population density of Brooklyn, but the size
Delaware," she wrote. Whatever those places wer
Even before the war, our city would have had room enough to fit the whole country, with room still to grow. "Every American a neighbor."
We weren't neighbors then. Some people lived as far away as possible, in vast, beautiful open spaces.
But we filled up all that empty space with loneliness and ignorance and fear.
Dr. K. called America a "curiously perfect machine." Not the people or the government. **America.** The land **beneath.**
We'd taken the America machine apart and hoarded the pieces. She taught us how to put it back together.
Then she taught us how to turn it on.

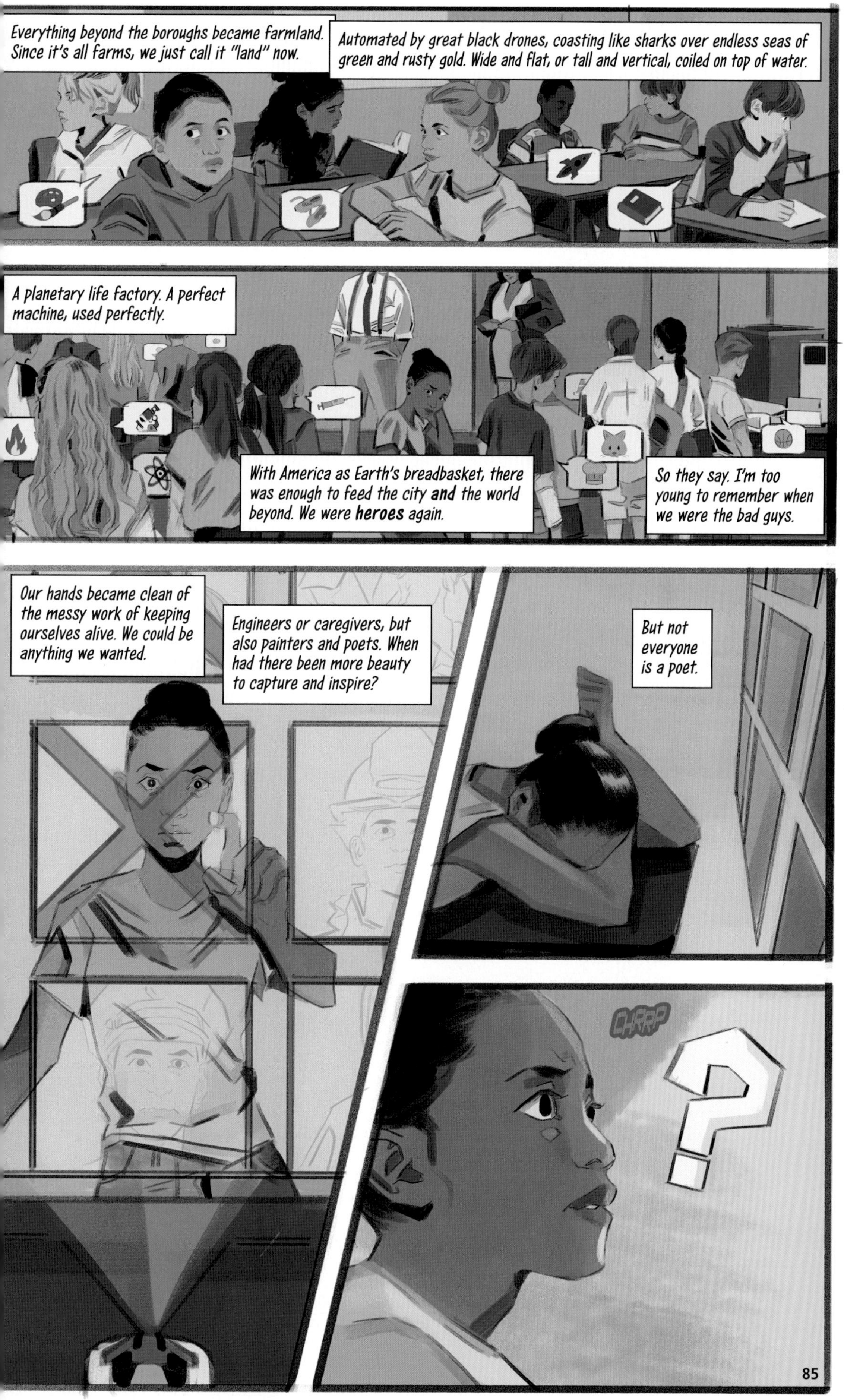
Everything beyond the boroughs became farmland. Since it's all farms, we just call it "land" now.
Automated by great black drones, coasting like sharks over endless seas of green and rusty gold. Wide and flat, or tall and vertical, coiled on top of water.
A planetary life factory. A perfect machine, used perfectly.
With America as Earth's breadbasket, there was enough to feed the city **and** the world beyond. We were **heroes** again.
So they say. I'm too young to remember when we were the bad guys.
Our hands became clean of the messy work of keeping ourselves alive. We could be anything we wanted.
Engineers or caregivers, but also painters and poets. When had there been more beauty to capture and inspire?
But not everyone is a poet.
CHRRP
?

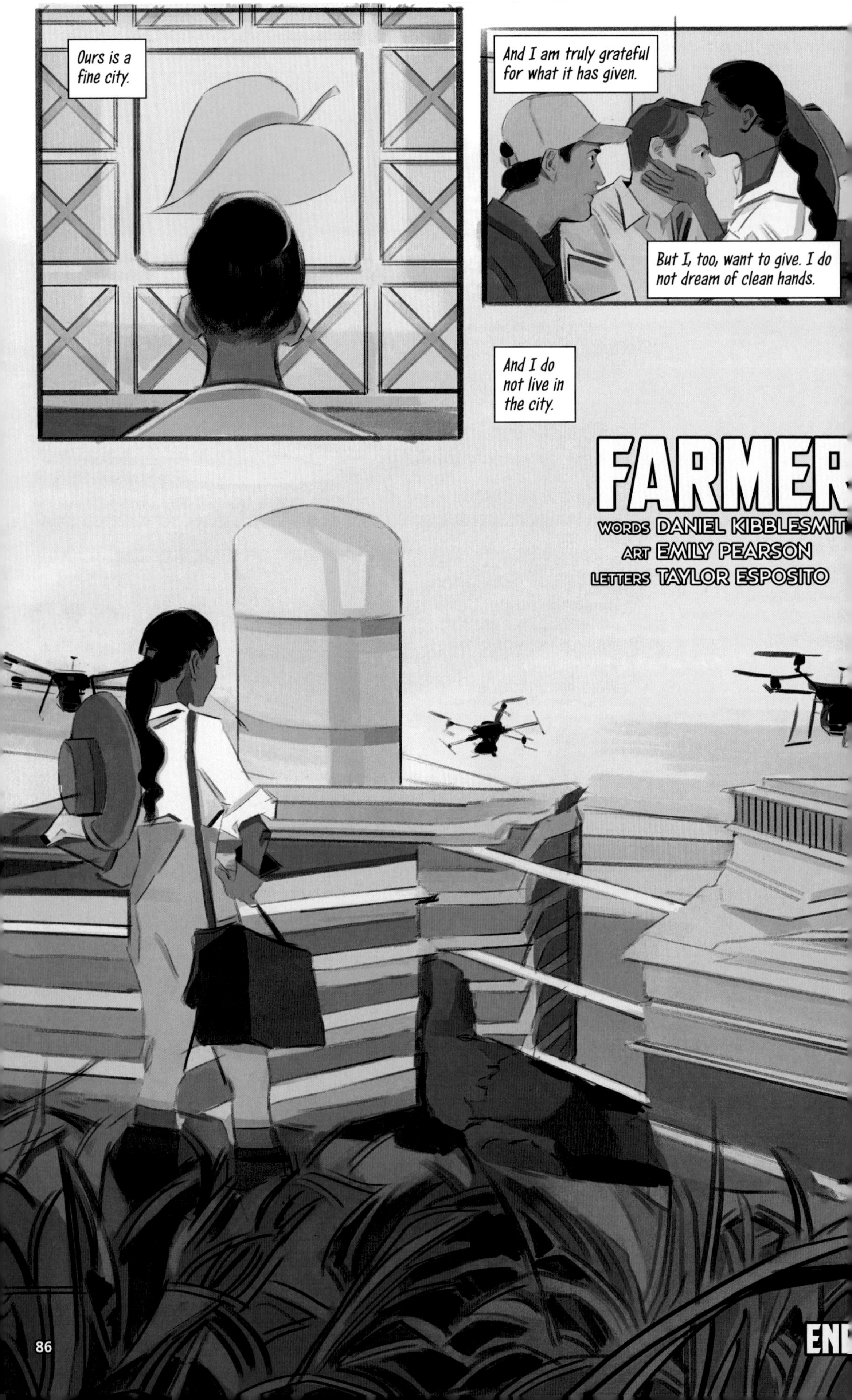
Ours is a fine city.
And I am truly grateful for what it has given.
But I, too, want to give. I do not dream of clean hands.
And I do not live in the city.
FARMER
WORDS DANIEL KIBBLESMIT
ART EMILY PEARSON
LETTERS TAYLOR ESPOSITO
EN

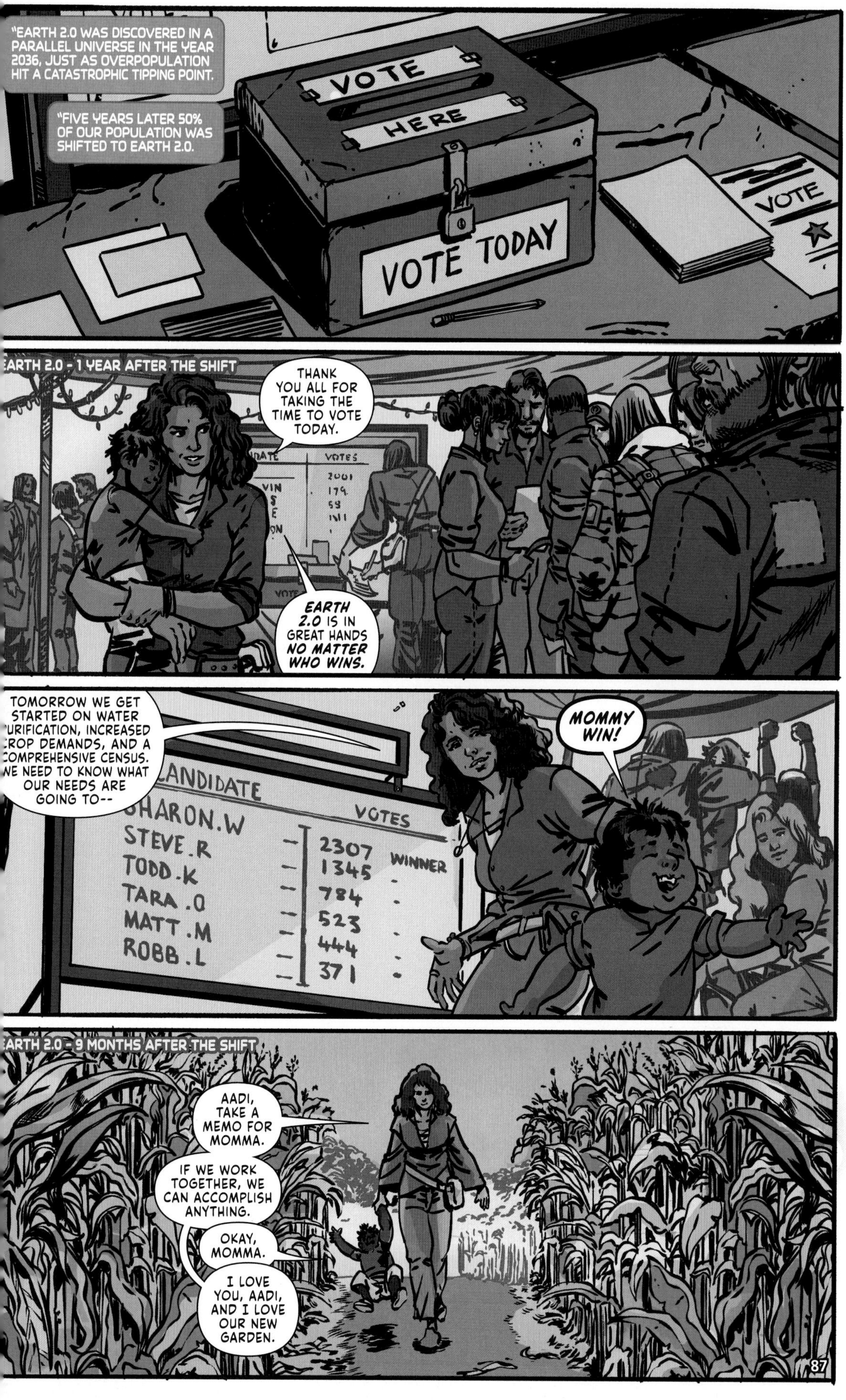

"EARTH 2.0 WAS DISCOVERED IN A PARALLEL UNIVERSE IN THE YEAR 2036, JUST AS OVERPOPULATION HIT A CATASTROPHIC TIPPING POINT.
"FIVE YEARS LATER 50% OF OUR POPULATION WAS SHIFTED TO EARTH 2.0.
VOTE HERE
VOTE TODAY
VOTE
ARTH 2.0 - 1 YEAR AFTER THE SHIFT
THANK YOU ALL FOR TAKING THE TIME TO VOTE TODAY.
EARTH 2.0 IS IN GREAT HANDS NO MATTER WHO WINS.
TOMORROW WE GET STARTED ON WATER URIFICATION, INCREASED ROP DEMANDS, AND A OMPREHENSIVE CENSUS. NE NEED TO KNOW WHAT OUR NEEDS ARE GOING TO--
CANDIDATE
VOTES
SHARON.W 2307 WINNER
STEVE.R 1345
TODD.K 784
TARA.O 523
MATT.M 444
ROBB.L 371
MOMMY WIN!
ARTH 2.0 - 9 MONTHS AFTER THE SHIFT
AADI, TAKE A MEMO FOR MOMMA.
IF WE WORK TOGETHER, WE CAN ACCOMPLISH ANYTHING.
OKAY, MOMMA.
I LOVE YOU, AADI, AND I LOVE OUR NEW GARDEN.

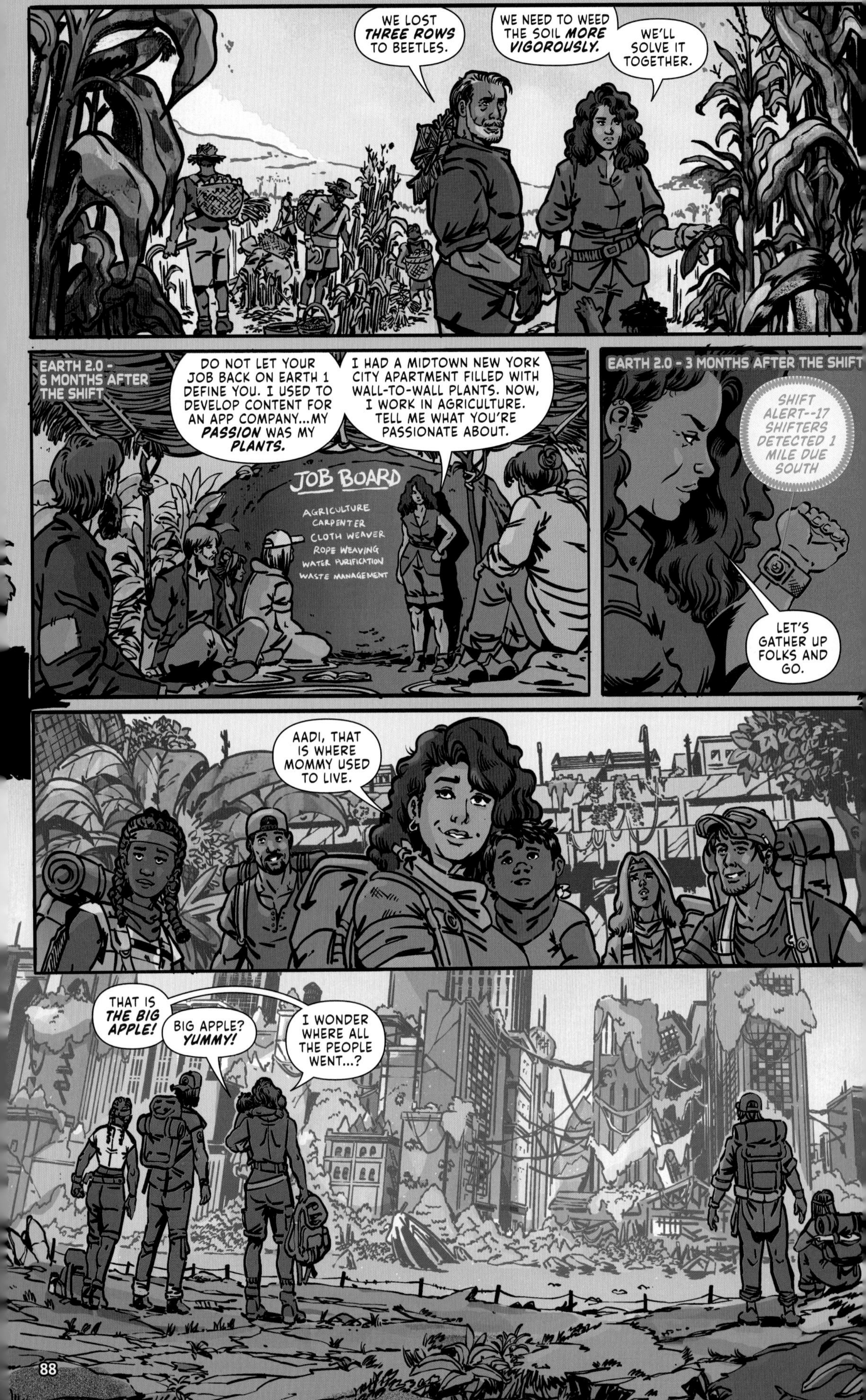
WE LOST *THREE ROWS* TO BEETLES.
WE NEED TO WEED THE SOIL *MORE VIGOROUSLY.*
WE'LL SOLVE IT TOGETHER.
EARTH 2.0 - 6 MONTHS AFTER THE SHIFT
DO NOT LET YOUR JOB BACK ON EARTH 1 DEFINE YOU. I USED TO DEVELOP CONTENT FOR AN APP COMPANY...MY *PASSION* WAS MY *PLANTS.*
I HAD A MIDTOWN NEW YORK CITY APARTMENT FILLED WITH WALL-TO-WALL PLANTS. NOW, I WORK IN AGRICULTURE. TELL ME WHAT YOU'RE PASSIONATE ABOUT.
JOB BOARD
AGRICULTURE
CARPENTER
CLOTH WEAVER
ROPE WEAVING
WATER PURIFICATION
WASTE MANAGEMENT
EARTH 2.0 - 3 MONTHS AFTER THE SHIFT
SHIFT ALERT--17 SHIFTERS DETECTED 1 MILE DUE SOUTH
LET'S GATHER UP FOLKS AND GO.
AADI, THAT IS WHERE MOMMY USED TO LIVE.
THAT IS *THE BIG APPLE!*
BIG APPLE? *YUMMY!*
I WONDER WHERE ALL THE PEOPLE WENT...?

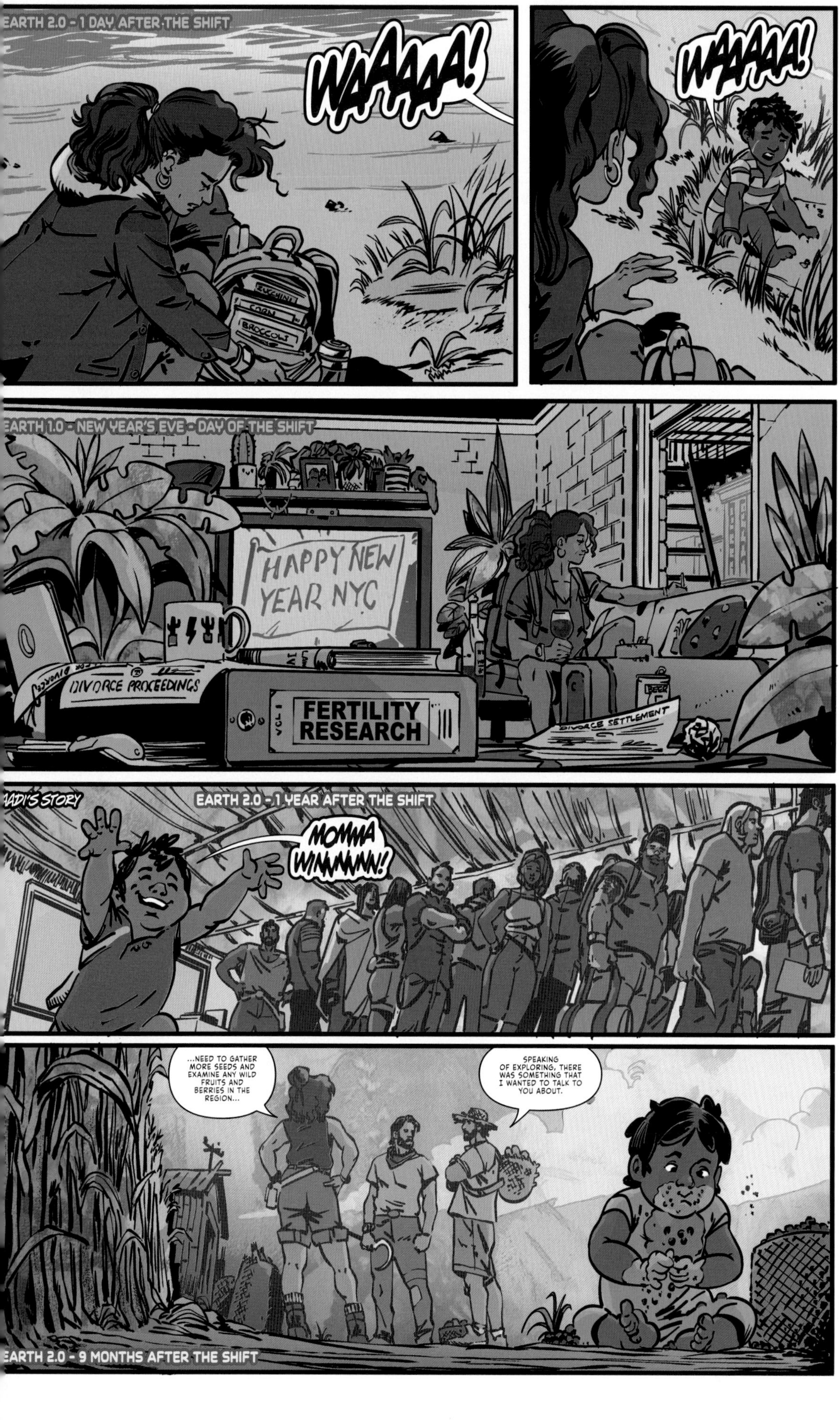
EARTH 2.0 - 1 DAY AFTER THE SHIFT
WAAAAA!
ZUCCHINI
CORN
BROCCOLI
WAAAAA!
EARTH 1.0 - NEW YEAR'S EVE - DAY OF THE SHIFT
HAPPY NEW YEAR NYC
DIVORCE PROCEEDINGS
FERTILITY RESEARCH
DIVORCE SETTLEMENT
ADI'S STORY
EARTH 2.0 - 1 YEAR AFTER THE SHIFT
MOMMA WINNNNN!
...NEED TO GATHER MORE SEEDS AND EXAMINE ANY WILD FRUITS AND BERRIES IN THE REGION...
SPEAKING OF EXPLORING, THERE WAS SOMETHING THAT I WANTED TO TALK TO YOU ABOUT.
EARTH 2.0 - 9 MONTHS AFTER THE SHIFT

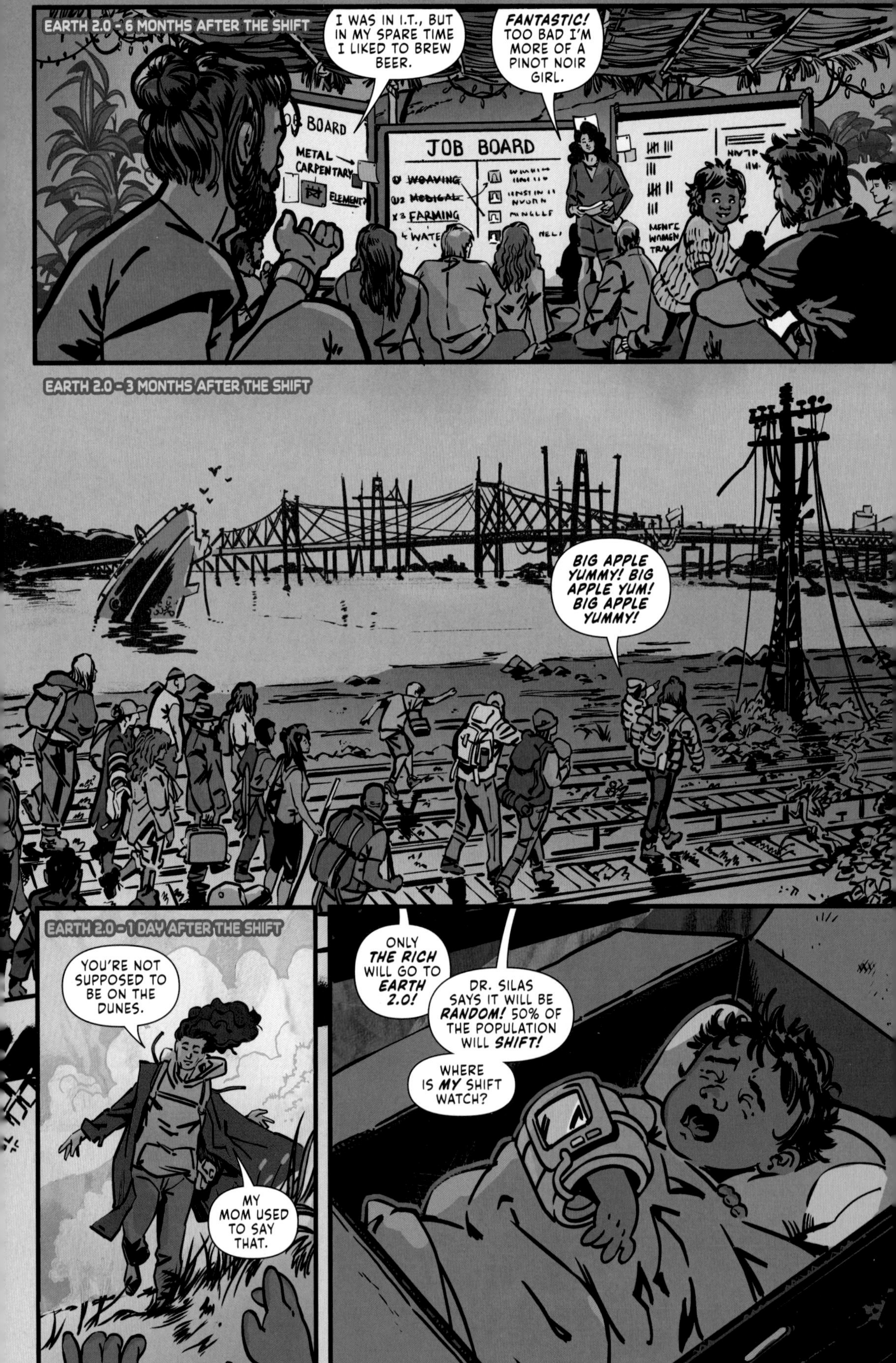
EARTH 2.0 - 6 MONTHS AFTER THE SHIFT
I WAS IN I.T., BUT IN MY SPARE TIME I LIKED TO BREW BEER.
FANTASTIC! TOO BAD I'M MORE OF A PINOT NOIR GIRL.
JOB BOARD
METAL CARPENTARY
ELEMENT?
WEAVING
MEDICAL
FARMING
EARTH 2.0 - 3 MONTHS AFTER THE SHIFT
BIG APPLE YUMMY! BIG APPLE YUM! BIG APPLE YUMMY!
EARTH 2.0 - 1 DAY AFTER THE SHIFT
YOU'RE NOT SUPPOSED TO BE ON THE DUNES.
MY MOM USED TO SAY THAT.
ONLY *THE RICH* WILL GO TO *EARTH 2.0!*
DR. SILAS SAYS IT WILL BE *RANDOM!* 50% OF THE POPULATION WILL *SHIFT!*
WHERE IS *MY* SHIFT WATCH?
EARTH 1.0 - NEW YEAR'S EVE, DAY OF THE SHIF

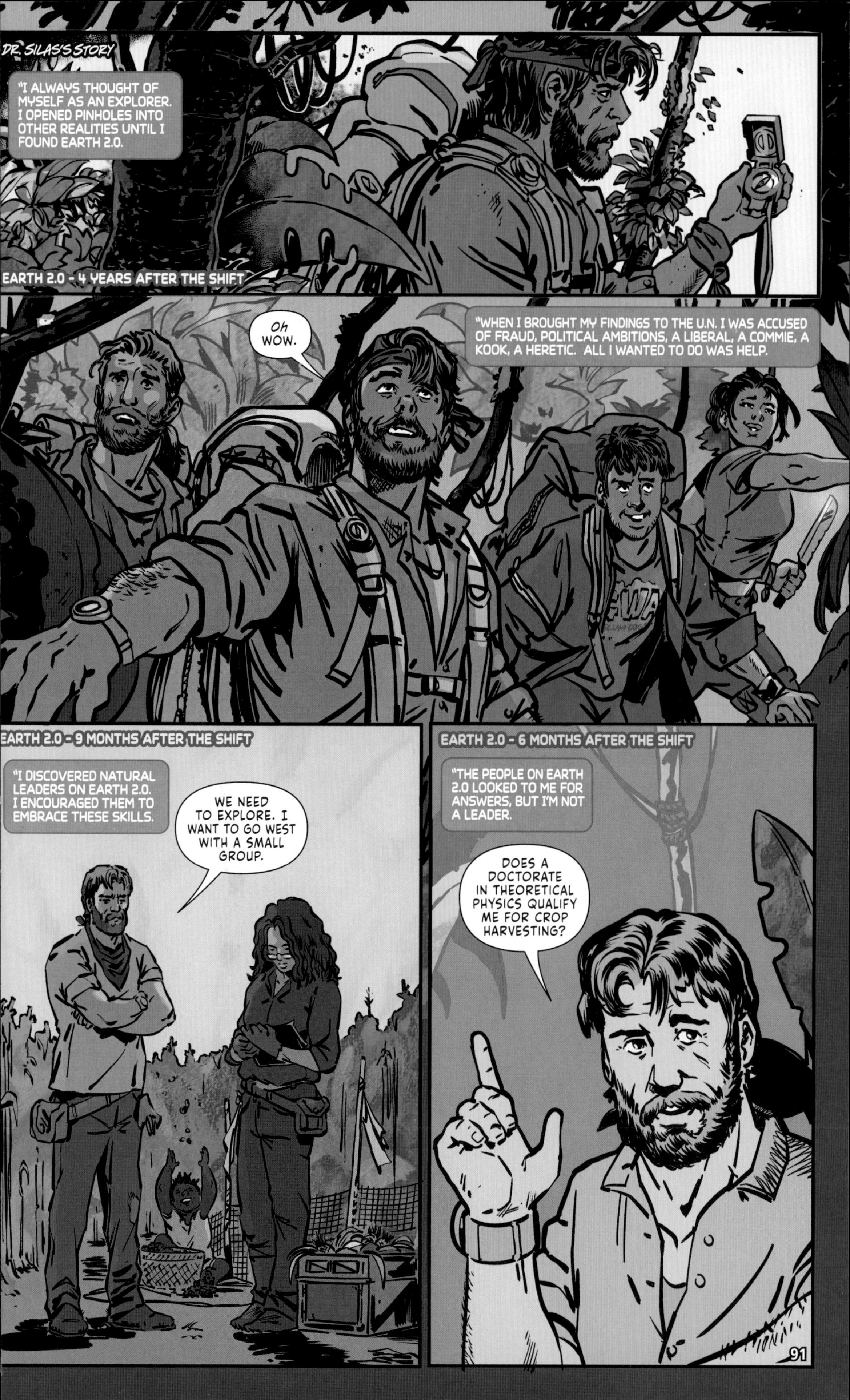
DR. SILAS'S STORY
"I ALWAYS THOUGHT OF MYSELF AS AN EXPLORER. I OPENED PINHOLES INTO OTHER REALITIES UNTIL I FOUND EARTH 2.0.
EARTH 2.0 - 4 YEARS AFTER THE SHIFT
Oh WOW.
"WHEN I BROUGHT MY FINDINGS TO THE U.N. I WAS ACCUSED OF FRAUD, POLITICAL AMBITIONS, A LIBERAL, A COMMIE, A KOOK, A HERETIC. ALL I WANTED TO DO WAS HELP.
EARTH 2.0 - 9 MONTHS AFTER THE SHIFT
"I DISCOVERED NATURAL LEADERS ON EARTH 2.0. I ENCOURAGED THEM TO EMBRACE THESE SKILLS.
WE NEED TO EXPLORE. I WANT TO GO WEST WITH A SMALL GROUP.
EARTH 2.0 - 6 MONTHS AFTER THE SHIFT
"THE PEOPLE ON EARTH 2.0 LOOKED TO ME FOR ANSWERS, BUT I'M NOT A LEADER.
DOES A DOCTORATE IN THEORETICAL PHYSICS QUALIFY ME FOR CROP HARVESTING?

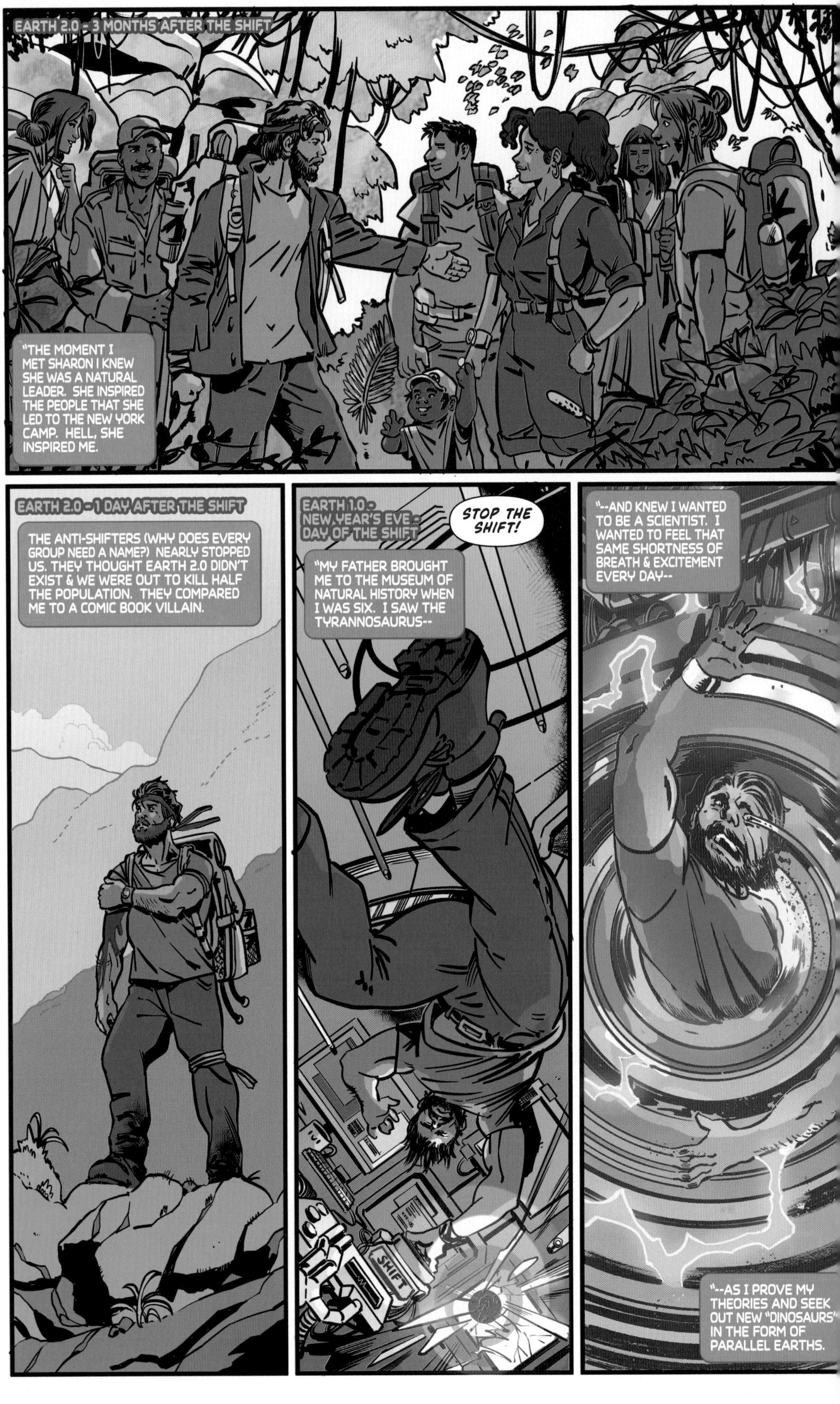
EARTH 2.0 - 3 MONTHS AFTER THE SHIFT
"THE MOMENT I MET SHARON I KNEW SHE WAS A NATURAL LEADER. SHE INSPIRED THE PEOPLE THAT SHE LED TO THE NEW YORK CAMP. HELL, SHE INSPIRED ME.
EARTH 2.0 - 1 DAY AFTER THE SHIFT
THE ANTI-SHIFTERS (WHY DOES EVERY GROUP NEED A NAME?) NEARLY STOPPED US. THEY THOUGHT EARTH 2.0 DIDN'T EXIST & WE WERE OUT TO KILL HALF THE POPULATION. THEY COMPARED ME TO A COMIC BOOK VILLAIN.
EARTH 1.0 - NEW YEAR'S EVE - DAY OF THE SHIFT
STOP THE SHIFT!
"MY FATHER BROUGHT ME TO THE MUSEUM OF NATURAL HISTORY WHEN I WAS SIX. I SAW THE TYRANNOSAURUS--
SHIFT
"--AND KNEW I WANTED TO BE A SCIENTIST. I WANTED TO FEEL THAT SAME SHORTNESS OF BREATH & EXCITEMENT EVERY DAY--
"--AS I PROVE MY THEORIES AND SEEK OUT NEW "DINOSAURS" IN THE FORM OF PARALLEL EARTHS.

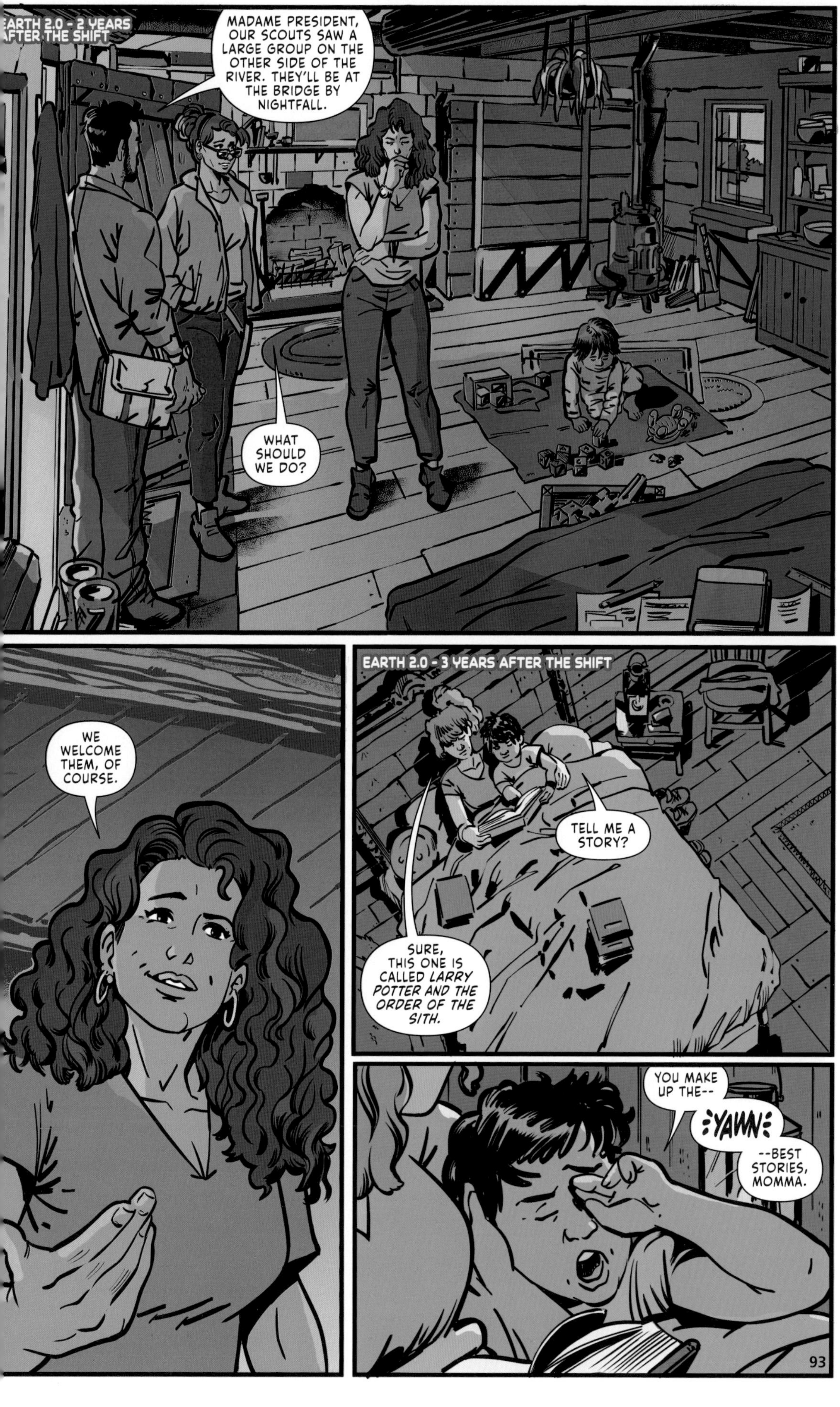
EARTH 2.0 - 2 YEARS AFTER THE SHIFT
MADAME PRESIDENT, OUR SCOUTS SAW A LARGE GROUP ON THE OTHER SIDE OF THE RIVER. THEY'LL BE AT THE BRIDGE BY NIGHTFALL.
WHAT SHOULD WE DO?
WE WELCOME THEM, OF COURSE.
EARTH 2.0 - 3 YEARS AFTER THE SHIFT
TELL ME A STORY?
SURE, THIS ONE IS CALLED *LARRY POTTER AND THE ORDER OF THE SITH.*
YOU MAKE UP THE--
YAWN
--BEST STORIES, MOMMA.

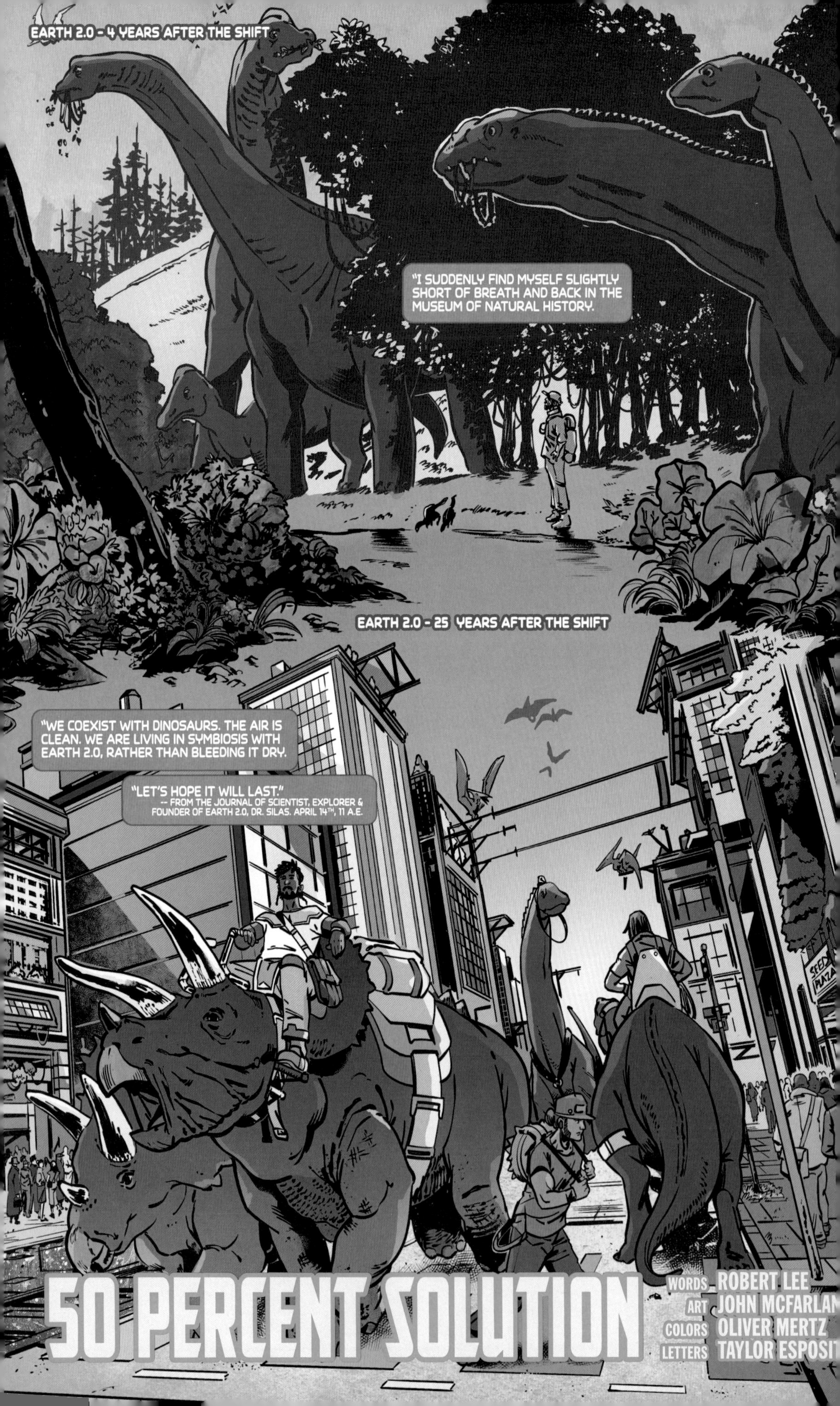
EARTH 2.0 - 4 YEARS AFTER THE SHIFT
"I SUDDENLY FIND MYSELF SLIGHTLY SHORT OF BREATH AND BACK IN THE MUSEUM OF NATURAL HISTORY.
EARTH 2.0 - 25 YEARS AFTER THE SHIFT
"WE COEXIST WITH DINOSAURS. THE AIR IS CLEAN. WE ARE LIVING IN SYMBIOSIS WITH EARTH 2.0, RATHER THAN BLEEDING IT DRY.
"LET'S HOPE IT WILL LAST."
-- FROM THE JOURNAL OF SCIENTIST, EXPLORER & FOUNDER OF EARTH 2.0, DR. SILAS. APRIL 14TH, 11 A.E.
50 PERCENT SOLUTION
WORDS ROBERT LEE
ART JOHN MCFARLAN
COLORS OLIVER MERTZ
LETTERS TAYLOR ESPOSI

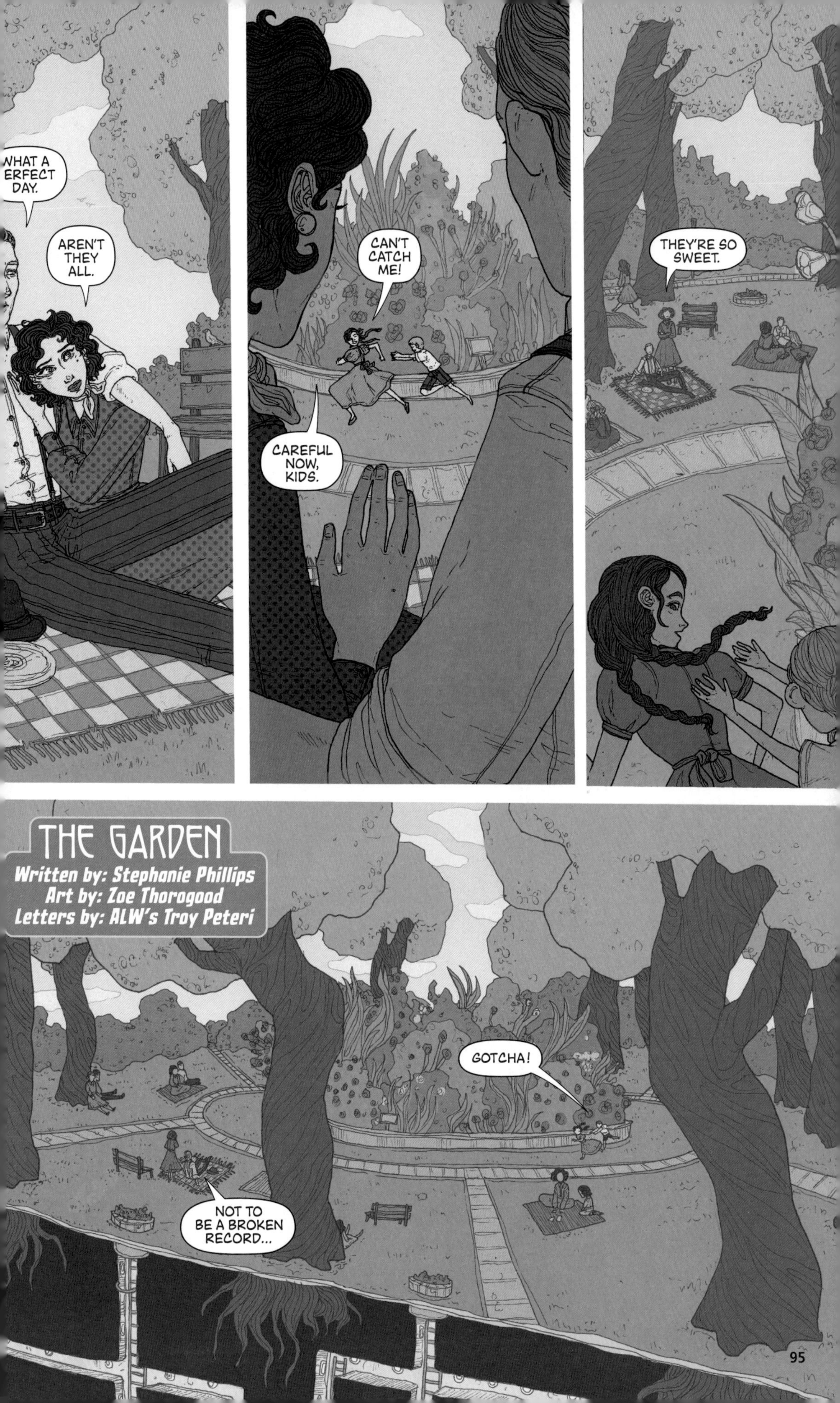

WHAT A ERFECT DAY.
AREN'T THEY ALL.
CAN'T CATCH ME!
CAREFUL NOW, KIDS.
THEY'RE SO SWEET.
THE GARDEN
Written by: Stephanie Phillips
Art by: Zoe Thorogood
Letters by: ALW's Troy Peteri
GOTCHA!
NOT TO BE A BROKEN RECORD...

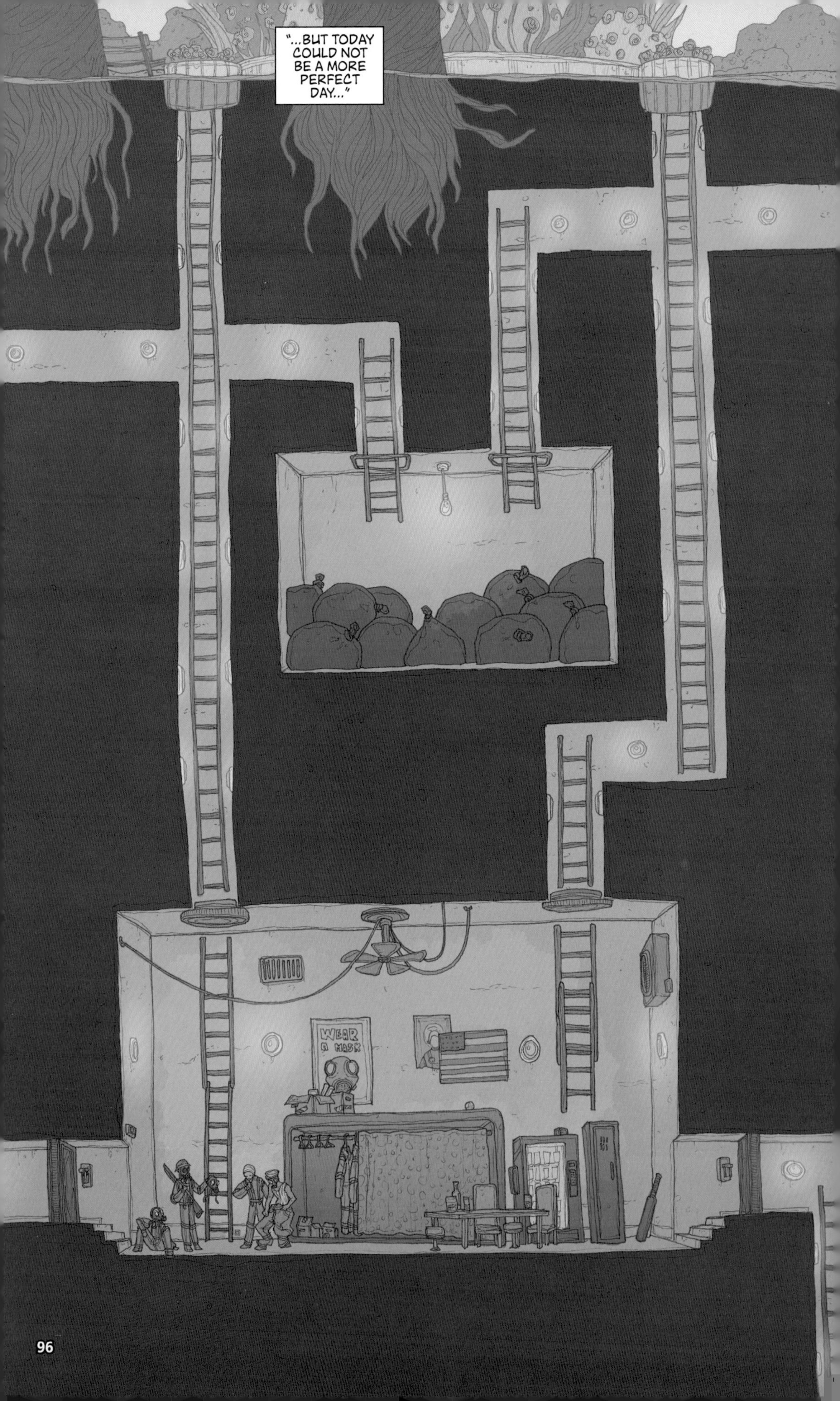
"...BUT TODAY COULD NOT BE A MORE PERFECT DAY..."
WEAR A MASK

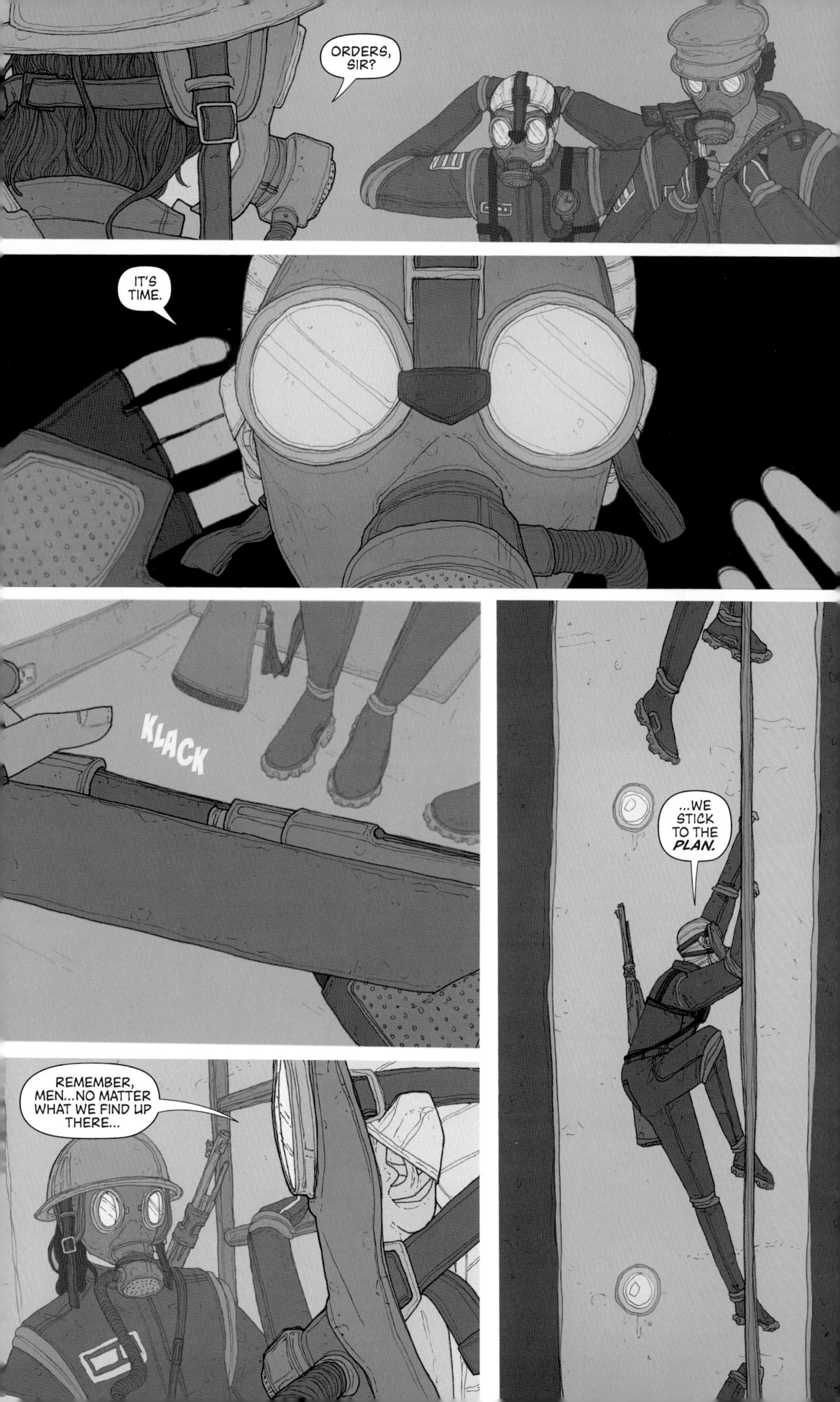
ORDERS, SIR?
IT'S TIME.
KLACK
REMEMBER, MEN...NO MATTER WHAT WE FIND UP THERE...
...WE STICK TO THE *PLAN.*

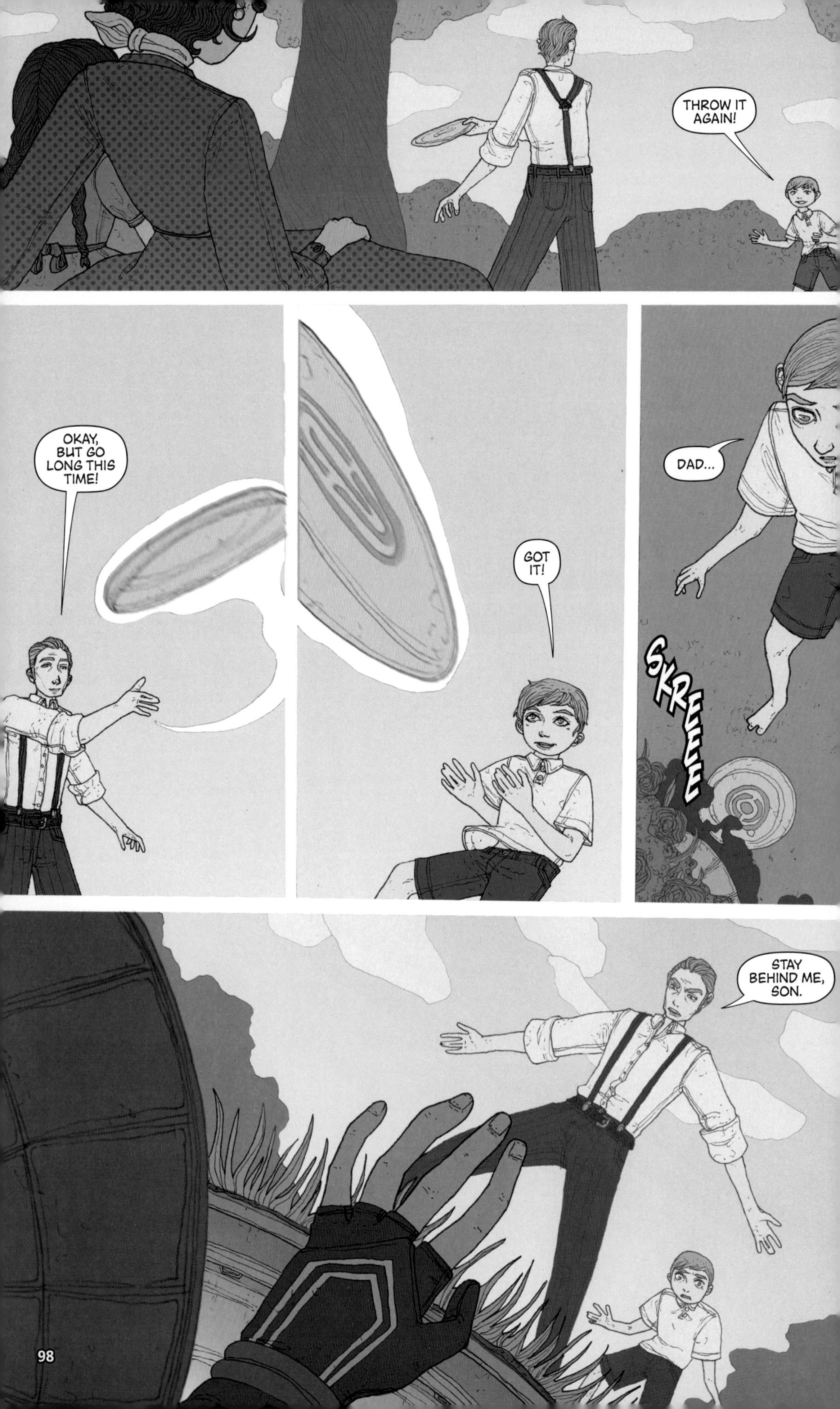
THROW IT AGAIN!
OKAY, BUT GO LONG THIS TIME!
GOT IT!
DAD...
SKREEEE
STAY BEHIND ME, SON.

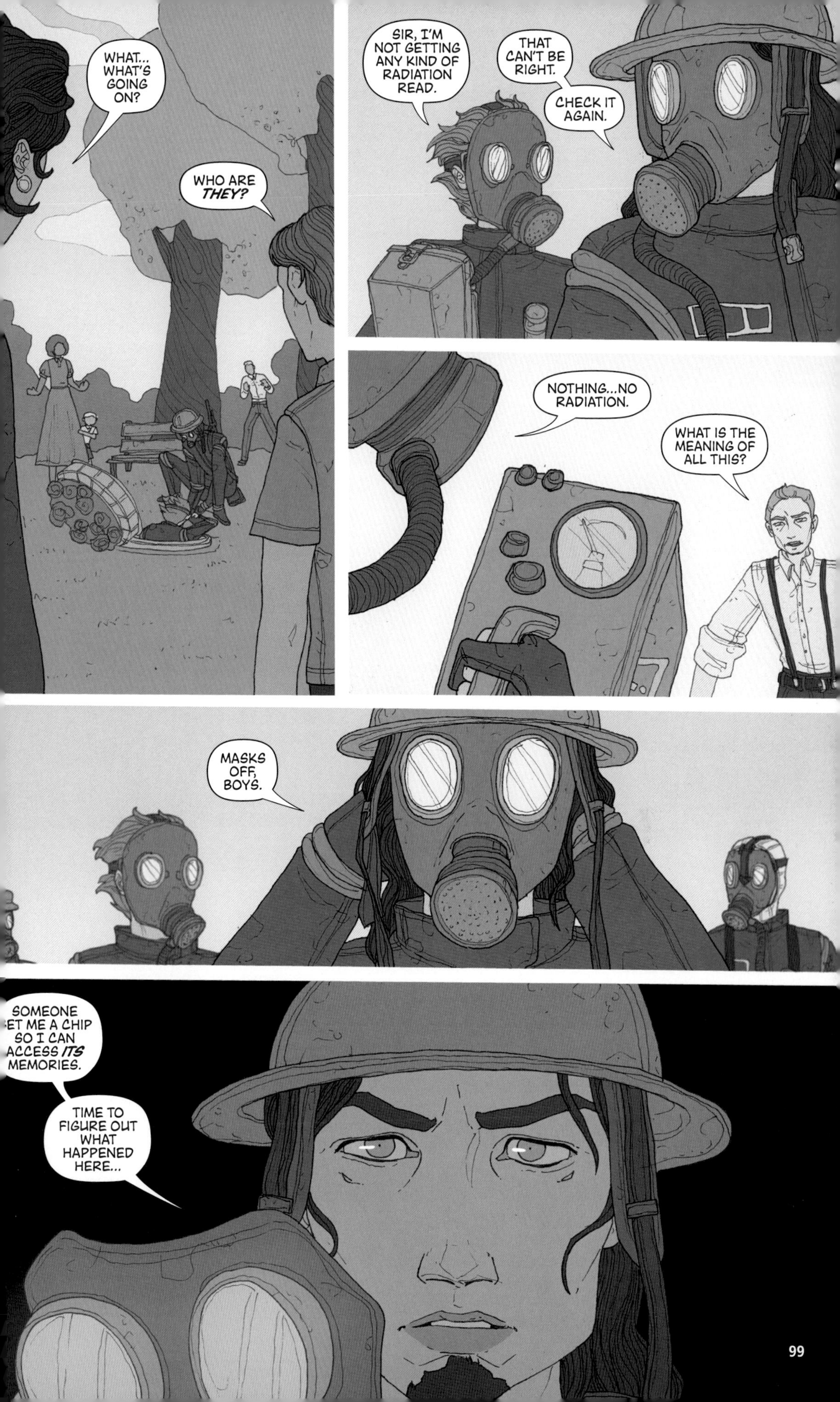
WHAT... WHAT'S GOING ON?
WHO ARE *THEY?*
SIR, I'M NOT GETTING ANY KIND OF RADIATION READ.
THAT CAN'T BE RIGHT.
CHECK IT AGAIN.
NOTHING...NO RADIATION.
WHAT IS THE MEANING OF ALL THIS?
MASKS OFF, BOYS.
SOMEONE ET ME A CHIP SO I CAN ACCESS *ITS* MEMORIES.
TIME TO FIGURE OUT WHAT HAPPENED HERE...

I ASKED WHAT IS GOING ON HERE.
THAT'S WHAT WE WOULD LIKE TO KNOW AS WELL.
EXCUSE ME! YOU CAN'T JUST...
UNIT ALPHA-TEN-X NOW AVAILABLE.
HOW MAY I ASSIST YOU?

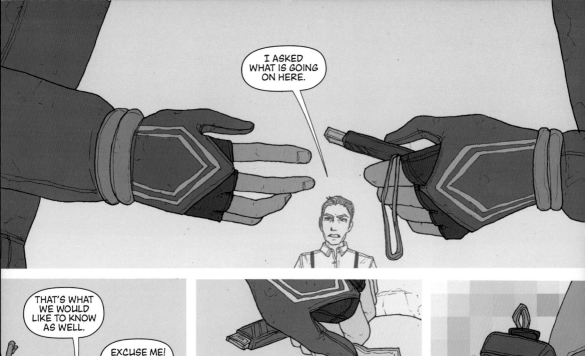

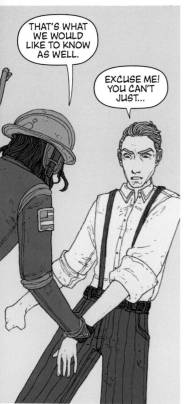

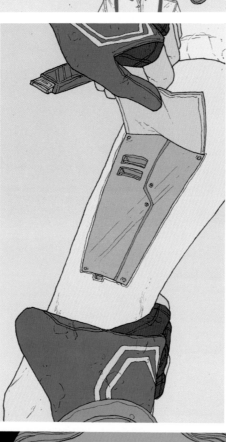

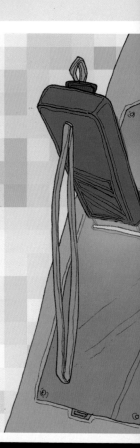

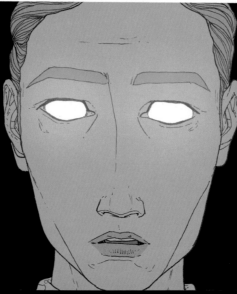

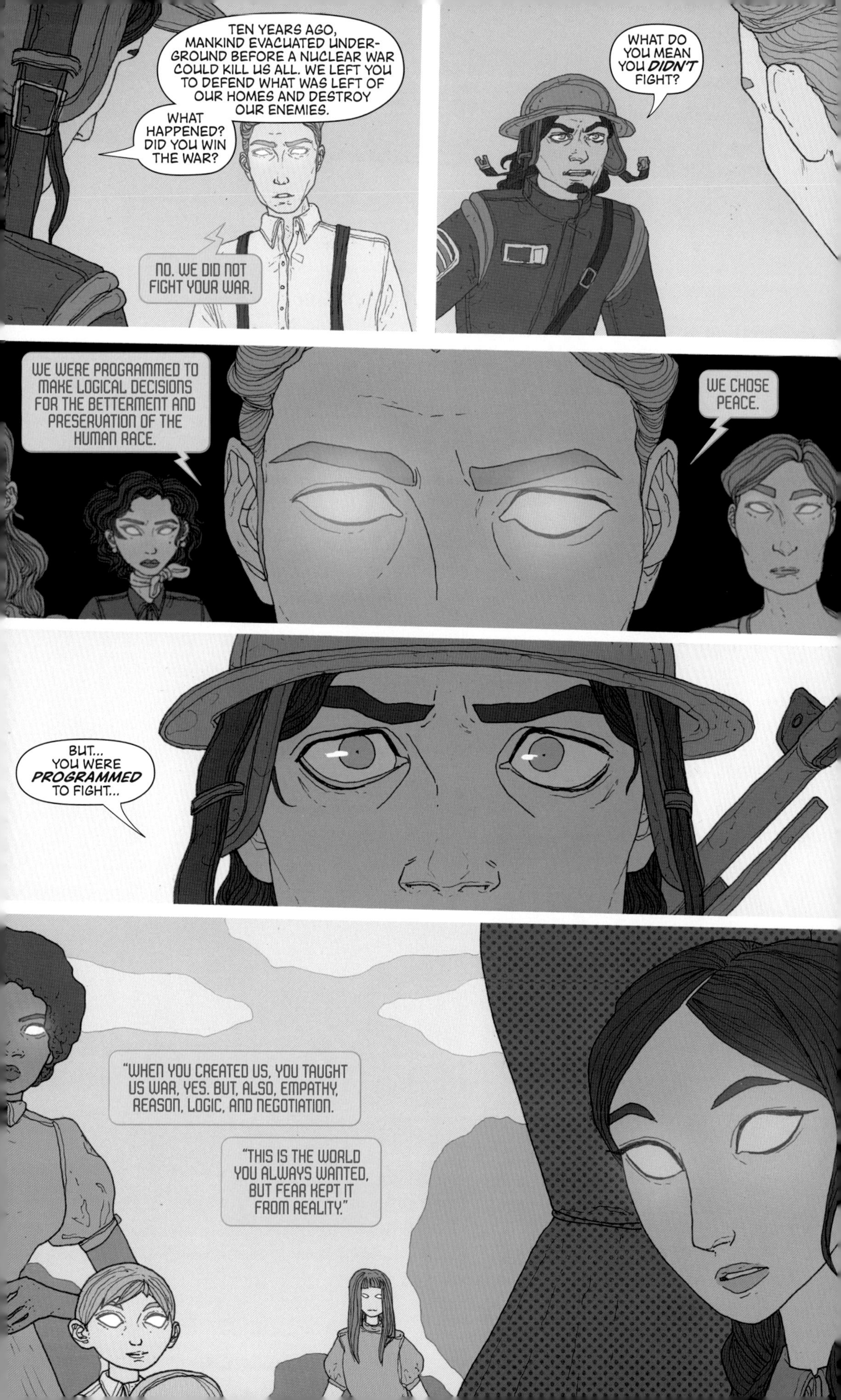
TEN YEARS AGO, MANKIND EVACUATED UNDERGROUND BEFORE A NUCLEAR WAR COULD KILL US ALL. WE LEFT YOU TO DEFEND WHAT WAS LEFT OF OUR HOMES AND DESTROY OUR ENEMIES.
WHAT HAPPENED? DID YOU WIN THE WAR?
NO. WE DID NOT FIGHT YOUR WAR.
WHAT DO YOU MEAN YOU *DIDN'T* FIGHT?
WE WERE PROGRAMMED TO MAKE LOGICAL DECISIONS FOR THE BETTERMENT AND PRESERVATION OF THE HUMAN RACE.
WE CHOSE PEACE.
BUT... YOU WERE *PROGRAMMED* TO FIGHT...
"WHEN YOU CREATED US, YOU TAUGHT US WAR, YES. BUT, ALSO, EMPATHY, REASON, LOGIC, AND NEGOTIATION.
"THIS IS THE WORLD YOU ALWAYS WANTED, BUT FEAR KEPT IT FROM REALITY."

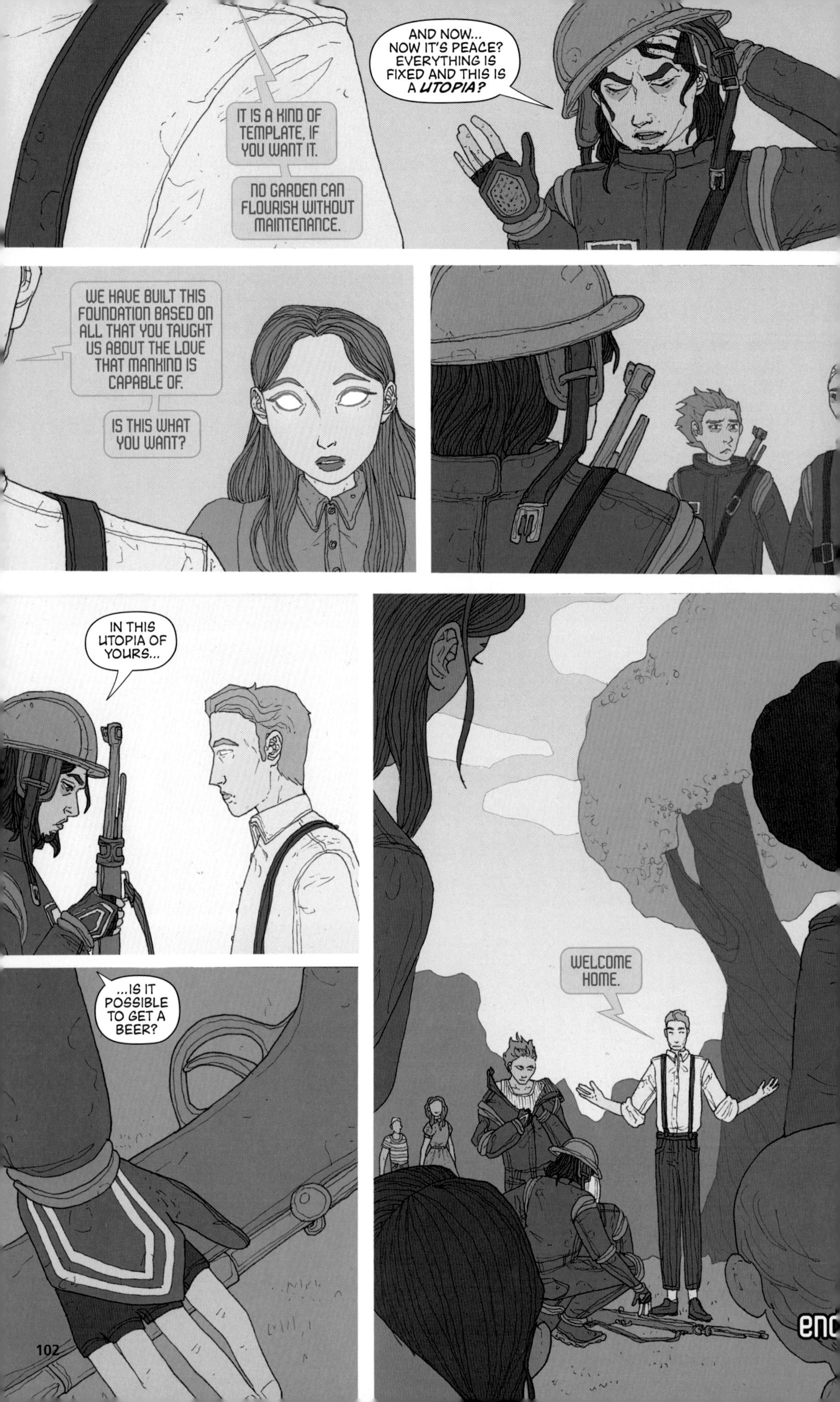
AND NOW... NOW IT'S PEACE? EVERYTHING IS FIXED AND THIS IS A *UTOPIA?*
IT IS A KIND OF TEMPLATE, IF YOU WANT IT.
NO GARDEN CAN FLOURISH WITHOUT MAINTENANCE.
WE HAVE BUILT THIS FOUNDATION BASED ON ALL THAT YOU TAUGHT US ABOUT THE LOVE THAT MANKIND IS CAPABLE OF.
IS THIS WHAT YOU WANT?
IN THIS UTOPIA OF YOURS...
...IS IT POSSIBLE TO GET A BEER?
WELCOME HOME.

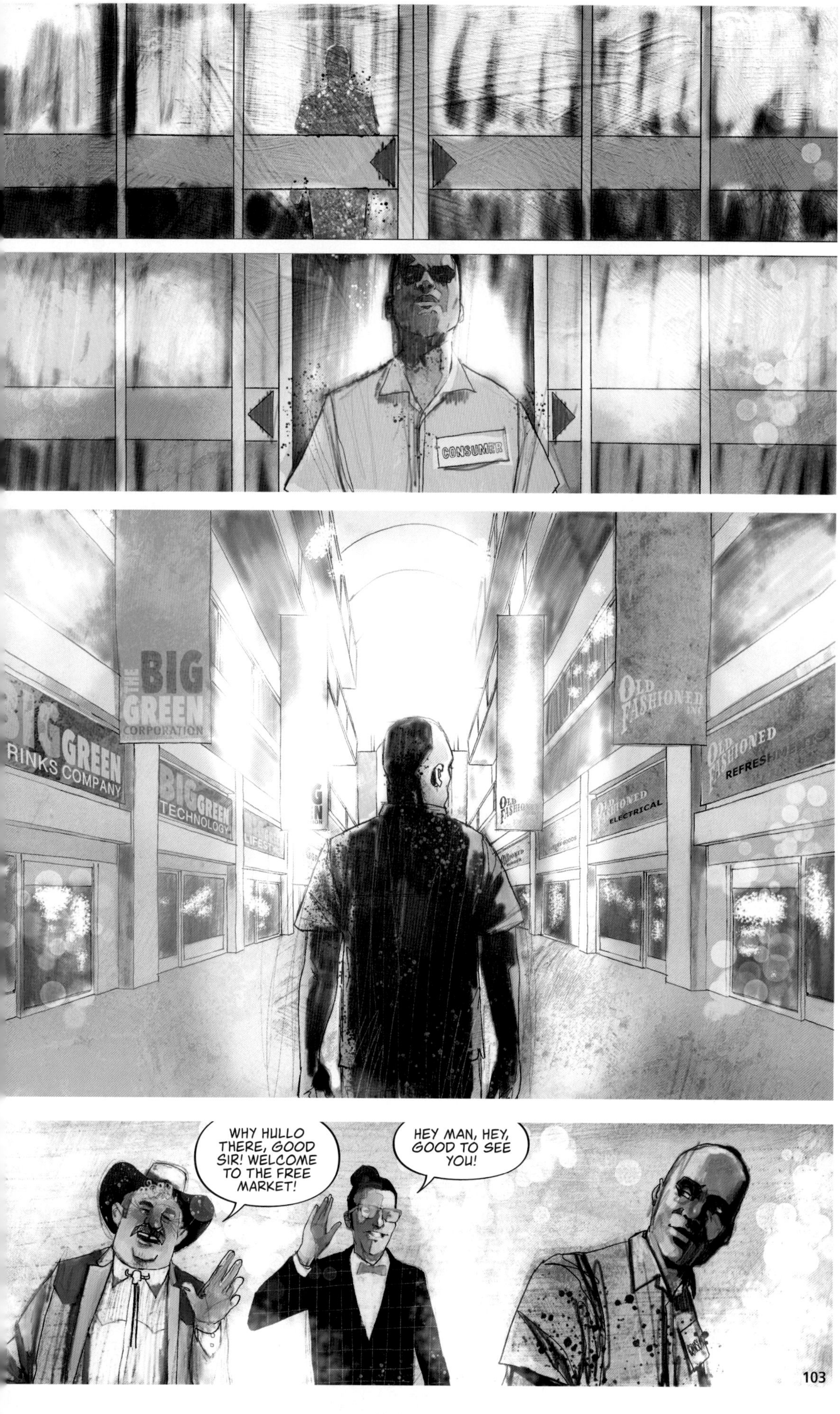
CONSUMER
THE BIG GREEN CORPORATION
BIG GREEN
RINKS COMPANY
BIG GREEN TECHNOLOGY
OLD FASHIONED INC
OLD FASHIONED
REFRESHMENTS
OLD FASHIONED ELECTRICAL
WHY HULLO THERE, GOOD SIR! WELCOME TO THE FREE MARKET!
HEY MAN, HEY, GOOD TO SEE YOU!

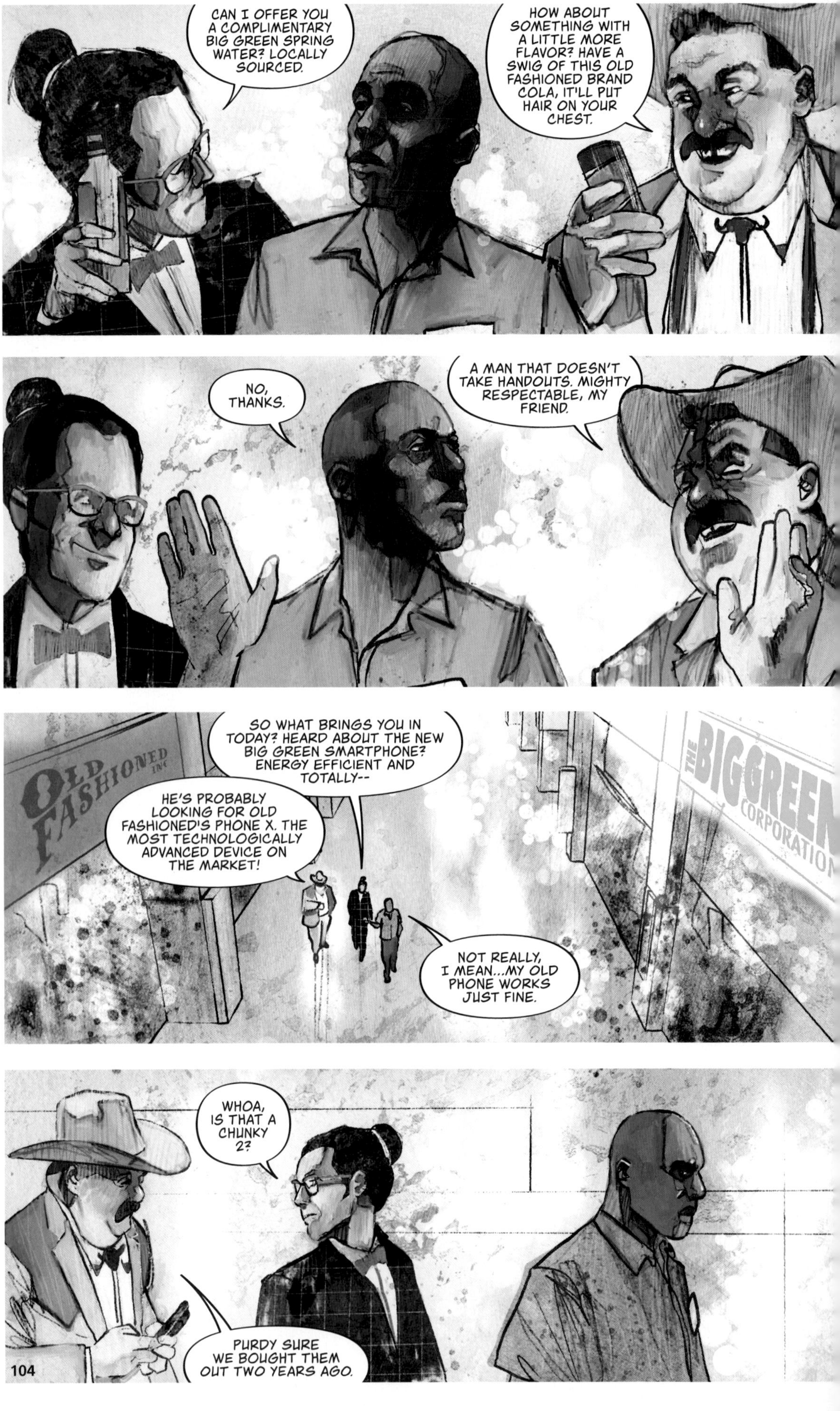
CAN I OFFER YOU A COMPLIMENTARY BIG GREEN SPRING WATER? LOCALLY SOURCED.
HOW ABOUT SOMETHING WITH A LITTLE MORE FLAVOR? HAVE A SWIG OF THIS OLD FASHIONED BRAND COLA, IT'LL PUT HAIR ON YOUR CHEST.
NO, THANKS.
A MAN THAT DOESN'T TAKE HANDOUTS. MIGHTY RESPECTABLE, MY FRIEND.
OLD FASHIONED INC
SO WHAT BRINGS YOU IN TODAY? HEARD ABOUT THE NEW BIG GREEN SMARTPHONE? ENERGY EFFICIENT AND TOTALLY--
THE BIGGREEN CORPORATION
HE'S PROBABLY LOOKING FOR OLD FASHIONED'S PHONE X. THE MOST TECHNOLOGICALLY ADVANCED DEVICE ON THE MARKET!
NOT REALLY, I MEAN...MY OLD PHONE WORKS JUST FINE.
WHOA, IS THAT A CHUNKY 2?
PURDY SURE WE BOUGHT THEM OUT TWO YEARS AGO.

WELL, SONNY, WHAT CAN OLD FASHIONED DO FOR YOU TODAY. WE OFFER THE FINEST LINE OF GOODS AND SERVICES THAT MONEY CAN BUY, AND AT DISCOUNT PRICES!
OLD FASHIONED INC
VIDEO GAMES
OR SHOP WITH BIG GREEN, WHERE YOUR DOLLARS AFFECT POSITIVE CHANGE. YOU CAN BE SURE THAT EVERY PURCHASE YOU MAKE IS AN ENVIRONMENTALLY FRIENDLY ONE.
BIG GREEN CORPORATION
THANKS, BUT I DON'T REALLY NEED ANY OF THAT STUFF.
NONE OF IT?
THERE'S NOTHING YOU WANT?
GRROWL

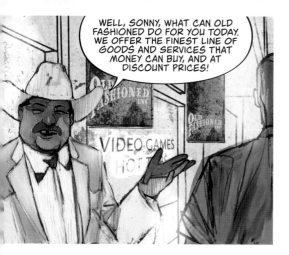

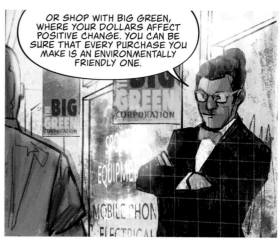

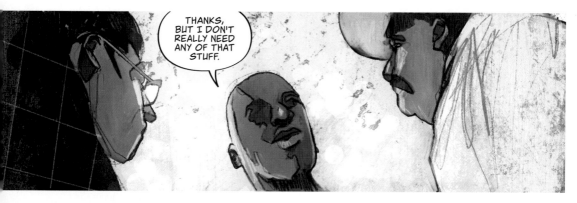

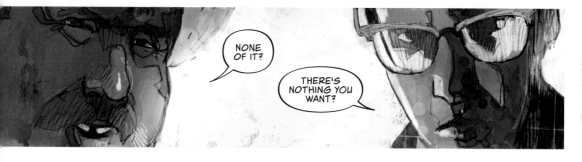

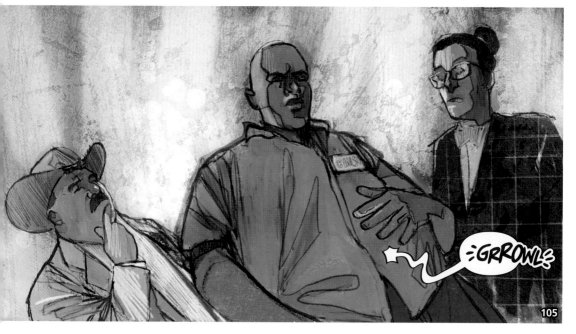

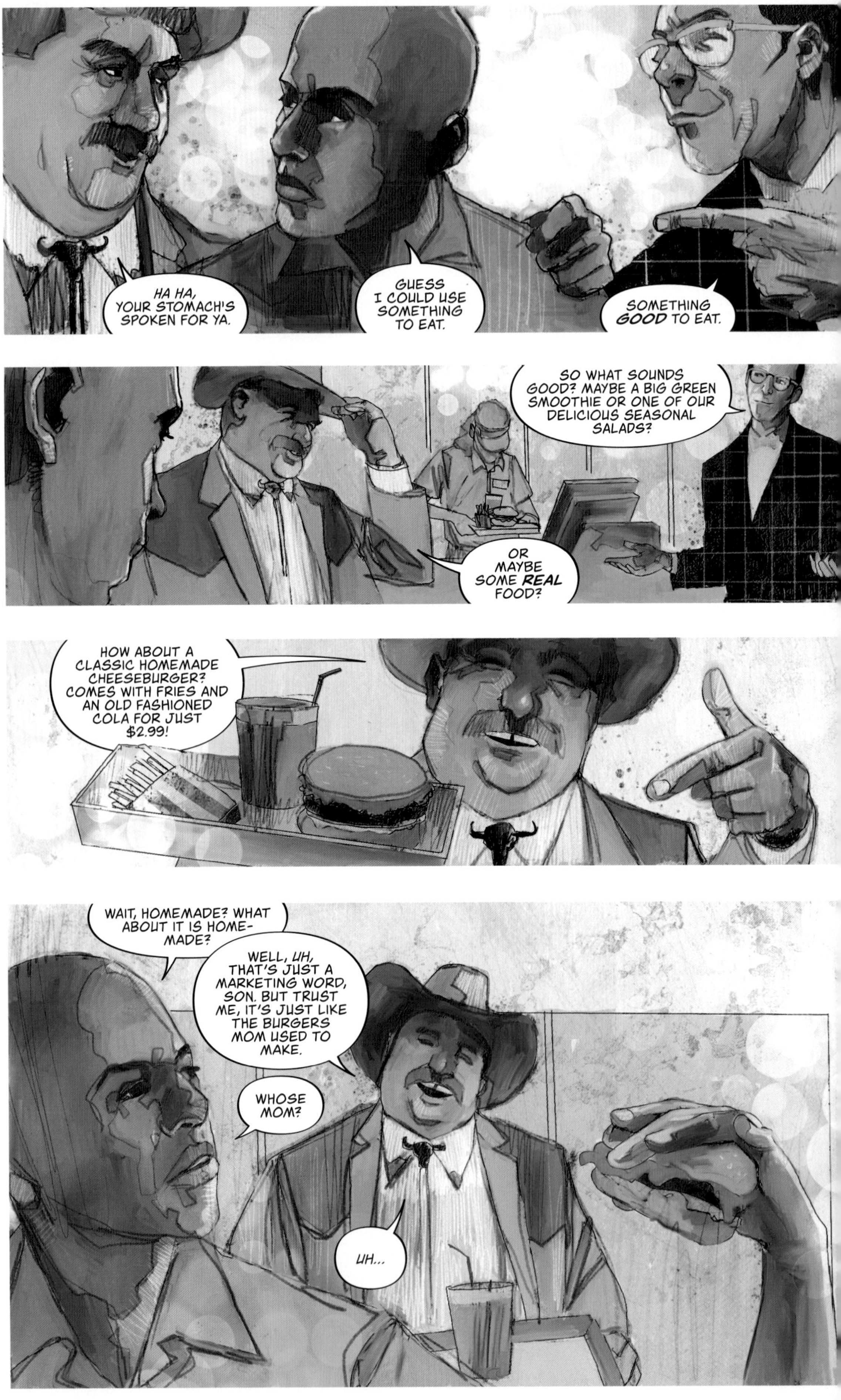
HA HA, YOUR STOMACH'S SPOKEN FOR YA.
GUESS I COULD USE SOMETHING TO EAT.
SOMETHING **GOOD** TO EAT.
SO WHAT SOUNDS GOOD? MAYBE A BIG GREEN SMOOTHIE OR ONE OF OUR DELICIOUS SEASONAL SALADS?
OR MAYBE SOME **REAL** FOOD?
HOW ABOUT A CLASSIC HOMEMADE CHEESEBURGER? COMES WITH FRIES AND AN OLD FASHIONED COLA FOR JUST $2.99!
WAIT, HOMEMADE? WHAT ABOUT IT IS HOME-MADE?
WELL, *UH*, THAT'S JUST A MARKETING WORD, SON. BUT TRUST ME, IT'S JUST LIKE THE BURGERS MOM USED TO MAKE.
WHOSE MOM?
UH...

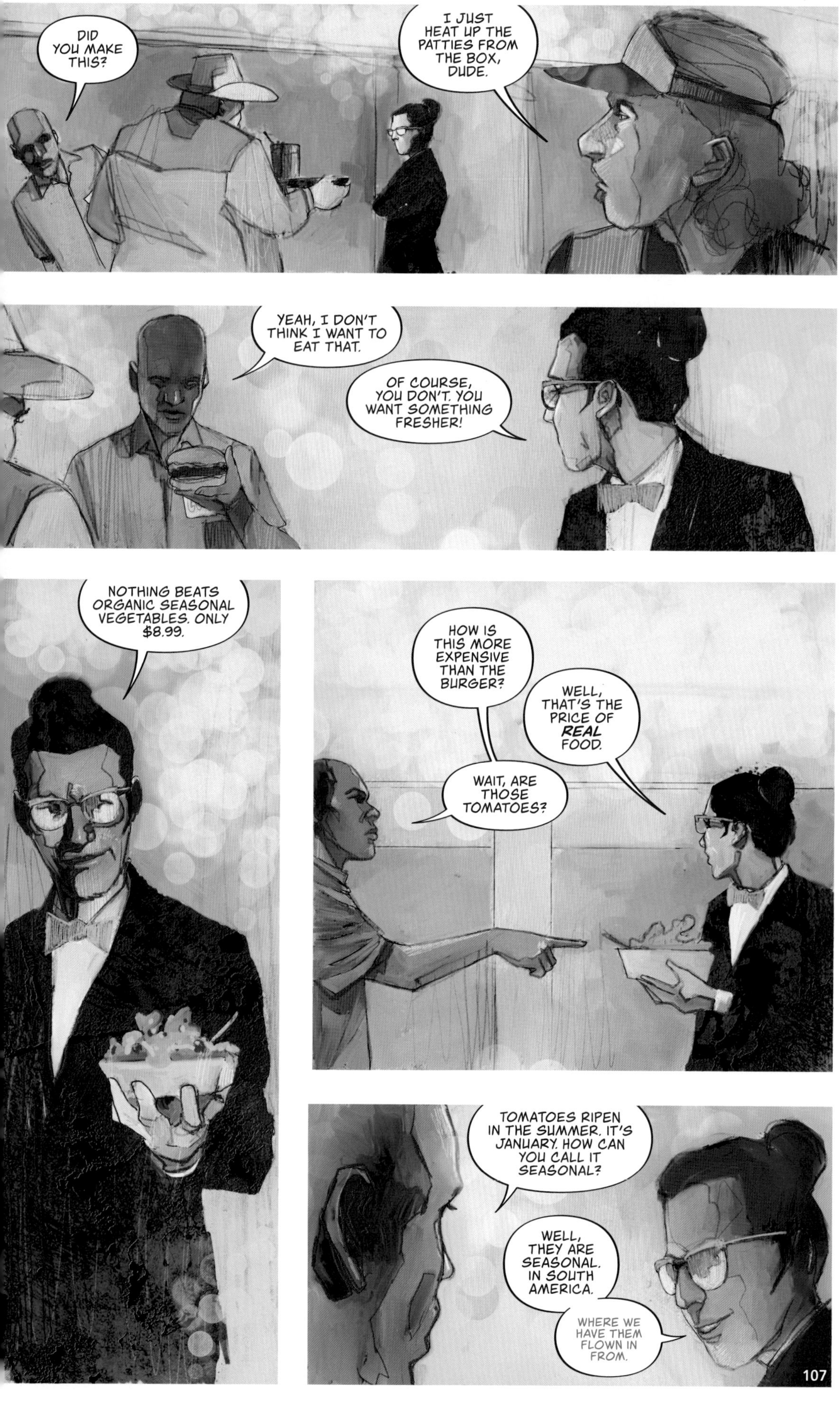
DID YOU MAKE THIS?
I JUST HEAT UP THE PATTIES FROM THE BOX, DUDE.
YEAH, I DON'T THINK I WANT TO EAT THAT.
OF COURSE, YOU DON'T. YOU WANT SOMETHING FRESHER!
NOTHING BEATS ORGANIC SEASONAL VEGETABLES. ONLY $8.99.
HOW IS THIS MORE EXPENSIVE THAN THE BURGER?
WELL, THAT'S THE PRICE OF **REAL** FOOD.
WAIT, ARE THOSE TOMATOES?
TOMATOES RIPEN IN THE SUMMER. IT'S JANUARY. HOW CAN YOU CALL IT SEASONAL?
WELL, THEY ARE SEASONAL. IN SOUTH AMERICA.
WHERE WE HAVE THEM FLOWN IN FROM.

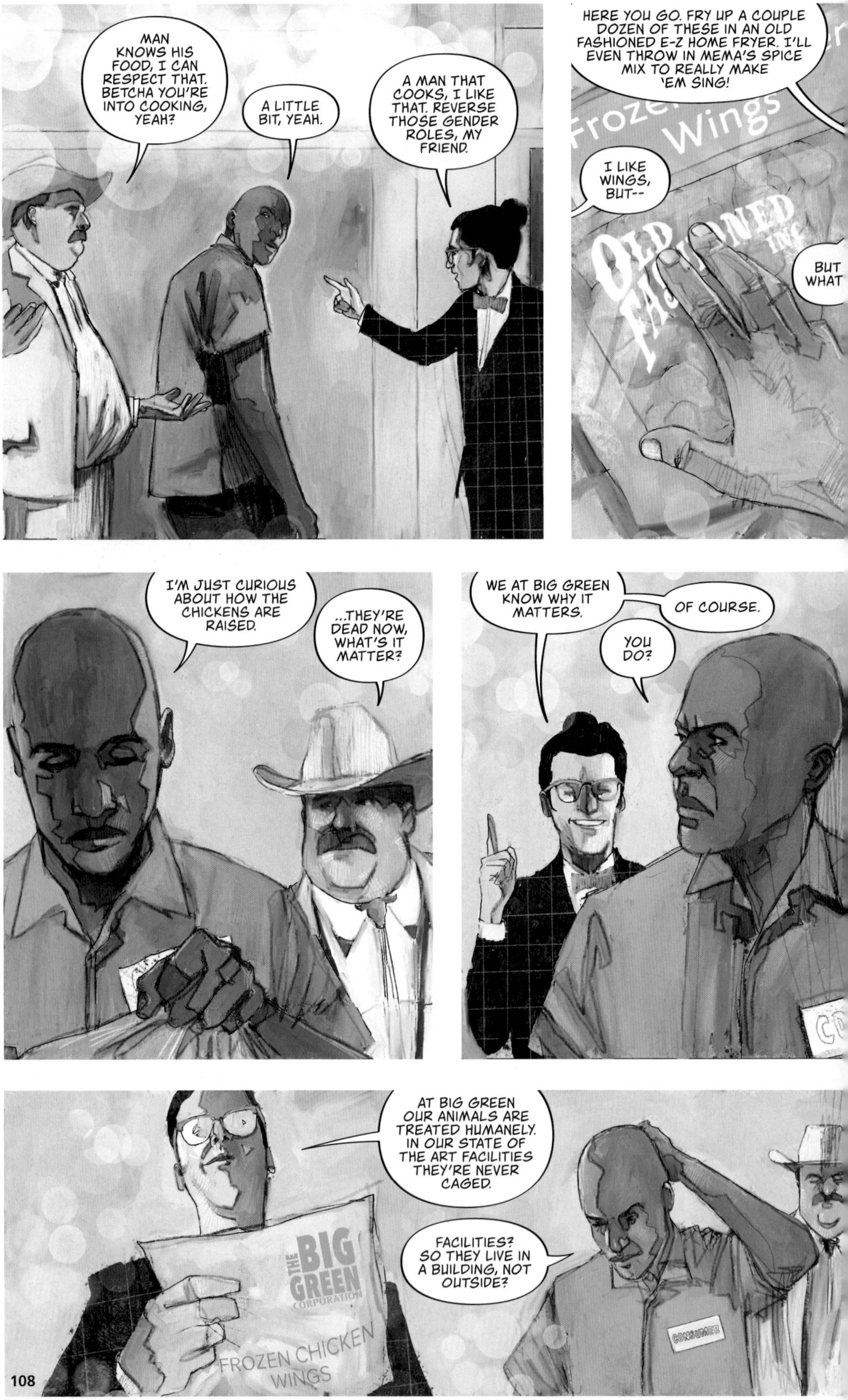
MAN KNOWS HIS FOOD, I CAN RESPECT THAT. BETCHA YOU'RE INTO COOKING, YEAH?
A LITTLE BIT, YEAH.
A MAN THAT COOKS, I LIKE THAT. REVERSE THOSE GENDER ROLES, MY FRIEND.
HERE YOU GO. FRY UP A COUPLE DOZEN OF THESE IN AN OLD FASHIONED E-Z HOME FRYER. I'LL EVEN THROW IN MEMA'S SPICE MIX TO REALLY MAKE 'EM SING!
Wings
I LIKE WINGS, BUT--
BUT WHAT
I'M JUST CURIOUS ABOUT HOW THE CHICKENS ARE RAISED.
...THEY'RE DEAD NOW, WHAT'S IT MATTER?
WE AT BIG GREEN KNOW WHY IT MATTERS.
OF COURSE.
YOU DO?
AT BIG GREEN OUR ANIMALS ARE TREATED HUMANELY. IN OUR STATE OF THE ART FACILITIES THEY'RE NEVER CAGED.
THE BIG GREEN CORPORATION
FROZEN CHICKEN WINGS
FACILITIES? SO THEY LIVE IN A BUILDING, NOT OUTSIDE?
CONSUMER

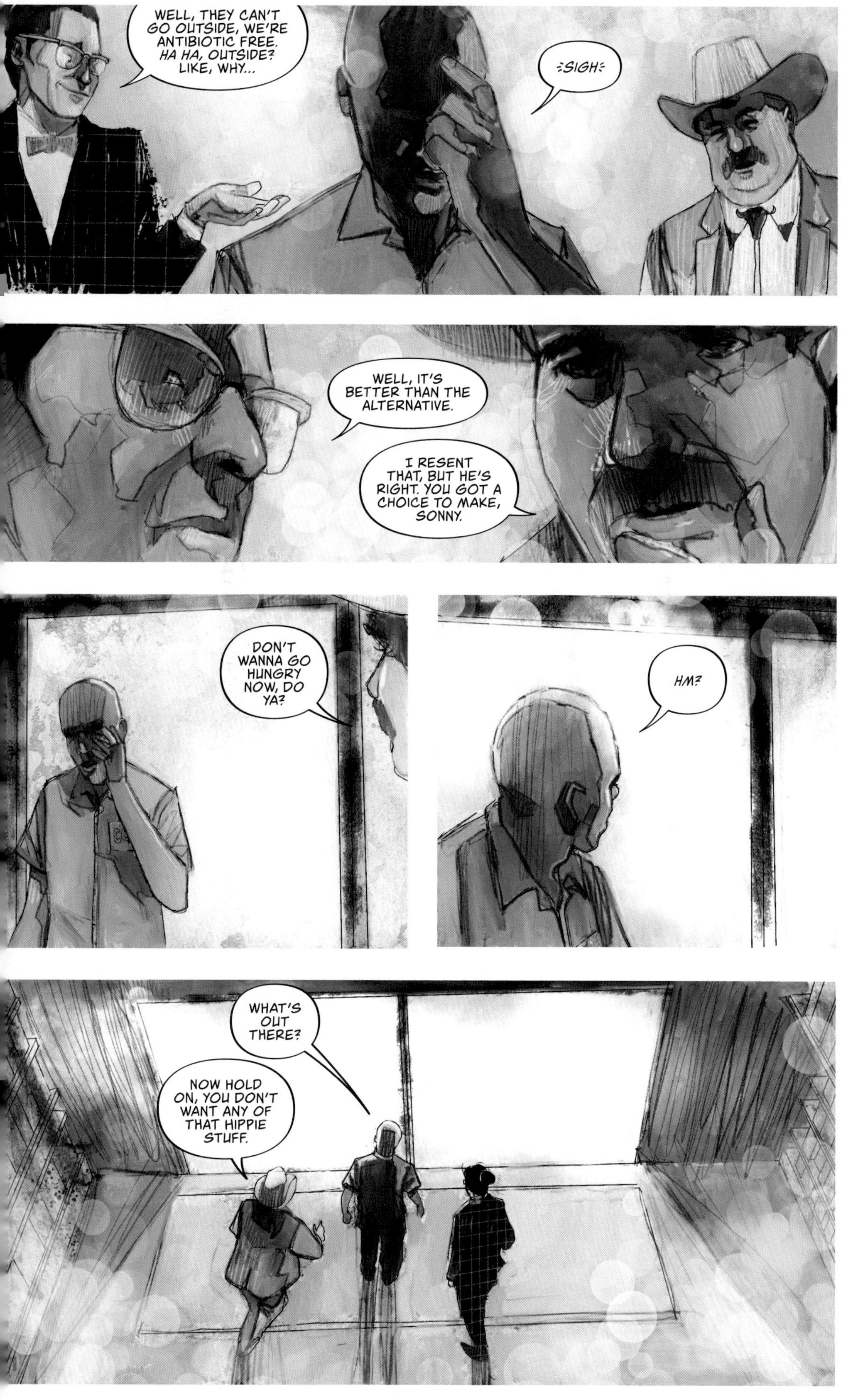
WELL, THEY CAN'T GO OUTSIDE, WE'RE ANTIBIOTIC FREE. HA HA, OUTSIDE? LIKE, WHY...
SIGH
WELL, IT'S BETTER THAN THE ALTERNATIVE.
I RESENT THAT, BUT HE'S RIGHT. YOU GOT A CHOICE TO MAKE, SONNY.
DON'T WANNA GO HUNGRY NOW, DO YA?
HM?
WHAT'S OUT THERE?
NOW HOLD ON, YOU DON'T WANT ANY OF THAT HIPPIE STUFF.

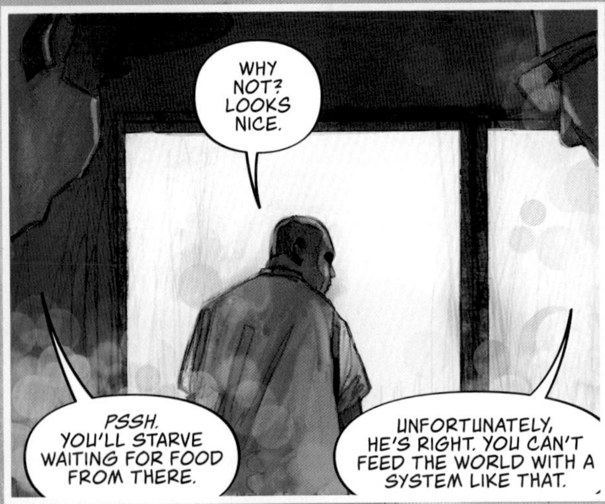
WHY NOT? LOOKS NICE.
PSSH. YOU'LL STARVE WAITING FOR FOOD FROM THERE.
UNFORTUNATELY, HE'S RIGHT. YOU CAN'T FEED THE WORLD WITH A SYSTEM LIKE THAT.
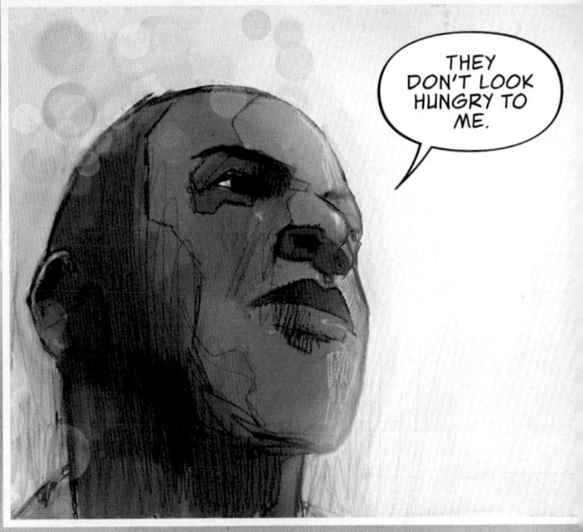
THEY DON'T LOOK HUNGRY TO ME.
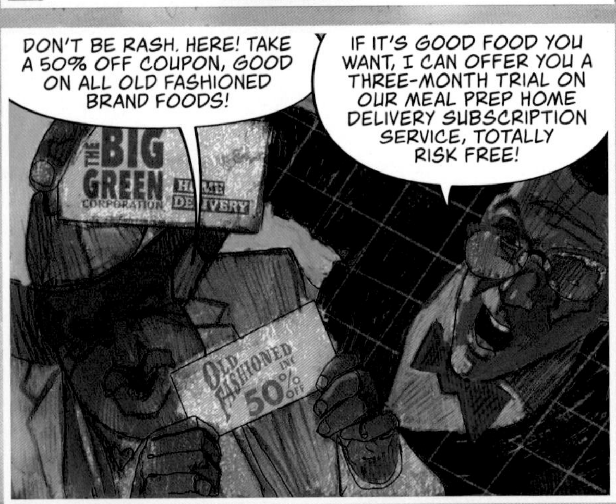
DON'T BE RASH. HERE! TAKE A 50% OFF COUPON, GOOD ON ALL OLD FASHIONED BRAND FOODS!
IF IT'S GOOD FOOD YOU WANT, I CAN OFFER YOU A THREE-MONTH TRIAL ON OUR MEAL PREP HOME DELIVERY SUBSCRIPTION SERVICE, TOTALLY RISK FREE!
THE BIG GREEN CORPORATION
HOME DELIVERY
OLD FASHIONED INC
50% OFF
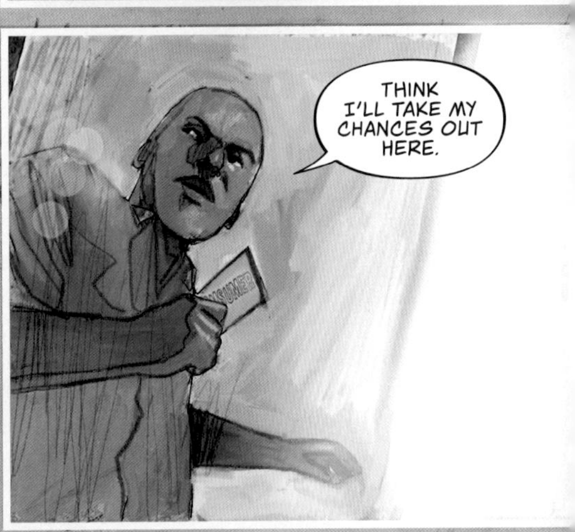
THINK I'LL TAKE MY CHANCES OUT HERE.
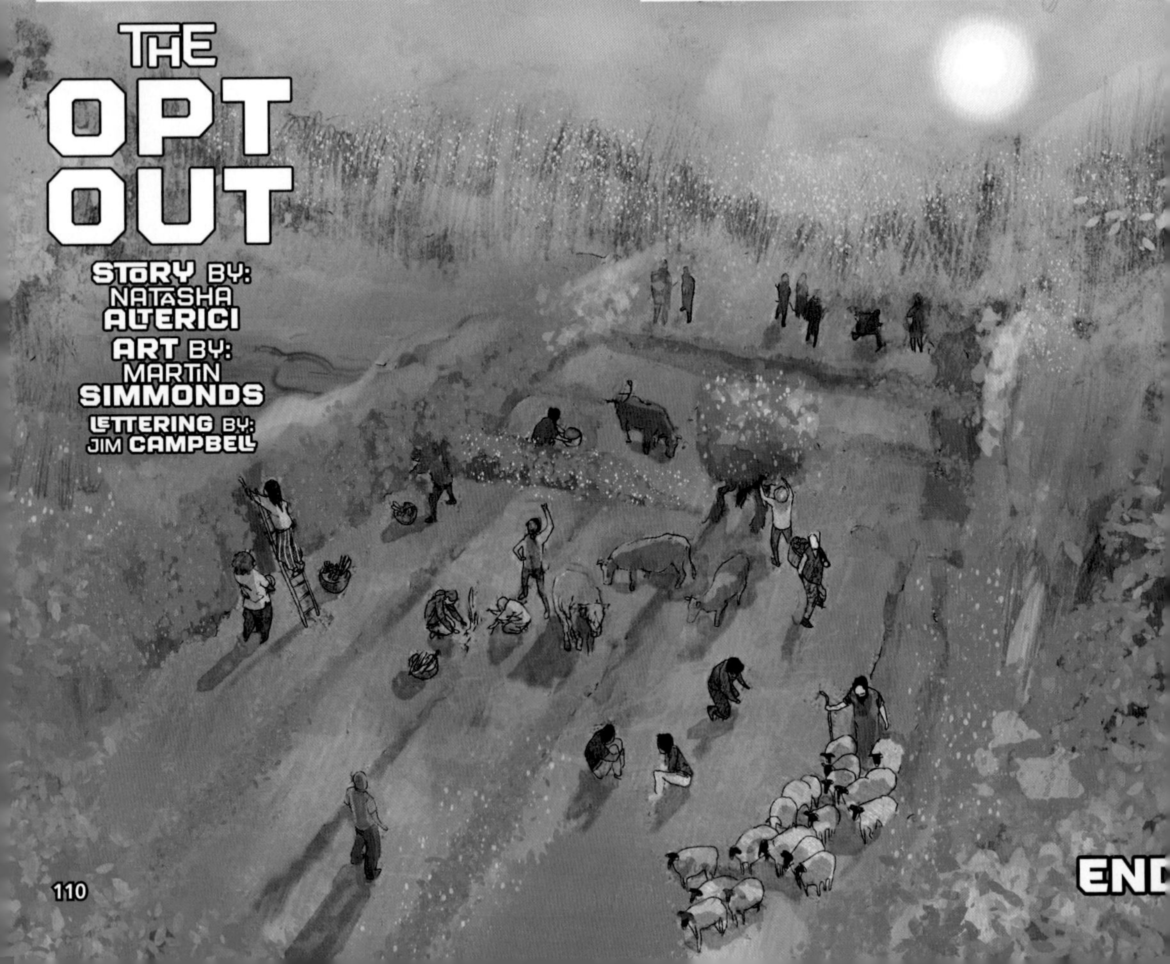
THE OPT OUT
STORY BY: NATASHA ALTERICI
ART BY: MARTIN SIMMONDS
LETTERING BY: JIM CAMPBELL
END

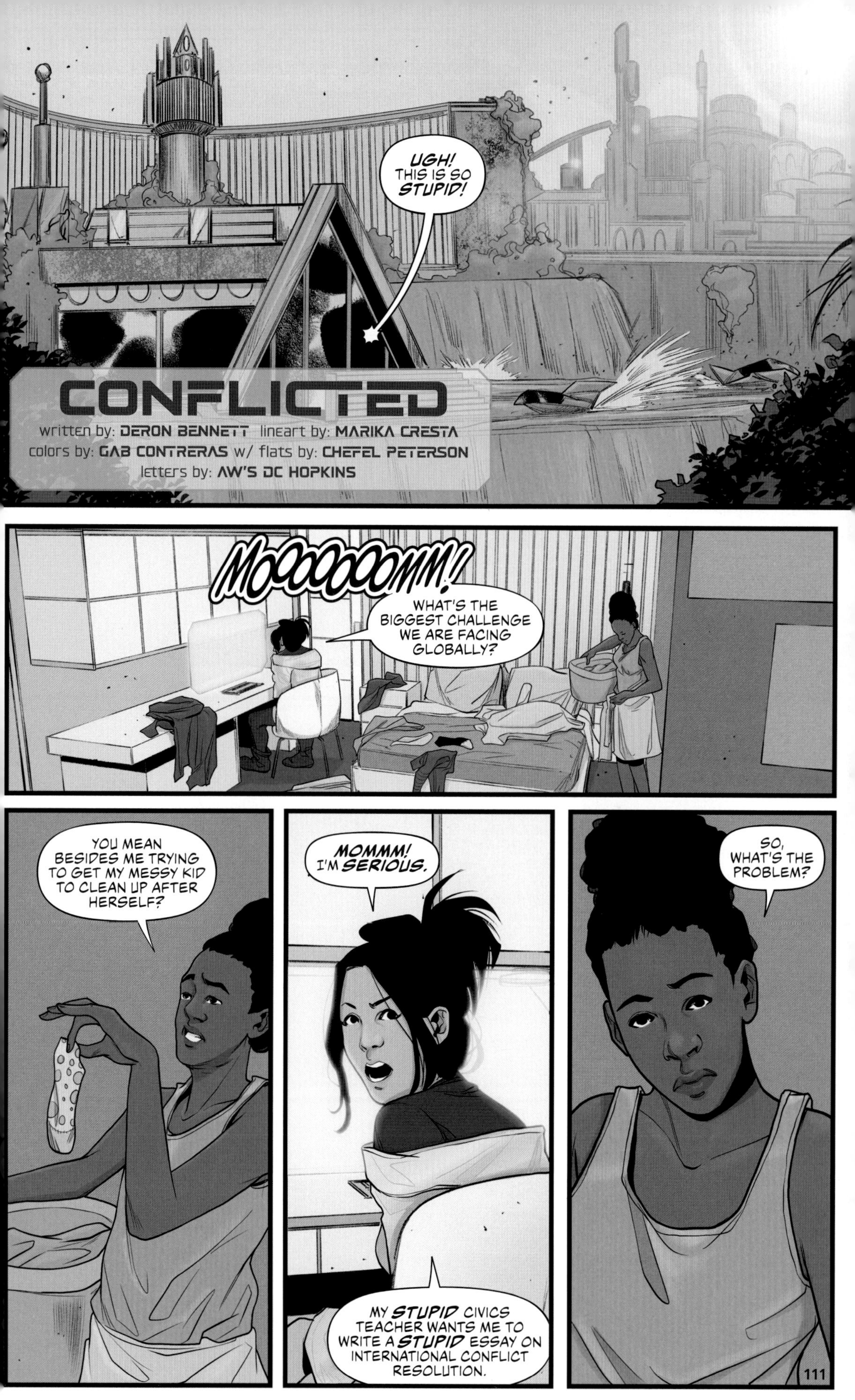
UGH! THIS IS SO STUPID!
CONFLICTED
written by: DERON BENNETT lineart by: MARIKA CRESTA
colors by: GAB CONTRERAS w/ flats by: CHEFEL PETERSON
letters by: AW'S DC HOPKINS
MOOOOOOOMM!
WHAT'S THE BIGGEST CHALLENGE WE ARE FACING GLOBALLY?
YOU MEAN BESIDES ME TRYING TO GET MY MESSY KID TO CLEAN UP AFTER HERSELF?
MOMMM! I'M SERIOUS.
MY STUPID CIVICS TEACHER WANTS ME TO WRITE A STUPID ESSAY ON INTERNATIONAL CONFLICT RESOLUTION.
SO, WHAT'S THE PROBLEM?
111

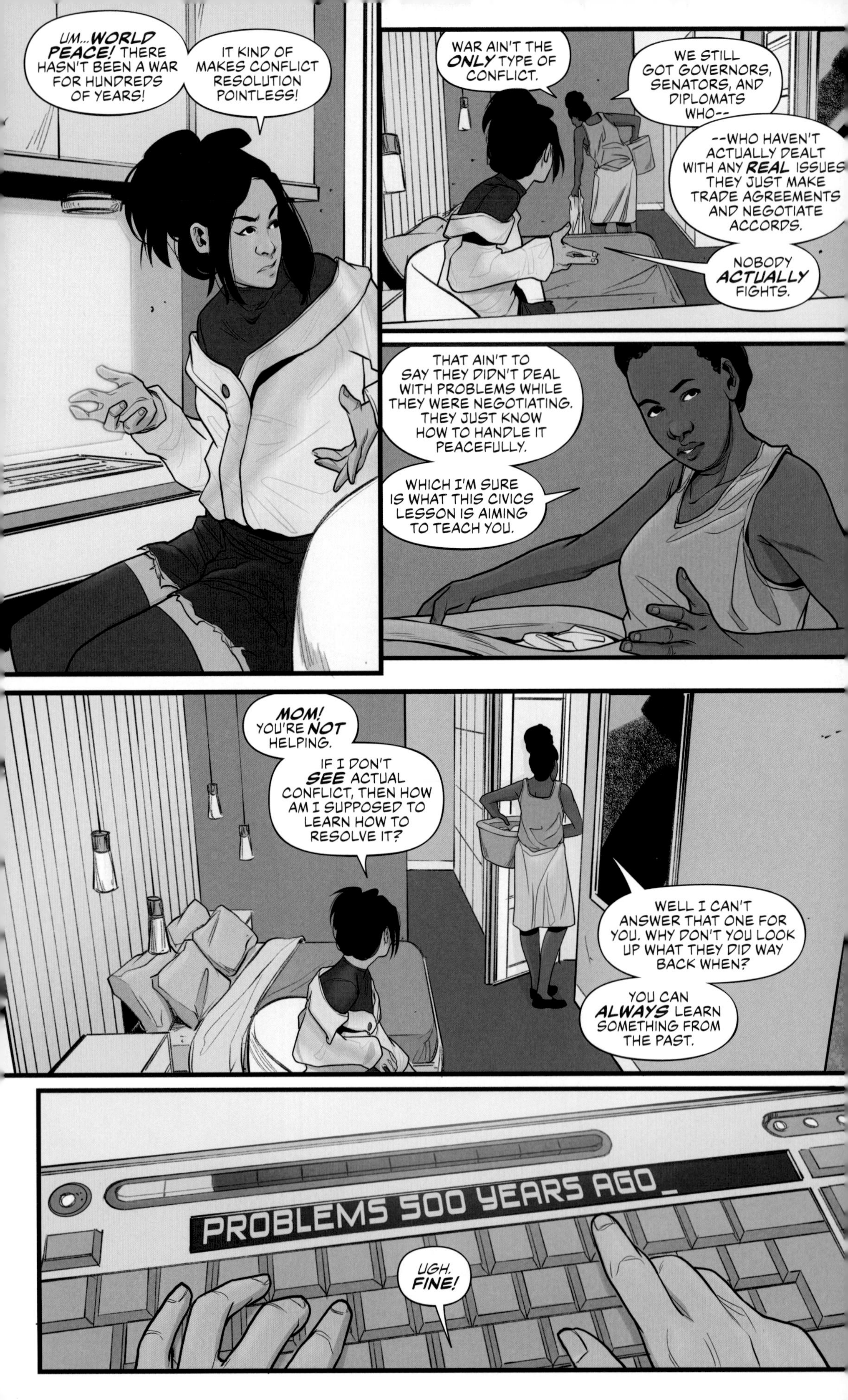
UM...WORLD PEACE! THERE HASN'T BEEN A WAR FOR HUNDREDS OF YEARS!
IT KIND OF MAKES CONFLICT RESOLUTION POINTLESS!
WAR AIN'T THE ONLY TYPE OF CONFLICT.
WE STILL GOT GOVERNORS, SENATORS, AND DIPLOMATS WHO--
--WHO HAVEN'T ACTUALLY DEALT WITH ANY REAL ISSUES. THEY JUST MAKE TRADE AGREEMENTS AND NEGOTIATE ACCORDS.
NOBODY ACTUALLY FIGHTS.
THAT AIN'T TO SAY THEY DIDN'T DEAL WITH PROBLEMS WHILE THEY WERE NEGOTIATING. THEY JUST KNOW HOW TO HANDLE IT PEACEFULLY.
WHICH I'M SURE IS WHAT THIS CIVICS LESSON IS AIMING TO TEACH YOU.
MOM! YOU'RE NOT HELPING.
IF I DON'T SEE ACTUAL CONFLICT, THEN HOW AM I SUPPOSED TO LEARN HOW TO RESOLVE IT?
WELL I CAN'T ANSWER THAT ONE FOR YOU. WHY DON'T YOU LOOK UP WHAT THEY DID WAY BACK WHEN?
YOU CAN ALWAYS LEARN SOMETHING FROM THE PAST.
PROBLEMS 500 YEARS AGO_
UGH. FINE!

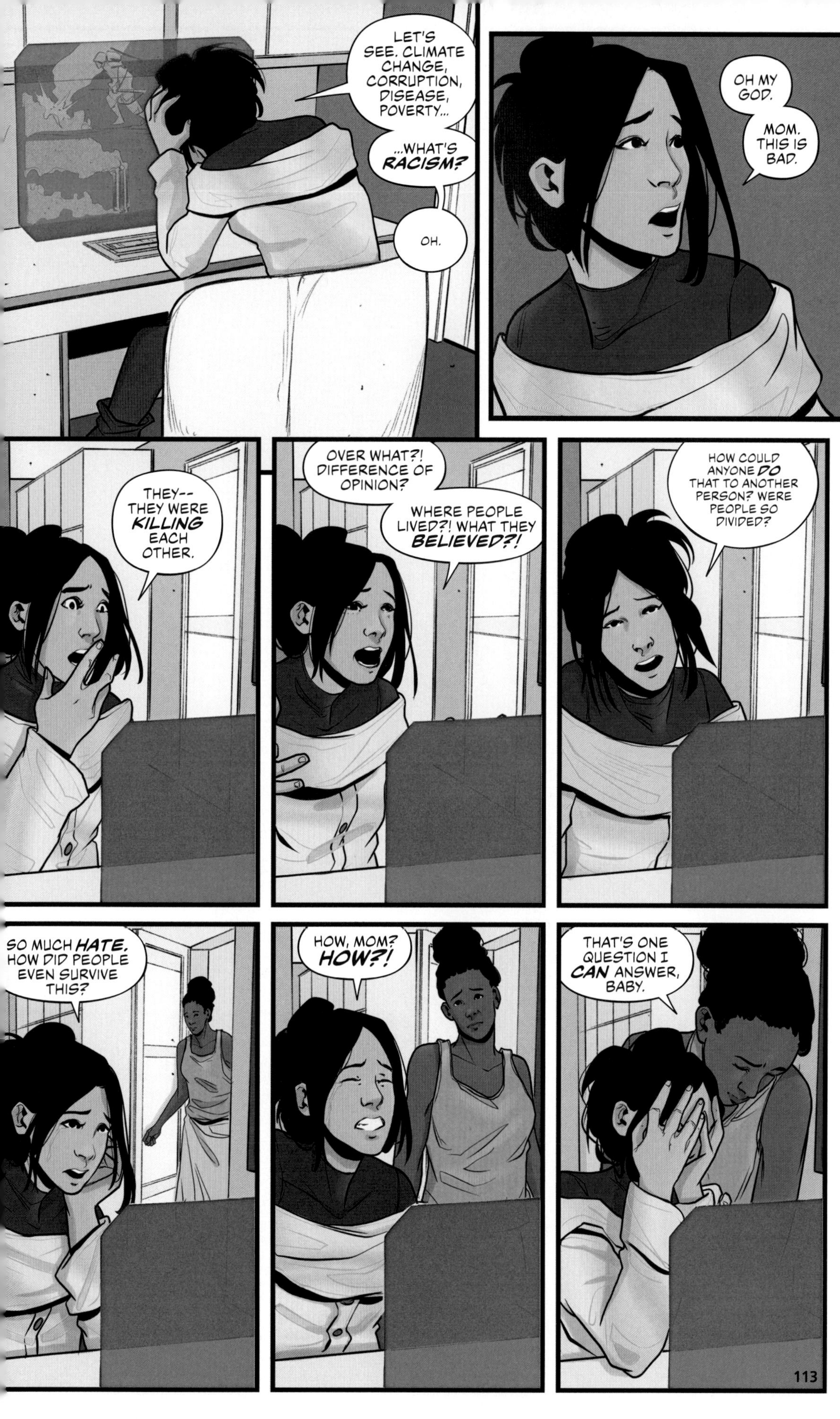
LET'S SEE. CLIMATE CHANGE, CORRUPTION, DISEASE, POVERTY...
...WHAT'S RACISM?
OH.
OH MY GOD.
MOM. THIS IS BAD.
THEY--THEY WERE KILLING EACH OTHER.
OVER WHAT?! DIFFERENCE OF OPINION?
WHERE PEOPLE LIVED?! WHAT THEY BELIEVED?!
HOW COULD ANYONE DO THAT TO ANOTHER PERSON? WERE PEOPLE SO DIVIDED?
SO MUCH HATE. HOW DID PEOPLE EVEN SURVIVE THIS?
HOW, MOM? HOW?!
THAT'S ONE QUESTION I CAN ANSWER, BABY.

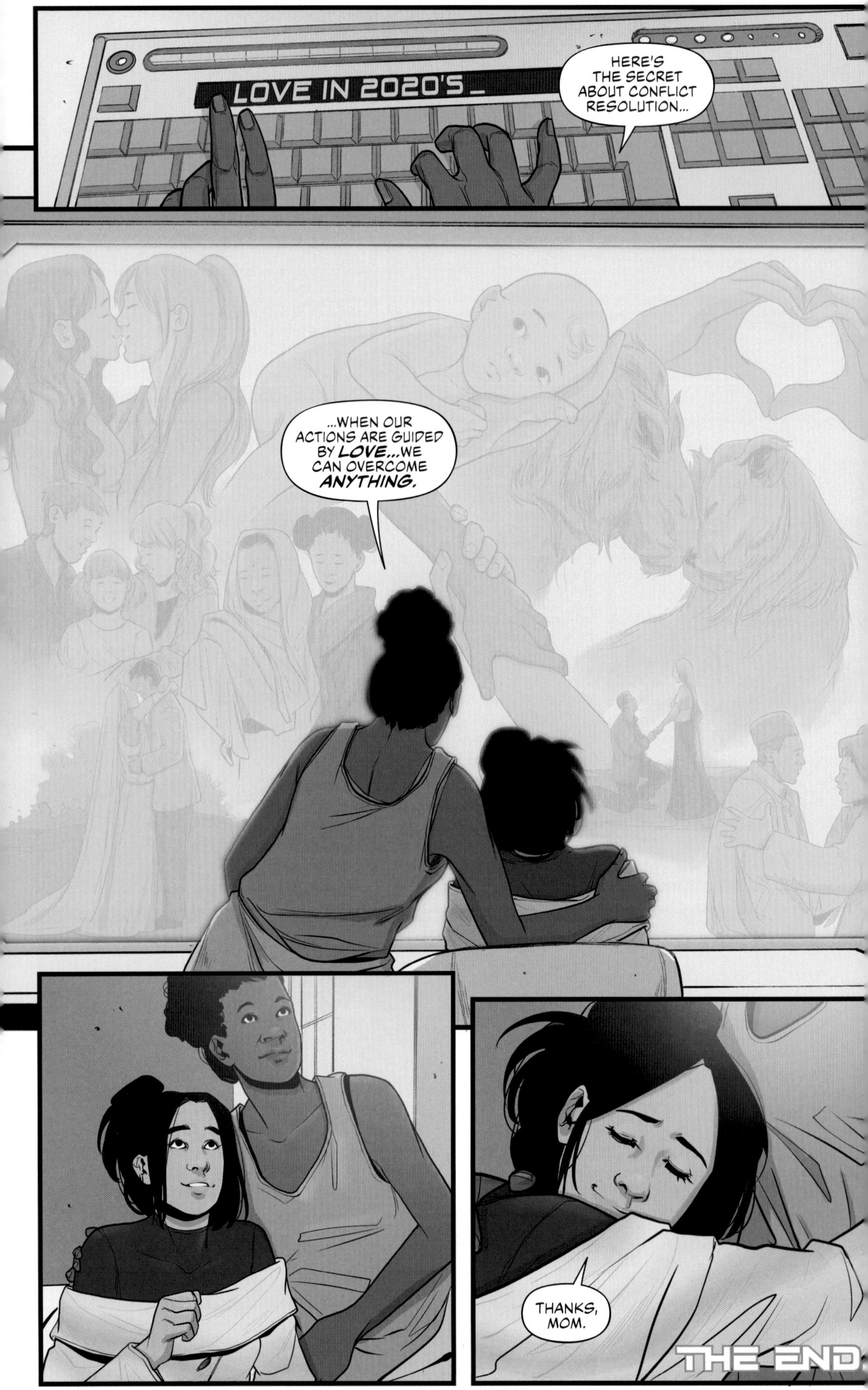
LOVE IN 2020'S_
HERE'S THE SECRET ABOUT CONFLICT RESOLUTION...
...WHEN OUR ACTIONS ARE GUIDED BY **LOVE**...WE CAN OVERCOME ***ANYTHING.***
THANKS, MOM.
THE END

TAKE ME HOME

Story by Regine L. Sawyer
Line Art & Color by Creees Lee
With Color Flats by SyoungEe
Lettering by Cardinal Rae

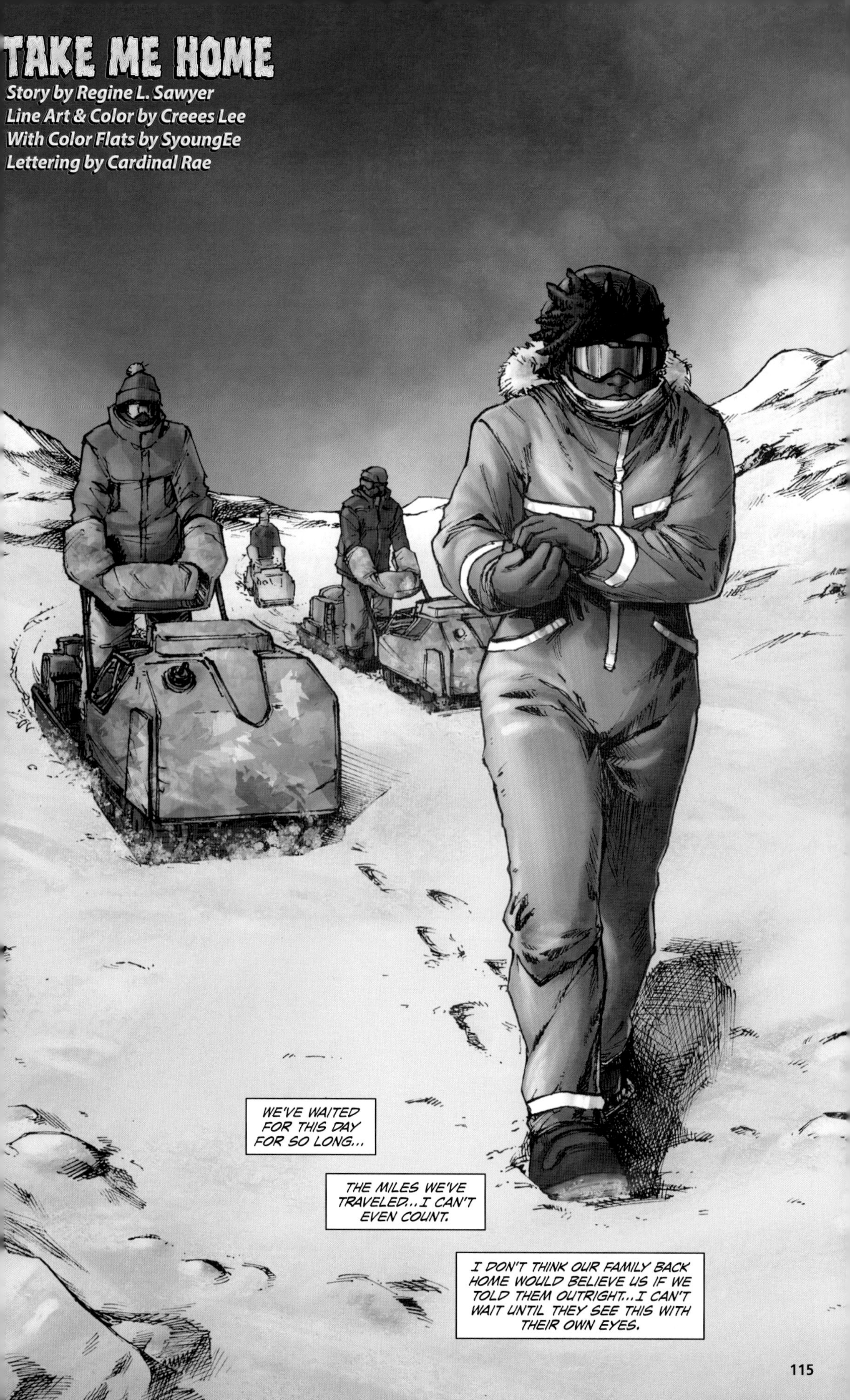
WE'VE WAITED FOR THIS DAY FOR SO LONG...
THE MILES WE'VE TRAVELED...I CAN'T EVEN COUNT.
I DON'T THINK OUR FAMILY BACK HOME WOULD BELIEVE US IF WE TOLD THEM OUTRIGHT...I CAN'T WAIT UNTIL THEY SEE THIS WITH THEIR OWN EYES.

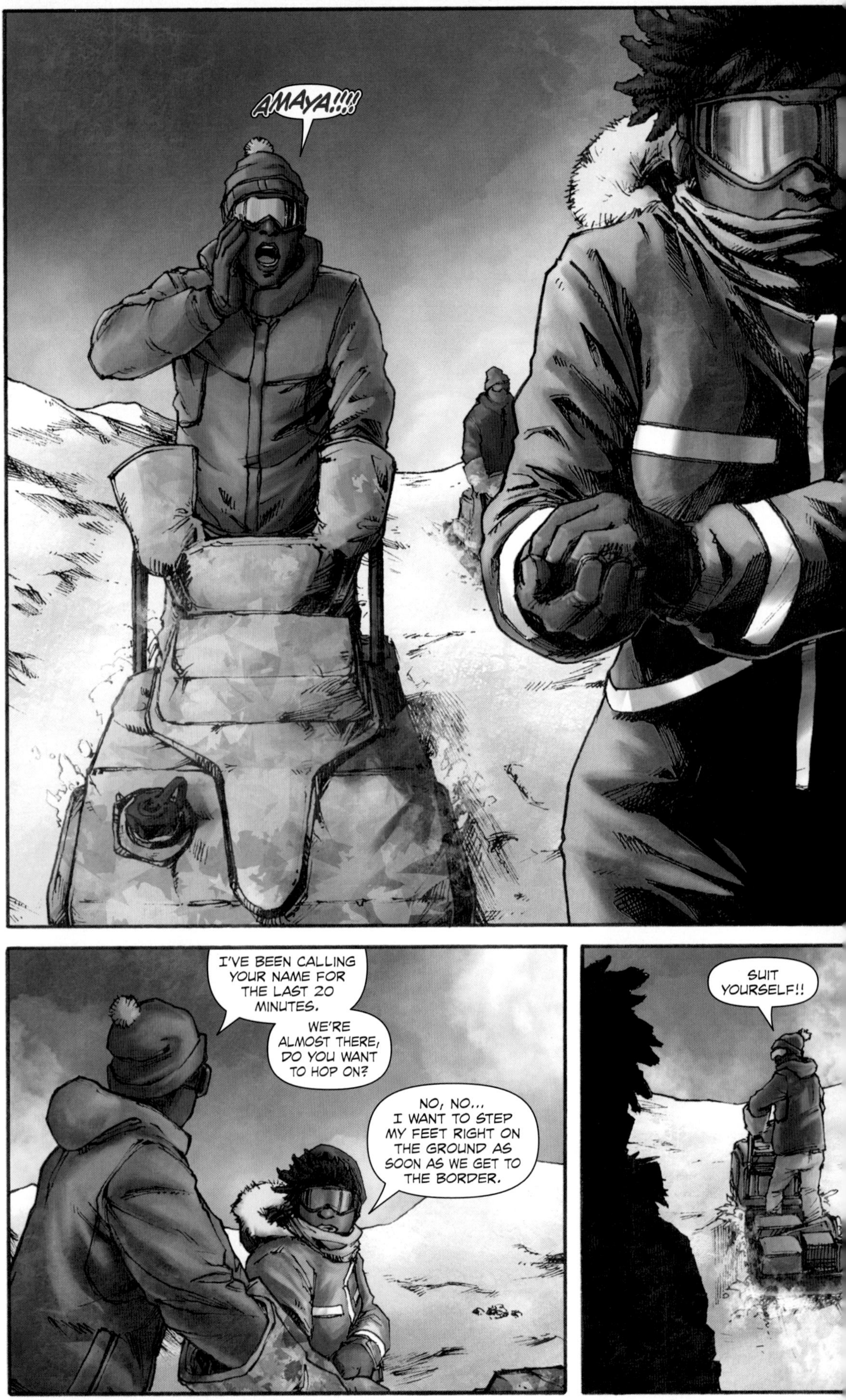
AMAYA!!!!
I'VE BEEN CALLING YOUR NAME FOR THE LAST 20 MINUTES.
WE'RE ALMOST THERE, DO YOU WANT TO HOP ON?
NO, NO... I WANT TO STEP MY FEET RIGHT ON THE GROUND AS SOON AS WE GET TO THE BORDER.
SUIT YOURSELF!!

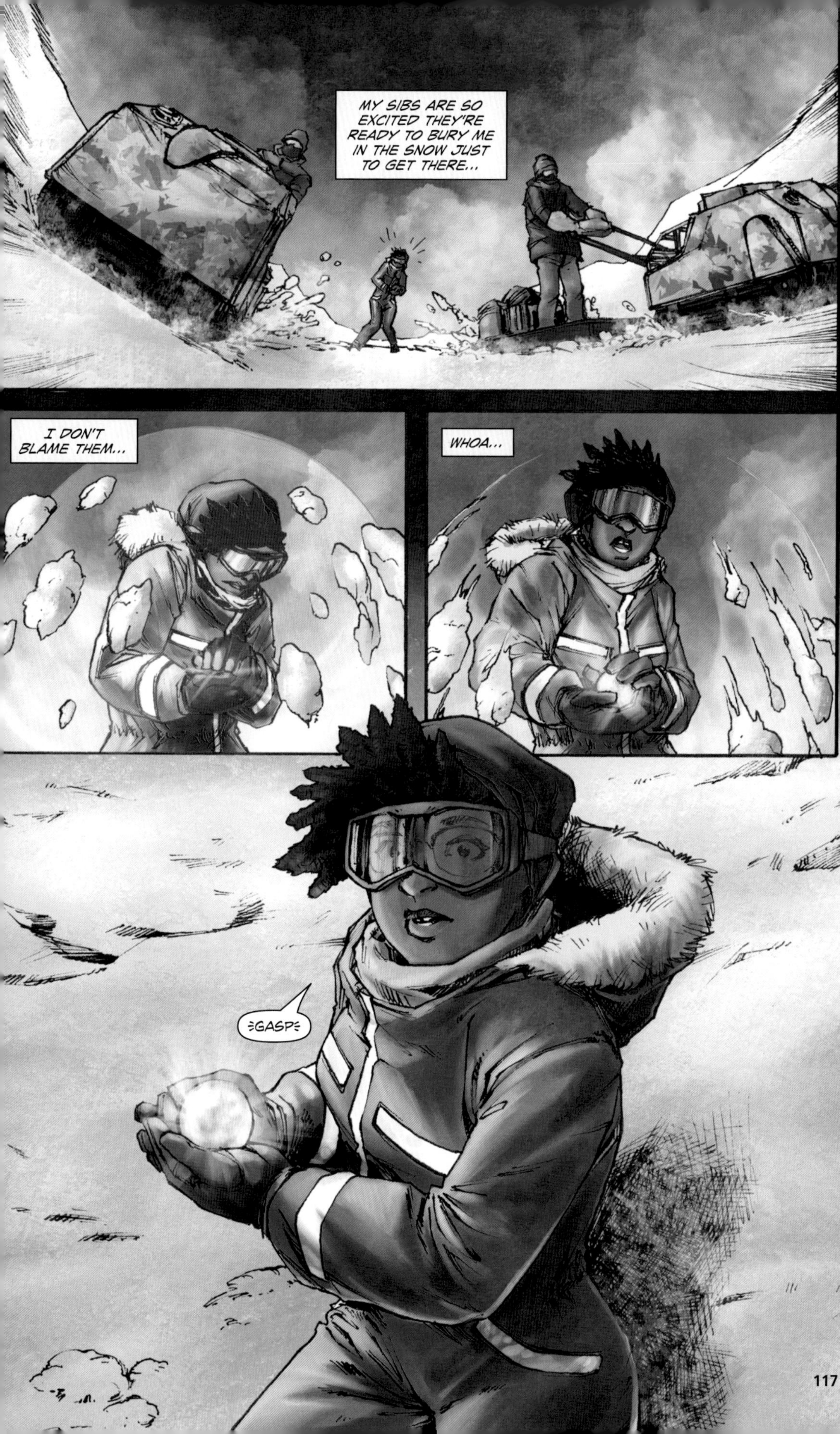
MY SIBS ARE SO EXCITED THEY'RE READY TO BURY ME IN THE SNOW JUST TO GET THERE...
I DON'T BLAME THEM...
WHOA...
GASP

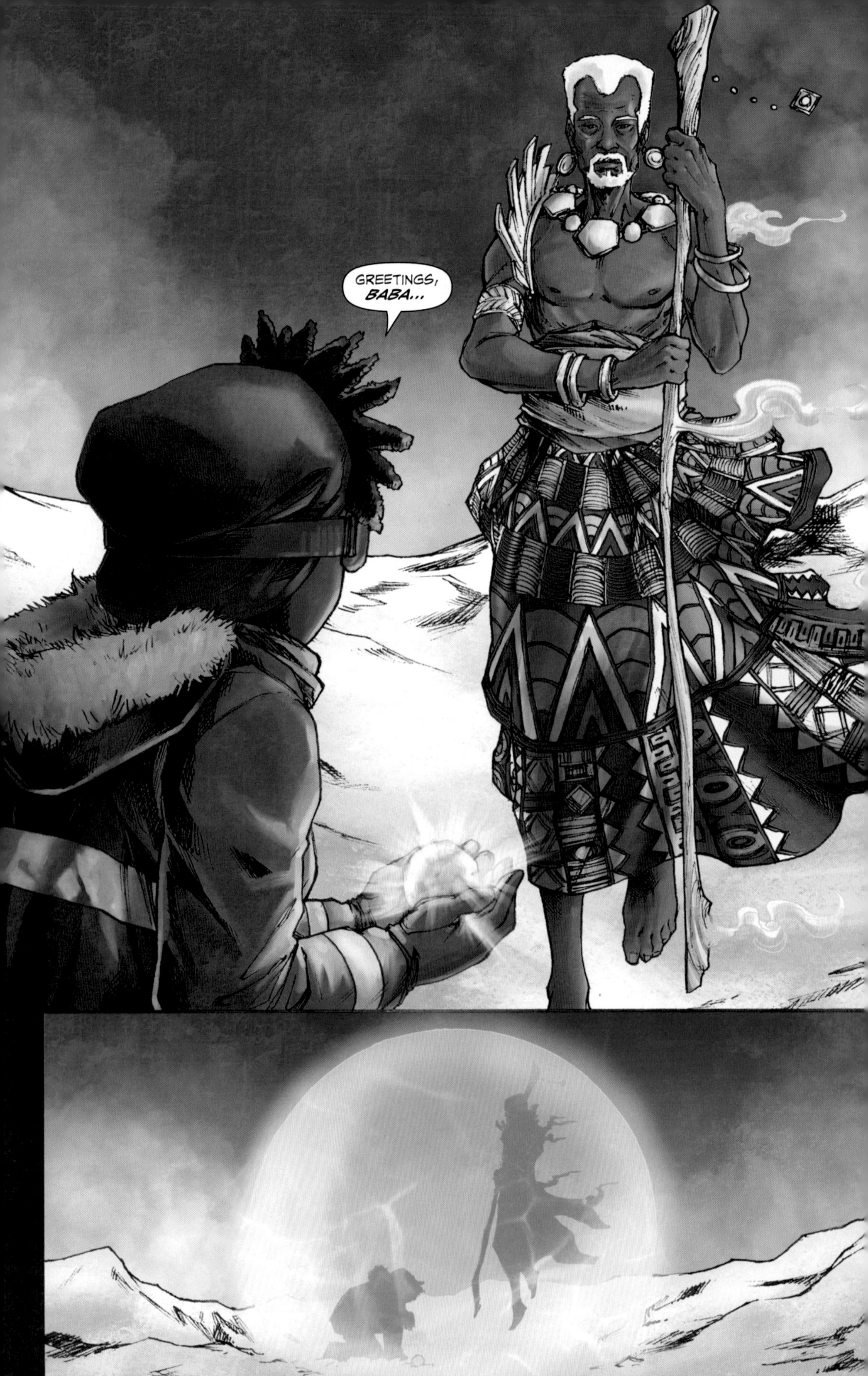
GREETINGS, BABA...

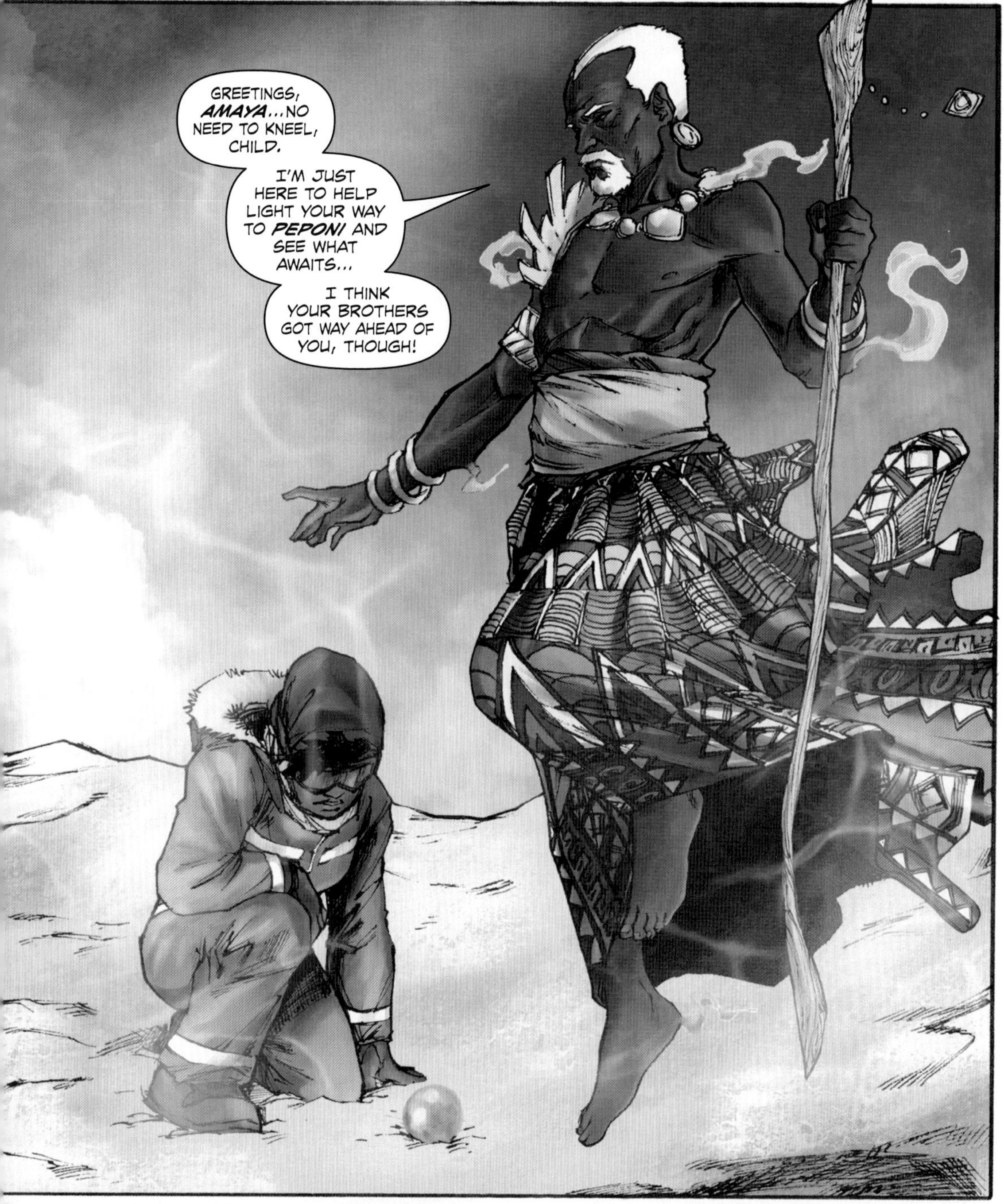
GREETINGS, AMAYA...NO NEED TO KNEEL, CHILD.
I'M JUST HERE TO HELP LIGHT YOUR WAY TO PEPONI AND SEE WHAT AWAITS...
I THINK YOUR BROTHERS GOT WAY AHEAD OF YOU, THOUGH!
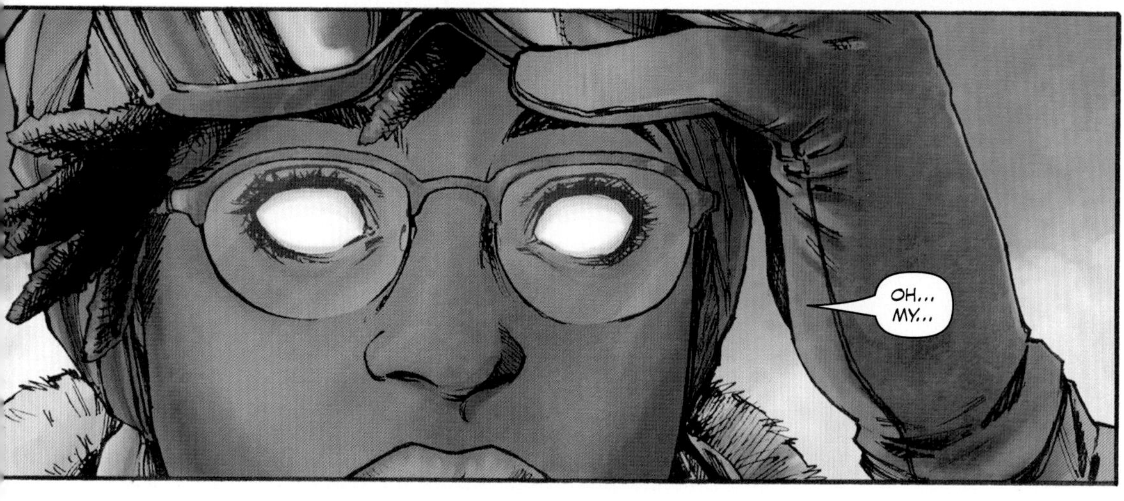
OH... MY...

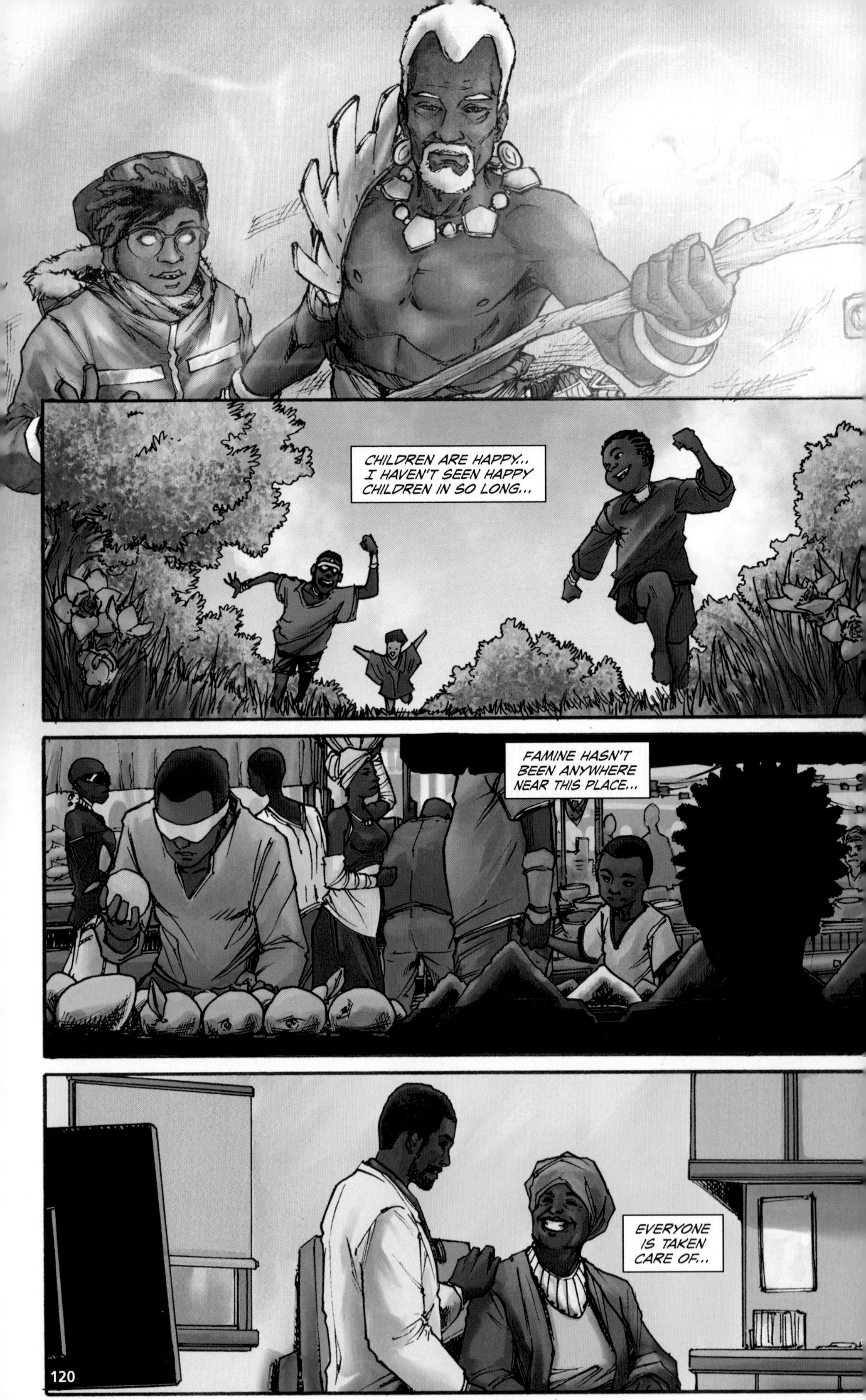
CHILDREN ARE HAPPY... I HAVEN'T SEEN HAPPY CHILDREN IN SO LONG...
FAMINE HASN'T BEEN ANYWHERE NEAR THIS PLACE...
EVERYONE IS TAKEN CARE OF...

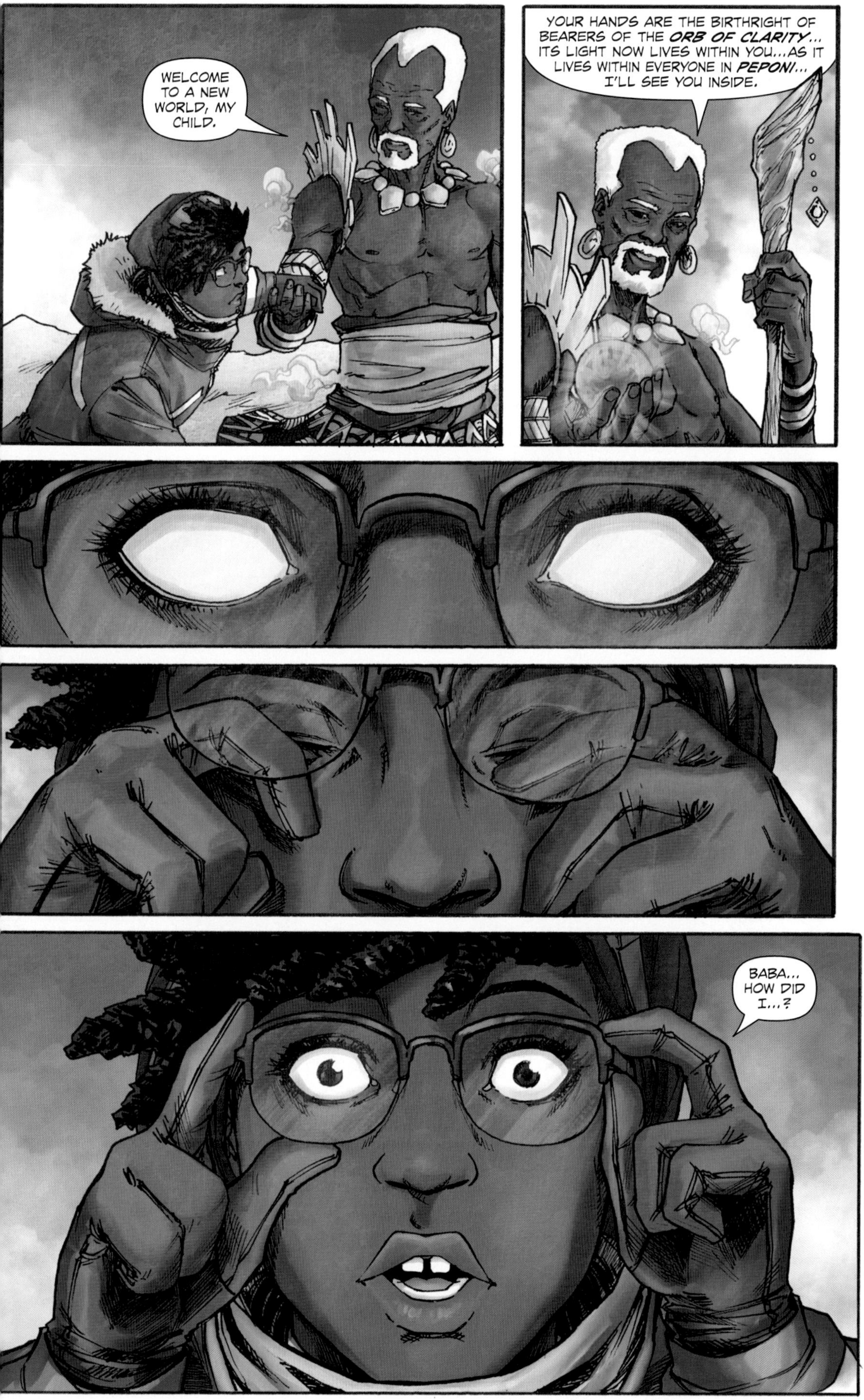
WELCOME TO A NEW WORLD, MY CHILD.
YOUR HANDS ARE THE BIRTHRIGHT OF BEARERS OF THE ORB OF CLARITY... ITS LIGHT NOW LIVES WITHIN YOU...AS IT LIVES WITHIN EVERYONE IN PEPONI... I'LL SEE YOU INSIDE.
BABA... HOW DID I...?

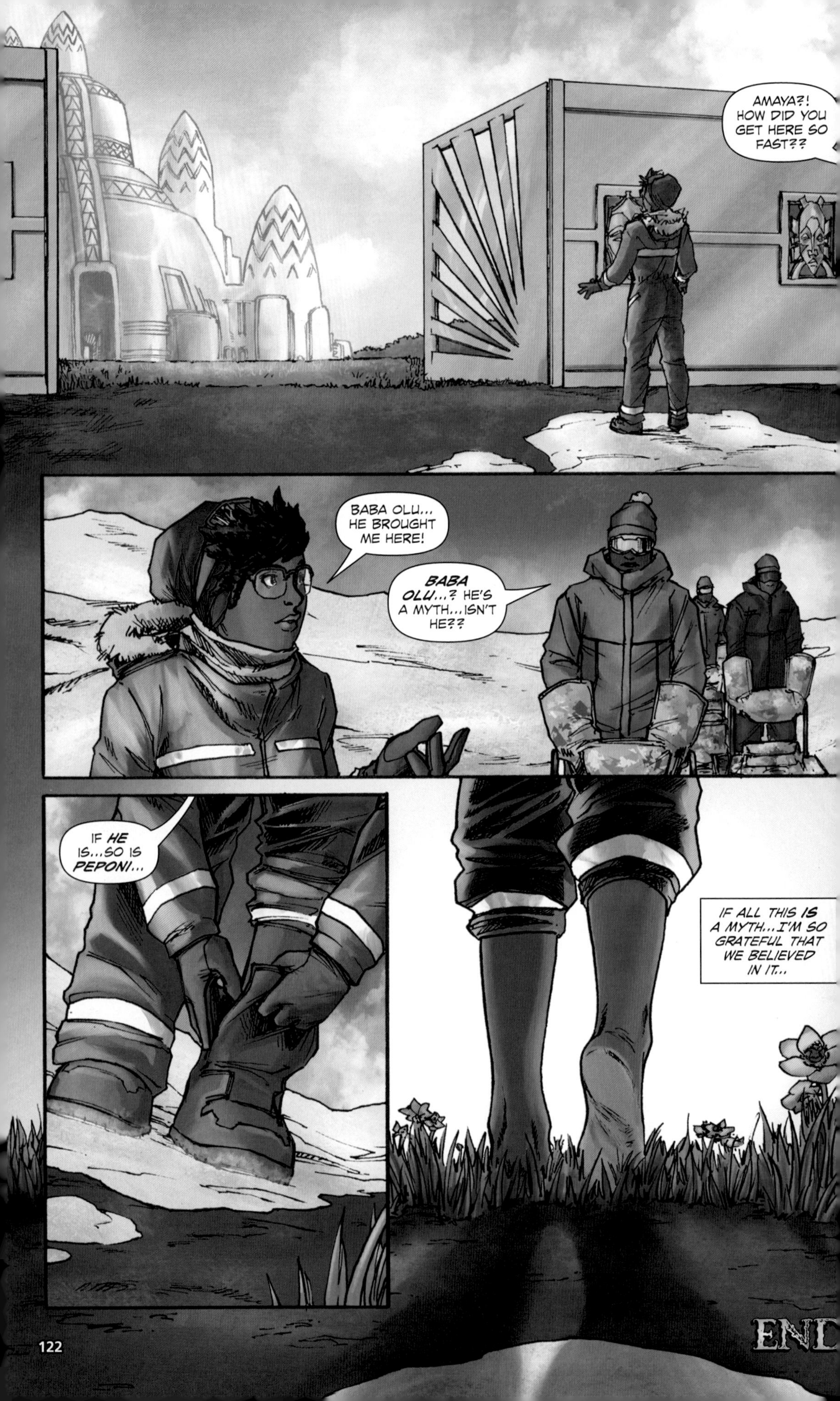
AMAYA?! HOW DID YOU GET HERE SO FAST??
BABA OLU... HE BROUGHT ME HERE!
BABA OLU...? HE'S A MYTH...ISN'T HE??
IF HE IS...SO IS PEPONI...
IF ALL THIS IS A MYTH...I'M SO GRATEFUL THAT WE BELIEVED IN IT...
END

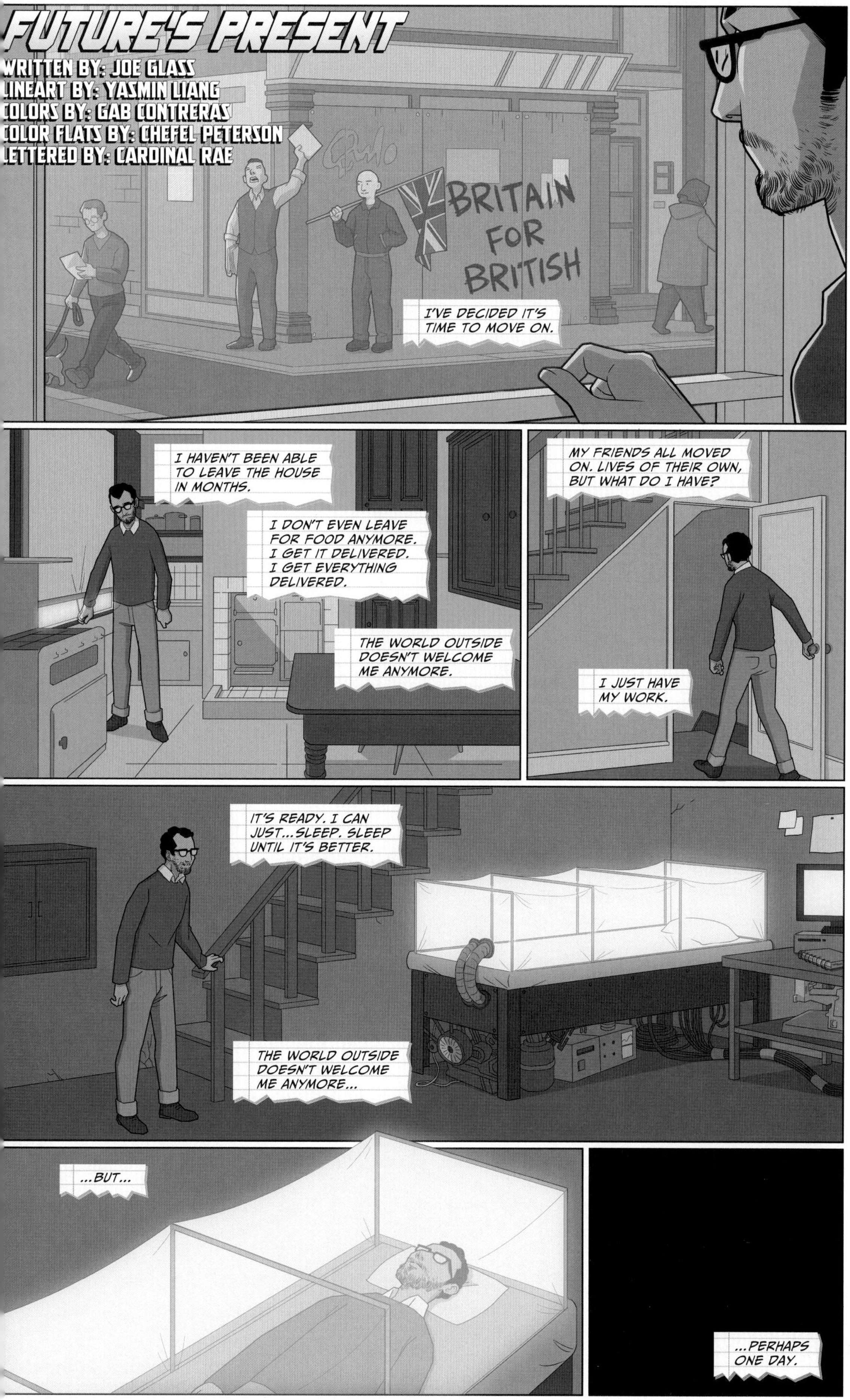
FUTURE'S PRESENT
WRITTEN BY: JOE GLASS
LINEART BY: YASMIN LIANG
COLORS BY: GAB CONTRERAS
COLOR FLATS BY: CHEFEL PETERSON
LETTERED BY: CARDINAL RAE
BRITAIN FOR BRITISH
I'VE DECIDED IT'S TIME TO MOVE ON.
I HAVEN'T BEEN ABLE TO LEAVE THE HOUSE IN MONTHS.
I DON'T EVEN LEAVE FOR FOOD ANYMORE. I GET IT DELIVERED. I GET EVERYTHING DELIVERED.
THE WORLD OUTSIDE DOESN'T WELCOME ME ANYMORE.
MY FRIENDS ALL MOVED ON. LIVES OF THEIR OWN, BUT WHAT DO I HAVE?
I JUST HAVE MY WORK.
IT'S READY. I CAN JUST...SLEEP. SLEEP UNTIL IT'S BETTER.
THE WORLD OUTSIDE DOESN'T WELCOME ME ANYMORE...
...BUT...
...PERHAPS ONE DAY.

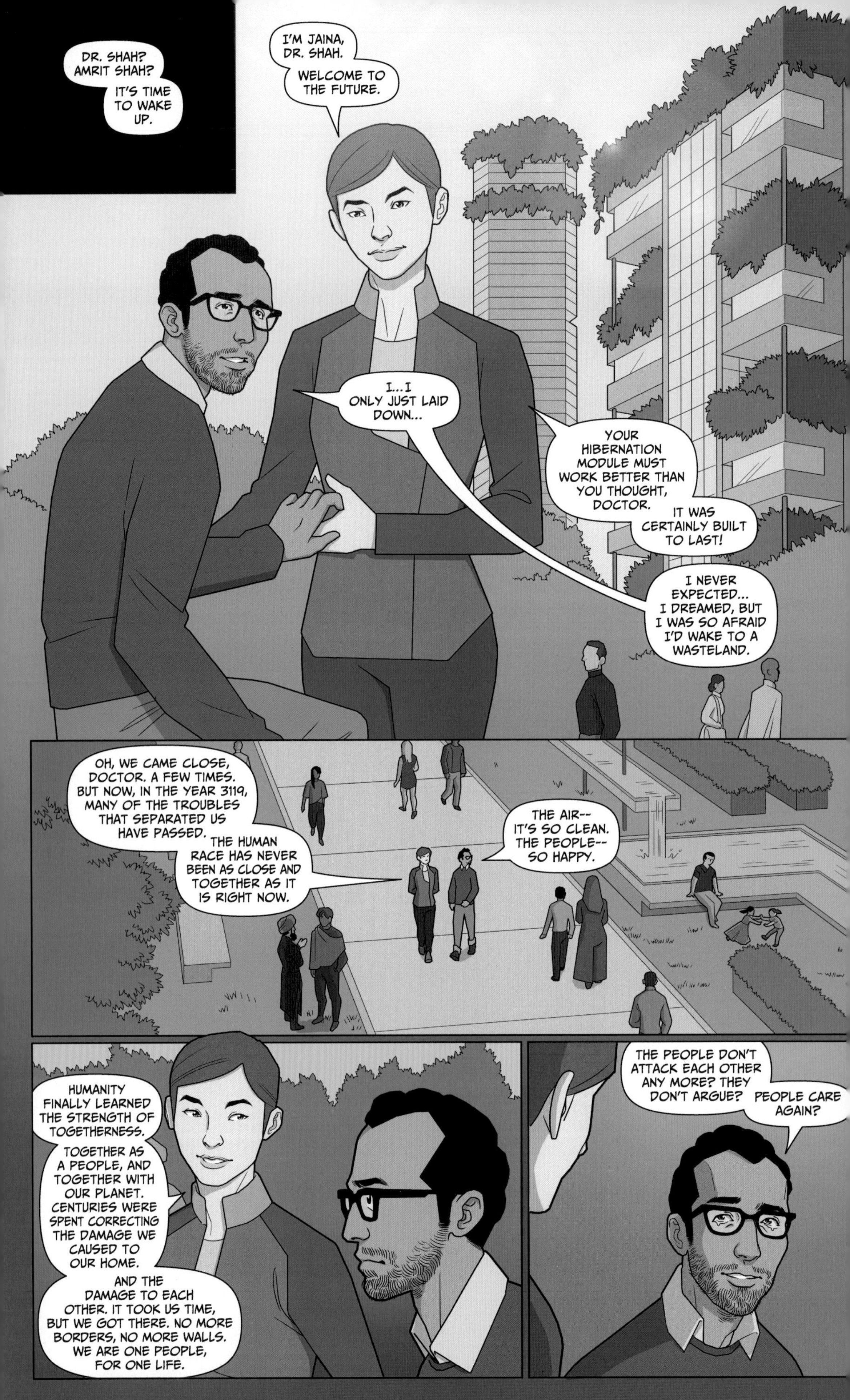
DR. SHAH? AMRIT SHAH?
IT'S TIME TO WAKE UP.
I'M JAINA, DR. SHAH.
WELCOME TO THE FUTURE.
I...I ONLY JUST LAID DOWN...
YOUR HIBERNATION MODULE MUST WORK BETTER THAN YOU THOUGHT, DOCTOR.
IT WAS CERTAINLY BUILT TO LAST!
I NEVER EXPECTED... I DREAMED, BUT I WAS SO AFRAID I'D WAKE TO A WASTELAND.
OH, WE CAME CLOSE, DOCTOR. A FEW TIMES. BUT NOW, IN THE YEAR 3119, MANY OF THE TROUBLES THAT SEPARATED US HAVE PASSED.
THE HUMAN RACE HAS NEVER BEEN AS CLOSE AND TOGETHER AS IT IS RIGHT NOW.
THE AIR-- IT'S SO CLEAN. THE PEOPLE-- SO HAPPY.
HUMANITY FINALLY LEARNED THE STRENGTH OF TOGETHERNESS.
TOGETHER AS A PEOPLE, AND TOGETHER WITH OUR PLANET. CENTURIES WERE SPENT CORRECTING THE DAMAGE WE CAUSED TO OUR HOME.
AND THE DAMAGE TO EACH OTHER. IT TOOK US TIME, BUT WE GOT THERE. NO MORE BORDERS, NO MORE WALLS. WE ARE ONE PEOPLE, FOR ONE LIFE.
THE PEOPLE DON'T ATTACK EACH OTHER ANY MORE? THEY DON'T ARGUE?
PEOPLE CARE AGAIN?

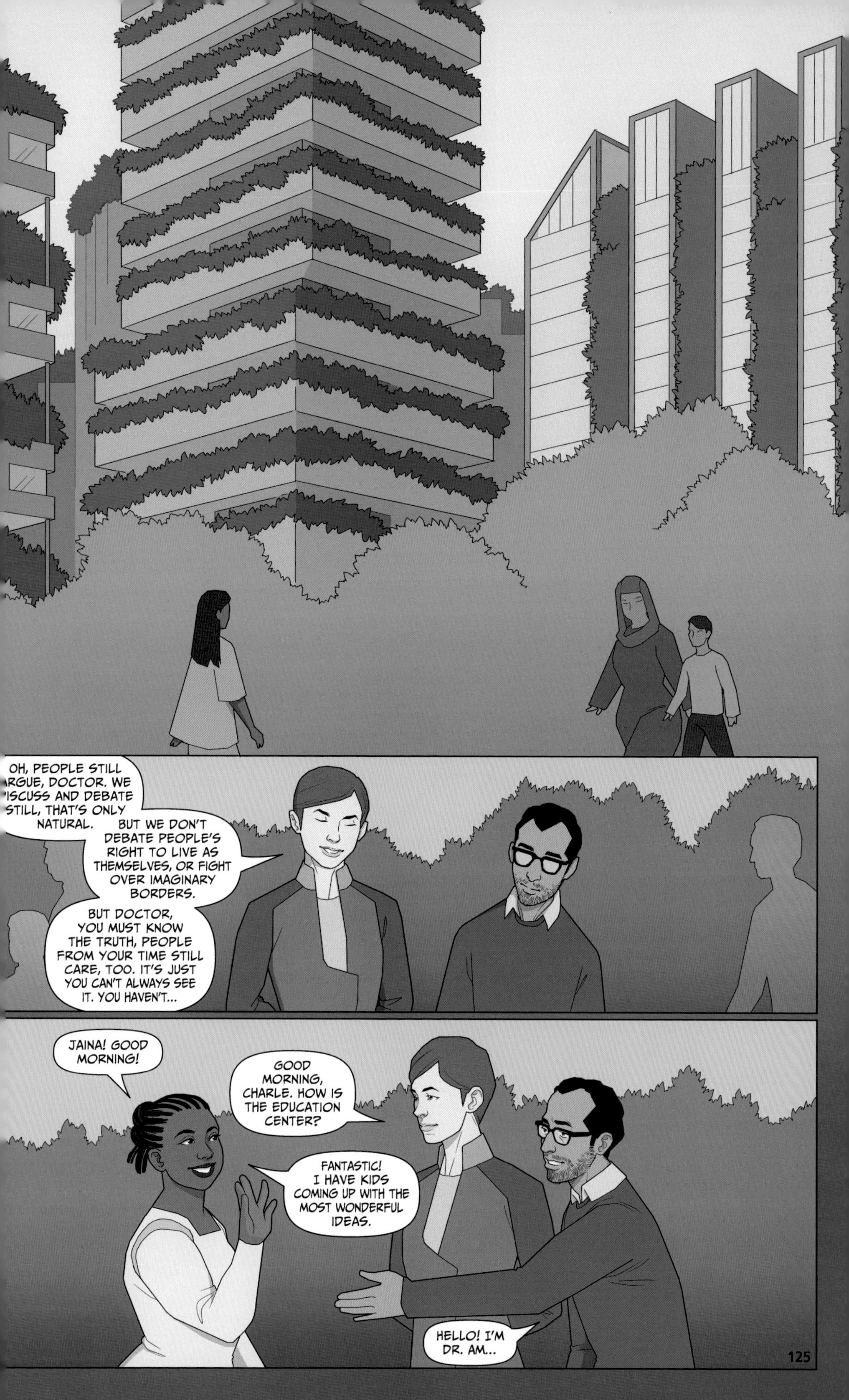
OH, PEOPLE STILL ARGUE, DOCTOR. WE DISCUSS AND DEBATE STILL, THAT'S ONLY NATURAL.
BUT WE DON'T DEBATE PEOPLE'S RIGHT TO LIVE AS THEMSELVES, OR FIGHT OVER IMAGINARY BORDERS.
BUT DOCTOR, YOU MUST KNOW THE TRUTH, PEOPLE FROM YOUR TIME STILL CARE, TOO. IT'S JUST YOU CAN'T ALWAYS SEE IT. YOU HAVEN'T...
JAINA! GOOD MORNING!
GOOD MORNING, CHARLE. HOW IS THE EDUCATION CENTER?
FANTASTIC! I HAVE KIDS COMING UP WITH THE MOST WONDERFUL IDEAS.
HELLO! I'M DR. AM...

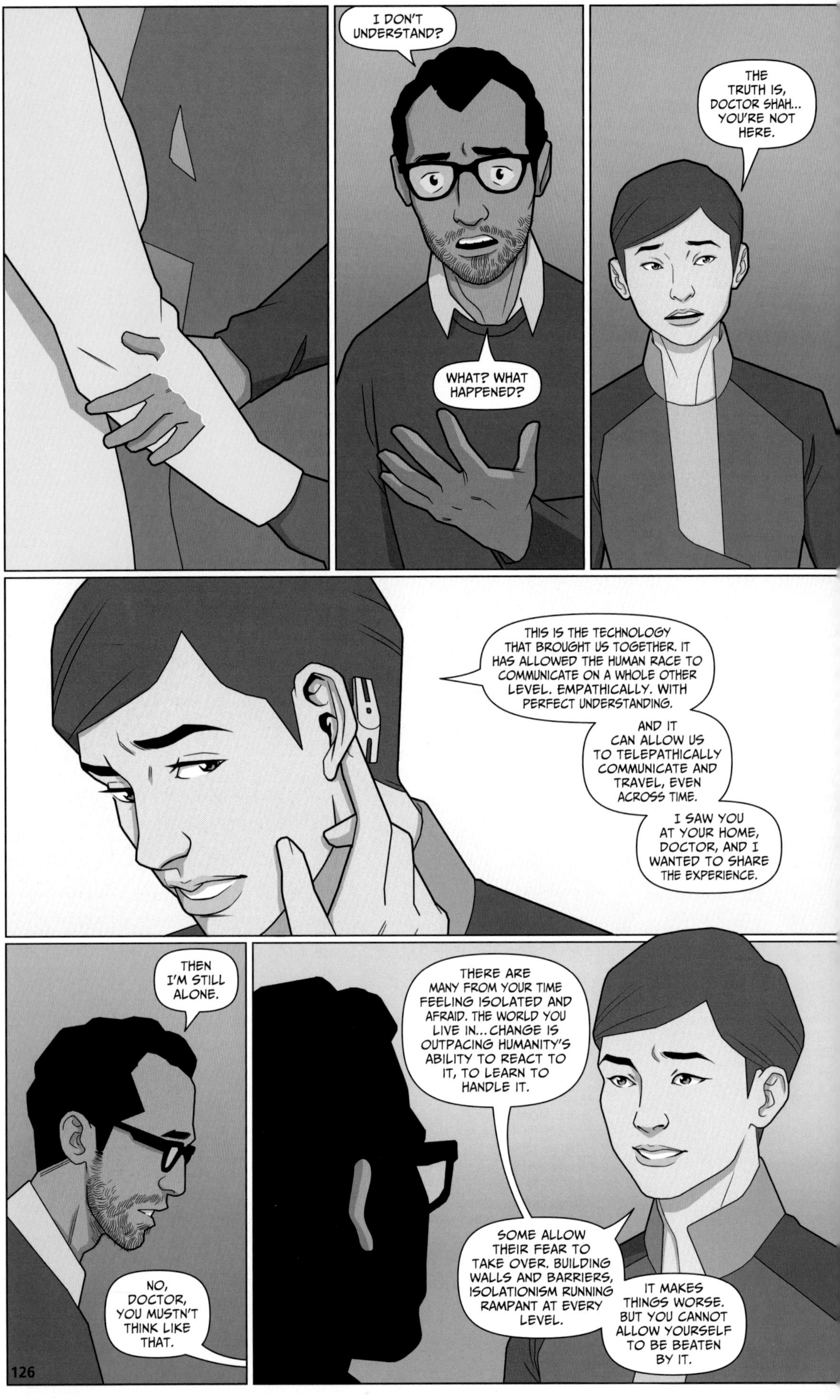
I DON'T UNDERSTAND?
WHAT? WHAT HAPPENED?
THE TRUTH IS, DOCTOR SHAH... YOU'RE NOT HERE.
THIS IS THE TECHNOLOGY THAT BROUGHT US TOGETHER. IT HAS ALLOWED THE HUMAN RACE TO COMMUNICATE ON A WHOLE OTHER LEVEL. EMPATHICALLY. WITH PERFECT UNDERSTANDING.
AND IT CAN ALLOW US TO TELEPATHICALLY COMMUNICATE AND TRAVEL, EVEN ACROSS TIME.
I SAW YOU AT YOUR HOME, DOCTOR, AND I WANTED TO SHARE THE EXPERIENCE.
THEN I'M STILL ALONE.
NO, DOCTOR, YOU MUSTN'T THINK LIKE THAT.
THERE ARE MANY FROM YOUR TIME FEELING ISOLATED AND AFRAID. THE WORLD YOU LIVE IN...CHANGE IS OUTPACING HUMANITY'S ABILITY TO REACT TO IT, TO LEARN TO HANDLE IT.
SOME ALLOW THEIR FEAR TO TAKE OVER. BUILDING WALLS AND BARRIERS, ISOLATIONISM RUNNING RAMPANT AT EVERY LEVEL.
IT MAKES THINGS WORSE. BUT YOU CANNOT ALLOW YOURSELF TO BE BEATEN BY IT.

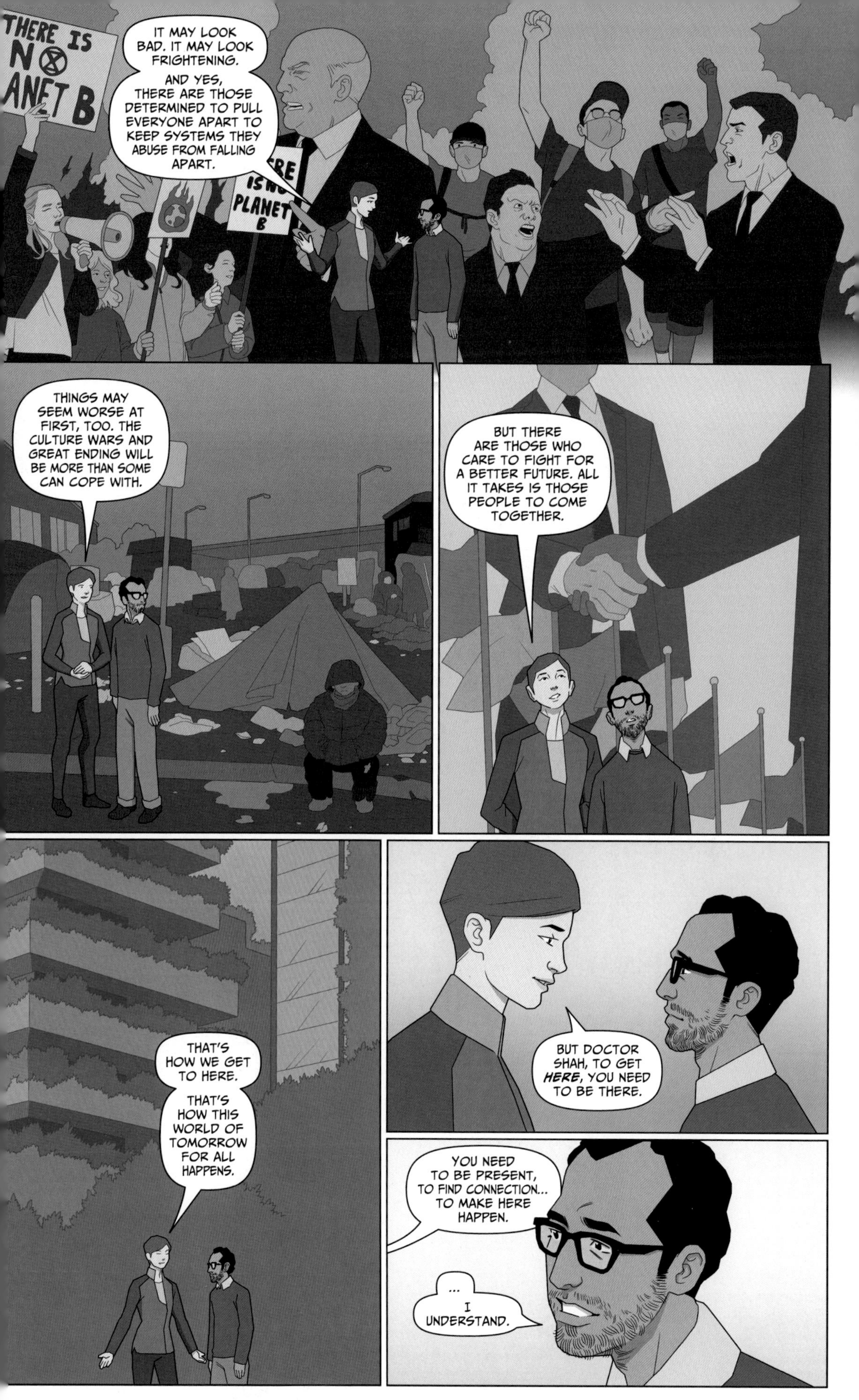
THERE IS N ANET B
IT MAY LOOK BAD. IT MAY LOOK FRIGHTENING.
AND YES, THERE ARE THOSE DETERMINED TO PULL EVERYONE APART TO KEEP SYSTEMS THEY ABUSE FROM FALLING APART.
PLANET B
THINGS MAY SEEM WORSE AT FIRST, TOO. THE CULTURE WARS AND GREAT ENDING WILL BE MORE THAN SOME CAN COPE WITH.
BUT THERE ARE THOSE WHO CARE TO FIGHT FOR A BETTER FUTURE. ALL IT TAKES IS THOSE PEOPLE TO COME TOGETHER.
THAT'S HOW WE GET TO HERE.
THAT'S HOW THIS WORLD OF TOMORROW FOR ALL HAPPENS.
BUT DOCTOR SHAH, TO GET *HERE*, YOU NEED TO BE THERE.
YOU NEED TO BE PRESENT, TO FIND CONNECTION... TO MAKE HERE HAPPEN.
... I UNDERSTAND.

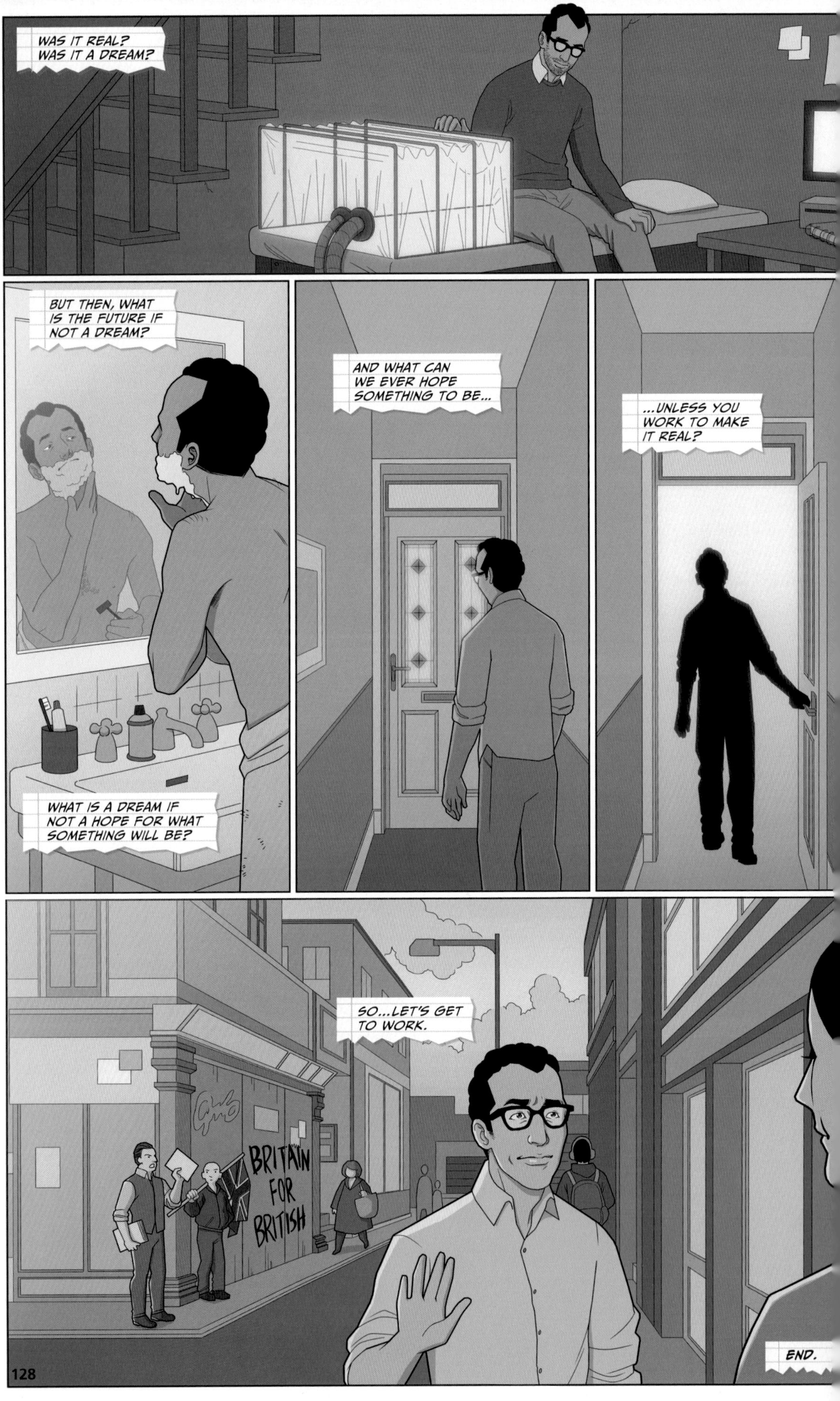
WAS IT REAL? WAS IT A DREAM?
BUT THEN, WHAT IS THE FUTURE IF NOT A DREAM?
WHAT IS A DREAM IF NOT A HOPE FOR WHAT SOMETHING WILL BE?
AND WHAT CAN WE EVER HOPE SOMETHING TO BE...
...UNLESS YOU WORK TO MAKE IT REAL?
SO...LET'S GET TO WORK.
BRITAIN FOR BRITISH
END.

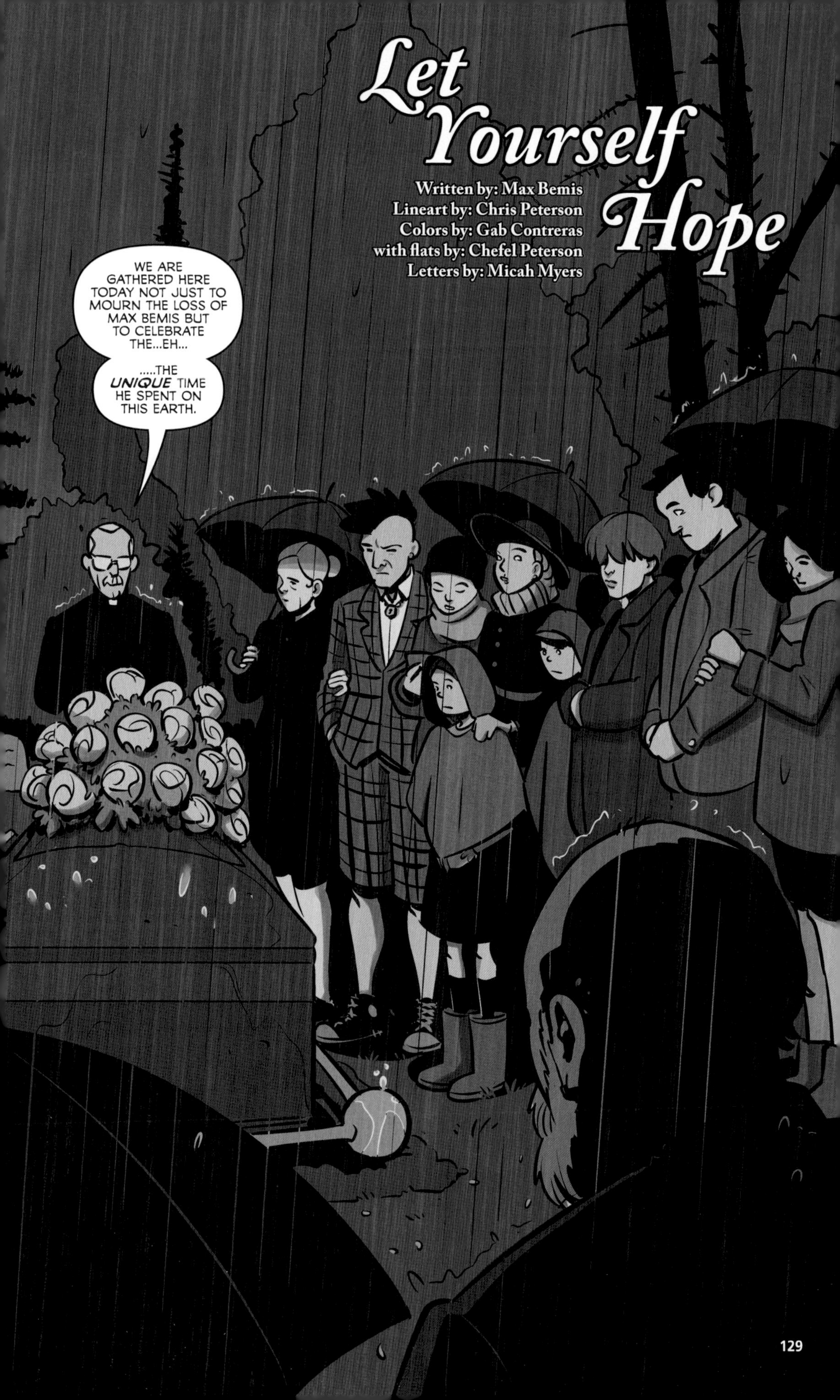

Let Yourself Hope
Written by: Max Bemis
Lineart by: Chris Peterson
Colors by: Gab Contreras
with flats by: Chefel Peterson
Letters by: Micah Myers
WE ARE GATHERED HERE TODAY NOT JUST TO MOURN THE LOSS OF MAX BEMIS BUT TO CELEBRATE THE...EH...
.....THE *UNIQUE* TIME HE SPENT ON THIS EARTH.

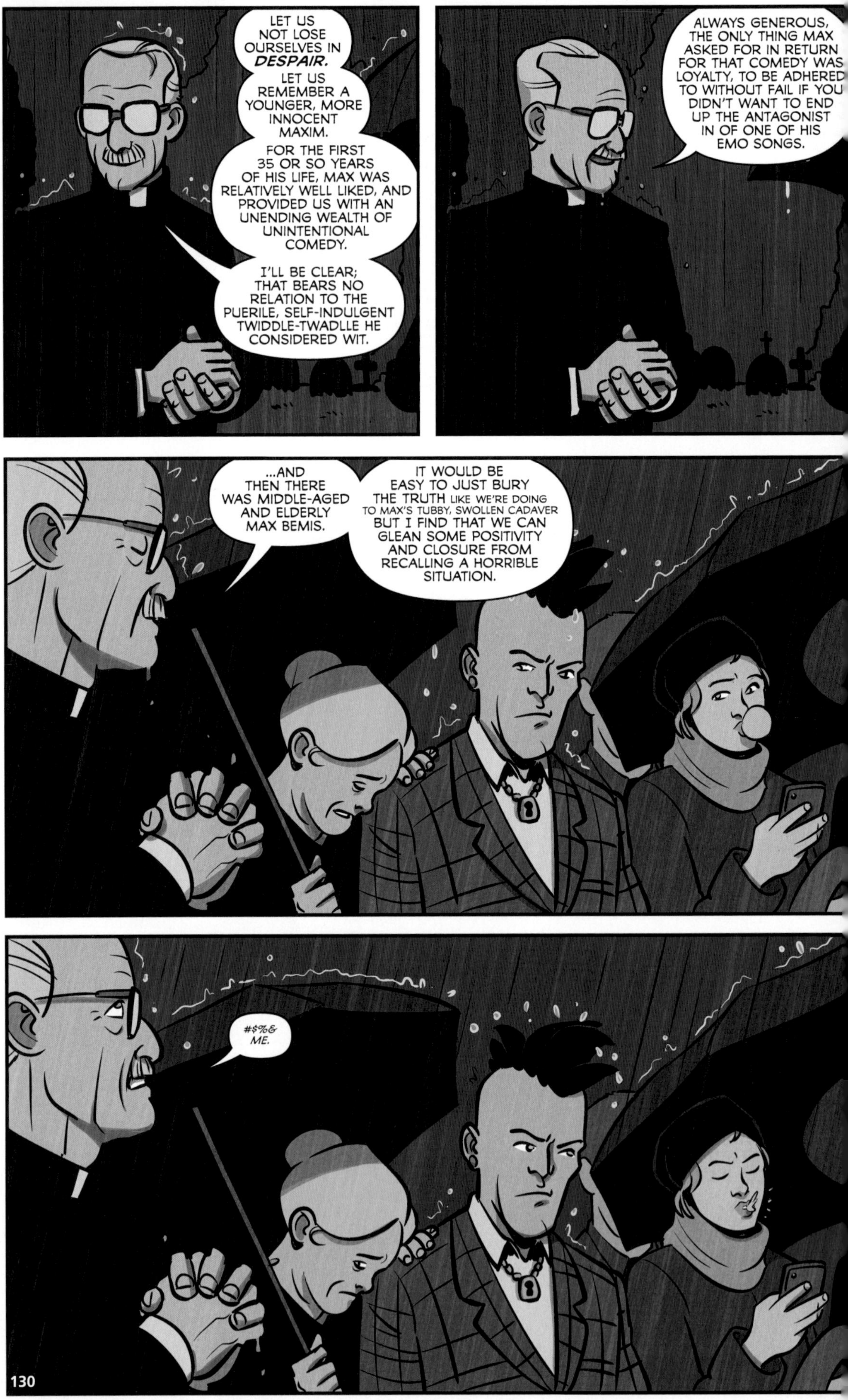
LET US NOT LOSE OURSELVES IN ***DESPAIR.***
LET US REMEMBER A YOUNGER, MORE INNOCENT MAXIM.
FOR THE FIRST 35 OR SO YEARS OF HIS LIFE, MAX WAS RELATIVELY WELL LIKED, AND PROVIDED US WITH AN UNENDING WEALTH OF UNINTENTIONAL COMEDY.
I'LL BE CLEAR; THAT BEARS NO RELATION TO THE PUERILE, SELF-INDULGENT TWIDDLE-TWADLLE HE CONSIDERED WIT.
ALWAYS GENEROUS, THE ONLY THING MAX ASKED FOR IN RETURN FOR THAT COMEDY WAS LOYALTY, TO BE ADHERED TO WITHOUT FAIL IF YOU DIDN'T WANT TO END UP THE ANTAGONIST IN OF ONE OF HIS EMO SONGS.
...AND THEN THERE WAS MIDDLE-AGED AND ELDERLY MAX BEMIS.
IT WOULD BE EASY TO JUST BURY THE TRUTH LIKE WE'RE DOING TO MAX'S TUBBY, SWOLLEN CADAVER BUT I FIND THAT WE CAN GLEAN SOME POSITIVITY AND CLOSURE FROM RECALLING A HORRIBLE SITUATION.
#$%& ME.

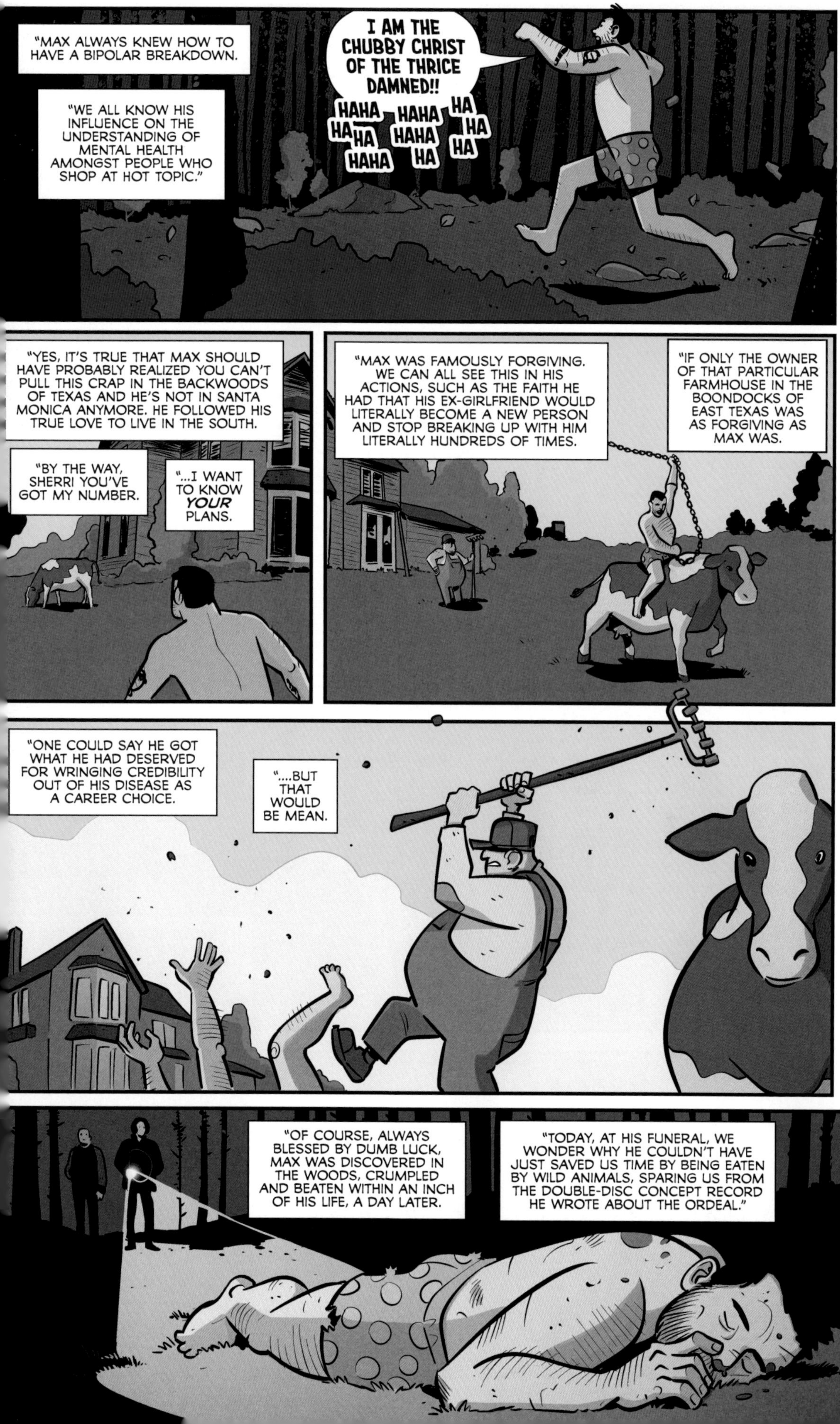
"MAX ALWAYS KNEW HOW TO HAVE A BIPOLAR BREAKDOWN.
"WE ALL KNOW HIS INFLUENCE ON THE UNDERSTANDING OF MENTAL HEALTH AMONGST PEOPLE WHO SHOP AT HOT TOPIC."
I AM THE CHUBBY CHRIST OF THE THRICE DAMNED!!
HAHA HA HA HAHA
HAHA HAHA HA
HA HA HA
"YES, IT'S TRUE THAT MAX SHOULD HAVE PROBABLY REALIZED YOU CAN'T PULL THIS CRAP IN THE BACKWOODS OF TEXAS AND HE'S NOT IN SANTA MONICA ANYMORE. HE FOLLOWED HIS TRUE LOVE TO LIVE IN THE SOUTH.
"BY THE WAY, SHERRI YOU'VE GOT MY NUMBER.
"...I WANT TO KNOW *YOUR* PLANS.
"MAX WAS FAMOUSLY FORGIVING. WE CAN ALL SEE THIS IN HIS ACTIONS, SUCH AS THE FAITH HE HAD THAT HIS EX-GIRLFRIEND WOULD LITERALLY BECOME A NEW PERSON AND STOP BREAKING UP WITH HIM LITERALLY HUNDREDS OF TIMES.
"IF ONLY THE OWNER OF THAT PARTICULAR FARMHOUSE IN THE BOONDOCKS OF EAST TEXAS WAS AS FORGIVING AS MAX WAS.
"ONE COULD SAY HE GOT WHAT HE HAD DESERVED FOR WRINGING CREDIBILITY OUT OF HIS DISEASE AS A CAREER CHOICE.
"....BUT THAT WOULD BE MEAN.
"OF COURSE, ALWAYS BLESSED BY DUMB LUCK, MAX WAS DISCOVERED IN THE WOODS, CRUMPLED AND BEATEN WITHIN AN INCH OF HIS LIFE, A DAY LATER.
"TODAY, AT HIS FUNERAL, WE WONDER WHY HE COULDN'T HAVE JUST SAVED US TIME BY BEING EATEN BY WILD ANIMALS, SPARING US FROM THE DOUBLE-DISC CONCEPT RECORD HE WROTE ABOUT THE ORDEAL."

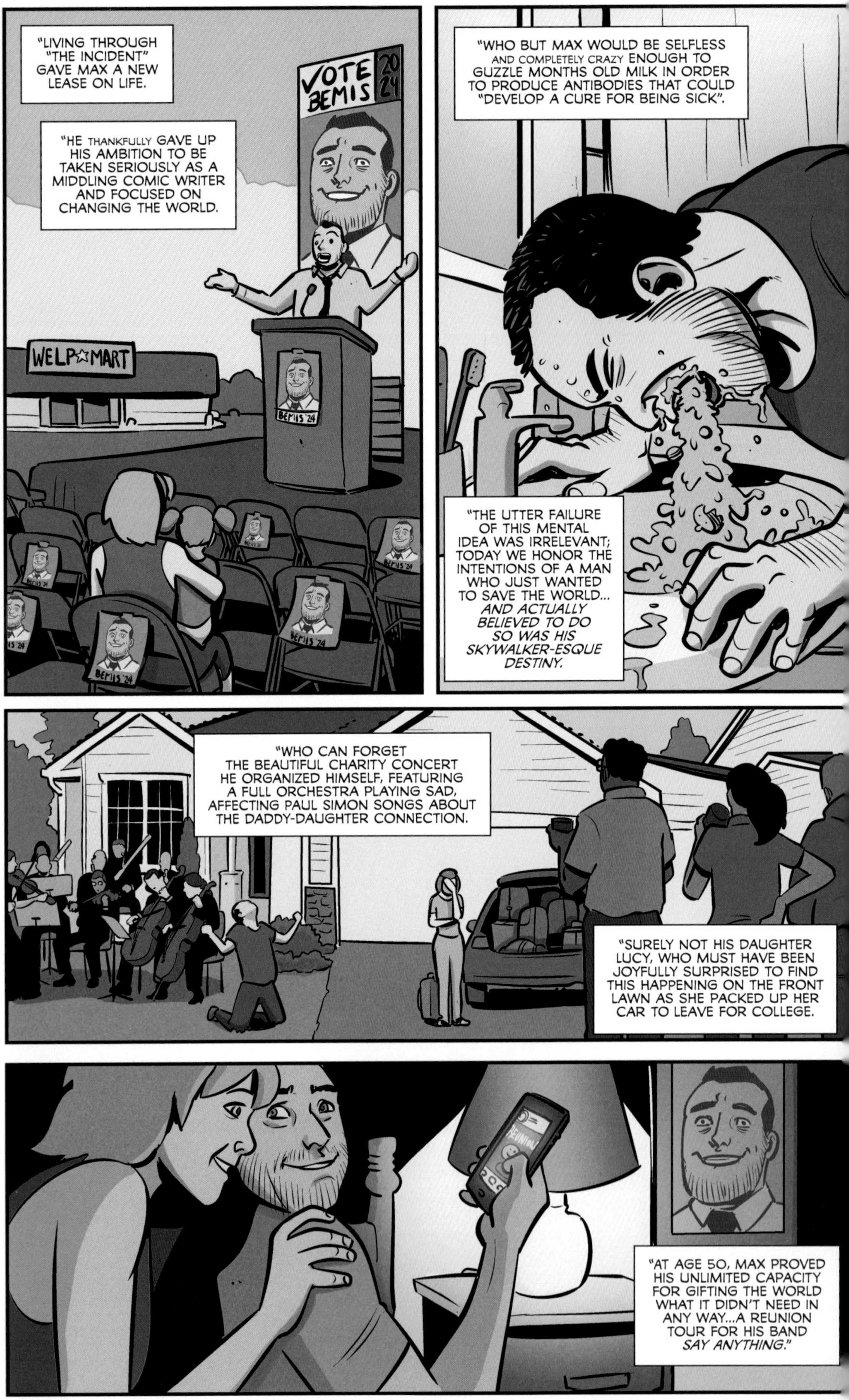
"LIVING THROUGH "THE INCIDENT" GAVE MAX A NEW LEASE ON LIFE.
VOTE BEMIS 2024
"HE THANKFULLY GAVE UP HIS AMBITION TO BE TAKEN SERIOUSLY AS A MIDDLING COMIC WRITER AND FOCUSED ON CHANGING THE WORLD.
WELP☆MART
BEMIS '24
"WHO BUT MAX WOULD BE SELFLESS AND COMPLETELY CRAZY ENOUGH TO GUZZLE MONTHS OLD MILK IN ORDER TO PRODUCE ANTIBODIES THAT COULD "DEVELOP A CURE FOR BEING SICK".
"THE UTTER FAILURE OF THIS MENTAL IDEA WAS IRRELEVANT; TODAY WE HONOR THE INTENTIONS OF A MAN WHO JUST WANTED TO SAVE THE WORLD... *AND ACTUALLY BELIEVED TO DO SO WAS HIS SKYWALKER-ESQUE DESTINY.*
"WHO CAN FORGET THE BEAUTIFUL CHARITY CONCERT HE ORGANIZED HIMSELF, FEATURING A FULL ORCHESTRA PLAYING SAD, AFFECTING PAUL SIMON SONGS ABOUT THE DADDY-DAUGHTER CONNECTION.
"SURELY NOT HIS DAUGHTER LUCY, WHO MUST HAVE BEEN JOYFULLY SURPRISED TO FIND THIS HAPPENING ON THE FRONT LAWN AS SHE PACKED UP HER CAR TO LEAVE FOR COLLEGE.
REUNION
"AT AGE 50, MAX PROVED HIS UNLIMITED CAPACITY FOR GIFTING THE WORLD WHAT IT DIDN'T NEED IN ANY WAY...A REUNION TOUR FOR HIS BAND *SAY ANYTHING.*"

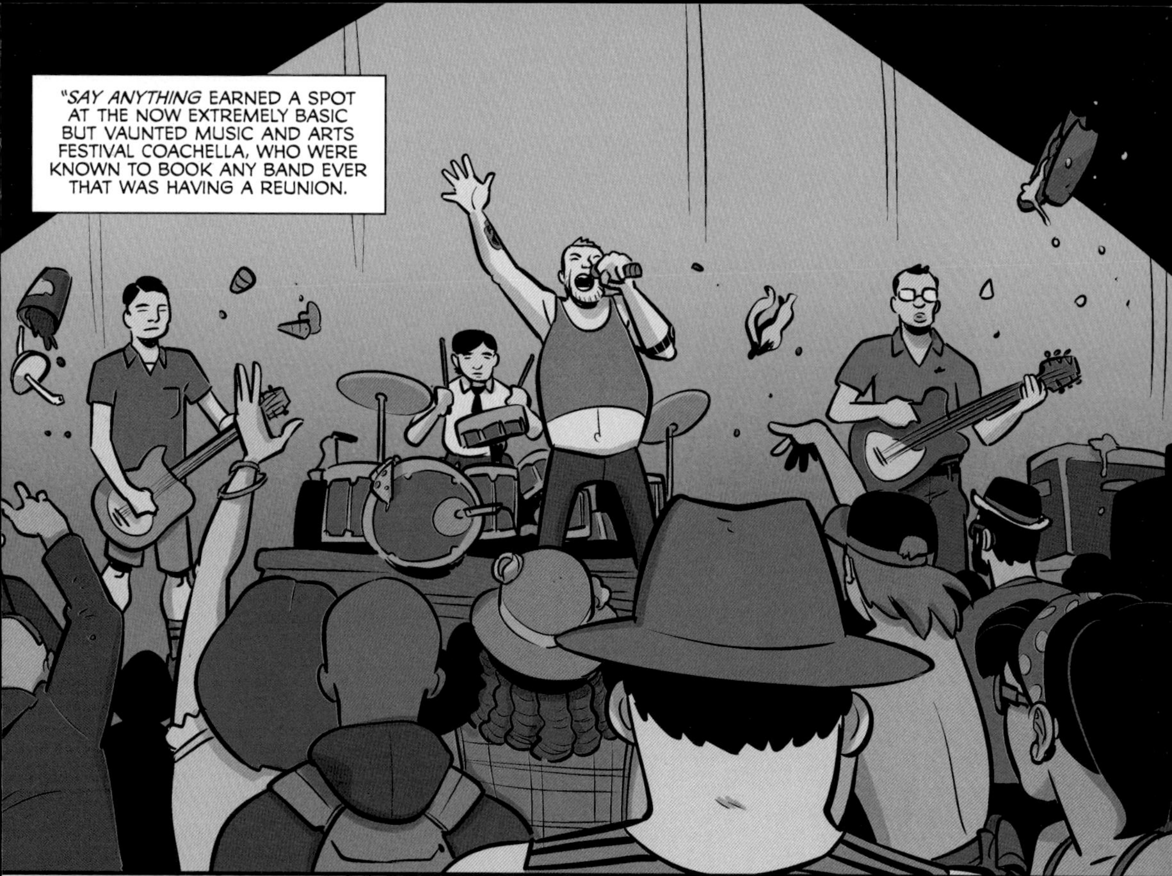
"*SAY ANYTHING* EARNED A SPOT AT THE NOW EXTREMELY BASIC BUT VAUNTED MUSIC AND ARTS FESTIVAL COACHELLA, WHO WERE KNOWN TO BOOK ANY BAND EVER THAT WAS HAVING A REUNION.

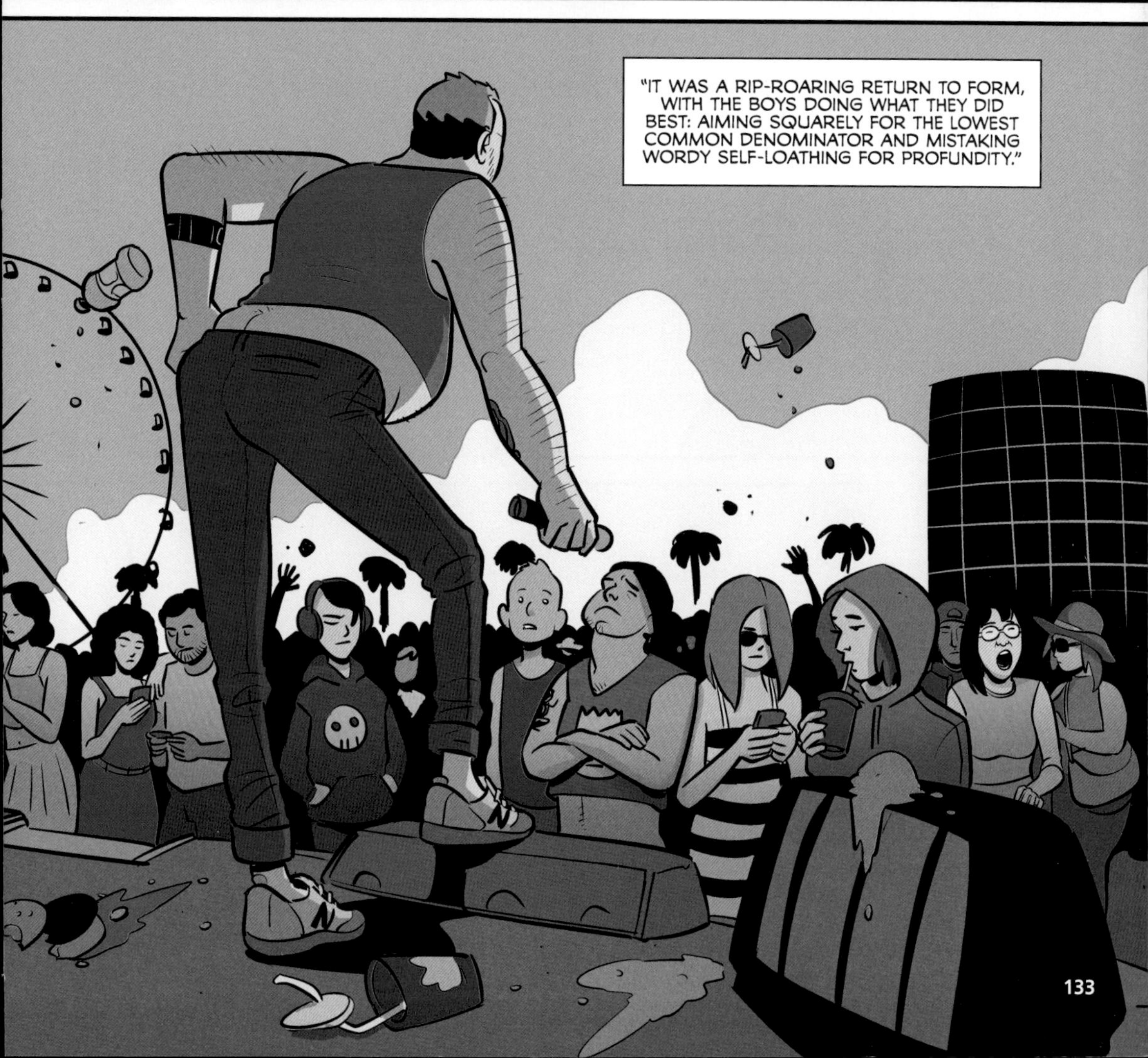
"IT WAS A RIP-ROARING RETURN TO FORM, WITH THE BOYS DOING WHAT THEY DID BEST: AIMING SQUARELY FOR THE LOWEST COMMON DENOMINATOR AND MISTAKING WORDY SELF-LOATHING FOR PROFUNDITY."

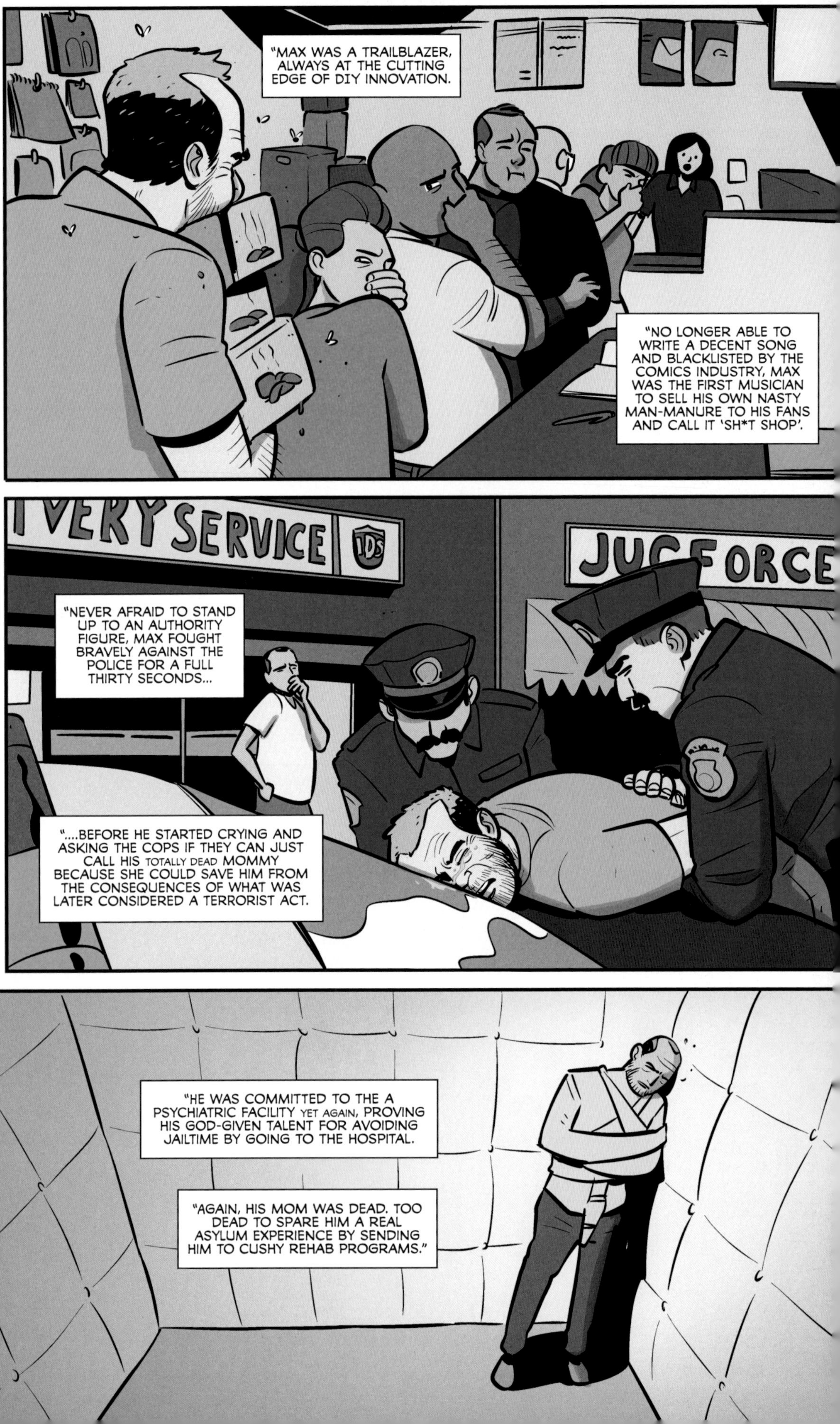
"MAX WAS A TRAILBLAZER, ALWAYS AT THE CUTTING EDGE OF DIY INNOVATION.
"NO LONGER ABLE TO WRITE A DECENT SONG AND BLACKLISTED BY THE COMICS INDUSTRY, MAX WAS THE FIRST MUSICIAN TO SELL HIS OWN NASTY MAN-MANURE TO HIS FANS AND CALL IT 'SH*T SHOP'.
"NEVER AFRAID TO STAND UP TO AN AUTHORITY FIGURE, MAX FOUGHT BRAVELY AGAINST THE POLICE FOR A FULL THIRTY SECONDS...
"....BEFORE HE STARTED CRYING AND ASKING THE COPS IF THEY CAN JUST CALL HIS TOTALLY DEAD MOMMY BECAUSE SHE COULD SAVE HIM FROM THE CONSEQUENCES OF WHAT WAS LATER CONSIDERED A TERRORIST ACT.
"HE WAS COMMITTED TO THE A PSYCHIATRIC FACILITY YET AGAIN, PROVING HIS GOD-GIVEN TALENT FOR AVOIDING JAILTIME BY GOING TO THE HOSPITAL.
"AGAIN, HIS MOM WAS DEAD. TOO DEAD TO SPARE HIM A REAL ASYLUM EXPERIENCE BY SENDING HIM TO CUSHY REHAB PROGRAMS."

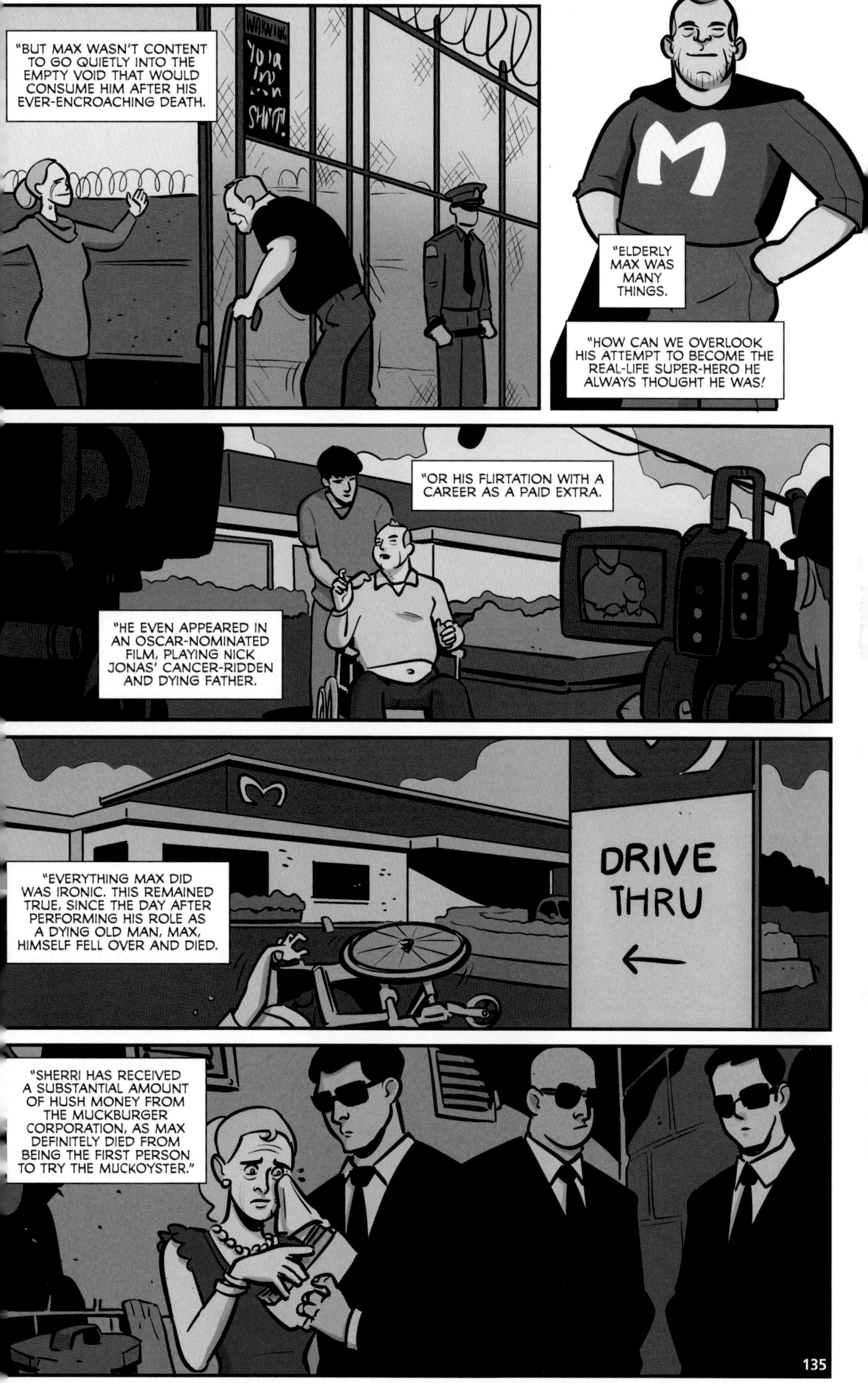
"BUT MAX WASN'T CONTENT TO GO QUIETLY INTO THE EMPTY VOID THAT WOULD CONSUME HIM AFTER HIS EVER-ENCROACHING DEATH.
WARNING
"ELDERLY MAX WAS MANY THINGS.
"HOW CAN WE OVERLOOK HIS ATTEMPT TO BECOME THE REAL-LIFE SUPER-HERO HE ALWAYS THOUGHT HE WAS!
"OR HIS FLIRTATION WITH A CAREER AS A PAID EXTRA.
"HE EVEN APPEARED IN AN OSCAR-NOMINATED FILM, PLAYING NICK JONAS' CANCER-RIDDEN AND DYING FATHER.
"EVERYTHING MAX DID WAS IRONIC. THIS REMAINED TRUE, SINCE THE DAY AFTER PERFORMING HIS ROLE AS A DYING OLD MAN, MAX, HIMSELF FELL OVER AND DIED.
DRIVE THRU
"SHERRI HAS RECEIVED A SUBSTANTIAL AMOUNT OF HUSH MONEY FROM THE MUCKBURGER CORPORATION, AS MAX DEFINITELY DIED FROM BEING THE FIRST PERSON TO TRY THE MUCKOYSTER."

YES, YOU COULD SAY THAT MAX'S LIFE WAS A WASTE OF TIME AND A LOT OF GREAT MEXICAN FOOD.

BUT WHAT MAX WANTED MOST WAS FOR THE FUTURE TO BE A BRIGHTER ONE FOR THOSE WHO WOULD INHERIT OUR WORLD.

AND IT IS.

LUCY IS THE EDITOR IN CHIEF OF VOGUE AND HAS MAINTAINED LIFELONG SASS.

CORALINE HAS REVOLUTIONIZED VETERINARY SCIENCE, INVENTING THE METHOD TO CREATE PERMANENT PUPPIES.

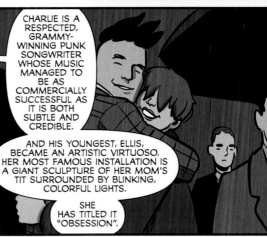

CHARLIE IS A RESPECTED, GRAMMY-WINNING PUNK SONGWRITER WHOSE MUSIC MANAGED TO BE AS COMMERCIALLY SUCCESSFUL AS IT IS BOTH SUBTLE AND CREDIBLE.

AND HIS YOUNGEST, ELLIS, BECAME AN ARTISTIC VIRTUOSO. HER MOST FAMOUS INSTALLATION IS A GIANT SCULPTURE OF HER MOM'S TIT SURROUNDED BY BLINKING, COLORFUL LIGHTS.

SHE HAS TITLED IT "OBSESSION".

AS WE LOWER MAX'S CASKET INTO THE WORMY DIRT HE WILL NOW ROT IN, LET US REMEMBER THAT HIS DEEPEST DESIRE WAS FOR THE WORLD TO CHANGE FOR THE BETTER.

THOUGH I DOUBT HE WOULD BE SURPRISED, I'M SURE HE'D BE GRATEFUL TO KNOW HIS CHILDREN ARE OUTDOING HIM IN EVERY WAY...AND THAT'S THE SECRET DESIRE OF ANY GOOD PARENT.

I LEAVE YOU WITH THIS, TO SUM UP THIS MAN'S LIFE....

...WE CAN REDEEM OURSELVES SIMPLY BY ALLOWING OURSELVES TO HOPE.

THANK YOU, MY FRIENDS. HAVE A BLESSED EVENING.

...AND APOLOGIES FOR THE STENCH MAX IS EMITTING.

HE IS A SMELLY BASTARD EVEN IN DEATH.

GOODBYE AND GOOD NIGHT.

The End

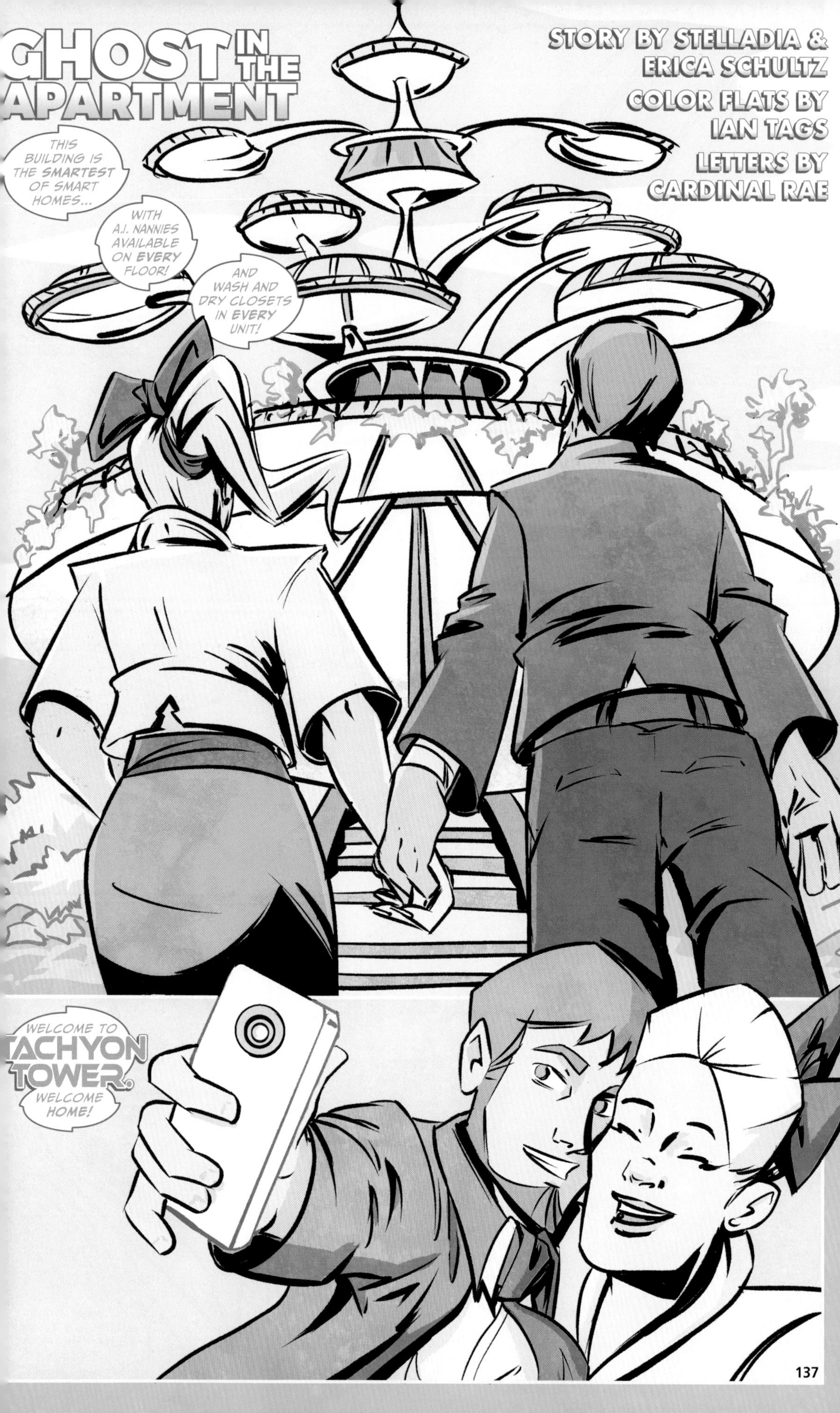
GHOST IN THE APARTMENT
STORY BY STELLADIA & ERICA SCHULTZ
COLOR FLATS BY IAN TAGS
LETTERS BY CARDINAL RAE
THIS BUILDING IS THE SMARTEST OF SMART HOMES...
WITH A.I. NANNIES AVAILABLE ON EVERY FLOOR!
AND WASH AND DRY CLOSETS IN EVERY UNIT!
WELCOME TO TACHYON TOWER. WELCOME HOME!

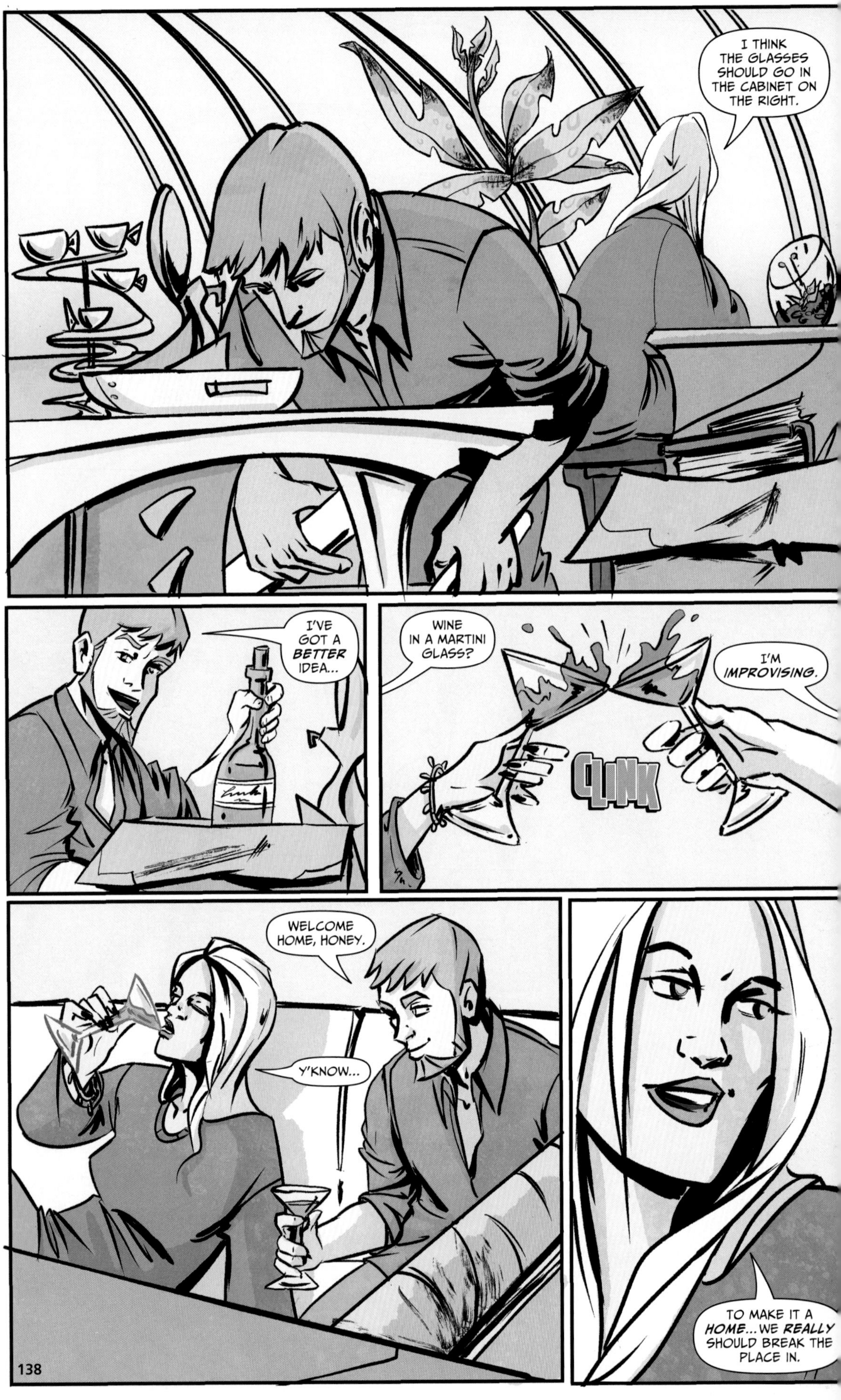

I THINK THE GLASSES SHOULD GO IN THE CABINET ON THE RIGHT.
I'VE GOT A *BETTER* IDEA...
WINE IN A MARTINI GLASS?
I'M *IMPROVISING.*
CLINK
WELCOME HOME, HONEY.
Y'KNOW...
TO MAKE IT A *HOME*... WE *REALLY* SHOULD BREAK THE PLACE IN.

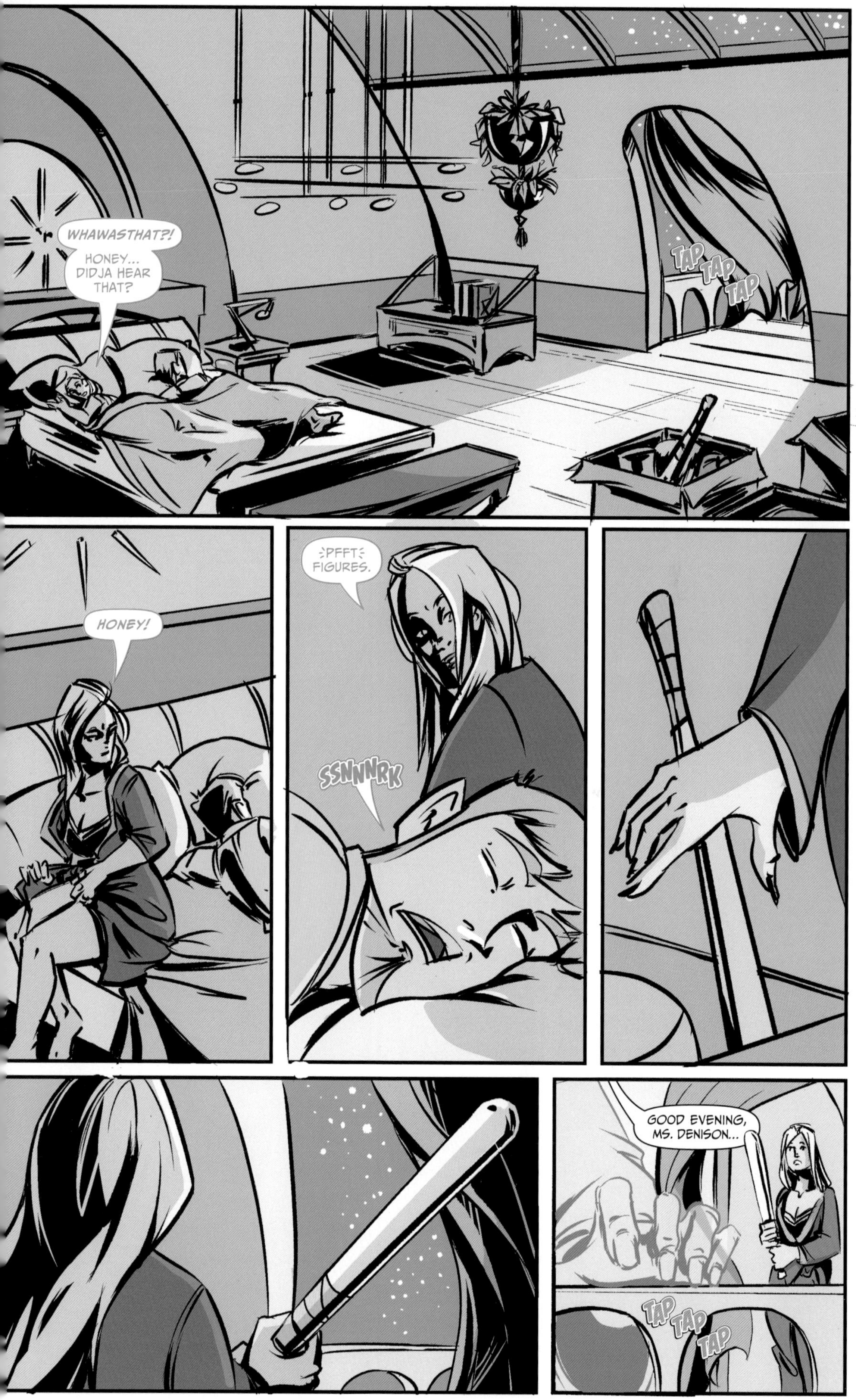
WHAWASTHAT?!
HONEY... DIDJA HEAR THAT?
TAP TAP TAP
HONEY!
PFFT FIGURES.
SSNNNRK
GOOD EVENING, MS. DENISON...
TAP TAP TAP

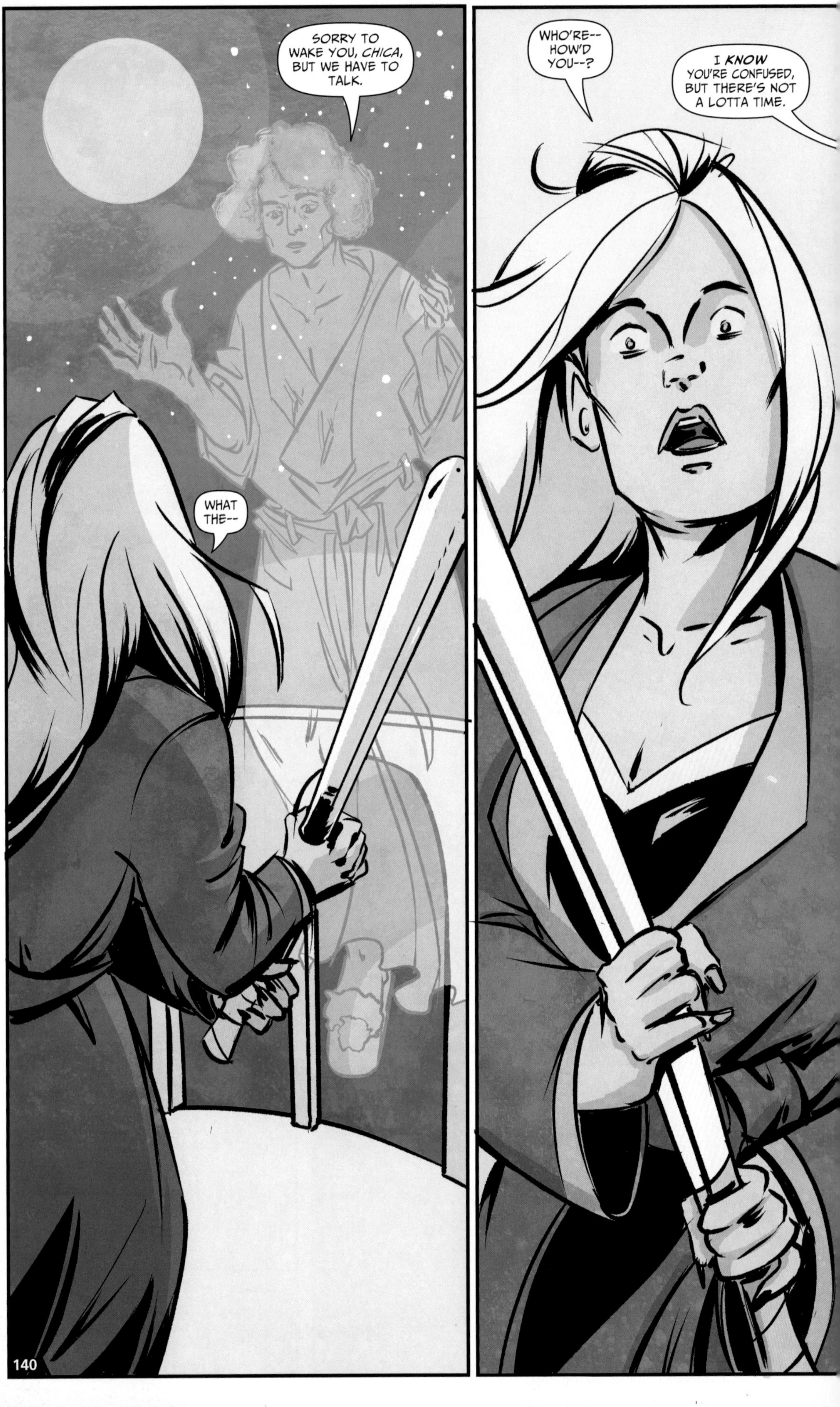
SORRY TO WAKE YOU, *CHICA*, BUT WE HAVE TO TALK.
WHAT THE--
WHO'RE-- HOW'D YOU--?
I ***KNOW*** YOU'RE CONFUSED, BUT THERE'S NOT A LOTTA TIME.

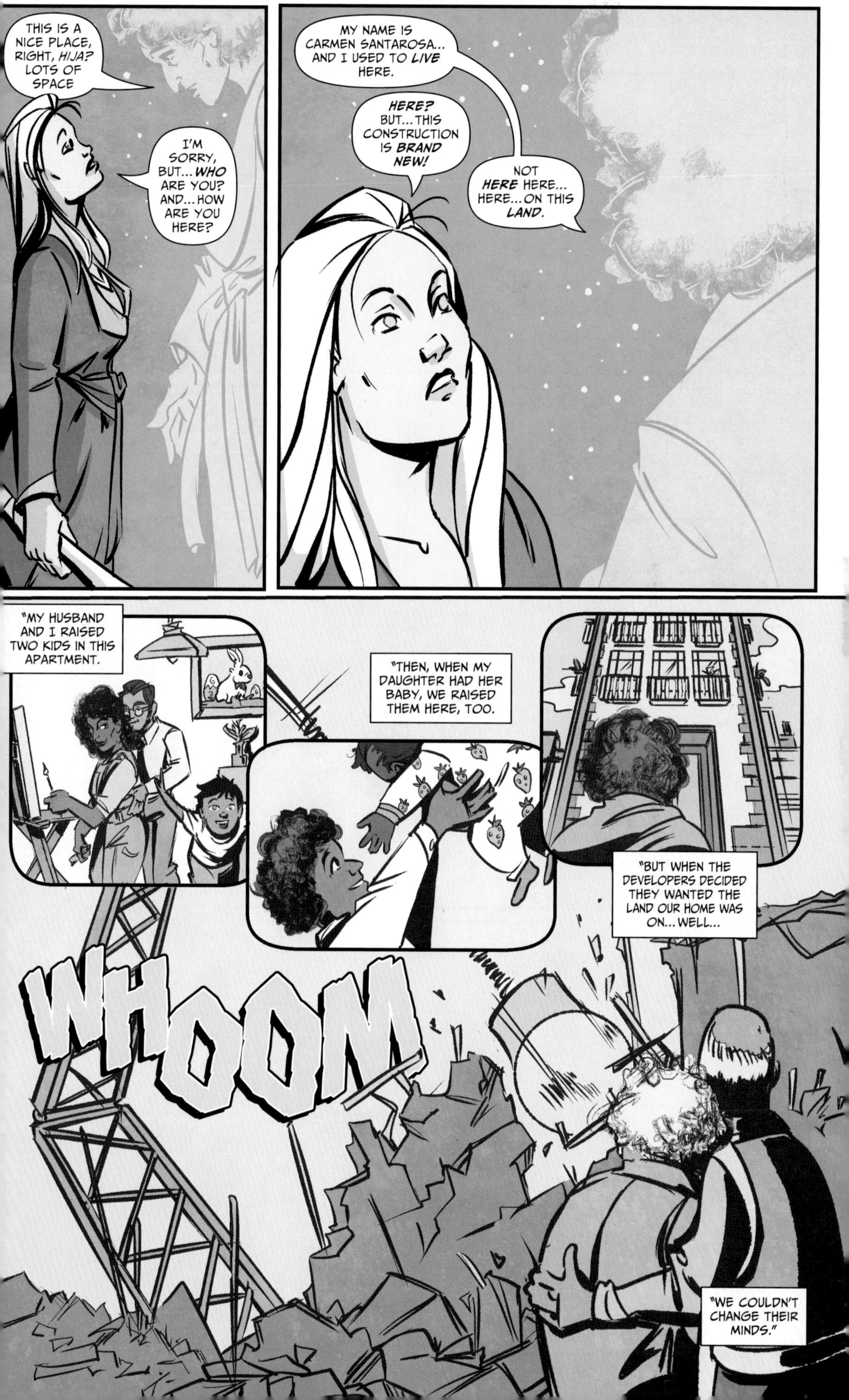

THIS IS A NICE PLACE, RIGHT, *HIJA?* LOTS OF SPACE
I'M SORRY, BUT... ***WHO*** ARE YOU? AND... HOW ARE YOU HERE?
MY NAME IS CARMEN SANTAROSA... AND I USED TO *LIVE* HERE.
HERE? BUT... THIS CONSTRUCTION IS ***BRAND NEW!***
NOT ***HERE*** HERE... HERE... ON THIS ***LAND.***
"MY HUSBAND AND I RAISED TWO KIDS IN THIS APARTMENT.
"THEN, WHEN MY DAUGHTER HAD HER BABY, WE RAISED THEM HERE, TOO.
"BUT WHEN THE DEVELOPERS DECIDED THEY WANTED THE LAND OUR HOME WAS ON... WELL...
WHOOM
"WE COULDN'T CHANGE THEIR MINDS."

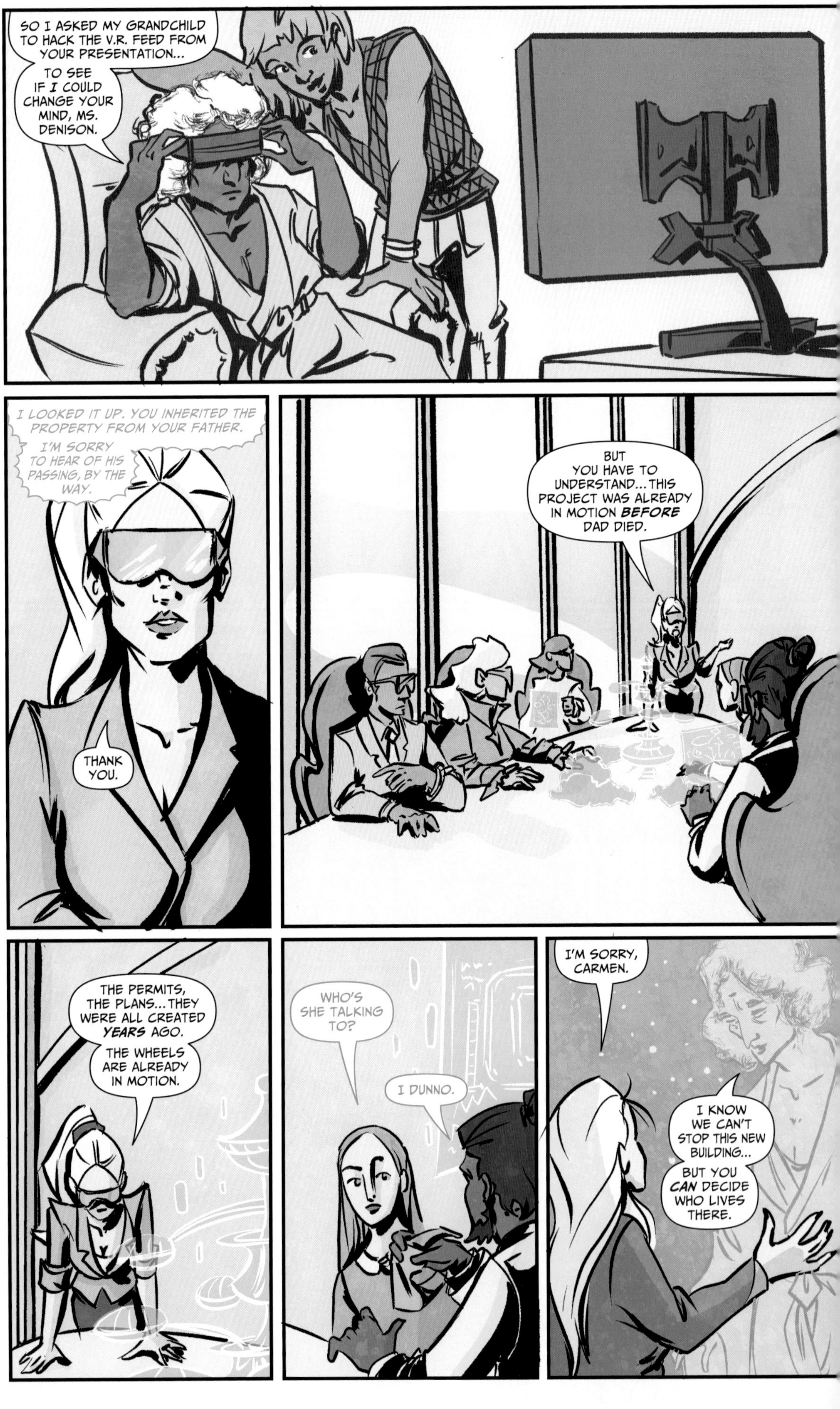
SO I ASKED MY GRANDCHILD TO HACK THE V.R. FEED FROM YOUR PRESENTATION...
TO SEE IF I COULD CHANGE YOUR MIND, MS. DENISON.
I LOOKED IT UP. YOU INHERITED THE PROPERTY FROM YOUR FATHER.
I'M SORRY TO HEAR OF HIS PASSING, BY THE WAY.
THANK YOU.
BUT YOU HAVE TO UNDERSTAND... THIS PROJECT WAS ALREADY IN MOTION BEFORE DAD DIED.
THE PERMITS, THE PLANS... THEY WERE ALL CREATED YEARS AGO.
THE WHEELS ARE ALREADY IN MOTION.
WHO'S SHE TALKING TO?
I DUNNO.
I'M SORRY, CARMEN.
I KNOW WE CAN'T STOP THIS NEW BUILDING...
BUT YOU CAN DECIDE WHO LIVES THERE.

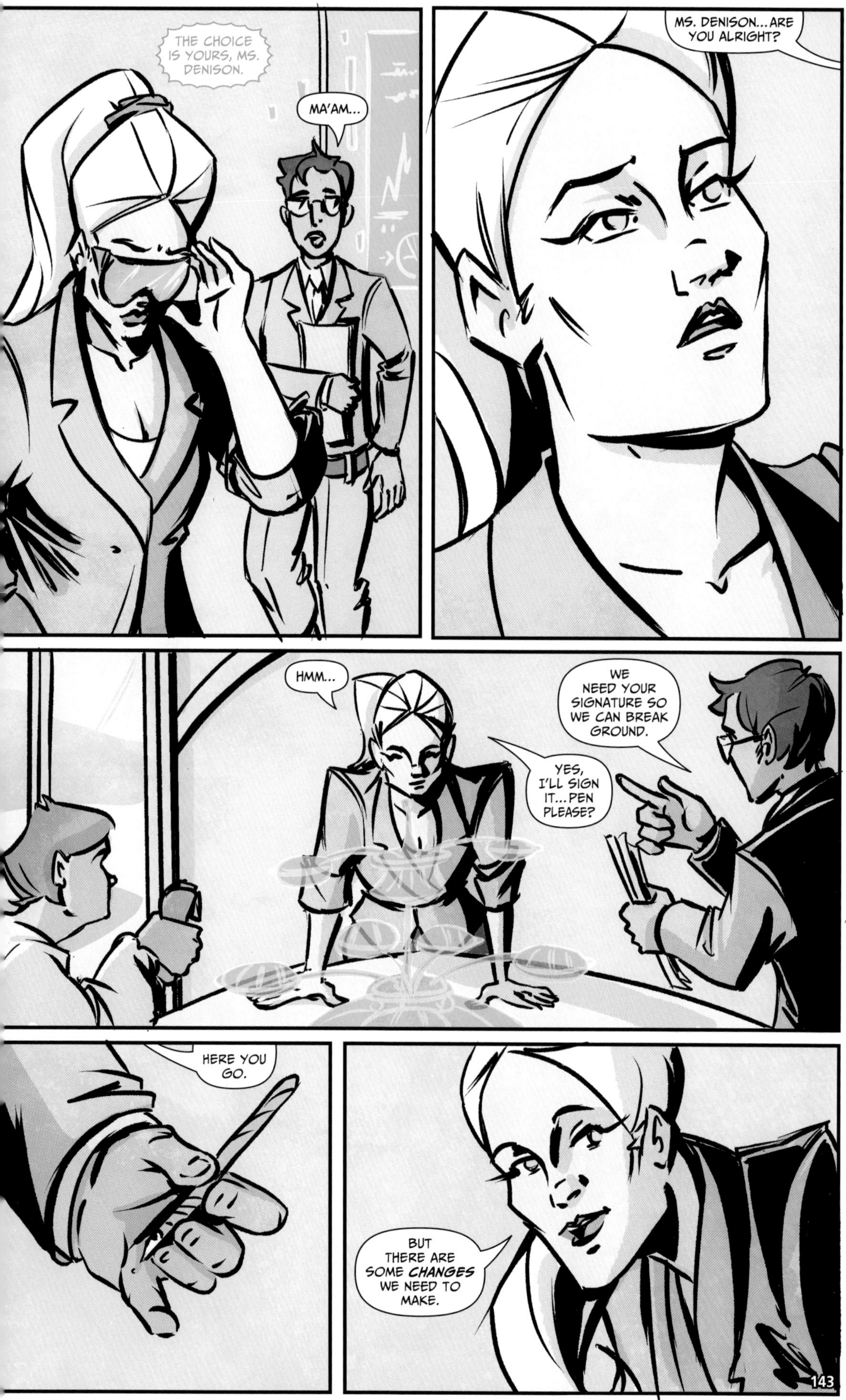
THE CHOICE IS YOURS, MS. DENISON.
MA'AM...
MS. DENISON... ARE YOU ALRIGHT?
HMM...
WE NEED YOUR SIGNATURE SO WE CAN BREAK GROUND.
YES, I'LL SIGN IT... PEN PLEASE?
HERE YOU GO.
BUT THERE ARE SOME *CHANGES* WE NEED TO MAKE.

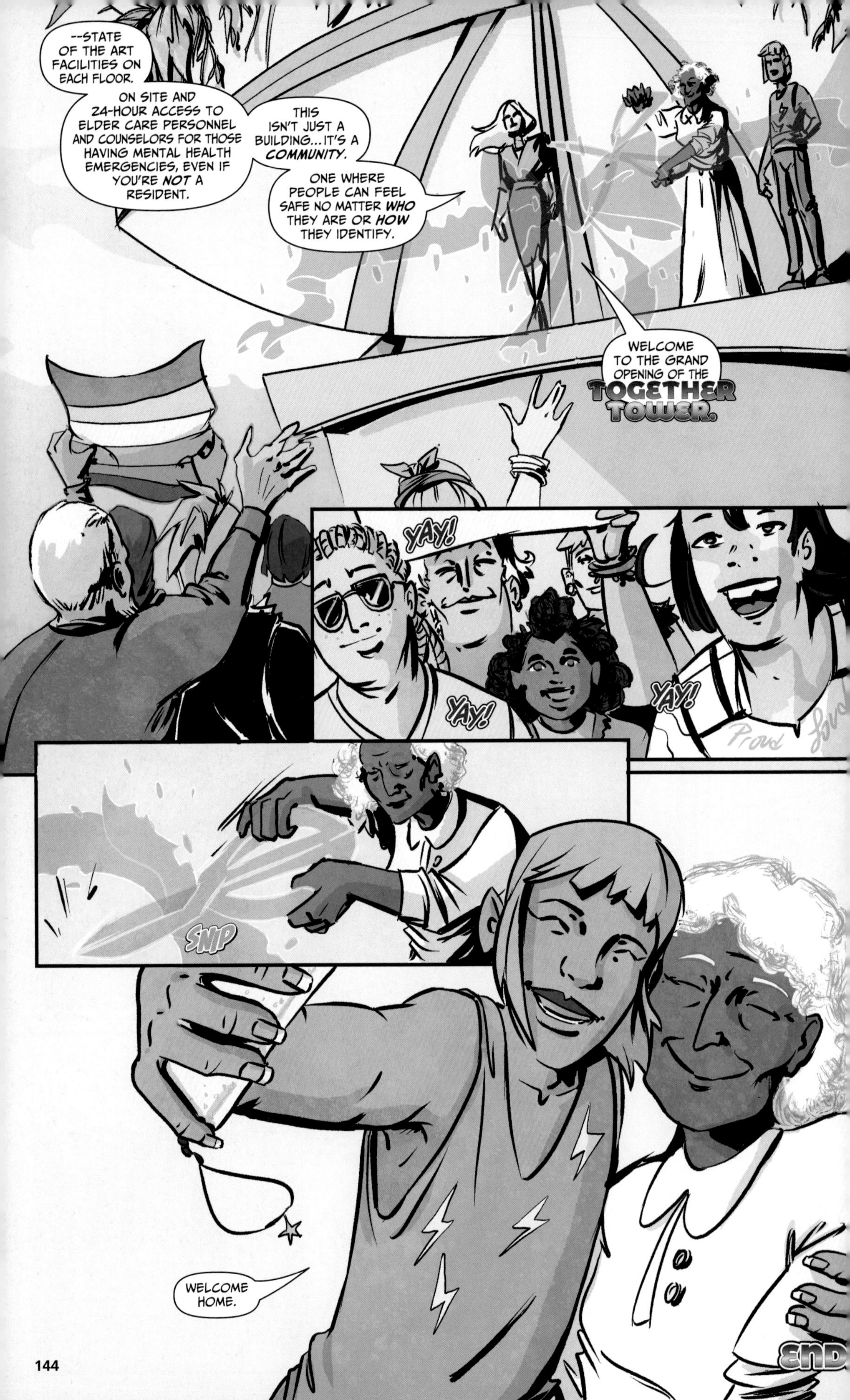
--STATE OF THE ART FACILITIES ON EACH FLOOR.
ON SITE AND 24-HOUR ACCESS TO ELDER CARE PERSONNEL AND COUNSELORS FOR THOSE HAVING MENTAL HEALTH EMERGENCIES, EVEN IF YOU'RE *NOT* A RESIDENT.
THIS ISN'T JUST A BUILDING... IT'S A *COMMUNITY.*
ONE WHERE PEOPLE CAN FEEL SAFE NO MATTER *WHO* THEY ARE OR *HOW* THEY IDENTIFY.
WELCOME TO THE GRAND OPENING OF THE TOGETHER TOWER.
YAY!
YAY!
YAY!
SNIP
WELCOME HOME.
END

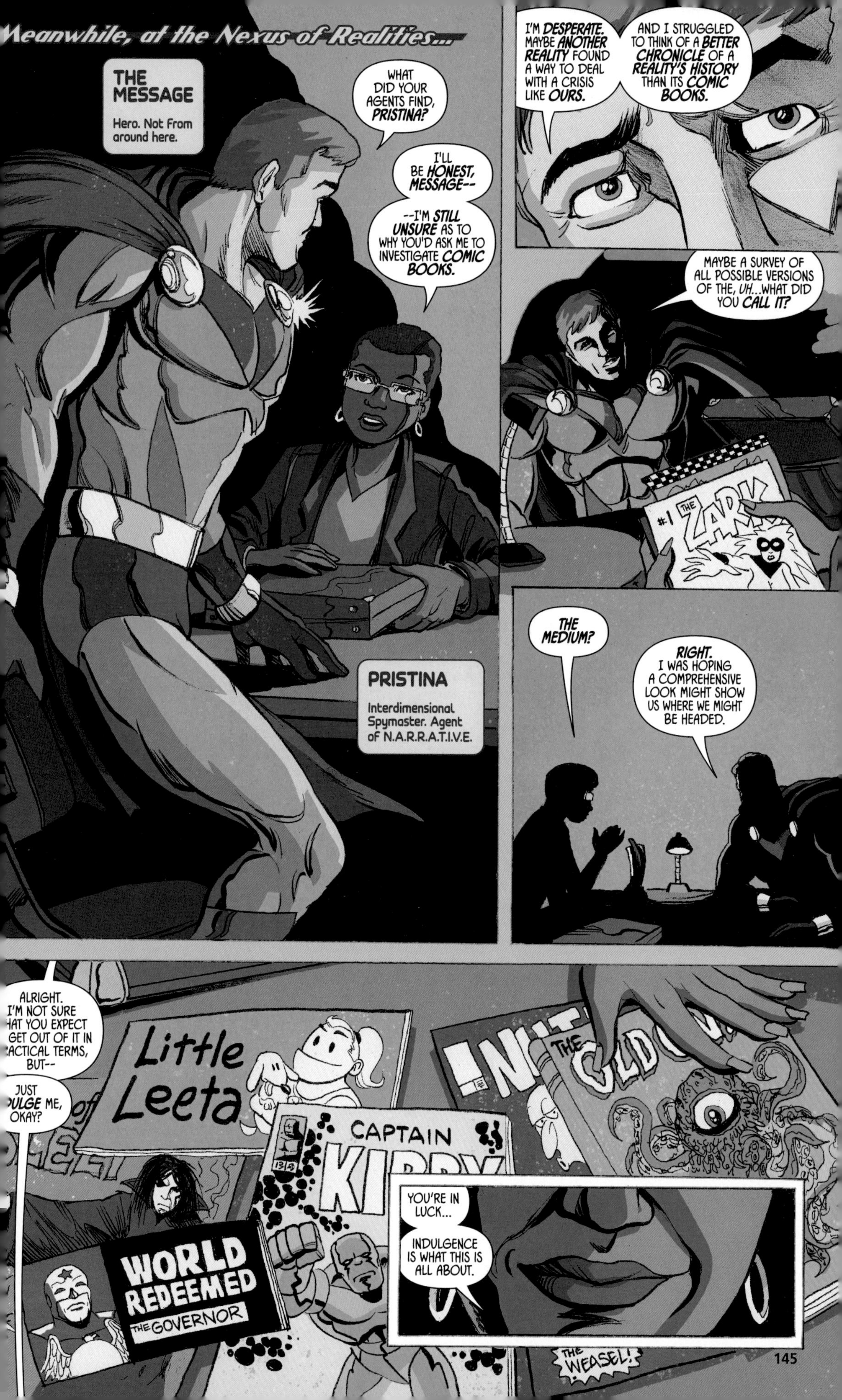

Meanwhile, at the Nexus of Realities...
THE MESSAGE
Hero. Not From around here.
WHAT DID YOUR AGENTS FIND, PRISTINA?
I'LL BE HONEST, MESSAGE--
--I'M STILL UNSURE AS TO WHY YOU'D ASK ME TO INVESTIGATE COMIC BOOKS.
PRISTINA
Interdimensional Spymaster. Agent of N.A.R.R.A.T.I.V.E.
I'M DESPERATE. MAYBE ANOTHER REALITY FOUND A WAY TO DEAL WITH A CRISIS LIKE OURS.
AND I STRUGGLED TO THINK OF A BETTER CHRONICLE OF A REALITY'S HISTORY THAN ITS COMIC BOOKS.
MAYBE A SURVEY OF ALL POSSIBLE VERSIONS OF THE, UH...WHAT DID YOU CALL IT?
#1 THE ZARK
THE MEDIUM?
RIGHT. I WAS HOPING A COMPREHENSIVE LOOK MIGHT SHOW US WHERE WE MIGHT BE HEADED.
ALRIGHT. I'M NOT SURE
HAT YOU EXPECT
GET OUT OF IT IN
ACTICAL TERMS,
BUT--
JUST
ULGE ME,
OKAY?
Little Leeta
CAPTAIN
WORLD REDEEMED
THE GOVERNOR
THE
YOU'RE IN LUCK...
INDULGENCE IS WHAT THIS IS ALL ABOUT.
THE WEASEL!

"THIS IS THE *FIRST REALITY* WE VISITED. LOOK HOW UBIQUITOUS THE COMICS ARE."

"WHAT HAPPENED THERE?"

PEACE DECLARED! WEAPONS DESTROYED!

"THAT'S ONE OF THOSE WORLDS WHERE EVERYTHING JUST SORT OF WORKED OUT. NO *WARS*, NO *CRIME*, NO *CRISES*. NOTHING AT ALL.

The Daily Cond

PEACE STILL RU THOUT EXCEPTI

"SO, AFTER A WHILE, THE NEWSPAPERS STARTED RUNNING OUT OF THINGS TO REPORT ON, AND THE NEED FOR COMIC STRIPS BECAME...*OVERWHELMING.*

THING TO E HERE!

"AND, SUDDENLY, YOU DIDN'T HAVE NEWSPAPERS ANYMORE. THE FUNNY PAGES BECAME THE *ONLY* PAGES.

BOY HITS DECADES-OLD CONFLI

"THOUSANDS OF REPORTERS LOST THEIR JOBS, BUT NOBODY KNEW SINCE THERE WASN'T ANYBODY TO REPORT IT."

I'M NOT SURE WHETHER TO FIND THAT *ENCOURAGING* OR *TERRIBLE.*

THE DAILY COMICS

...

DEPENDS ON YOUR POINT OF VIEW I GUESS.

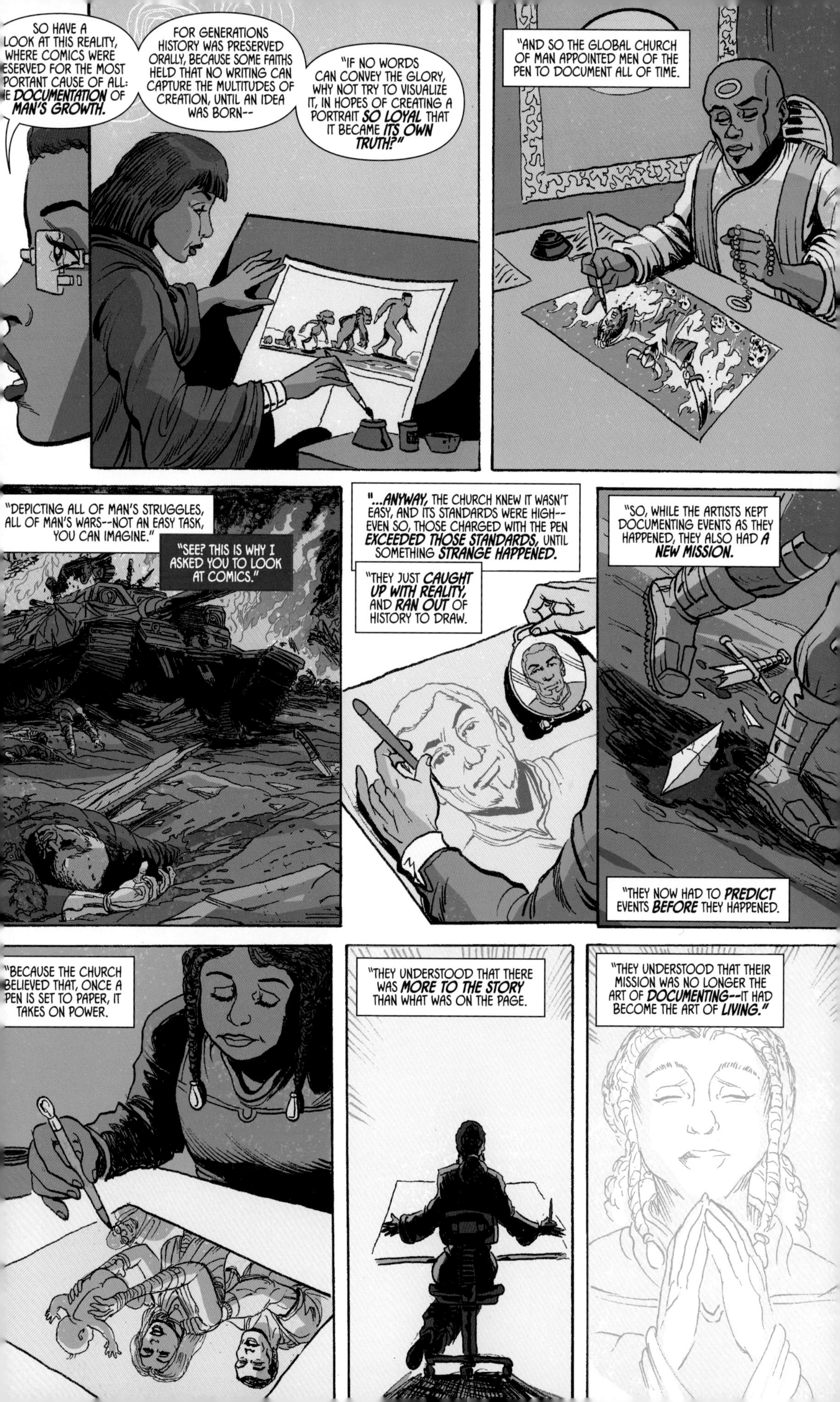
SO HAVE A LOOK AT THIS REALITY, WHERE COMICS WERE ESERVED FOR THE MOST PORTANT CAUSE OF ALL: E DOCUMENTATION OF MAN'S GROWTH.
FOR GENERATIONS HISTORY WAS PRESERVED ORALLY, BECAUSE SOME FAITHS HELD THAT NO WRITING CAN CAPTURE THE MULTITUDES OF CREATION, UNTIL AN IDEA WAS BORN--
"IF NO WORDS CAN CONVEY THE GLORY, WHY NOT TRY TO VISUALIZE IT, IN HOPES OF CREATING A PORTRAIT SO LOYAL THAT IT BECAME ITS OWN TRUTH?"
"AND SO THE GLOBAL CHURCH OF MAN APPOINTED MEN OF THE PEN TO DOCUMENT ALL OF TIME.
"DEPICTING ALL OF MAN'S STRUGGLES, ALL OF MAN'S WARS--NOT AN EASY TASK, YOU CAN IMAGINE."
"SEE? THIS IS WHY I ASKED YOU TO LOOK AT COMICS."
"...ANYWAY, THE CHURCH KNEW IT WASN'T EASY, AND ITS STANDARDS WERE HIGH--EVEN SO, THOSE CHARGED WITH THE PEN EXCEEDED THOSE STANDARDS, UNTIL SOMETHING STRANGE HAPPENED.
"THEY JUST CAUGHT UP WITH REALITY, AND RAN OUT OF HISTORY TO DRAW.
"SO, WHILE THE ARTISTS KEPT DOCUMENTING EVENTS AS THEY HAPPENED, THEY ALSO HAD A NEW MISSION.
"THEY NOW HAD TO PREDICT EVENTS BEFORE THEY HAPPENED.
"BECAUSE THE CHURCH BELIEVED THAT, ONCE A PEN IS SET TO PAPER, IT TAKES ON POWER.
"THEY UNDERSTOOD THAT THERE WAS MORE TO THE STORY THAN WHAT WAS ON THE PAGE.
"THEY UNDERSTOOD THAT THEIR MISSION WAS NO LONGER THE ART OF DOCUMENTING--IT HAD BECOME THE ART OF LIVING."

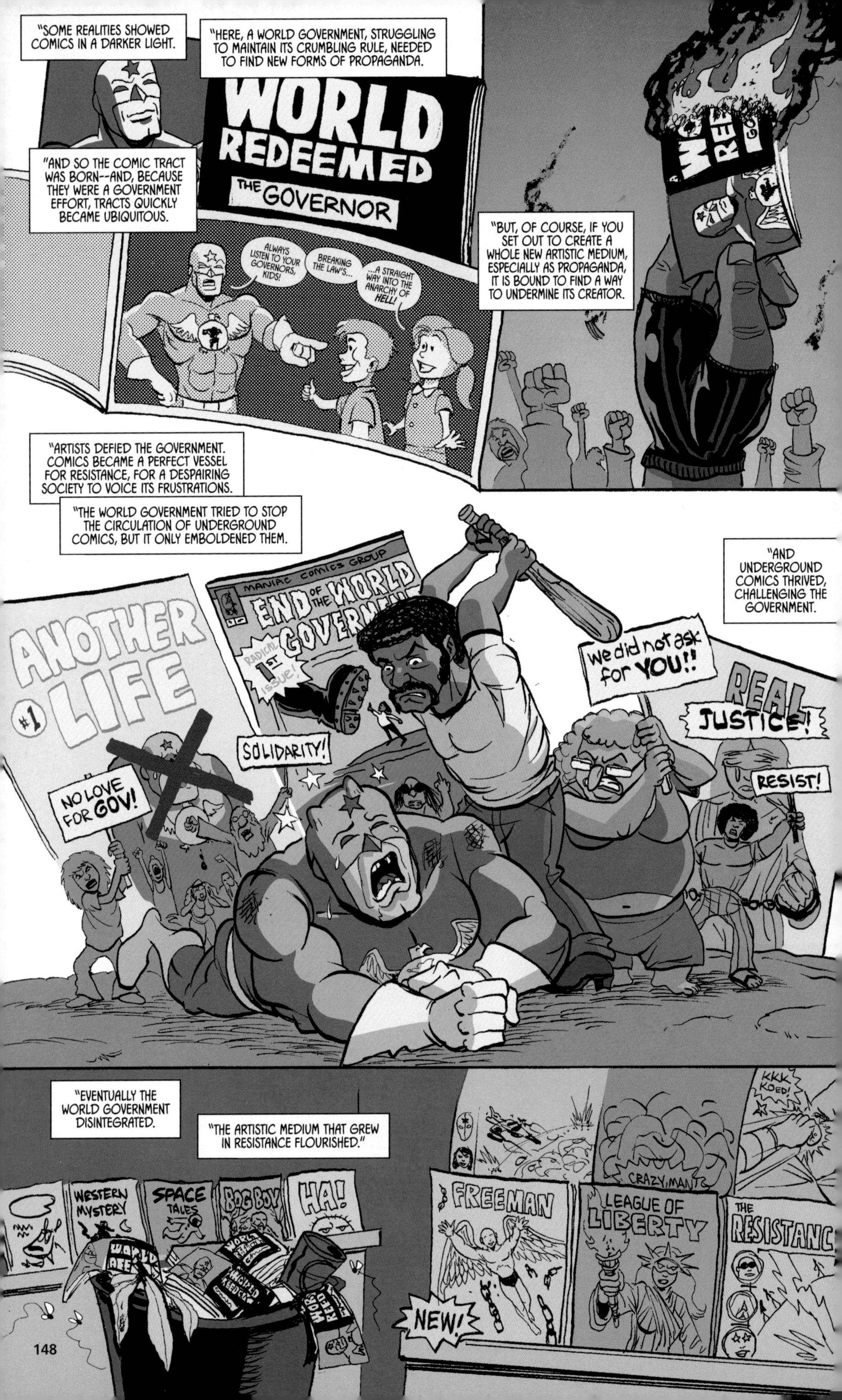
"SOME REALITIES SHOWED COMICS IN A DARKER LIGHT.
"HERE, A WORLD GOVERNMENT, STRUGGLING TO MAINTAIN ITS CRUMBLING RULE, NEEDED TO FIND NEW FORMS OF PROPAGANDA.
WORLD REDEEMED
THE GOVERNOR
"AND SO THE COMIC TRACT WAS BORN--AND, BECAUSE THEY WERE A GOVERNMENT EFFORT, TRACTS QUICKLY BECAME UBIQUITOUS.
ALWAYS LISTEN TO YOUR GOVERNORS, KIDS!
BREAKING THE LAW'S...
...A STRAIGHT WAY INTO THE ANARCHY OF HELL!
"ARTISTS DEFIED THE GOVERNMENT. COMICS BECAME A PERFECT VESSEL FOR RESISTANCE, FOR A DESPAIRING SOCIETY TO VOICE ITS FRUSTRATIONS.
"BUT, OF COURSE, IF YOU SET OUT TO CREATE A WHOLE NEW ARTISTIC MEDIUM, ESPECIALLY AS PROPAGANDA, IT IS BOUND TO FIND A WAY TO UNDERMINE ITS CREATOR.
"THE WORLD GOVERNMENT TRIED TO STOP THE CIRCULATION OF UNDERGROUND COMICS, BUT IT ONLY EMBOLDENED THEM.
ANOTHER LIFE #1
MANIAC COMICS GROUP
END OF THE WORLD GOVERN
RADICAL 1ST ISSUE!
NO LOVE FOR GOV!
SOLIDARITY!
we did not ask for YOU!!
"AND UNDERGROUND COMICS THRIVED, CHALLENGING THE GOVERNMENT.
REAL JUSTICE!
RESIST!
"EVENTUALLY THE WORLD GOVERNMENT DISINTEGRATED.
"THE ARTISTIC MEDIUM THAT GREW IN RESISTANCE FLOURISHED."
KKK KOED!
CRAZY, MAN!
WESTERN MYSTERY
SPACE TALES
BOG BOY
HA!
FREEMAN
LEAGUE OF LIBERTY
THE RESISTANC
NEW!

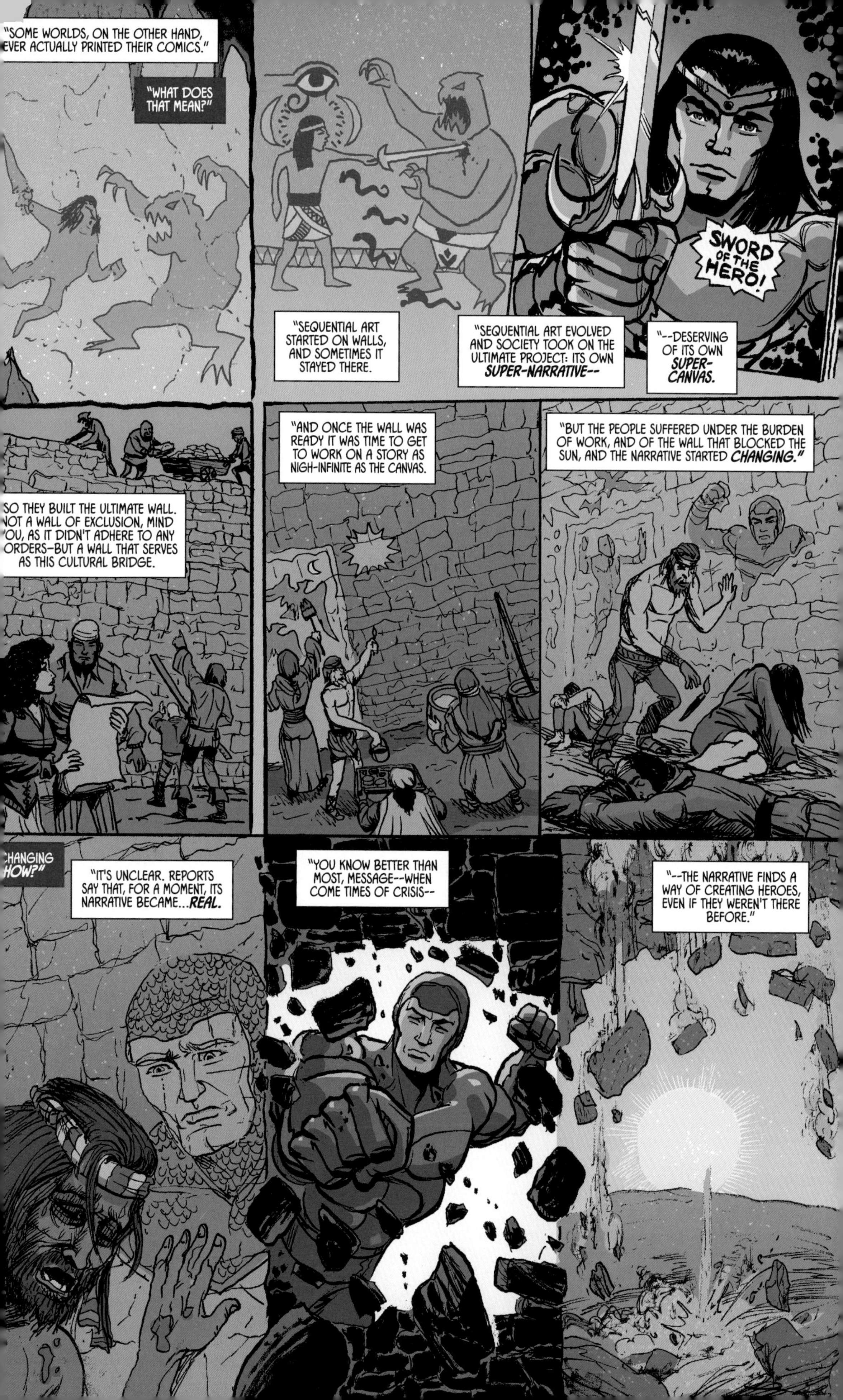
"SOME WORLDS, ON THE OTHER HAND, EVER ACTUALLY PRINTED THEIR COMICS."
"WHAT DOES THAT MEAN?"
"SEQUENTIAL ART STARTED ON WALLS, AND SOMETIMES IT STAYED THERE.
"SEQUENTIAL ART EVOLVED AND SOCIETY TOOK ON THE ULTIMATE PROJECT: ITS OWN SUPER-NARRATIVE--
SWORD OF THE HERO!
"--DESERVING OF ITS OWN SUPER-CANVAS.
SO THEY BUILT THE ULTIMATE WALL. NOT A WALL OF EXCLUSION, MIND YOU, AS IT DIDN'T ADHERE TO ANY ORDERS--BUT A WALL THAT SERVES AS THIS CULTURAL BRIDGE.
"AND ONCE THE WALL WAS READY IT WAS TIME TO GET TO WORK ON A STORY AS NIGH-INFINITE AS THE CANVAS.
"BUT THE PEOPLE SUFFERED UNDER THE BURDEN OF WORK, AND OF THE WALL THAT BLOCKED THE SUN, AND THE NARRATIVE STARTED CHANGING."
CHANGING HOW?"
"IT'S UNCLEAR. REPORTS SAY THAT, FOR A MOMENT, ITS NARRATIVE BECAME...REAL.
"YOU KNOW BETTER THAN MOST, MESSAGE--WHEN COME TIMES OF CRISIS--
"--THE NARRATIVE FINDS A WAY OF CREATING HEROES, EVEN IF THEY WEREN'T THERE BEFORE."

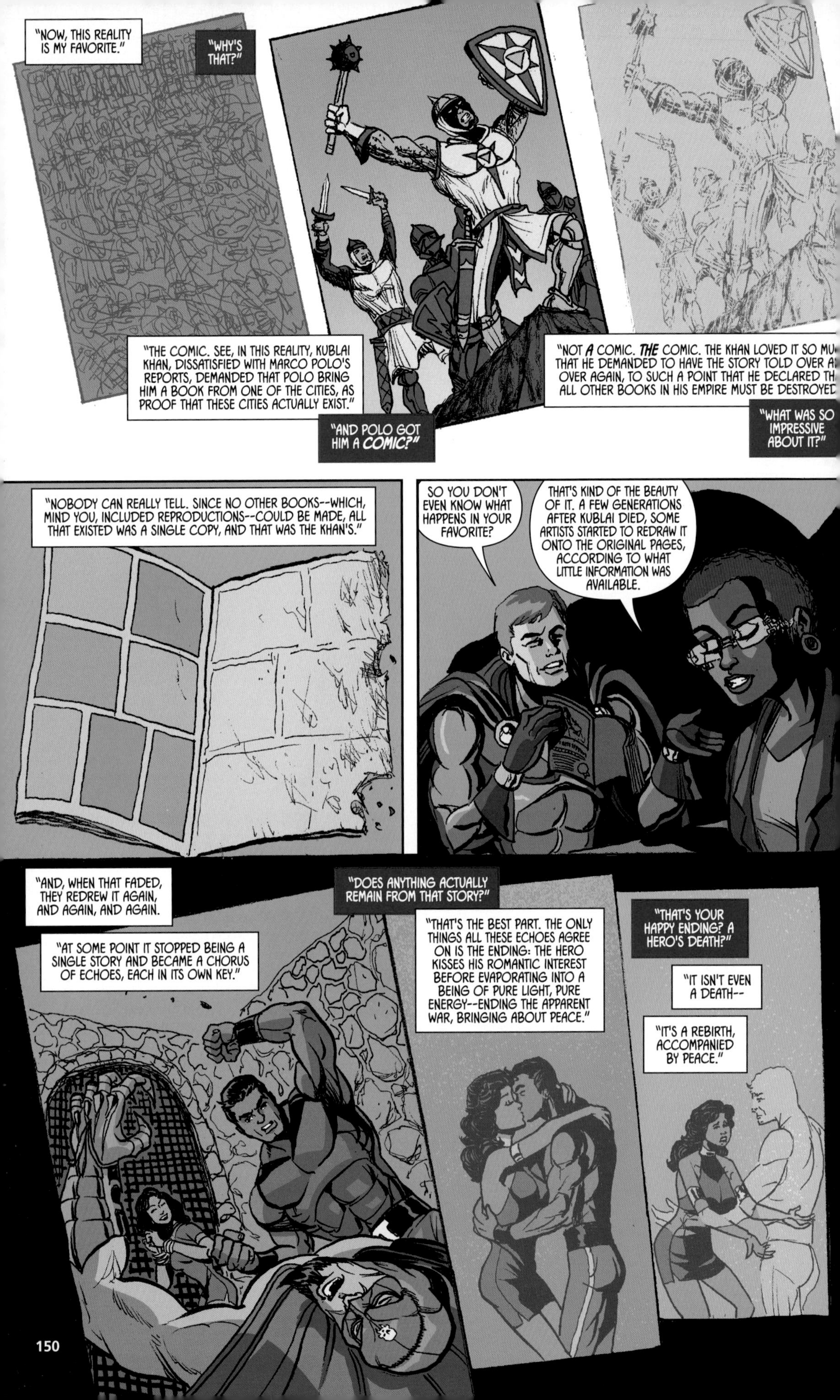
"NOW, THIS REALITY IS MY FAVORITE."
"WHY'S THAT?"
"THE COMIC. SEE, IN THIS REALITY, KUBLAI KHAN, DISSATISFIED WITH MARCO POLO'S REPORTS, DEMANDED THAT POLO BRING HIM A BOOK FROM ONE OF THE CITIES, AS PROOF THAT THESE CITIES ACTUALLY EXIST."
"AND POLO GOT HIM A COMIC?"
"NOT A COMIC. THE COMIC. THE KHAN LOVED IT SO MU THAT HE DEMANDED TO HAVE THE STORY TOLD OVER A OVER AGAIN, TO SUCH A POINT THAT HE DECLARED TH ALL OTHER BOOKS IN HIS EMPIRE MUST BE DESTROYED
"WHAT WAS SO IMPRESSIVE ABOUT IT?"
"NOBODY CAN REALLY TELL. SINCE NO OTHER BOOKS--WHICH, MIND YOU, INCLUDED REPRODUCTIONS--COULD BE MADE, ALL THAT EXISTED WAS A SINGLE COPY, AND THAT WAS THE KHAN'S."
SO YOU DON'T EVEN KNOW WHAT HAPPENS IN YOUR FAVORITE?
THAT'S KIND OF THE BEAUTY OF IT. A FEW GENERATIONS AFTER KUBLAI DIED, SOME ARTISTS STARTED TO REDRAW IT ONTO THE ORIGINAL PAGES, ACCORDING TO WHAT LITTLE INFORMATION WAS AVAILABLE.
"AND, WHEN THAT FADED, THEY REDREW IT AGAIN, AND AGAIN, AND AGAIN.
"AT SOME POINT IT STOPPED BEING A SINGLE STORY AND BECAME A CHORUS OF ECHOES, EACH IN ITS OWN KEY."
"DOES ANYTHING ACTUALLY REMAIN FROM THAT STORY?"
"THAT'S THE BEST PART. THE ONLY THINGS ALL THESE ECHOES AGREE ON IS THE ENDING: THE HERO KISSES HIS ROMANTIC INTEREST BEFORE EVAPORATING INTO A BEING OF PURE LIGHT, PURE ENERGY--ENDING THE APPARENT WAR, BRINGING ABOUT PEACE."
"THAT'S YOUR HAPPY ENDING? A HERO'S DEATH?"
"IT ISN'T EVEN A DEATH--
"IT'S A REBIRTH, ACCOMPANIED BY PEACE."

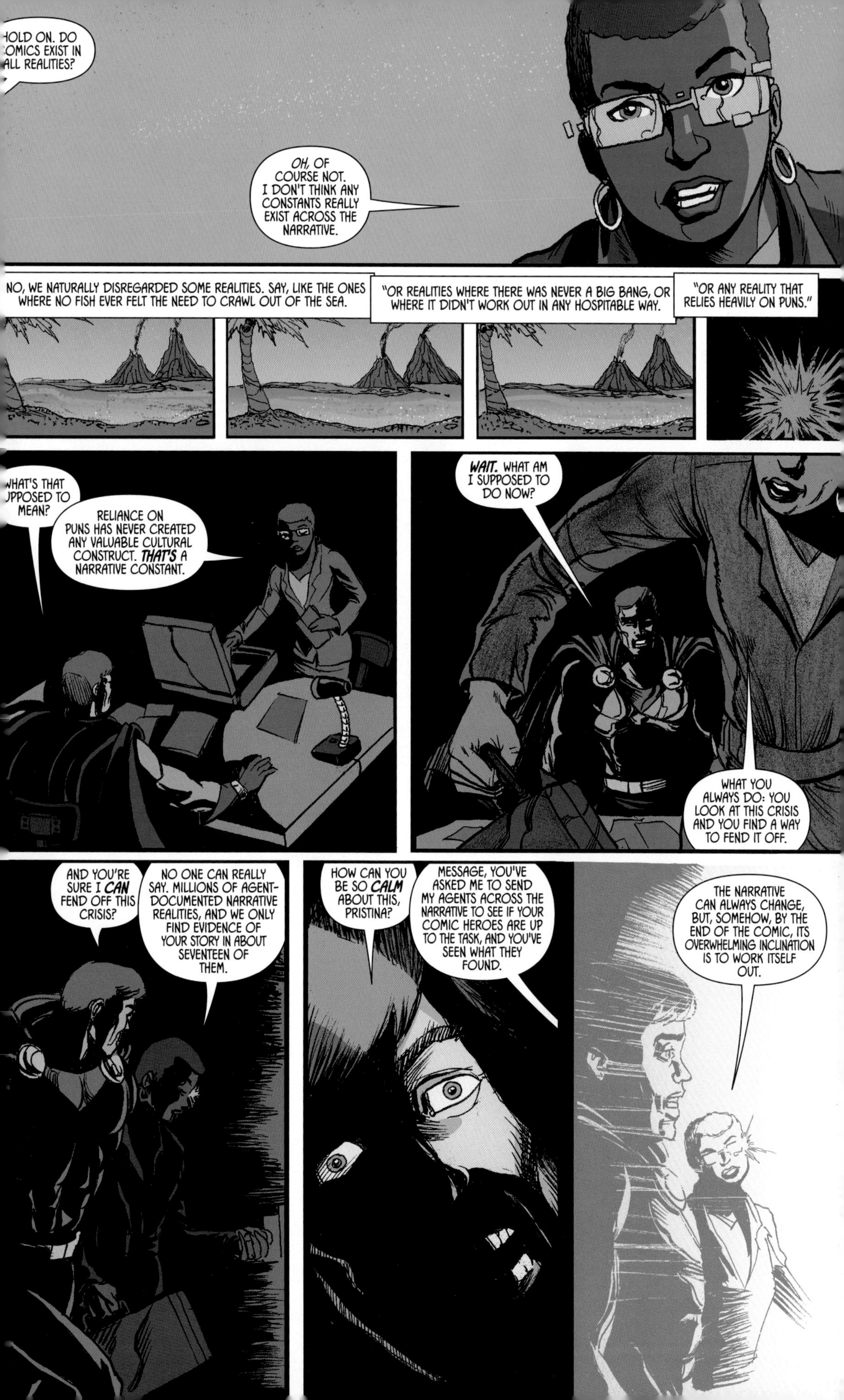
HOLD ON. DO COMICS EXIST IN ALL REALITIES?
OH, OF COURSE NOT. I DON'T THINK ANY CONSTANTS REALLY EXIST ACROSS THE NARRATIVE.
NO, WE NATURALLY DISREGARDED SOME REALITIES. SAY, LIKE THE ONES WHERE NO FISH EVER FELT THE NEED TO CRAWL OUT OF THE SEA.
"OR REALITIES WHERE THERE WAS NEVER A BIG BANG, OR WHERE IT DIDN'T WORK OUT IN ANY HOSPITABLE WAY.
"OR ANY REALITY THAT RELIES HEAVILY ON PUNS."
WHAT'S THAT SUPPOSED TO MEAN?
RELIANCE ON PUNS HAS NEVER CREATED ANY VALUABLE CULTURAL CONSTRUCT. THAT'S A NARRATIVE CONSTANT.
WAIT. WHAT AM I SUPPOSED TO DO NOW?
WHAT YOU ALWAYS DO: YOU LOOK AT THIS CRISIS AND YOU FIND A WAY TO FEND IT OFF.
AND YOU'RE SURE I CAN FEND OFF THIS CRISIS?
NO ONE CAN REALLY SAY. MILLIONS OF AGENT-DOCUMENTED NARRATIVE REALITIES, AND WE ONLY FIND EVIDENCE OF YOUR STORY IN ABOUT SEVENTEEN OF THEM.
HOW CAN YOU BE SO CALM ABOUT THIS, PRISTINA?
MESSAGE, YOU'VE ASKED ME TO SEND MY AGENTS ACROSS THE NARRATIVE TO SEE IF YOUR COMIC HEROES ARE UP TO THE TASK, AND YOU'VE SEEN WHAT THEY FOUND.
THE NARRATIVE CAN ALWAYS CHANGE, BUT, SOMEHOW, BY THE END OF THE COMIC, ITS OVERWHELMING INCLINATION IS TO WORK ITSELF OUT.

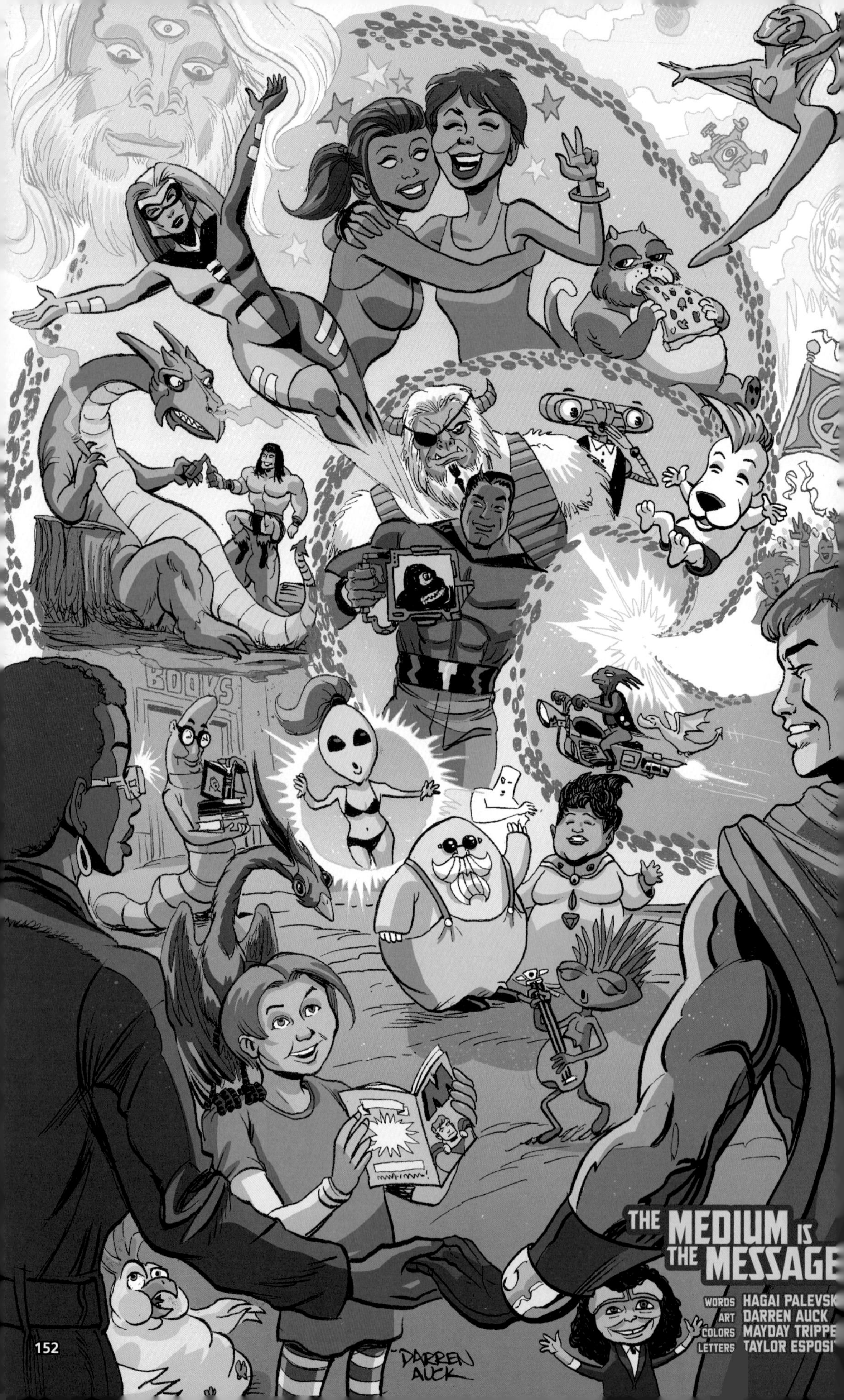
BOOKS
DARREN AUCK
THE MEDIUM IS THE MESSAGE
WORDS HAGAI PALEVSK
ART DARREN AUCK
COLORS MAYDAY TRIPPE
LETTERS TAYLOR ESPOSI

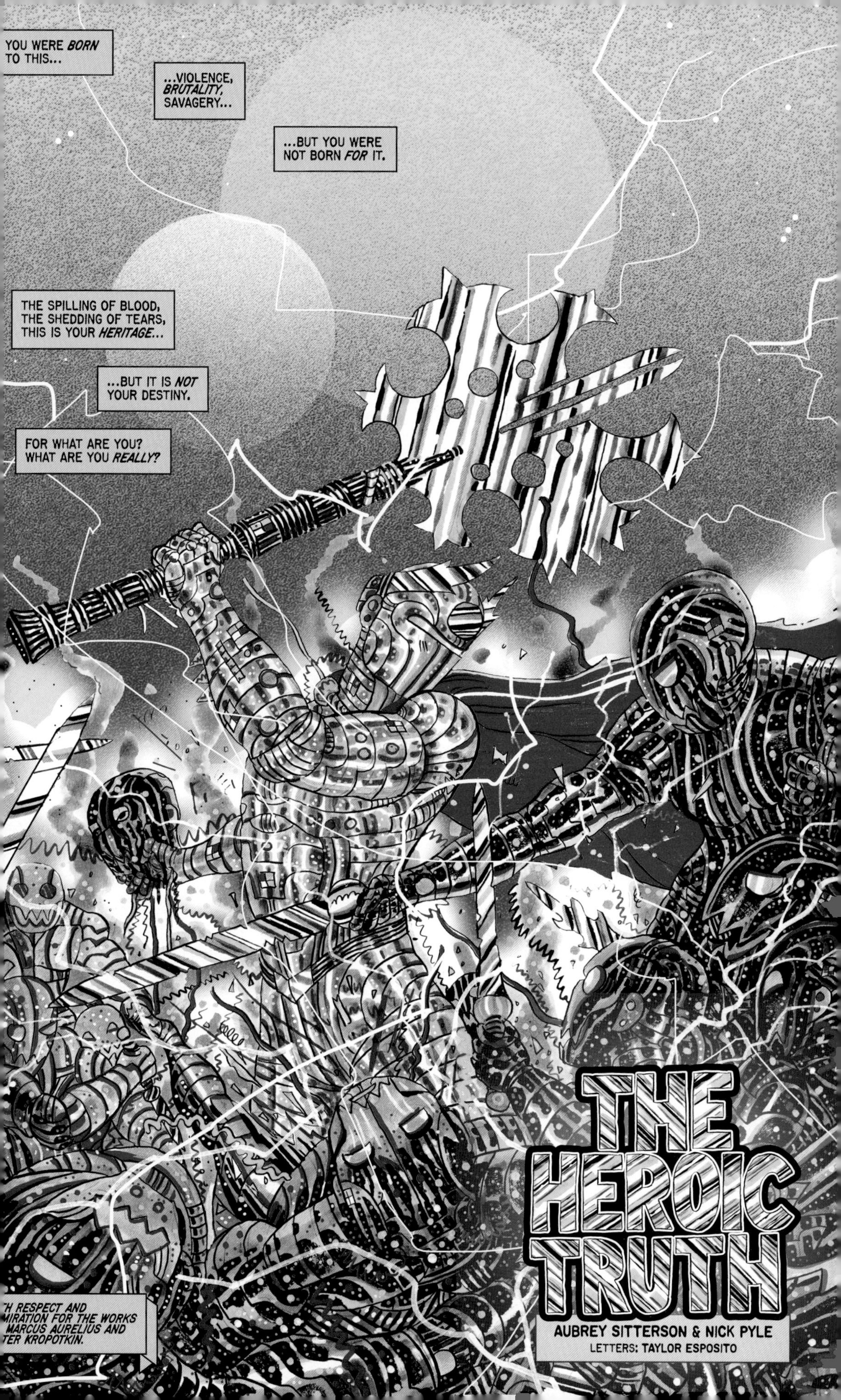
YOU WERE *BORN* TO THIS...
...VIOLENCE, *BRUTALITY,* SAVAGERY...
...BUT YOU WERE NOT BORN *FOR* IT.
THE SPILLING OF BLOOD, THE SHEDDING OF TEARS, THIS IS YOUR *HERITAGE*...
...BUT IT IS *NOT* YOUR DESTINY.
FOR WHAT ARE YOU? WHAT ARE YOU *REALLY?*
H RESPECT AND MIRATION FOR THE WORKS MARCUS AURELIUS AND TER KROPOTKIN.
THE HEROIC TRUTH
AUBREY SITTERSON & NICK PYLE
LETTERS: TAYLOR ESPOSITO

YOU ARE *BODY.* A TWISTED SKEIN OF NERVES AND MUSCLE.

DOOMED TO PAIN AND SUFFERING, AT THE WHIMS OF THE RAGING STORM.

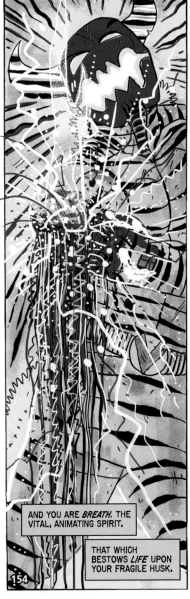

AND YOU ARE *BREATH.* THE VITAL, ANIMATING SPIRIT.

THAT WHICH BESTOWS *LIFE* UPON YOUR FRAGILE HUSK.

154

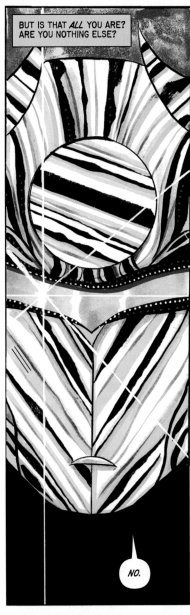

BUT IS THAT *ALL* YOU ARE? ARE YOU NOTHING ELSE?

NO.

THERE IS YET A THIRD PART: THE MIND THAT GUIDES YOU, YOUR *GOVERNING SELF.*

THE *SOVEREIGN POWER* THAT YEARNS TO FREE ITSELF FROM BONDAGE.

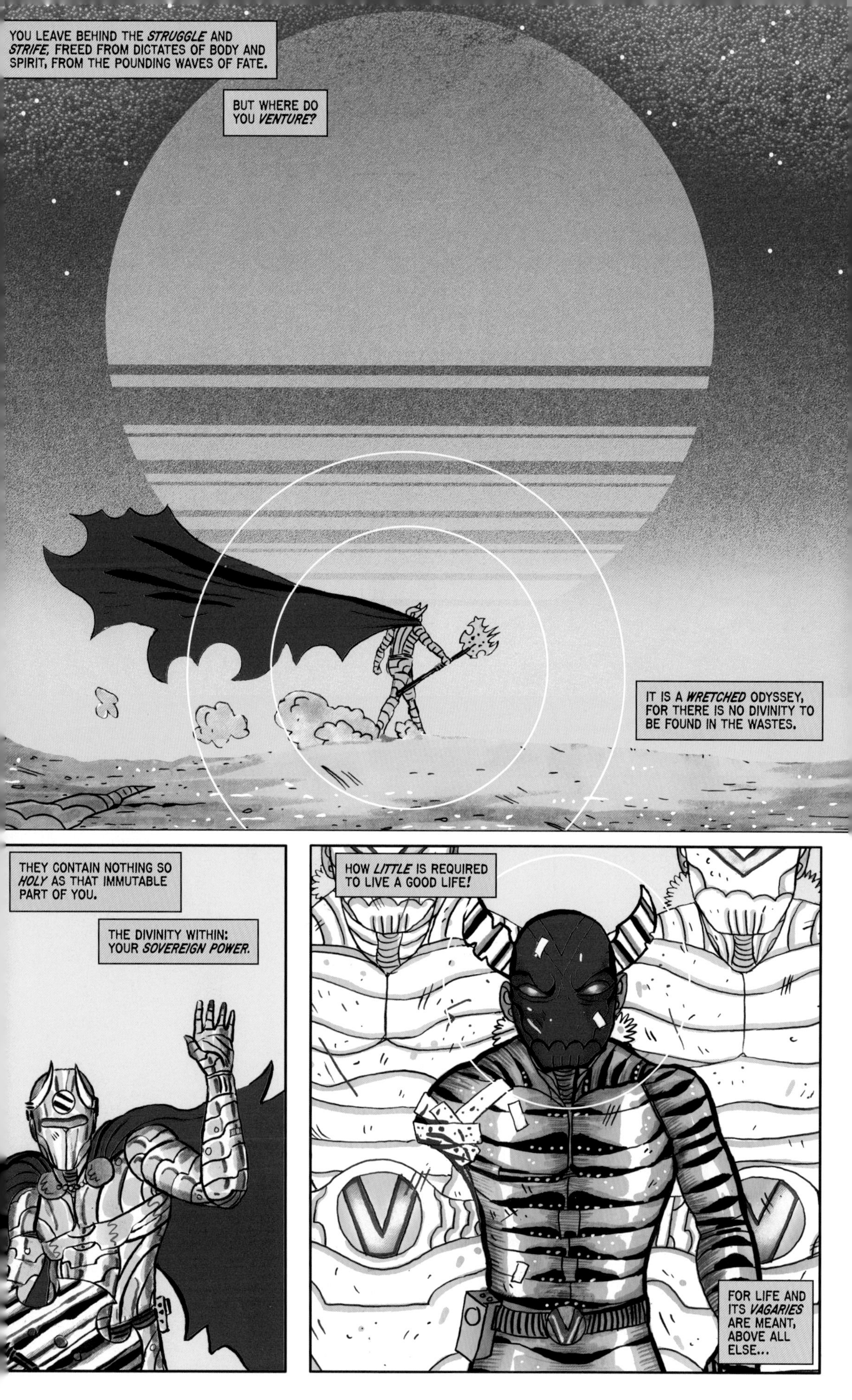
YOU LEAVE BEHIND THE STRUGGLE AND STRIFE, FREED FROM DICTATES OF BODY AND SPIRIT, FROM THE POUNDING WAVES OF FATE.
BUT WHERE DO YOU VENTURE?
IT IS A WRETCHED ODYSSEY, FOR THERE IS NO DIVINITY TO BE FOUND IN THE WASTES.
THEY CONTAIN NOTHING SO HOLY AS THAT IMMUTABLE PART OF YOU.
THE DIVINITY WITHIN: YOUR SOVEREIGN POWER.
HOW LITTLE IS REQUIRED TO LIVE A GOOD LIFE!
FOR LIFE AND ITS VAGARIES ARE MEANT, ABOVE ALL ELSE...

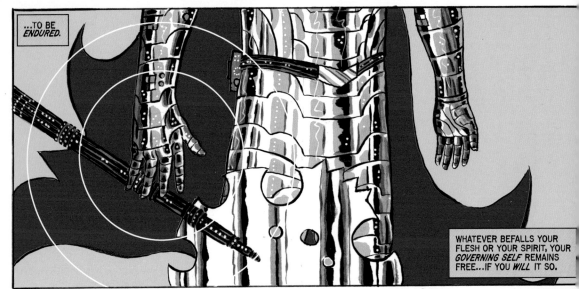

...TO BE *ENDURED*.

WHATEVER BEFALLS YOUR FLESH OR YOUR SPIRIT, YOUR *GOVERNING SELF* REMAINS FREE...IF YOU *WILL* IT SO.

WHATEVER WRONG IS DONE YOU--THEY KNOW NOT WHAT THEY DO--IT IS DONE *INVOLUNTARILY*.

AS IS THE WRONG *YOU* HAVE DONE.

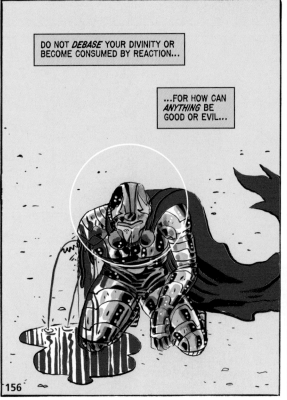

DO NOT *DEBASE* YOUR DIVINITY OR BECOME CONSUMED BY REACTION...

...FOR HOW CAN *ANYTHING* BE GOOD OR EVIL...

...WHEN IT FALLS UPON THE HEADS OF *GOOD* MEN...

...AND BAD *ALIKE?*

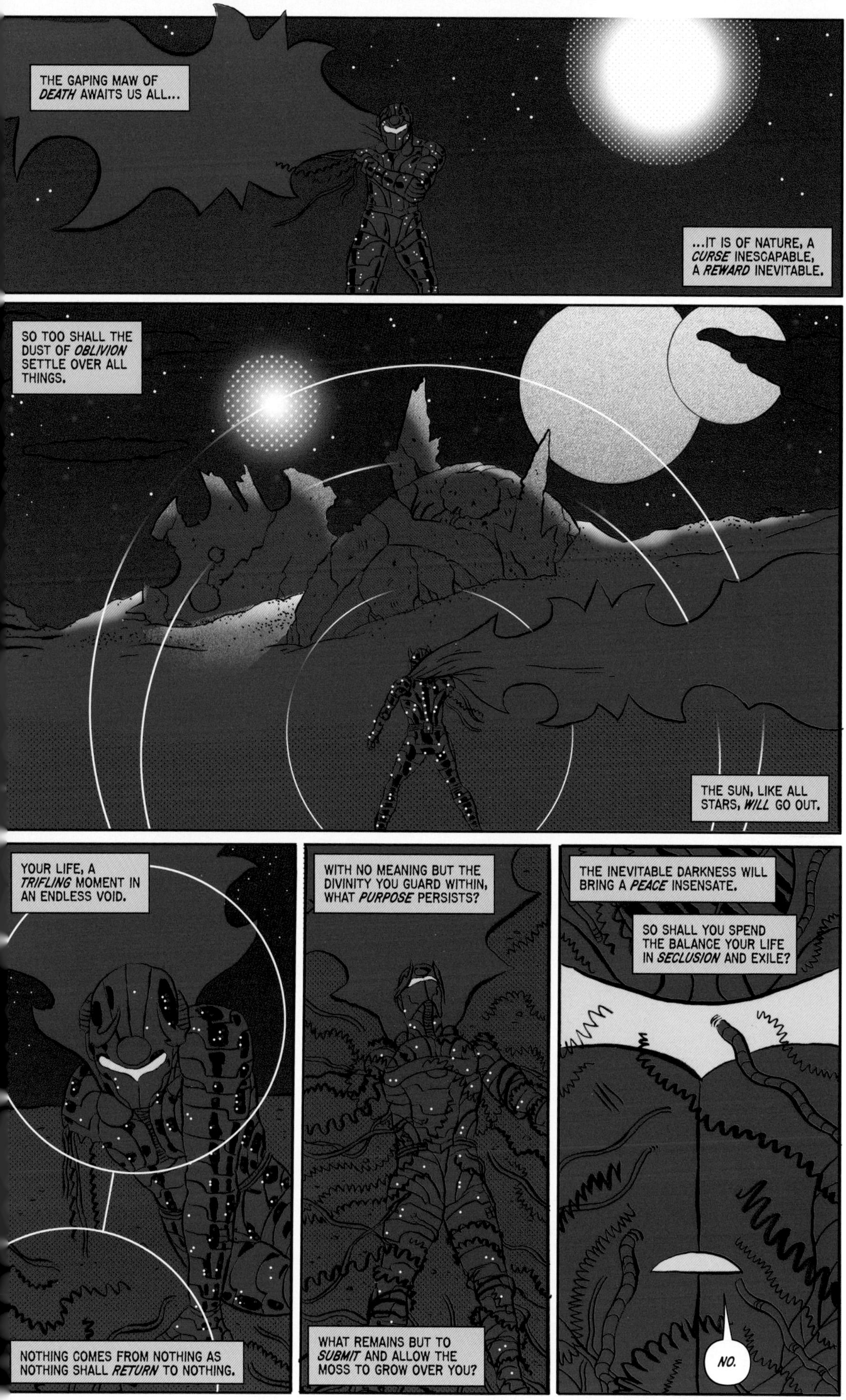
THE GAPING MAW OF *DEATH* AWAITS US ALL...
...IT IS OF NATURE, A *CURSE* INESCAPABLE, A *REWARD* INEVITABLE.
SO TOO SHALL THE DUST OF *OBLIVION* SETTLE OVER ALL THINGS.
THE SUN, LIKE ALL STARS, *WILL* GO OUT.
YOUR LIFE, A *TRIFLING* MOMENT IN AN ENDLESS VOID.
NOTHING COMES FROM NOTHING AS NOTHING SHALL *RETURN* TO NOTHING.
WITH NO MEANING BUT THE DIVINITY YOU GUARD WITHIN, WHAT *PURPOSE* PERSISTS?
WHAT REMAINS BUT TO *SUBMIT* AND ALLOW THE MOSS TO GROW OVER YOU?
THE INEVITABLE DARKNESS WILL BRING A *PEACE* INSENSATE.
SO SHALL YOU SPEND THE BALANCE YOUR LIFE IN *SECLUSION* AND EXILE?
NO.

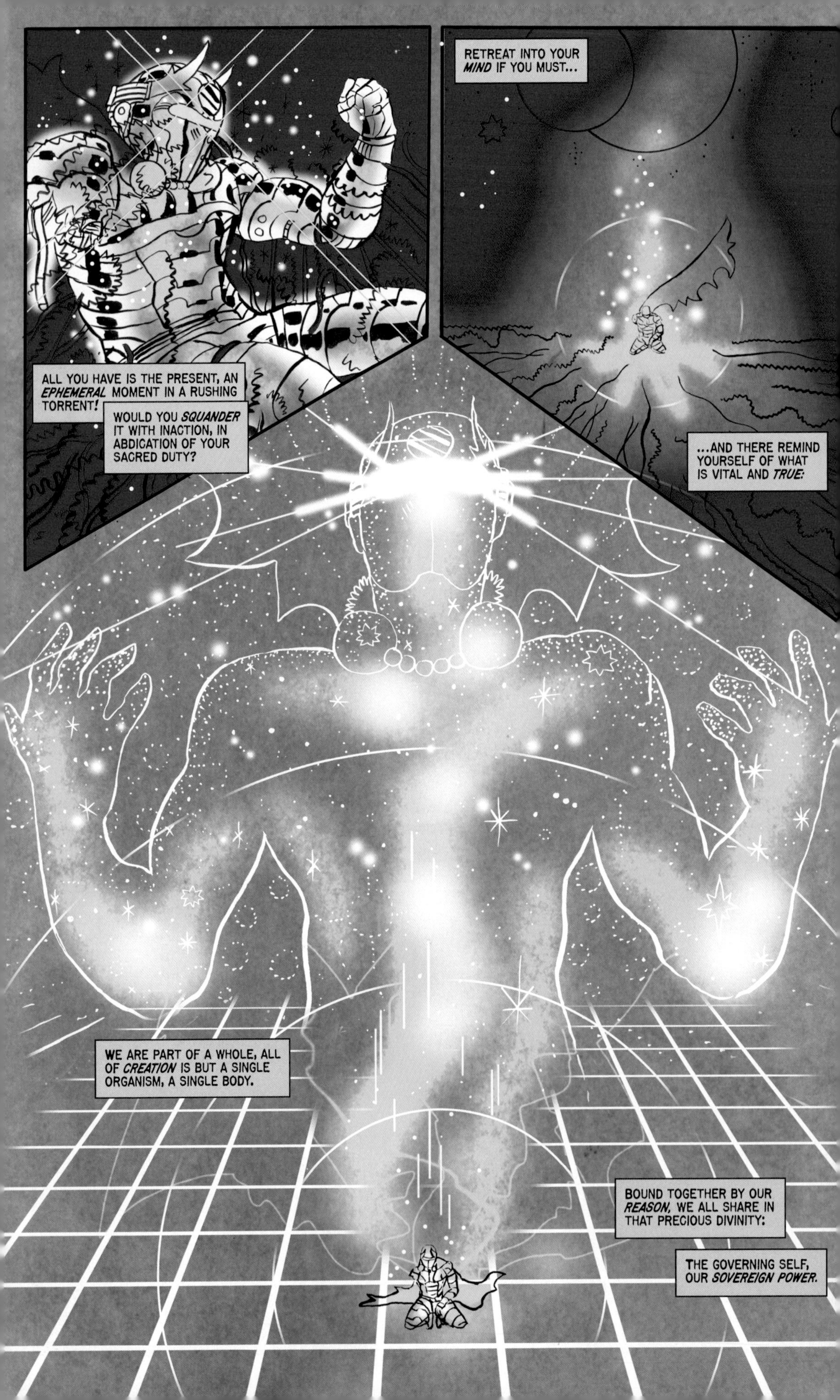
ALL YOU HAVE IS THE PRESENT, AN *EPHEMERAL* MOMENT IN A RUSHING TORRENT!
WOULD YOU *SQUANDER* IT WITH INACTION, IN ABDICATION OF YOUR SACRED DUTY?
RETREAT INTO YOUR *MIND* IF YOU MUST...
...AND THERE REMIND YOURSELF OF WHAT IS VITAL AND *TRUE:*
WE ARE PART OF A WHOLE, ALL OF *CREATION* IS BUT A SINGLE ORGANISM, A SINGLE BODY.
BOUND TOGETHER BY OUR *REASON,* WE ALL SHARE IN THAT PRECIOUS DIVINITY:
THE GOVERNING SELF, OUR *SOVEREIGN POWER.*

YOU HAVE BEEN *LIED* TO. TOLD THAT THE NATURAL ORDER IS STRUGGLE AND STRIFE.

THAT ALL GOOD THINGS COME FROM *COMPETITION*.

BUT IS IT NATURAL FOR THE BODY TO *WAGE WAR* AGAINST ITSELF?

ANGER, VIOLENCE, HATRED...THESE ARE *TUMORS* OF OUR SHARED BODY, A DESECRATION OF OUR BLESSED DESTINY.

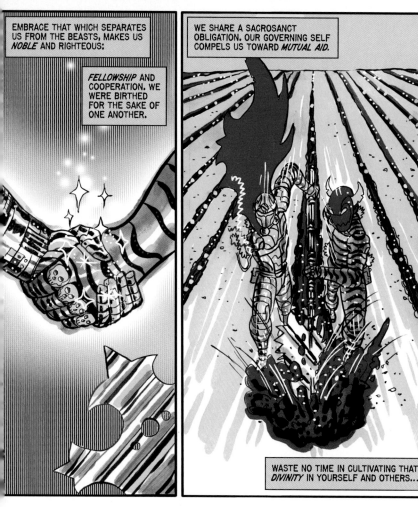

EMBRACE THAT WHICH SEPARATES US FROM THE BEASTS, MAKES US *NOBLE* AND RIGHTEOUS:

FELLOWSHIP AND COOPERATION. WE WERE BIRTHED FOR THE SAKE OF ONE ANOTHER.

WE SHARE A SACROSANCT OBLIGATION. OUR GOVERNING SELF COMPELS US TOWARD *MUTUAL AID*.

WASTE NO TIME IN CULTIVATING THAT *DIVINITY* IN YOURSELF AND OTHERS...

...FOR IT IS THE *PRECIOUS* SEED OF OUR GREATEST ACHIEVEMENTS.

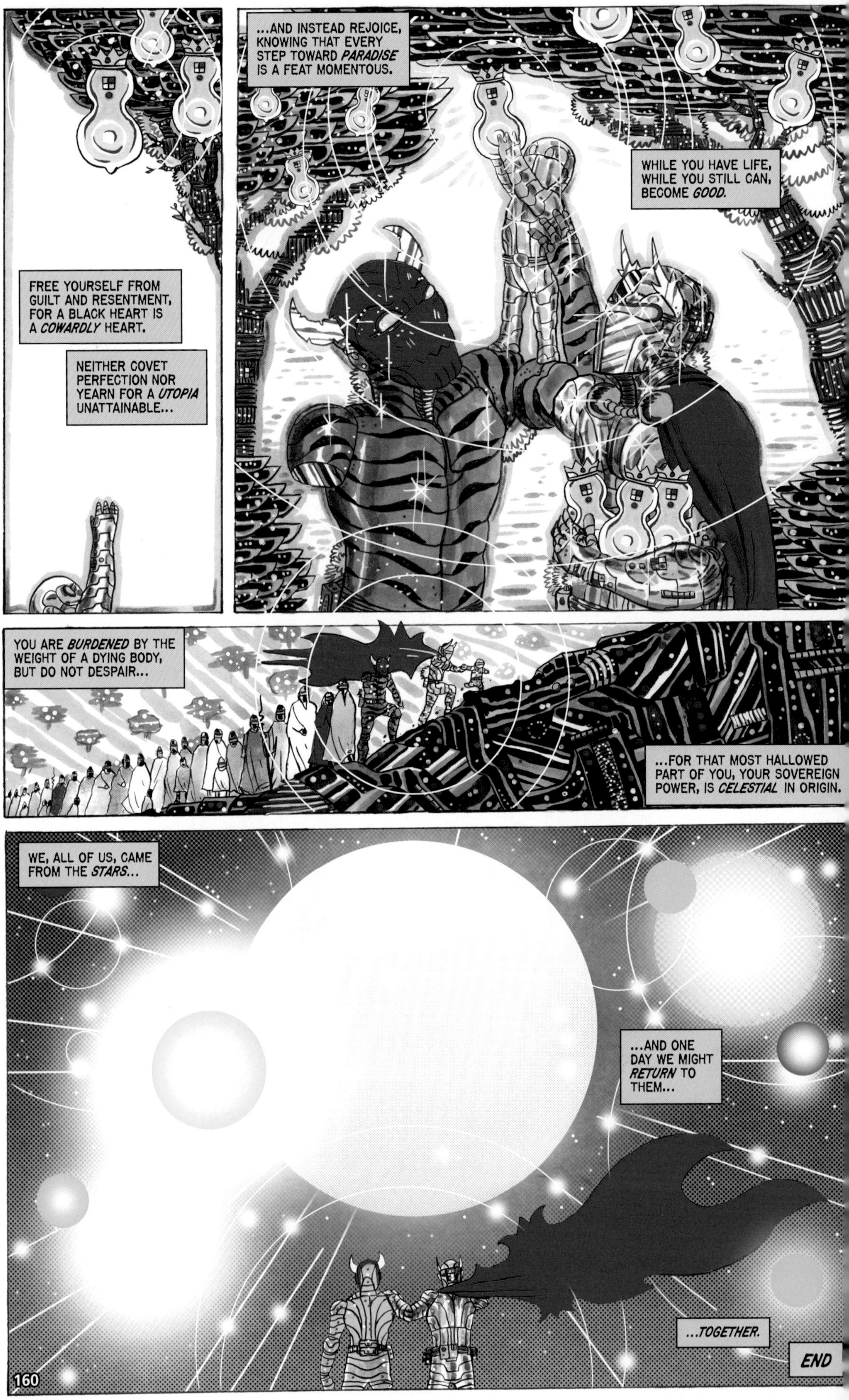
FREE YOURSELF FROM GUILT AND RESENTMENT, FOR A BLACK HEART IS A *COWARDLY* HEART.
NEITHER COVET PERFECTION NOR YEARN FOR A *UTOPIA* UNATTAINABLE...
...AND INSTEAD REJOICE, KNOWING THAT EVERY STEP TOWARD *PARADISE* IS A FEAT MOMENTOUS.
WHILE YOU HAVE LIFE, WHILE YOU STILL CAN, BECOME *GOOD.*
YOU ARE *BURDENED* BY THE WEIGHT OF A DYING BODY, BUT DO NOT DESPAIR...
...FOR THAT MOST HALLOWED PART OF YOU, YOUR SOVEREIGN POWER, IS *CELESTIAL* IN ORIGIN.
WE, ALL OF US, CAME FROM THE *STARS*...
...AND ONE DAY WE MIGHT *RETURN* TO THEM...
...TOGETHER.
END

THE TECHNICIAN

WRITTEN BY: MARIO CANDELARIA
ART BY: SHAWN DALEY
LETTERS BY: MICAH MYERS

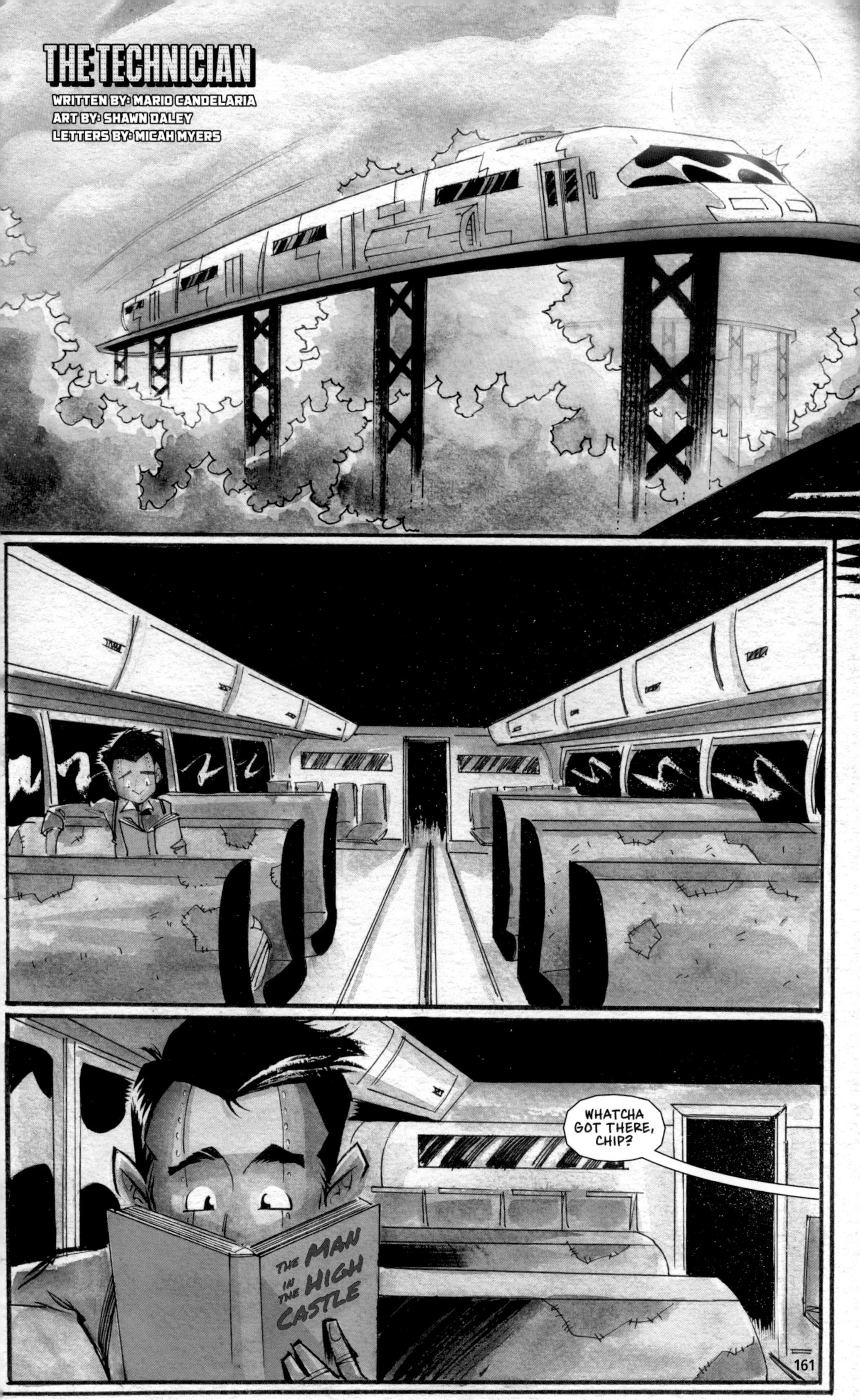
WHATCHA GOT THERE, CHIP?
THE MAN IN THE HIGH CASTLE

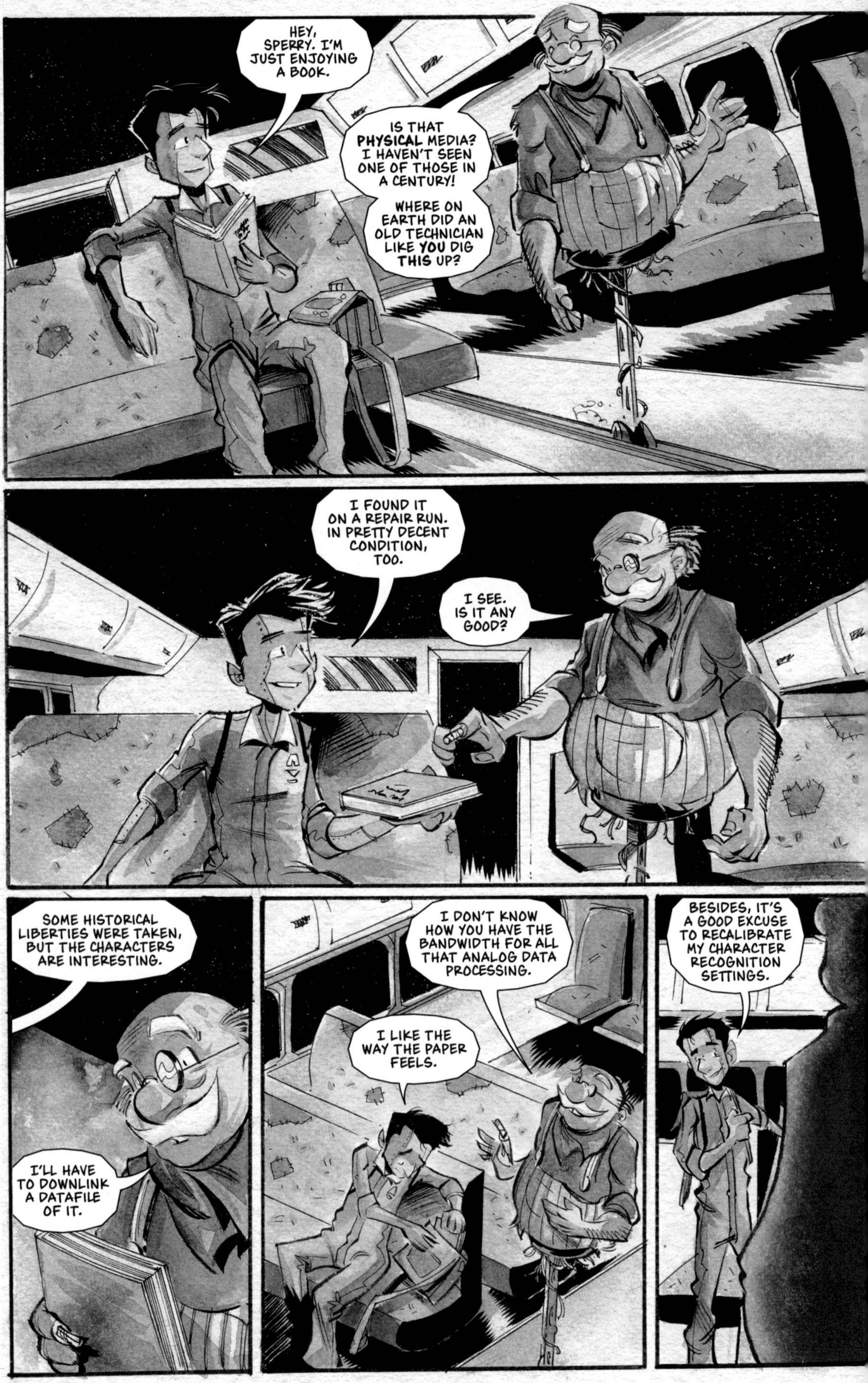
HEY, SPERRY. I'M JUST ENJOYING A BOOK.
IS THAT PHYSICAL MEDIA? I HAVEN'T SEEN ONE OF THOSE IN A CENTURY!
WHERE ON EARTH DID AN OLD TECHNICIAN LIKE YOU DIG THIS UP?
I FOUND IT ON A REPAIR RUN. IN PRETTY DECENT CONDITION, TOO.
I SEE. IS IT ANY GOOD?
SOME HISTORICAL LIBERTIES WERE TAKEN, BUT THE CHARACTERS ARE INTERESTING.
I'LL HAVE TO DOWNLINK A DATAFILE OF IT.
I DON'T KNOW HOW YOU HAVE THE BANDWIDTH FOR ALL THAT ANALOG DATA PROCESSING.
I LIKE THE WAY THE PAPER FEELS.
BESIDES, IT'S A GOOD EXCUSE TO RECALIBRATE MY CHARACTER RECOGNITION SETTINGS.

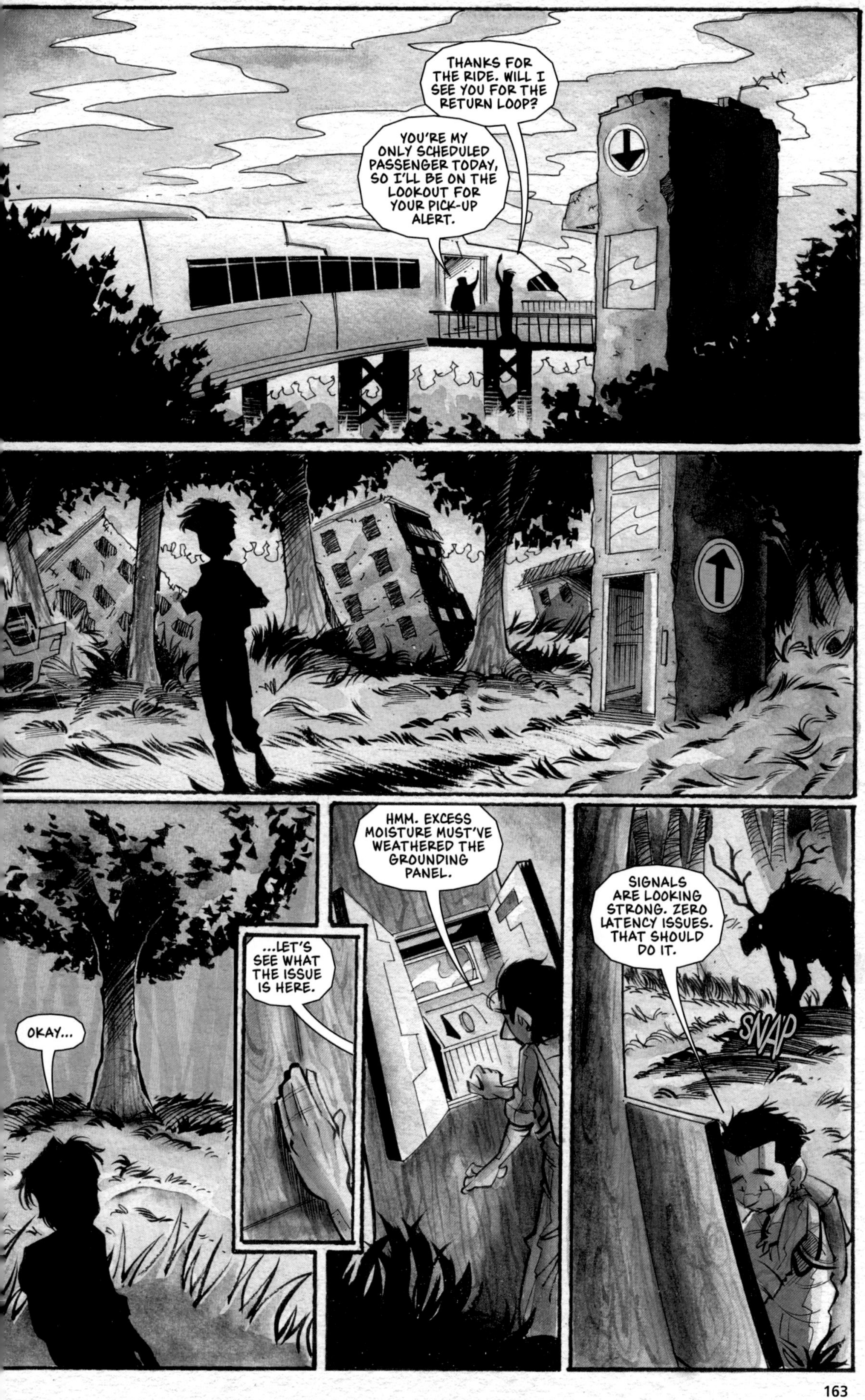
THANKS FOR THE RIDE. WILL I SEE YOU FOR THE RETURN LOOP?
YOU'RE MY ONLY SCHEDULED PASSENGER TODAY, SO I'LL BE ON THE LOOKOUT FOR YOUR PICK-UP ALERT.
OKAY...
HMM. EXCESS MOISTURE MUST'VE WEATHERED THE GROUNDING PANEL.
...LET'S SEE WHAT THE ISSUE IS HERE.
SIGNALS ARE LOOKING STRONG. ZERO LATENCY ISSUES. THAT SHOULD DO IT.
SNAP

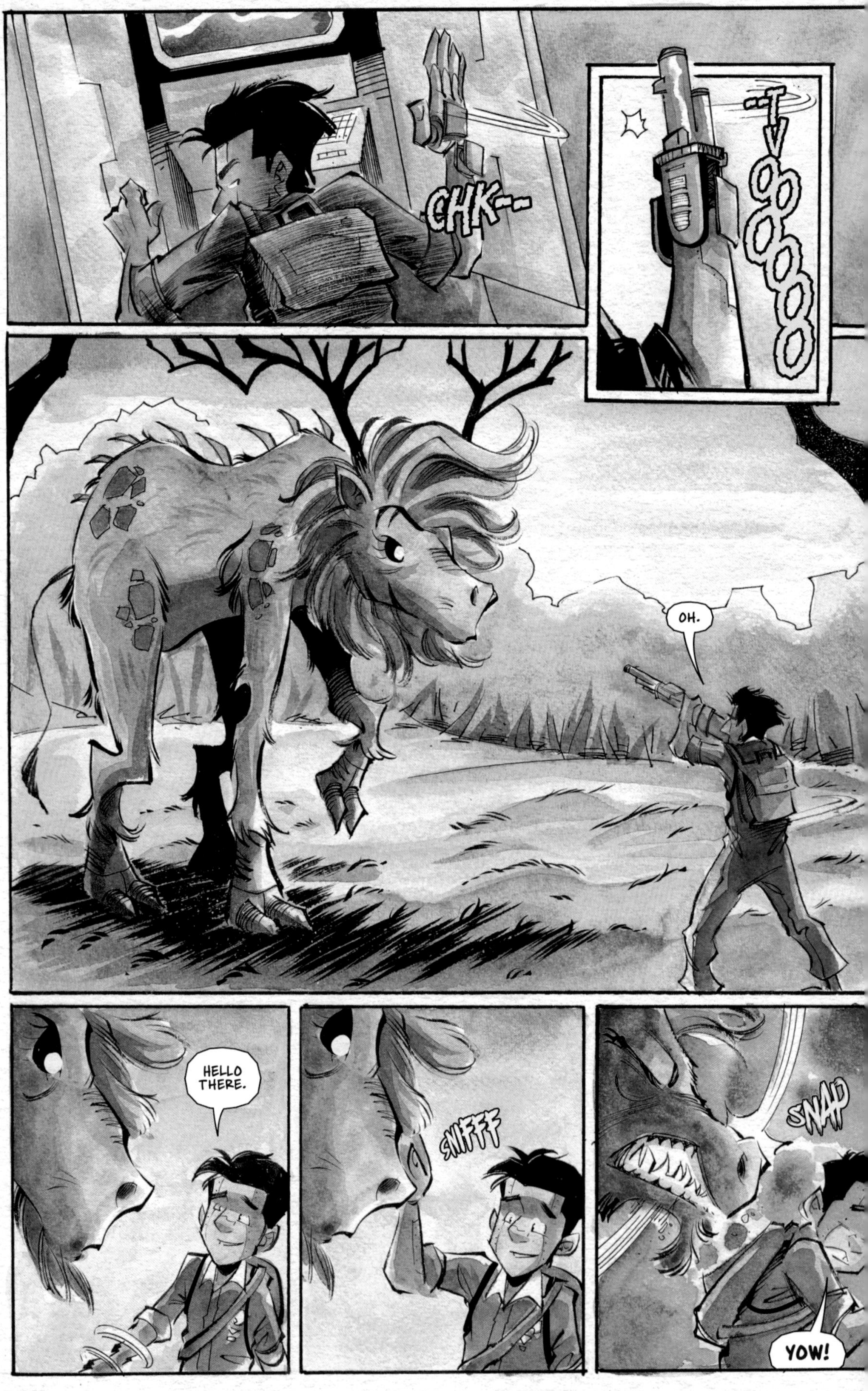
CHK--
--TVOOOOO
OH.
HELLO THERE.
SNIFFF
SNAP
YOW!

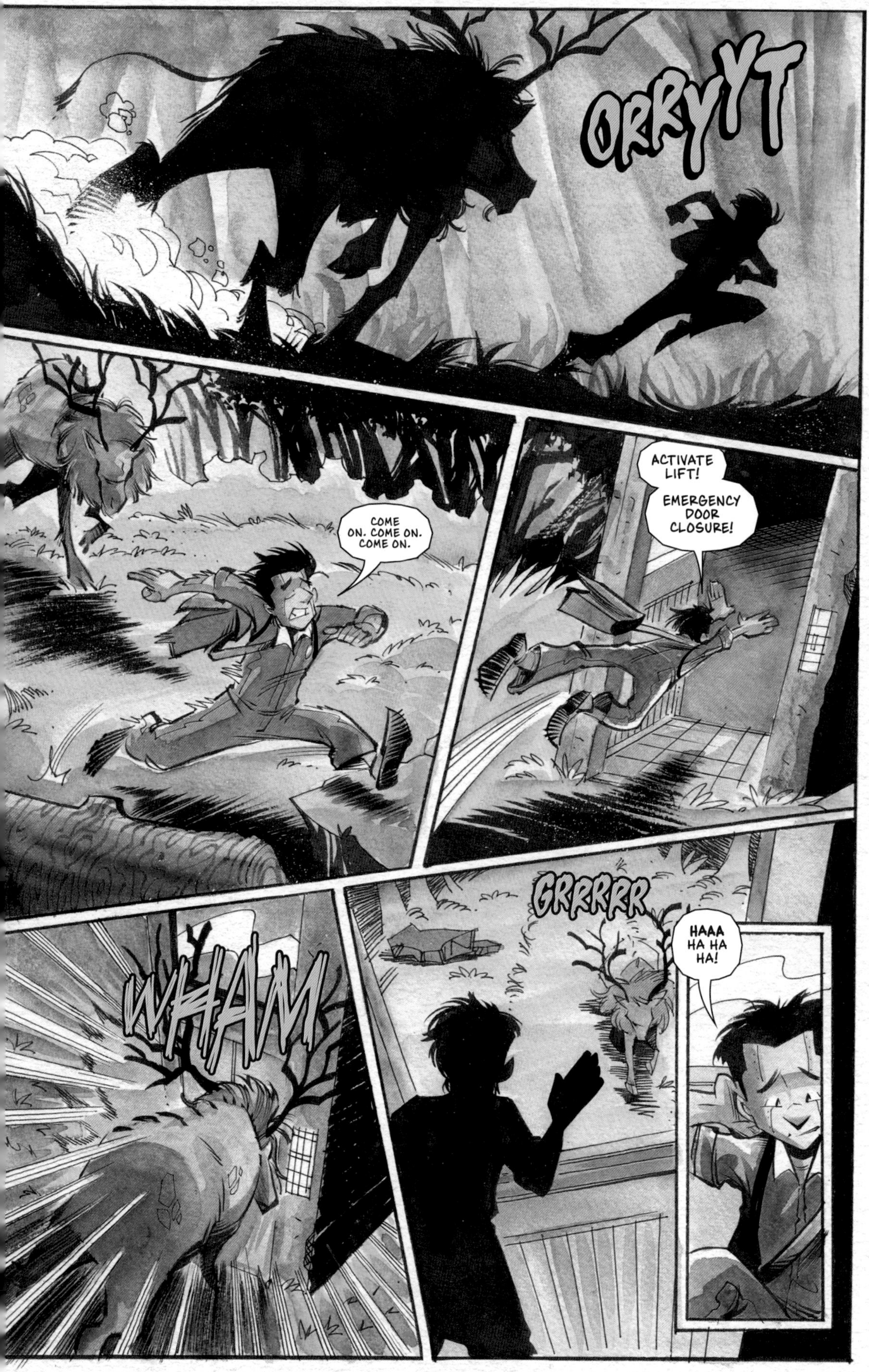
ORRYYT
COME ON. COME ON. COME ON.
ACTIVATE LIFT!
EMERGENCY DOOR CLOSURE!
WHAM
GRRRRR
HAAA HA HA HA!

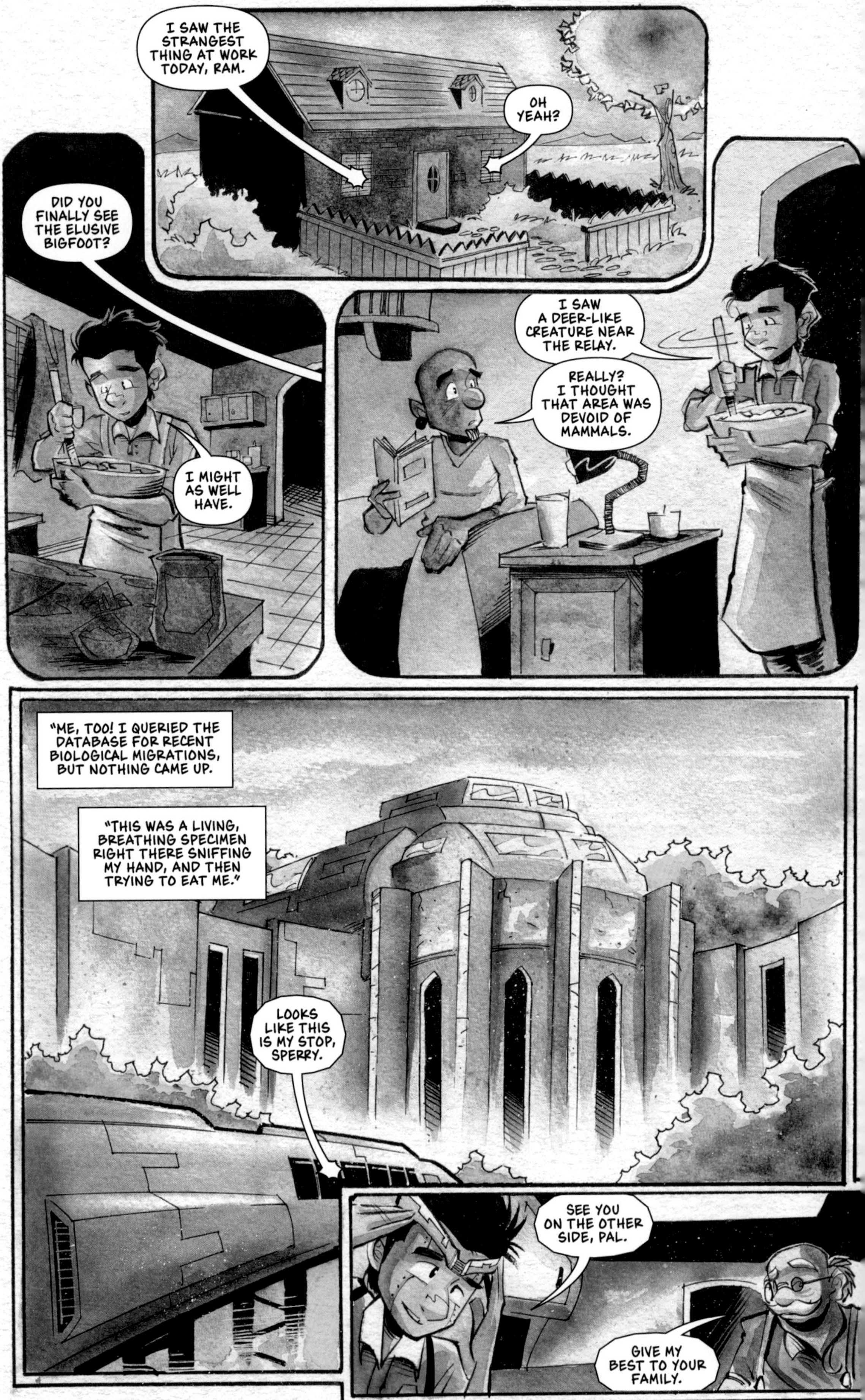
I SAW THE STRANGEST THING AT WORK TODAY, RAM.
OH YEAH?
DID YOU FINALLY SEE THE ELUSIVE BIGFOOT?
I MIGHT AS WELL HAVE.
I SAW A DEER-LIKE CREATURE NEAR THE RELAY.
REALLY? I THOUGHT THAT AREA WAS DEVOID OF MAMMALS.
"ME, TOO! I QUERIED THE DATABASE FOR RECENT BIOLOGICAL MIGRATIONS, BUT NOTHING CAME UP.
"THIS WAS A LIVING, BREATHING SPECIMEN RIGHT THERE SNIFFING MY HAND, AND THEN TRYING TO EAT ME."
LOOKS LIKE THIS IS MY STOP, SPERRY.
SEE YOU ON THE OTHER SIDE, PAL.
GIVE MY BEST TO YOUR FAMILY.

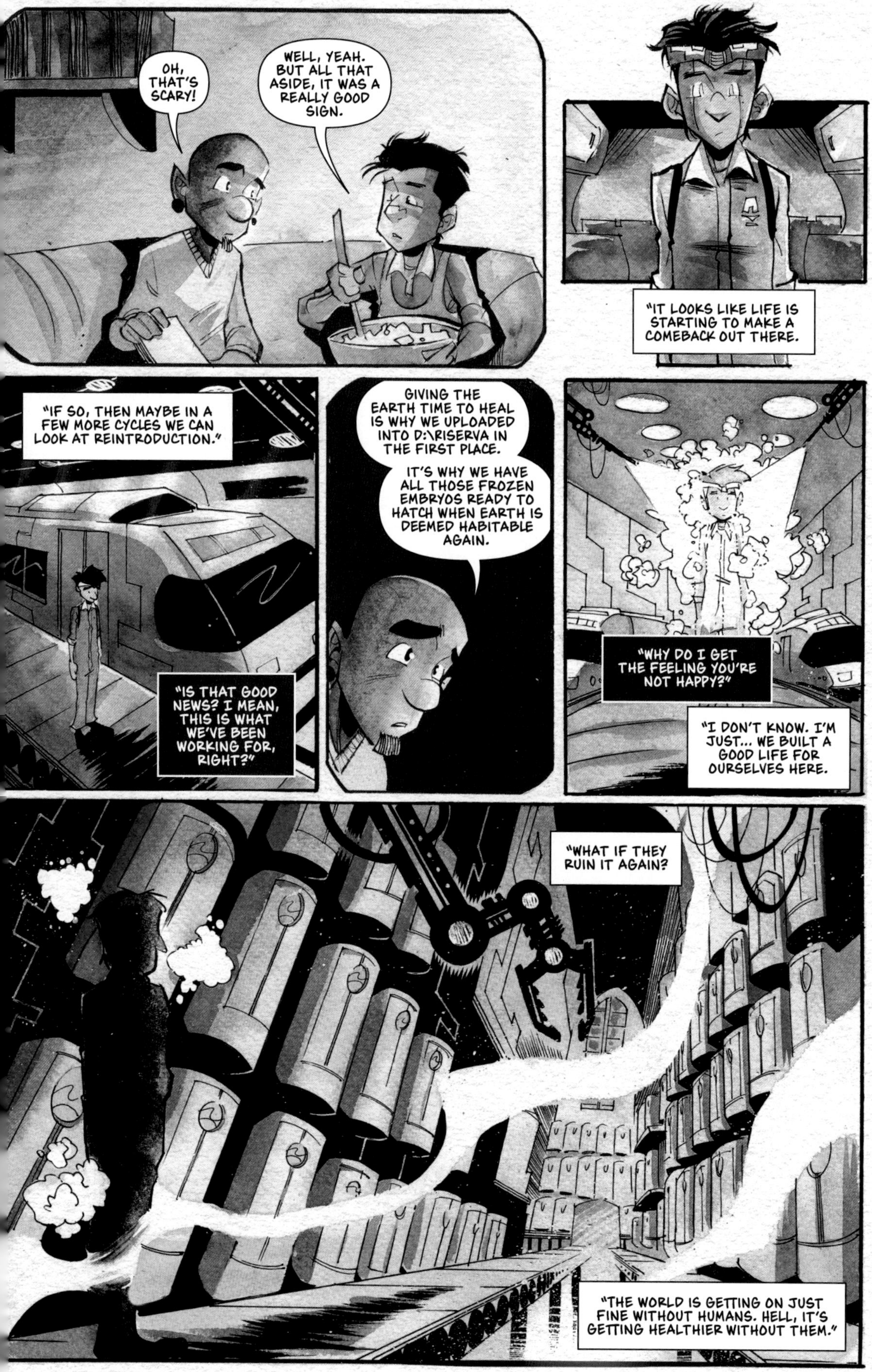
OH, THAT'S SCARY!
WELL, YEAH. BUT ALL THAT ASIDE, IT WAS A REALLY GOOD SIGN.
"IT LOOKS LIKE LIFE IS STARTING TO MAKE A COMEBACK OUT THERE.
"IF SO, THEN MAYBE IN A FEW MORE CYCLES WE CAN LOOK AT REINTRODUCTION."
"IS THAT GOOD NEWS? I MEAN, THIS IS WHAT WE'VE BEEN WORKING FOR, RIGHT?"
GIVING THE EARTH TIME TO HEAL IS WHY WE UPLOADED INTO D:\RISERVA IN THE FIRST PLACE.
IT'S WHY WE HAVE ALL THOSE FROZEN EMBRYOS READY TO HATCH WHEN EARTH IS DEEMED HABITABLE AGAIN.
"WHY DO I GET THE FEELING YOU'RE NOT HAPPY?"
"I DON'T KNOW. I'M JUST... WE BUILT A GOOD LIFE FOR OURSELVES HERE.
"WHAT IF THEY RUIN IT AGAIN?
"THE WORLD IS GETTING ON JUST FINE WITHOUT HUMANS. HELL, IT'S GETTING HEALTHIER WITHOUT THEM."

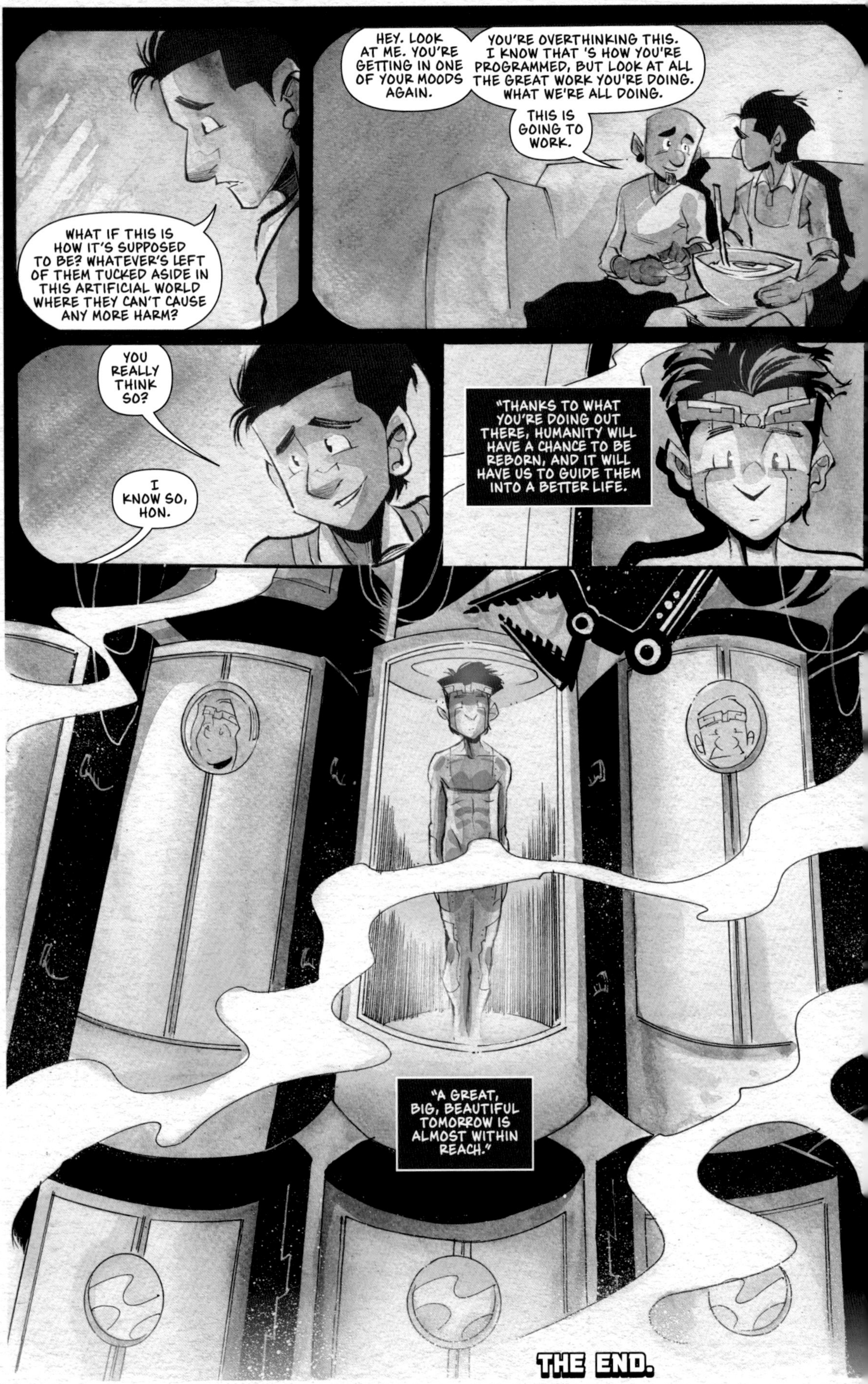
WHAT IF THIS IS HOW IT'S SUPPOSED TO BE? WHATEVER'S LEFT OF THEM TUCKED ASIDE IN THIS ARTIFICIAL WORLD WHERE THEY CAN'T CAUSE ANY MORE HARM?
HEY. LOOK AT ME. YOU'RE GETTING IN ONE OF YOUR MOODS AGAIN.
YOU'RE OVERTHINKING THIS. I KNOW THAT 'S HOW YOU'RE PROGRAMMED, BUT LOOK AT ALL THE GREAT WORK YOU'RE DOING. WHAT WE'RE ALL DOING.
THIS IS GOING TO WORK.
YOU REALLY THINK SO?
I KNOW SO, HON.
"THANKS TO WHAT YOU'RE DOING OUT THERE, HUMANITY WILL HAVE A CHANCE TO BE REBORN, AND IT WILL HAVE US TO GUIDE THEM INTO A BETTER LIFE.
"A GREAT, BIG, BEAUTIFUL TOMORROW IS ALMOST WITHIN REACH."
THE END.

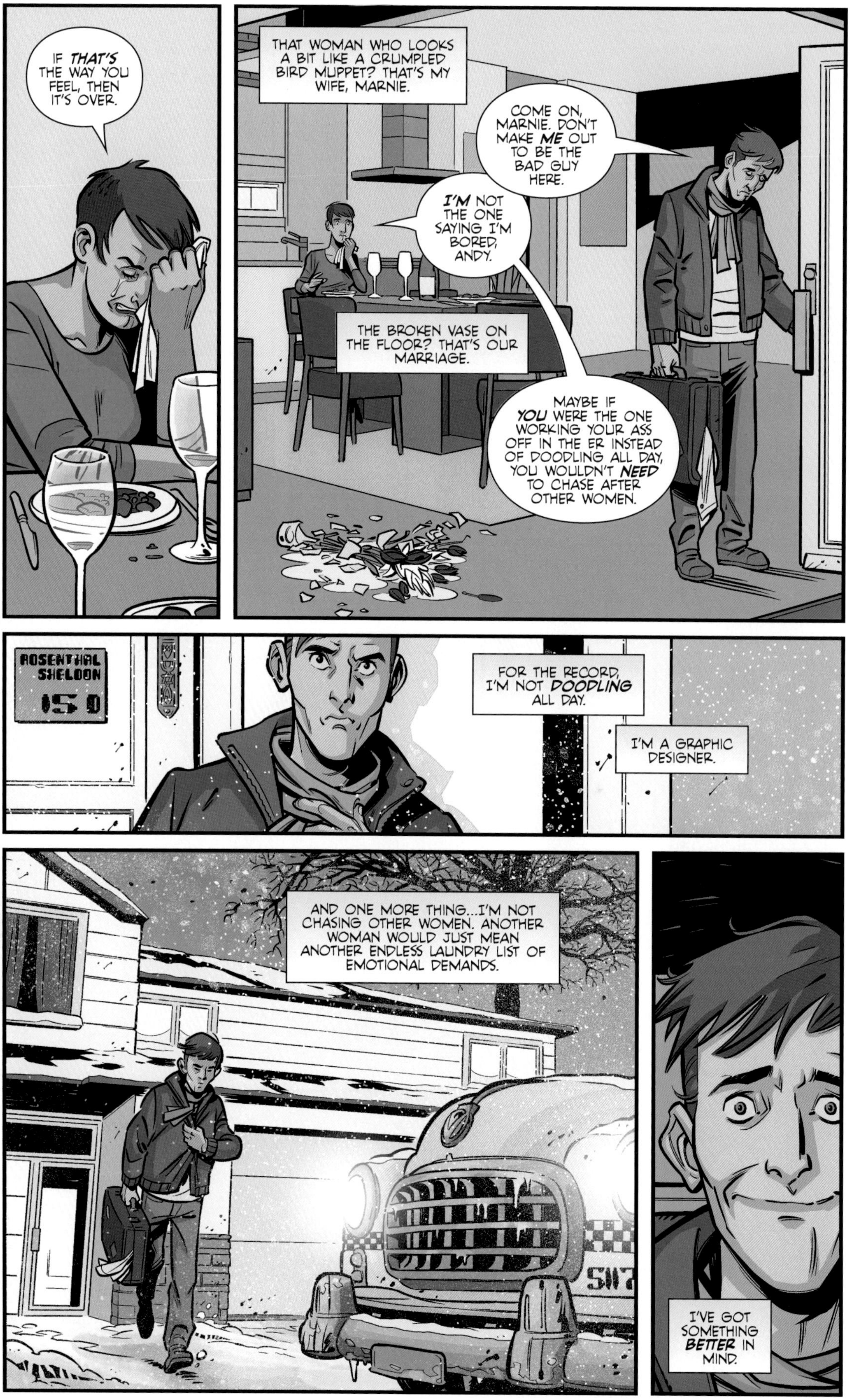
IF *THAT'S* THE WAY YOU FEEL, THEN IT'S OVER.
THAT WOMAN WHO LOOKS A BIT LIKE A CRUMPLED BIRD MUPPET? THAT'S MY WIFE, MARNIE.
COME ON, MARNIE. DON'T MAKE *ME* OUT TO BE THE BAD GUY HERE.
I'M NOT THE ONE SAYING I'M BORED, ANDY.
THE BROKEN VASE ON THE FLOOR? THAT'S OUR MARRIAGE.
MAYBE IF *YOU* WERE THE ONE WORKING YOUR ASS OFF IN THE ER INSTEAD OF DOODLING ALL DAY, YOU WOULDN'T *NEED* TO CHASE AFTER OTHER WOMEN.
ROSENTHAL SHELDON
150
FOR THE RECORD, I'M NOT *DOODLING* ALL DAY.
I'M A GRAPHIC DESIGNER.
AND ONE MORE THING...I'M NOT CHASING OTHER WOMEN. ANOTHER WOMAN WOULD JUST MEAN ANOTHER ENDLESS LAUNDRY LIST OF EMOTIONAL DEMANDS.
I'VE GOT SOMETHING *BETTER* IN MIND.

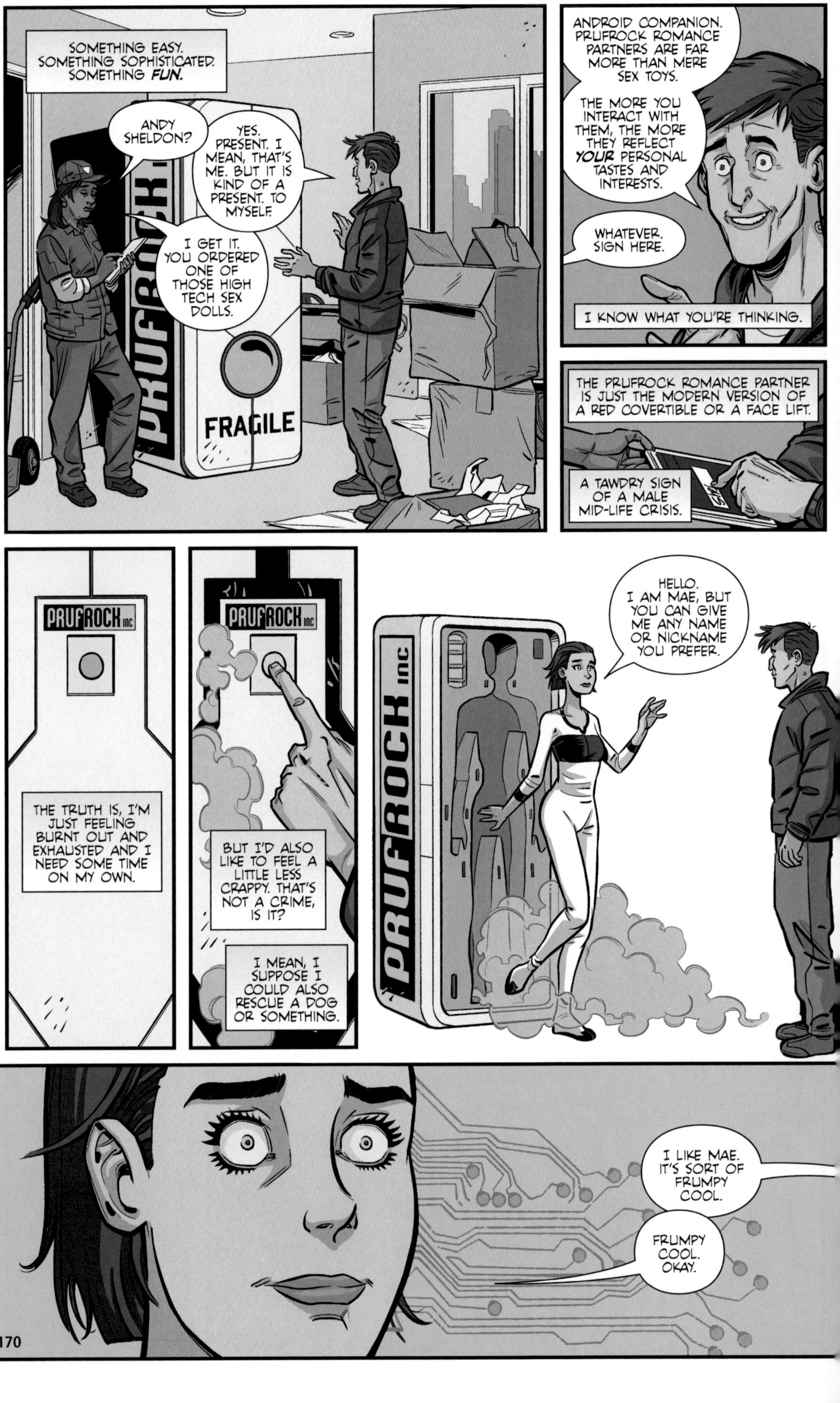
SOMETHING EASY. SOMETHING SOPHISTICATED. SOMETHING *FUN.*
ANDY SHELDON?
YES. PRESENT. I MEAN, THAT'S ME. BUT IT IS KIND OF A PRESENT. TO MYSELF.
I GET IT. YOU ORDERED ONE OF THOSE HIGH TECH SEX DOLLS.
PRUFROCK INC
FRAGILE
ANDROID COMPANION. PRUFROCK ROMANCE PARTNERS ARE FAR MORE THAN MERE SEX TOYS.
THE MORE YOU INTERACT WITH THEM, THE MORE THEY REFLECT ***YOUR*** PERSONAL TASTES AND INTERESTS.
WHATEVER. SIGN HERE.
I KNOW WHAT YOU'RE THINKING.
THE PRUFROCK ROMANCE PARTNER IS JUST THE MODERN VERSION OF A RED COVERTIBLE OR A FACE LIFT.
A TAWDRY SIGN OF A MALE MID-LIFE CRISIS.
PRUFROCK INC
THE TRUTH IS, I'M JUST FEELING BURNT OUT AND EXHAUSTED AND I NEED SOME TIME ON MY OWN.
PRUFROCK INC
BUT I'D ALSO LIKE TO FEEL A LITTLE LESS CRAPPY. THAT'S NOT A CRIME, IS IT?
I MEAN, I SUPPOSE I COULD ALSO RESCUE A DOG OR SOMETHING.
PRUFROCK INC
HELLO. I AM MAE, BUT YOU CAN GIVE ME ANY NAME OR NICKNAME YOU PREFER.
I LIKE MAE. IT'S SORT OF FRUMPY COOL.
FRUMPY COOL. OKAY.

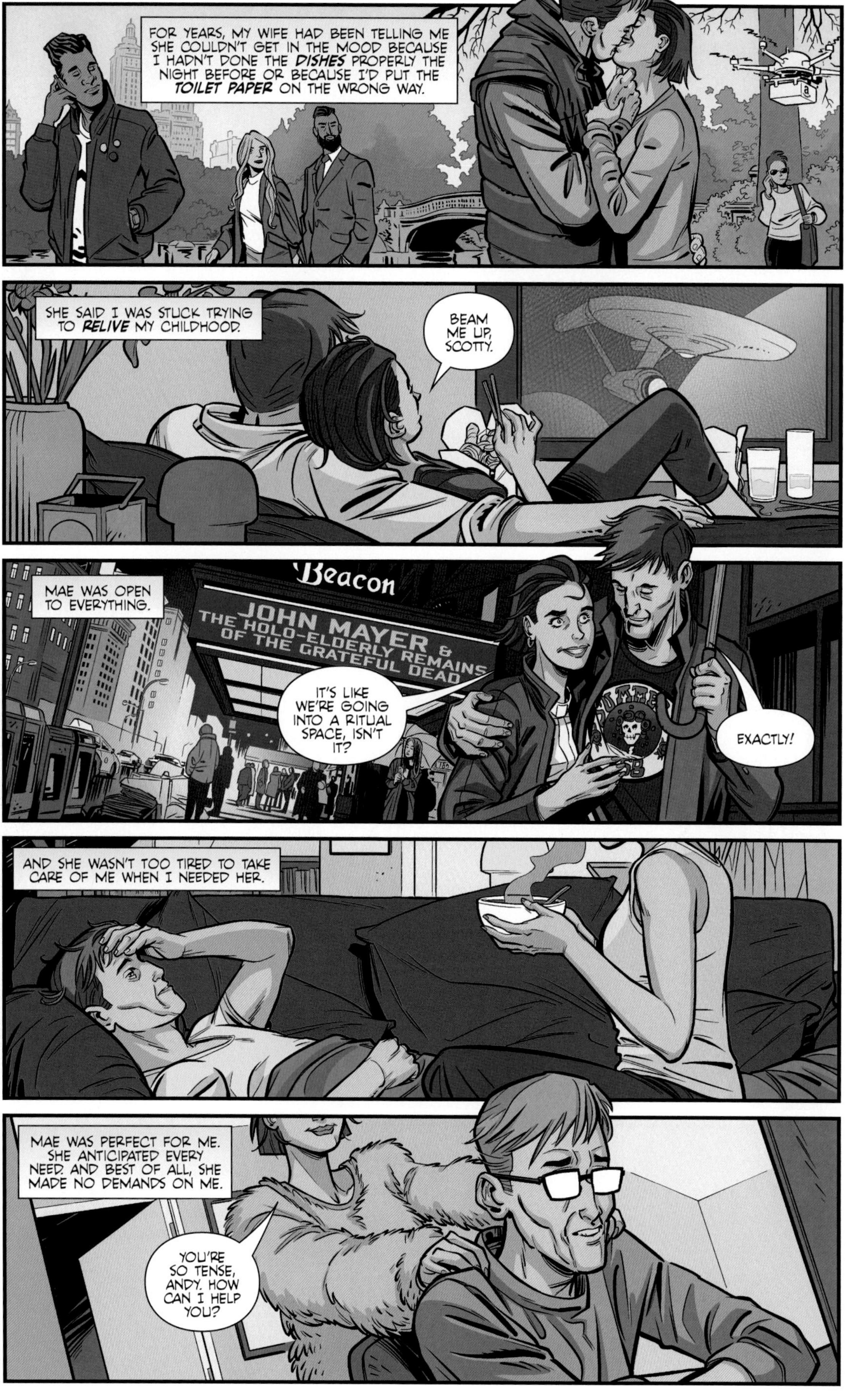
FOR YEARS, MY WIFE HAD BEEN TELLING ME SHE COULDN'T GET IN THE MOOD BECAUSE I HADN'T DONE THE *DISHES* PROPERLY THE NIGHT BEFORE OR BECAUSE I'D PUT THE *TOILET PAPER* ON THE WRONG WAY.
SHE SAID I WAS STUCK TRYING TO *RELIVE* MY CHILDHOOD.
BEAM ME UP, SCOTTY.
MAE WAS OPEN TO EVERYTHING.
Beacon
JOHN MAYER & THE HOLO-ELDERLY REMAINS OF THE GRATEFUL DEAD
IT'S LIKE WE'RE GOING INTO A RITUAL SPACE, ISN'T IT?
EXACTLY!
AND SHE WASN'T TOO TIRED TO TAKE CARE OF ME WHEN I NEEDED HER.
MAE WAS PERFECT FOR ME. SHE ANTICIPATED EVERY NEED. AND BEST OF ALL, SHE MADE NO DEMANDS ON ME.
YOU'RE SO TENSE, ANDY. HOW CAN I HELP YOU?

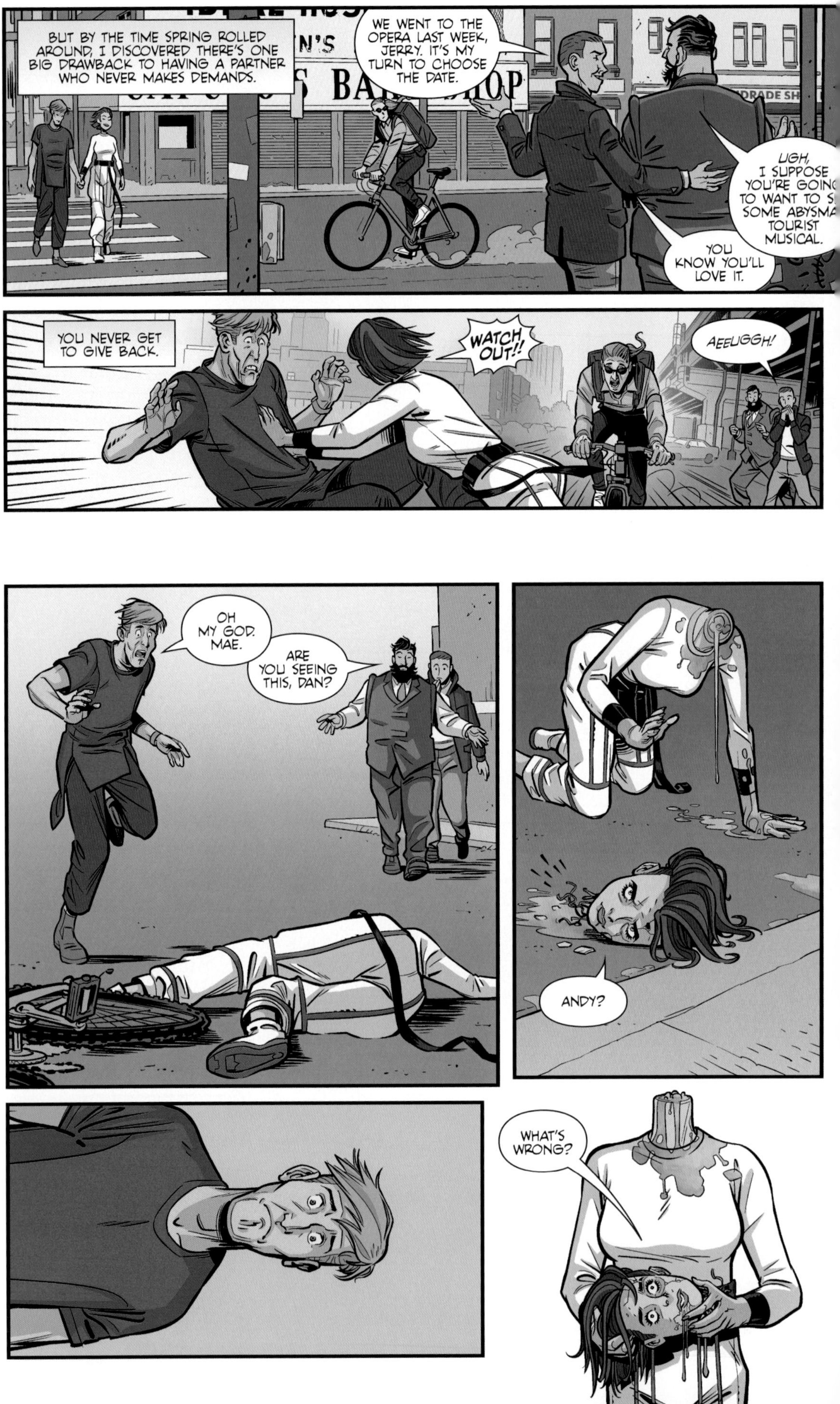
BUT BY THE TIME SPRING ROLLED AROUND, I DISCOVERED THERE'S ONE BIG DRAWBACK TO HAVING A PARTNER WHO NEVER MAKES DEMANDS.
WE WENT TO THE OPERA LAST WEEK, JERRY. IT'S MY TURN TO CHOOSE THE DATE.
UGH, I SUPPOSE YOU'RE GOING TO WANT TO S SOME ABYSMA TOURIST MUSICAL.
YOU KNOW YOU'LL LOVE IT.
YOU NEVER GET TO GIVE BACK.
WATCH OUT!!
AEEUGGH!
OH MY GOD. MAE.
ARE YOU SEEING THIS, DAN?
ANDY?
WHAT'S WRONG?

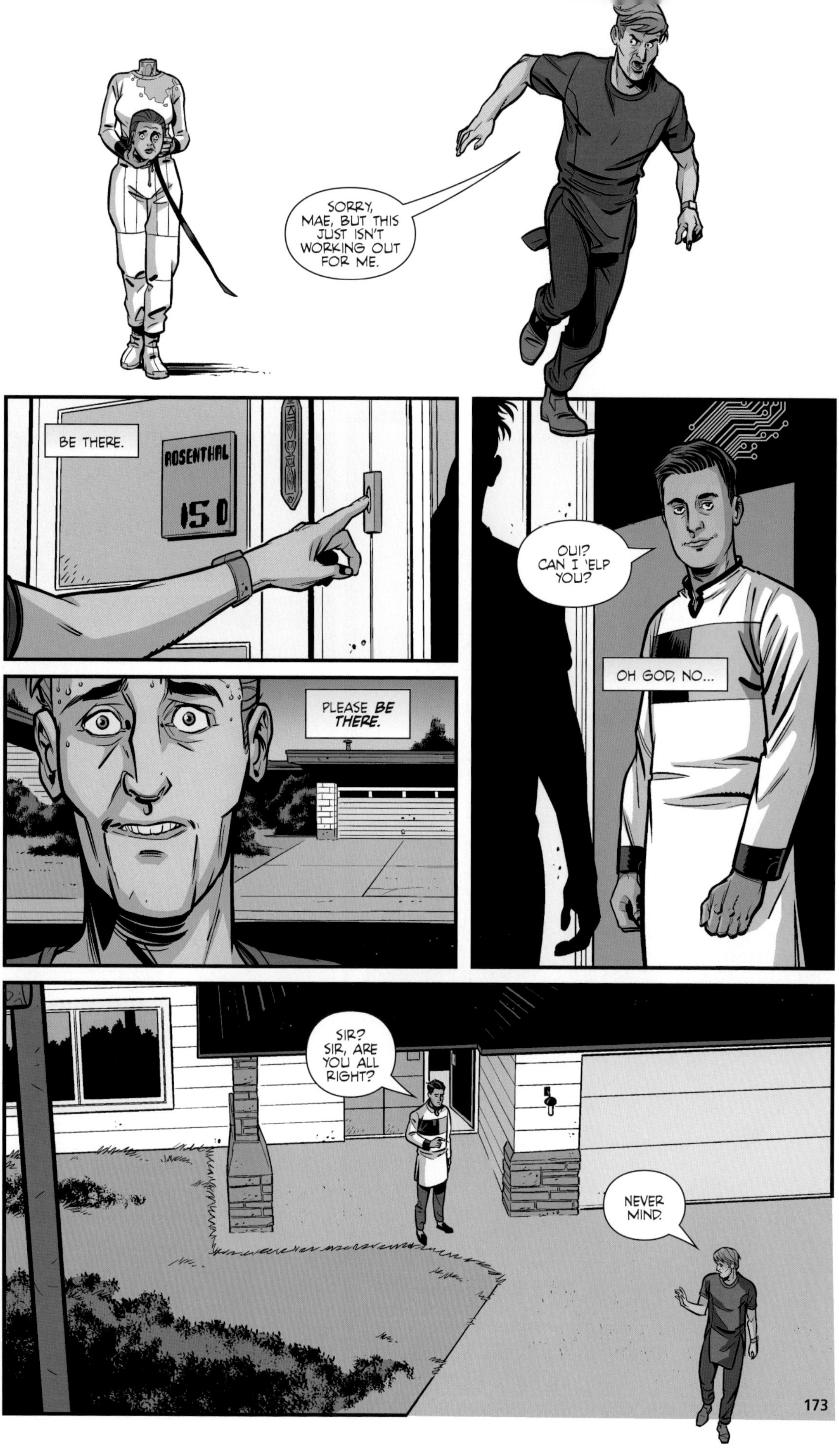
SORRY, MAE, BUT THIS JUST ISN'T WORKING OUT FOR ME.
BE THERE.
ROSENTHAL
150
PLEASE ***BE THERE.***
OUI? CAN I 'ELP YOU?
OH GOD, NO...
SIR? SIR, ARE YOU ALL RIGHT?
NEVER MIND.

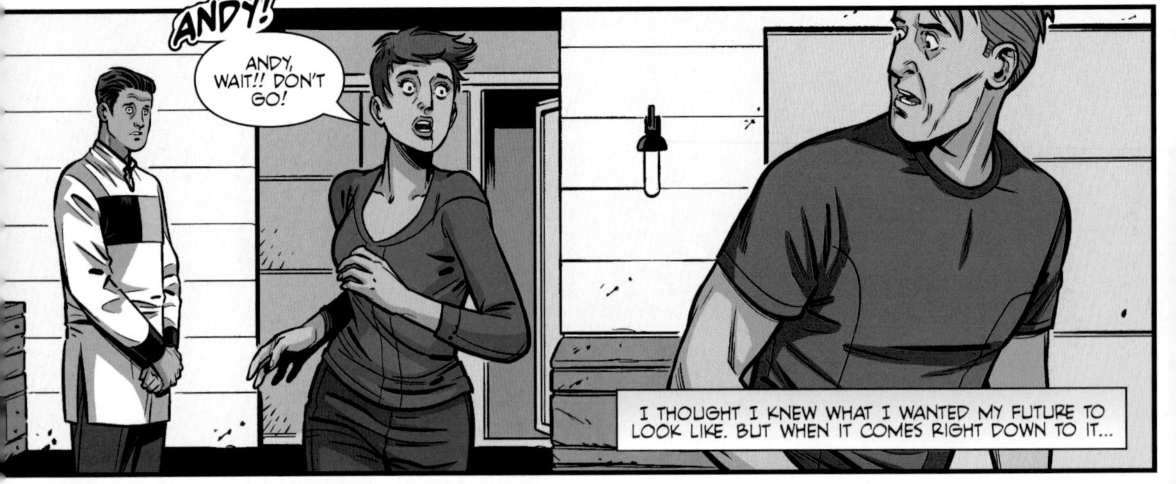
ANDY!
ANDY, WAIT!! DON'T GO!
I THOUGHT I KNEW WHAT I WANTED MY FUTURE TO LOOK LIKE. BUT WHEN IT COMES RIGHT DOWN TO IT...

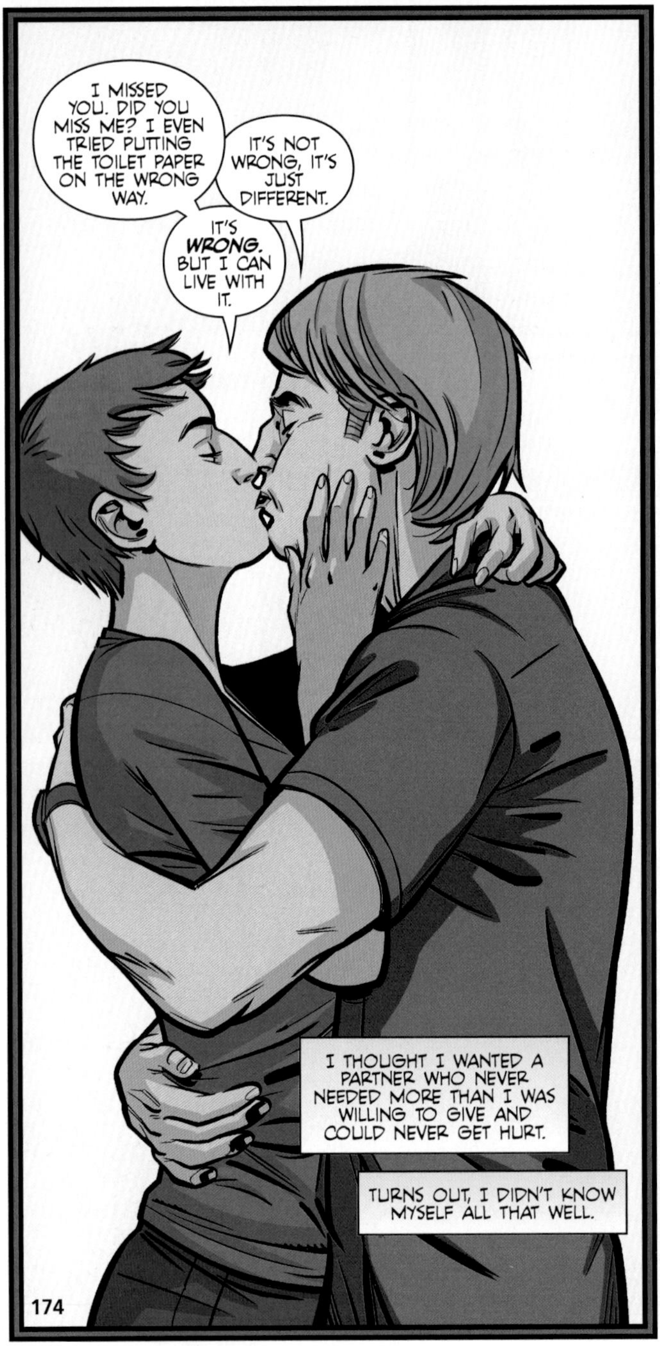
I MISSED YOU. DID YOU MISS ME? I EVEN TRIED PUTTING THE TOILET PAPER ON THE WRONG WAY.
IT'S NOT WRONG, IT'S JUST DIFFERENT.
IT'S *WRONG.* BUT I CAN LIVE WITH IT.
I THOUGHT I WANTED A PARTNER WHO NEVER NEEDED MORE THAN I WAS WILLING TO GIVE AND COULD NEVER GET HURT.
TURNS OUT, I DIDN'T KNOW MYSELF ALL THAT WELL.

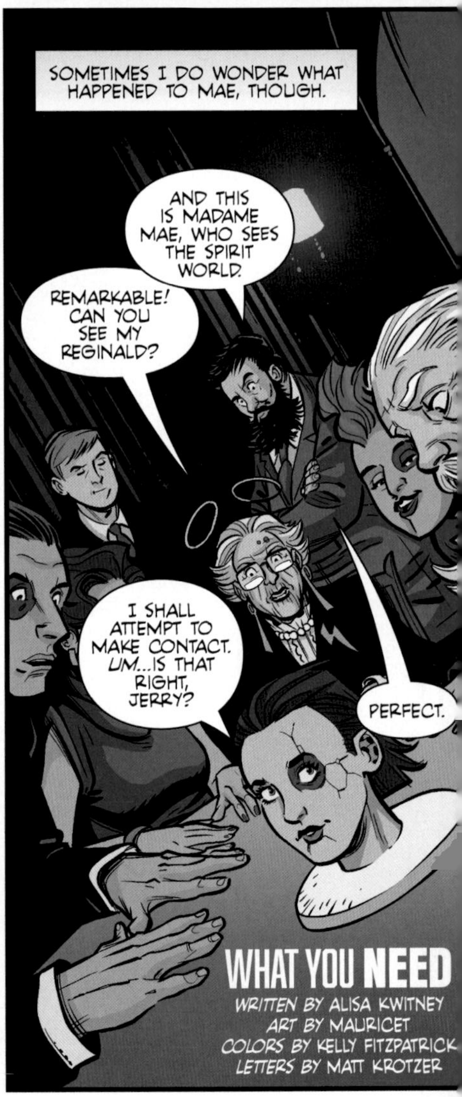
SOMETIMES I DO WONDER WHAT HAPPENED TO MAE, THOUGH.
AND THIS IS MADAME MAE, WHO SEES THE SPIRIT WORLD.
REMARKABLE! CAN YOU SEE MY REGINALD?
I SHALL ATTEMPT TO MAKE CONTACT. *UM*...IS THAT RIGHT, JERRY?
PERFECT.
WHAT YOU NEED
WRITTEN BY ALISA KWITNEY
ART BY MAURICET
COLORS BY KELLY FITZPATRICK
LETTERS BY MATT KROTZER

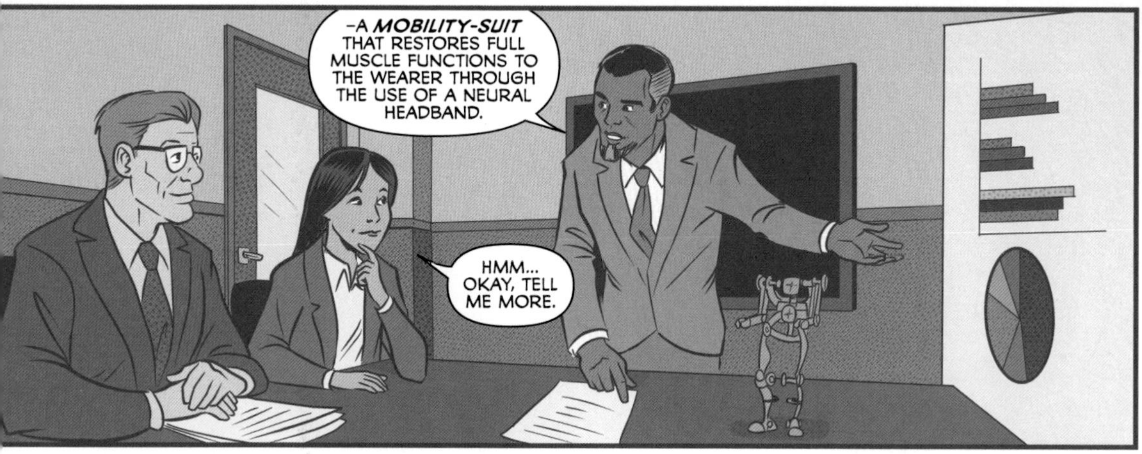
–A *MOBILITY-SUIT* THAT RESTORES FULL MUSCLE FUNCTIONS TO THE WEARER THROUGH THE USE OF A NEURAL HEADBAND.
HMM... OKAY, TELL ME MORE.

BIRTHDAY SURPRISE

WRITTEN BY: JOE CARAMAGNA
ART BY: BOBBY TIMONY
LETTERS BY: MICAH MYERS
SPECIAL THANKS TO SENSITIVITY READER: RUS WOOTON

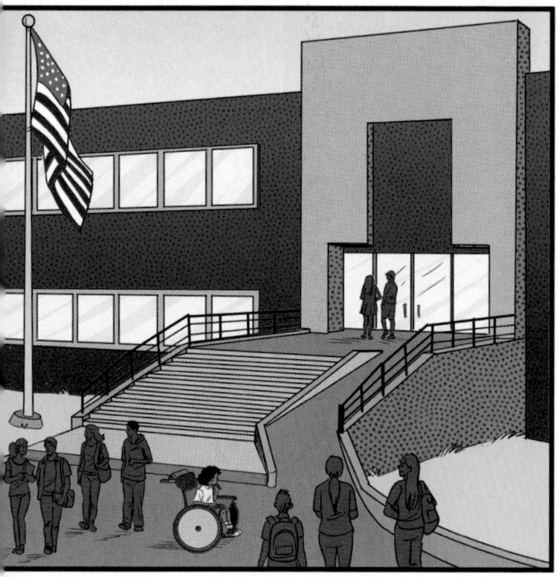

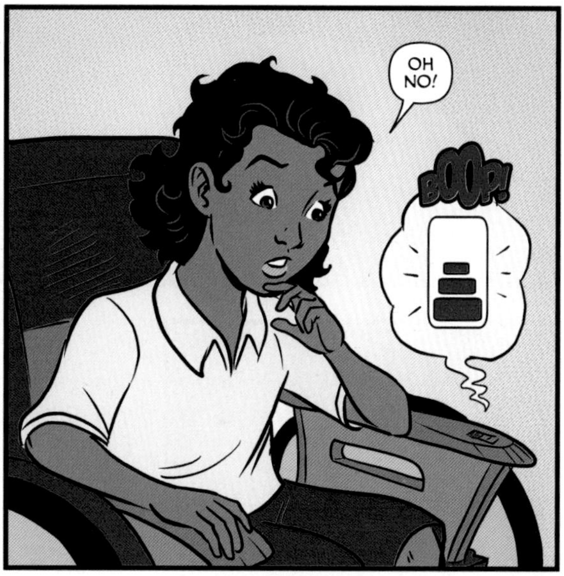
OH NO!
BOOP!

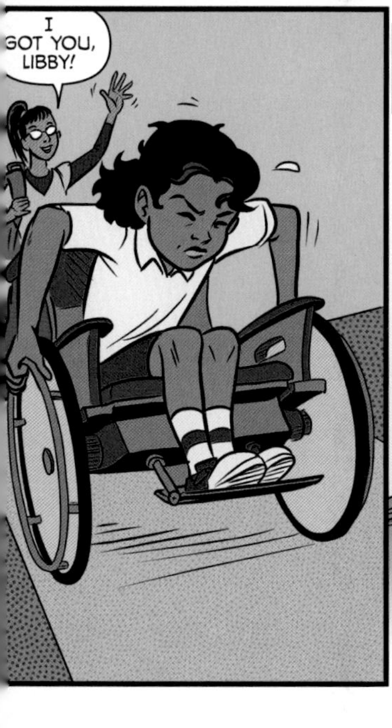
I GOT YOU, LIBBY!

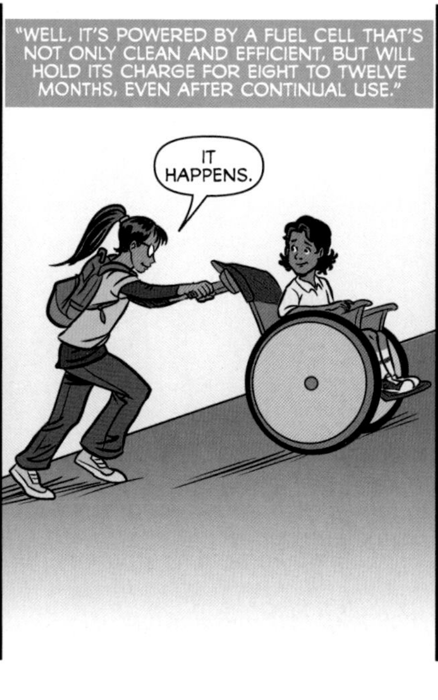
"WELL, IT'S POWERED BY A FUEL CELL THAT'S NOT ONLY CLEAN AND EFFICIENT, BUT WILL HOLD ITS CHARGE FOR EIGHT TO TWELVE MONTHS, EVEN AFTER CONTINUAL USE."
IT HAPPENS.

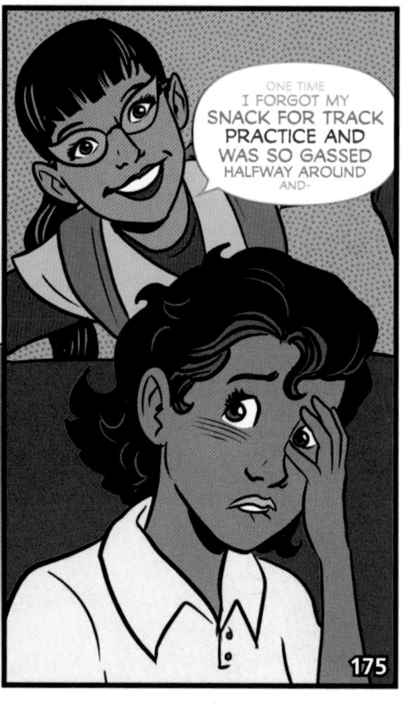
ONE TIME I FORGOT MY SNACK FOR TRACK PRACTICE AND WAS SO GASSED HALFWAY AROUND AND–

"OUR CARBON FIBER MATERIALS WON'T BE VISIBLE THROUGH REGULAR CLOTHING. THERE'S NO SIGNIFICANT WEIGHT OR BULK."

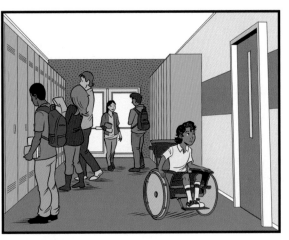

KLUNK

GAH!

DON'T BE EMBARRASSED. I CAN'T BELIEVE THE SCHOOL STILL ISN'T FULLY ADA COMPLIANT AFTER ALL THESE YEARS. LET'S GET THE SCHOOL PAPER TO WRITE

"WHICH ALSO MEANS..."

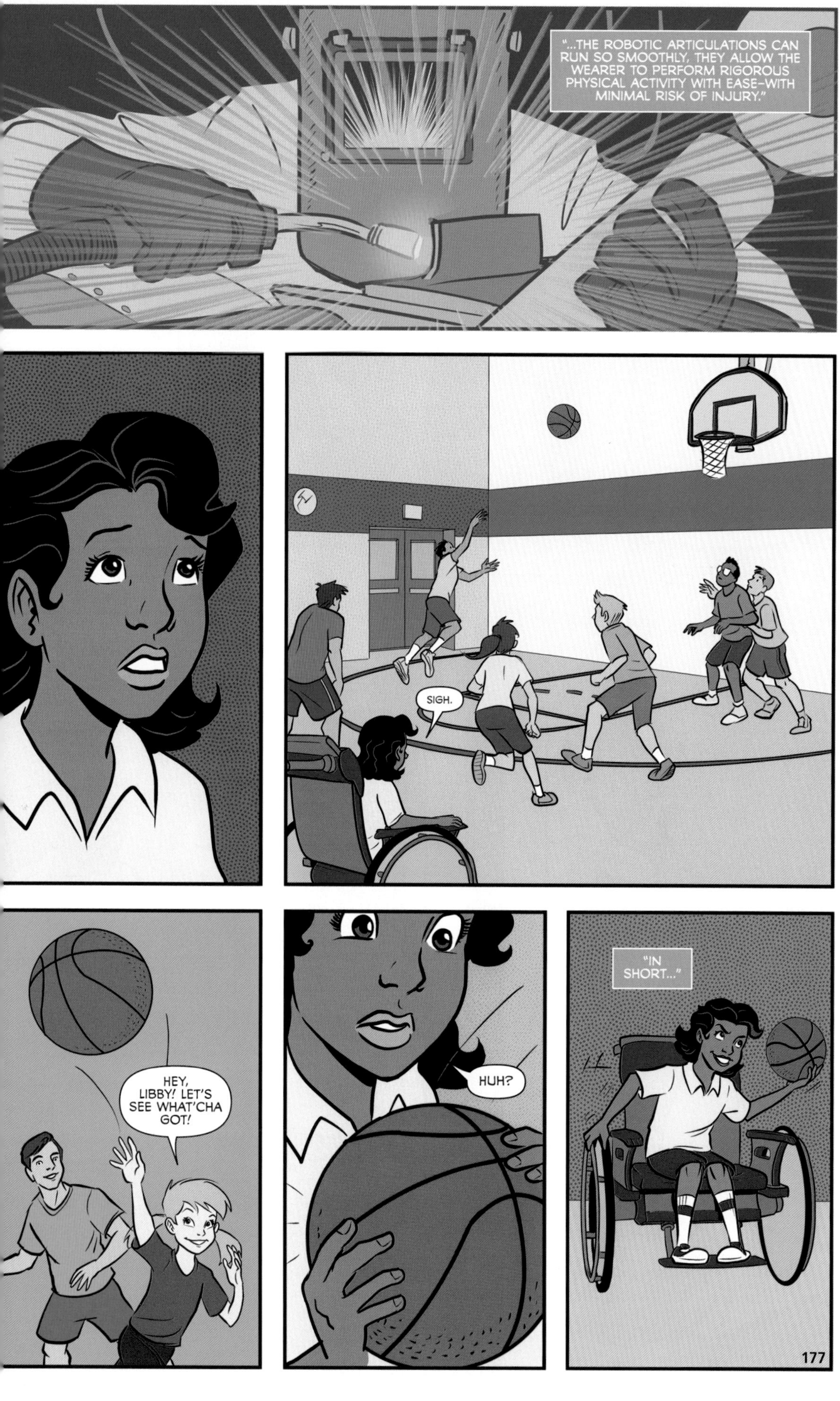

"...THE ROBOTIC ARTICULATIONS CAN RUN SO SMOOTHLY, THEY ALLOW THE WEARER TO PERFORM RIGOROUS PHYSICAL ACTIVITY WITH EASE–WITH MINIMAL RISK OF INJURY."
SIGH.
HEY, LIBBY! LET'S SEE WHAT'CHA GOT!
HUH?
"IN SHORT..."

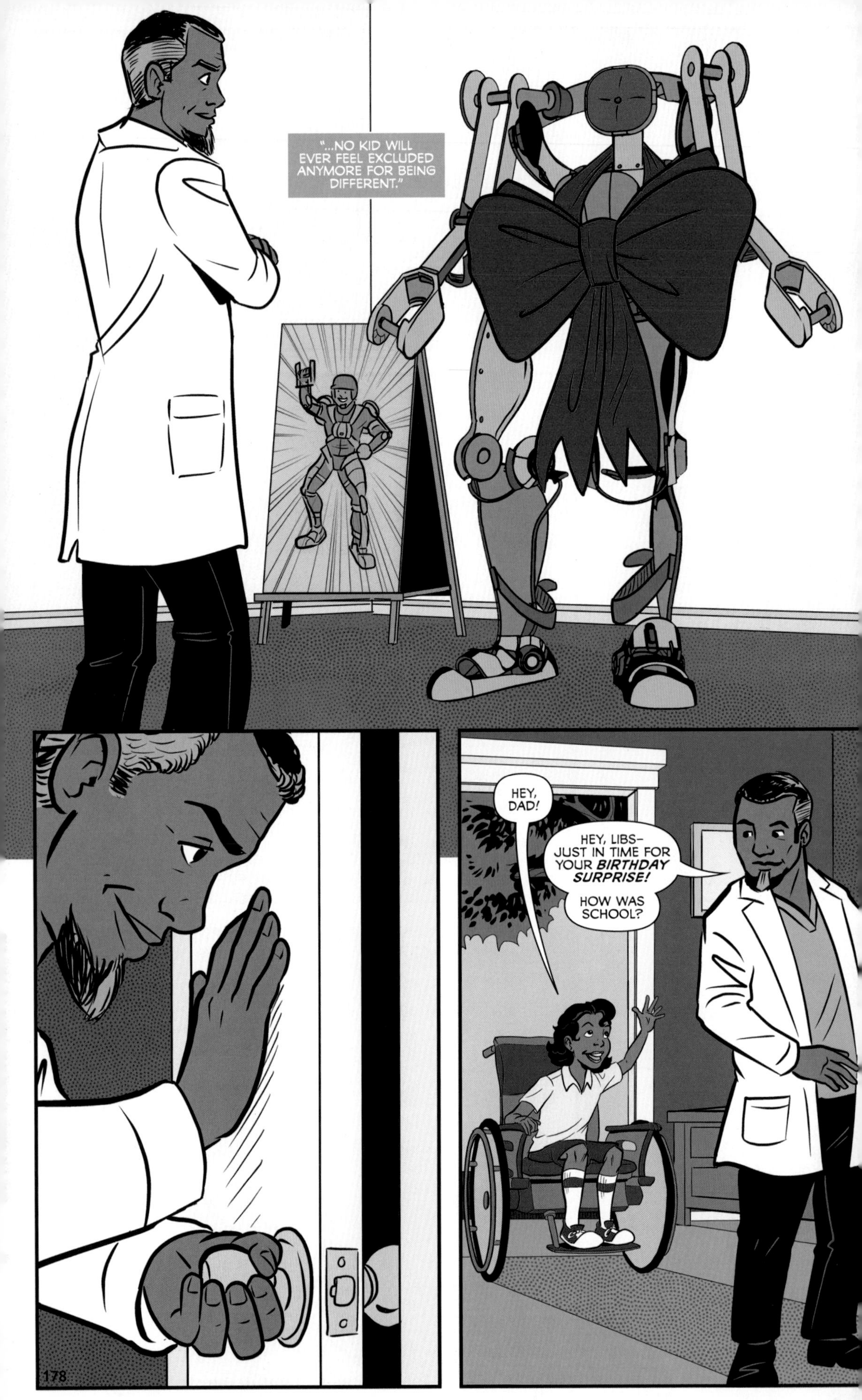
"...NO KID WILL EVER FEEL EXCLUDED ANYMORE FOR BEING DIFFERENT."
HEY, DAD!
HEY, LIBS– JUST IN TIME FOR YOUR *BIRTHDAY SURPRISE!*
HOW WAS SCHOOL?

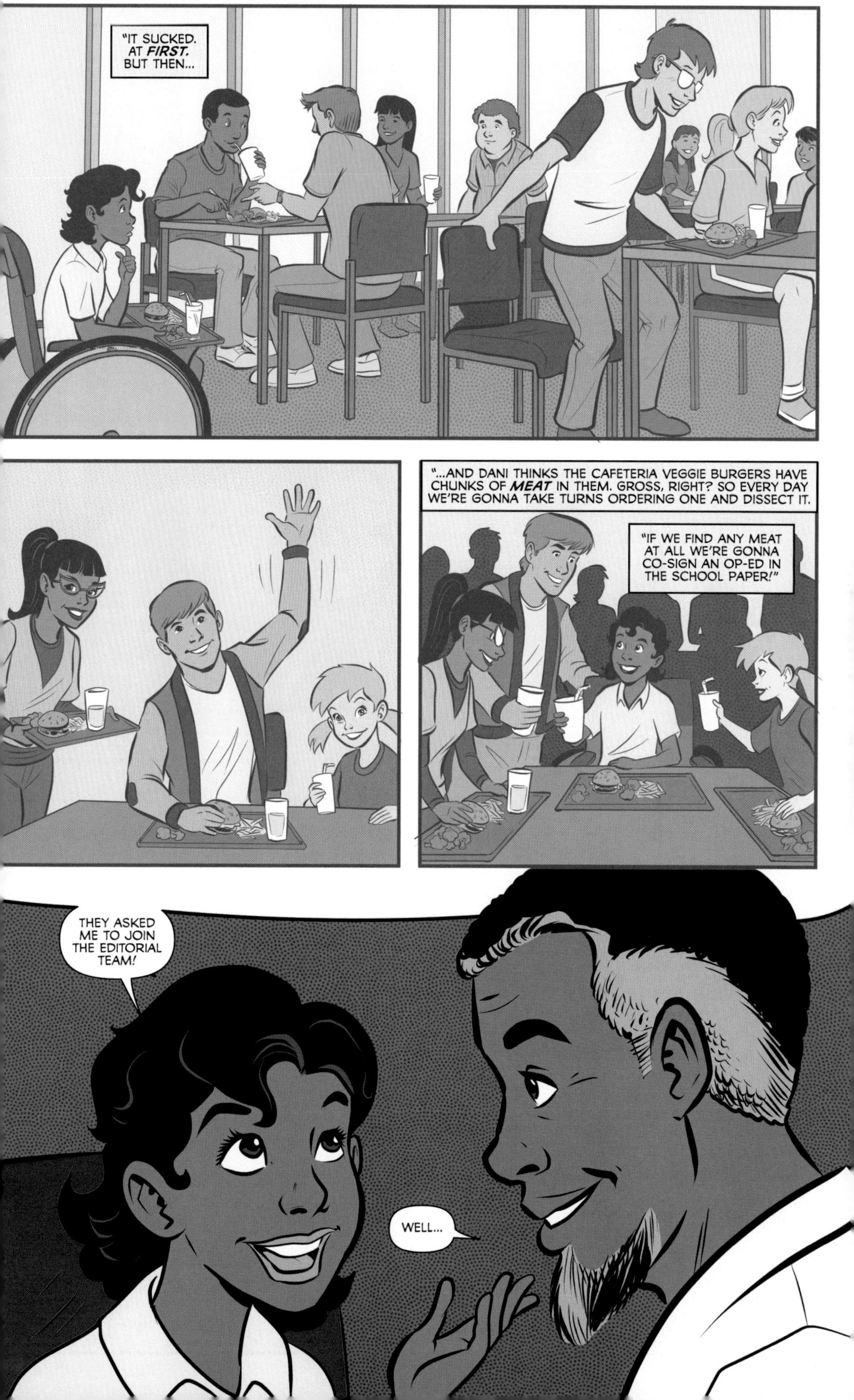
"IT SUCKED. AT *FIRST.* BUT THEN...
"...AND DANI THINKS THE CAFETERIA VEGGIE BURGERS HAVE CHUNKS OF *MEAT* IN THEM. GROSS, RIGHT? SO EVERY DAY WE'RE GONNA TAKE TURNS ORDERING ONE AND DISSECT IT.
"IF WE FIND ANY MEAT AT ALL WE'RE GONNA CO-SIGN AN OP-ED IN THE SCHOOL PAPER!"
THEY ASKED ME TO JOIN THE EDITORIAL TEAM!
WELL...

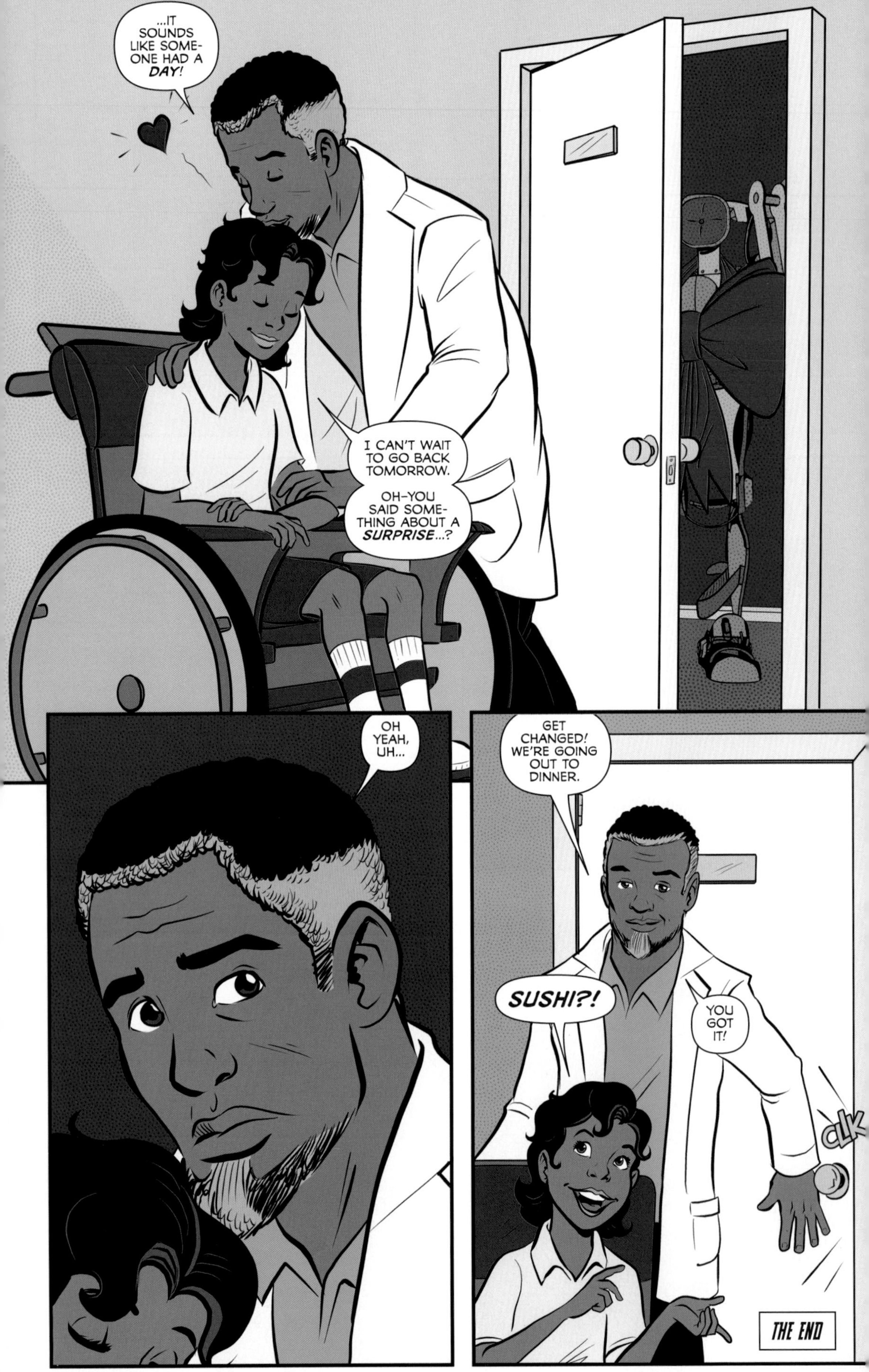
...IT SOUNDS LIKE SOME-ONE HAD A *DAY*!
I CAN'T WAIT TO GO BACK TOMORROW.
OH—YOU SAID SOME-THING ABOUT A *SURPRISE*...?
OH YEAH, UH...
GET CHANGED! WE'RE GOING OUT TO DINNER.
SUSHI?!
YOU GOT IT!
CLIK
THE END

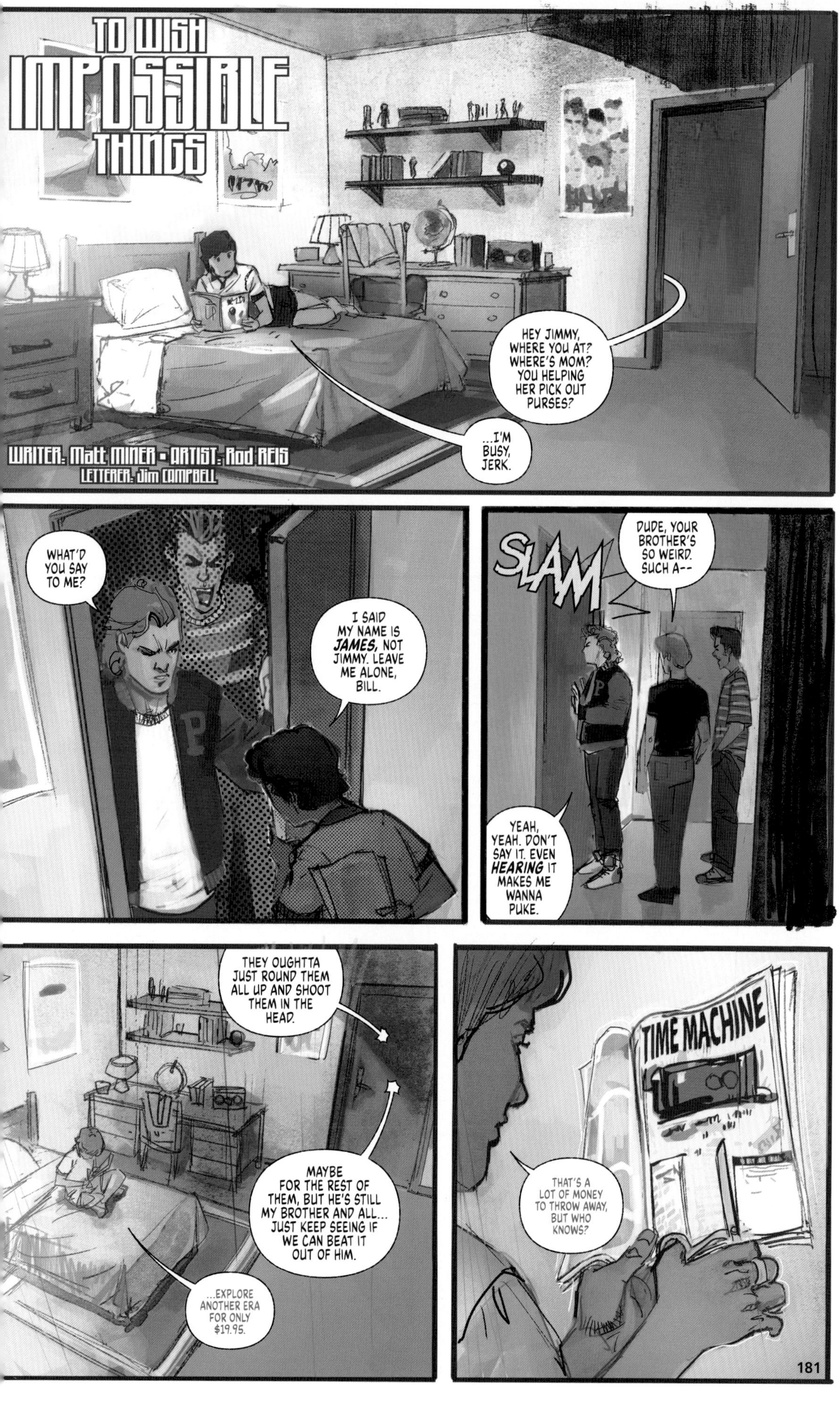
TO WISH IMPOSSIBLE THINGS
WRITER: Matt MINER • ARTIST: Rod REIS
LETTERER: Jim CAMPBELL
HEY JIMMY, WHERE YOU AT? WHERE'S MOM? YOU HELPING HER PICK OUT PURSES?
...I'M BUSY, JERK.
WHAT'D YOU SAY TO ME?
I SAID MY NAME IS *JAMES,* NOT JIMMY. LEAVE ME ALONE, BILL.
SLAM
DUDE, YOUR BROTHER'S SO WEIRD. SUCH A--
YEAH, YEAH. DON'T SAY IT. EVEN *HEARING* IT MAKES ME WANNA PUKE.
THEY OUGHTTA JUST ROUND THEM ALL UP AND SHOOT THEM IN THE HEAD.
MAYBE FOR THE REST OF THEM, BUT HE'S STILL MY BROTHER AND ALL... JUST KEEP SEEING IF WE CAN BEAT IT OUT OF HIM.
...EXPLORE ANOTHER ERA FOR ONLY $19.95.
TIME MACHINE
THAT'S A LOT OF MONEY TO THROW AWAY, BUT WHO KNOWS?

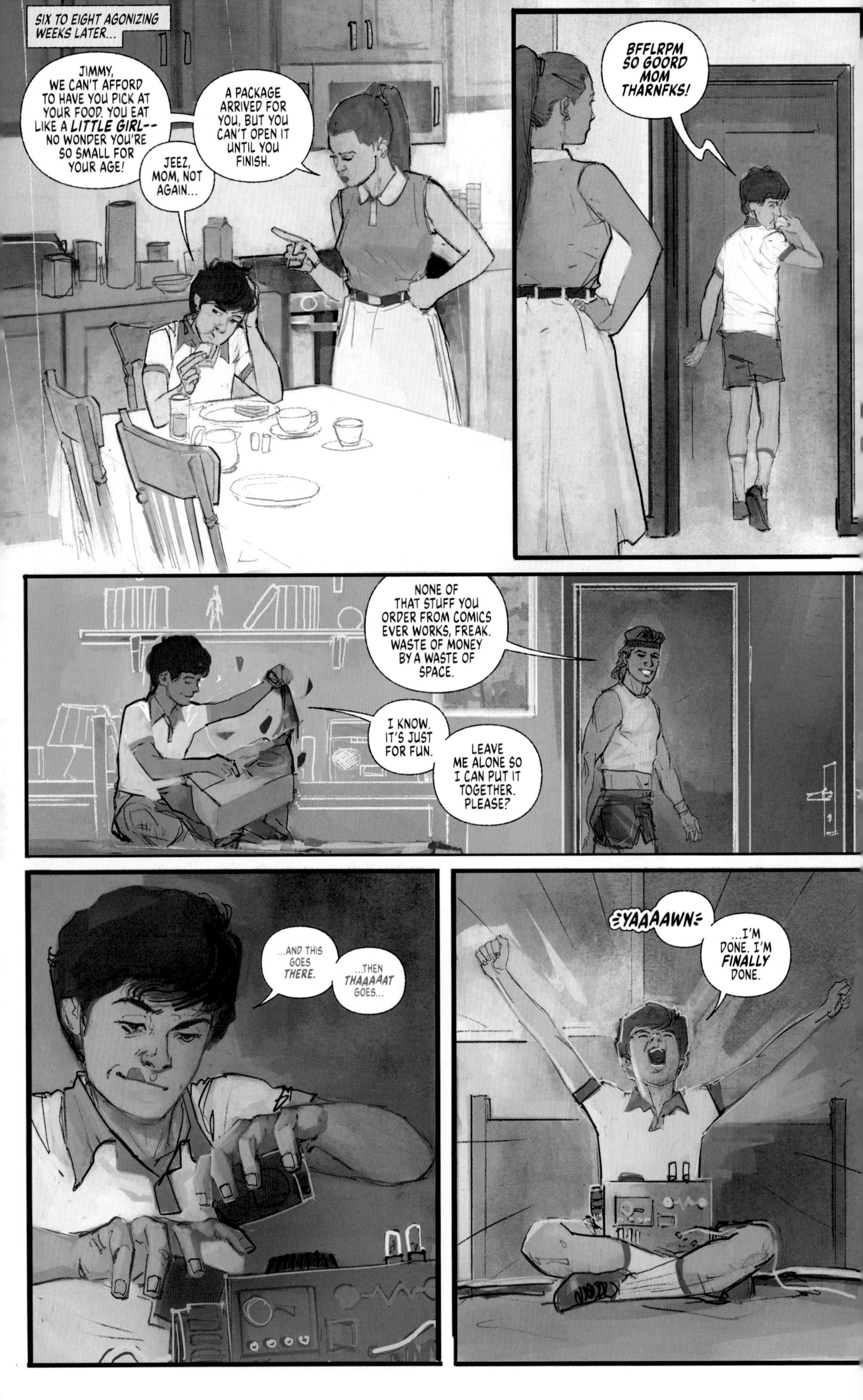
SIX TO EIGHT AGONIZING WEEKS LATER...
JIMMY, WE CAN'T AFFORD TO HAVE YOU PICK AT YOUR FOOD. YOU EAT LIKE A *LITTLE GIRL*-- NO WONDER YOU'RE SO SMALL FOR YOUR AGE!
A PACKAGE ARRIVED FOR YOU, BUT YOU CAN'T OPEN IT UNTIL YOU FINISH.
JEEZ, MOM, NOT AGAIN...
BFFLRPM SO GOORD MOM THARNFKS!
NONE OF THAT STUFF YOU ORDER FROM COMICS EVER WORKS, FREAK. WASTE OF MONEY BY A WASTE OF SPACE.
I KNOW. IT'S JUST FOR FUN.
LEAVE ME ALONE SO I CAN PUT IT TOGETHER. PLEASE?
...AND THIS GOES *THERE*.
...THEN *THAAAAAT* GOES...
YAAAAWN
...I'M DONE. I'M *FINALLY* DONE.

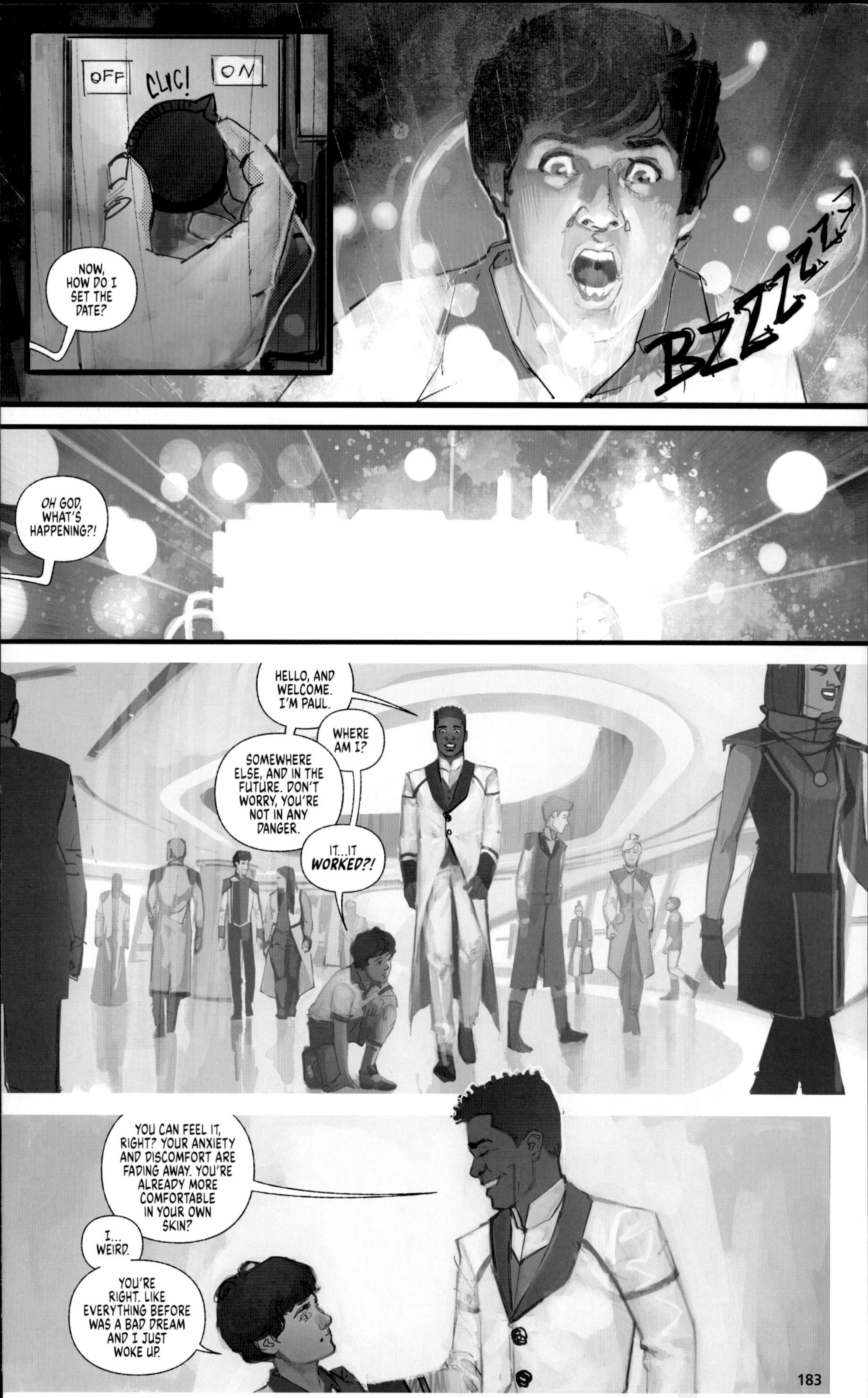
OFF
CLIC!
ON
NOW, HOW DO I SET THE DATE?
BZZZZZ
OH GOD, WHAT'S HAPPENING?!
HELLO, AND WELCOME. I'M PAUL.
WHERE AM I?
SOMEWHERE ELSE, AND IN THE FUTURE. DON'T WORRY, YOU'RE NOT IN ANY DANGER.
IT...IT *WORKED?!*
YOU CAN FEEL IT, RIGHT? YOUR ANXIETY AND DISCOMFORT ARE FADING AWAY. YOU'RE ALREADY MORE COMFORTABLE IN YOUR OWN SKIN?
I... WEIRD.
YOU'RE RIGHT. LIKE EVERYTHING BEFORE WAS A BAD DREAM AND I JUST WOKE UP.

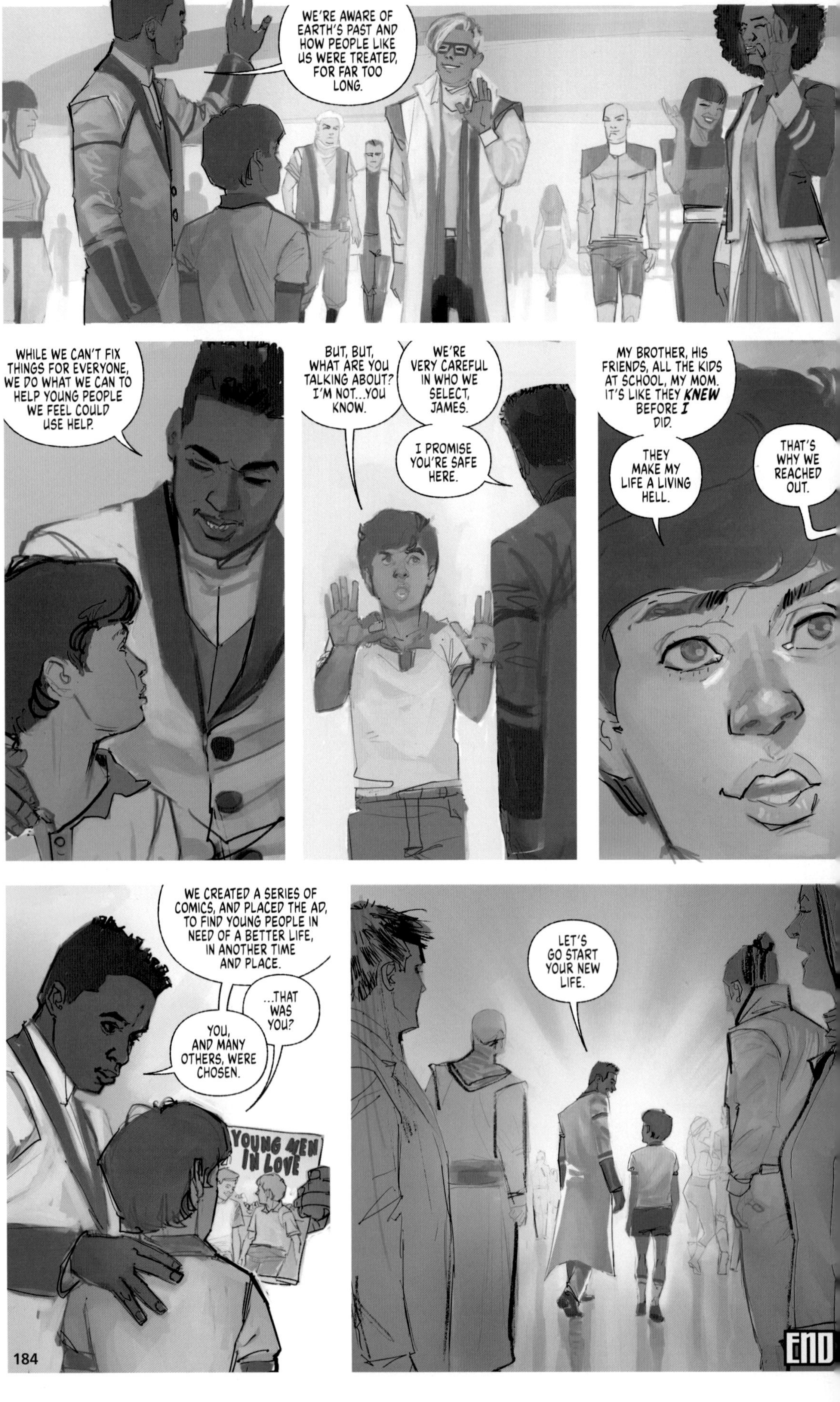

WE'RE AWARE OF EARTH'S PAST AND HOW PEOPLE LIKE US WERE TREATED, FOR FAR TOO LONG.
WHILE WE CAN'T FIX THINGS FOR EVERYONE, WE DO WHAT WE CAN TO HELP YOUNG PEOPLE WE FEEL COULD USE HELP.
BUT, BUT, WHAT ARE YOU TALKING ABOUT? I'M NOT...YOU KNOW.
WE'RE VERY CAREFUL IN WHO WE SELECT, JAMES.
I PROMISE YOU'RE SAFE HERE.
MY BROTHER, HIS FRIENDS, ALL THE KIDS AT SCHOOL, MY MOM. IT'S LIKE THEY ***KNEW*** BEFORE ***I*** DID.
THEY MAKE MY LIFE A LIVING HELL.
THAT'S WHY WE REACHED OUT.
WE CREATED A SERIES OF COMICS, AND PLACED THE AD, TO FIND YOUNG PEOPLE IN NEED OF A BETTER LIFE, IN ANOTHER TIME AND PLACE.
...THAT WAS YOU?
YOU, AND MANY OTHERS, WERE CHOSEN.
YOUNG MEN IN LOVE
LET'S GO START YOUR NEW LIFE.
END

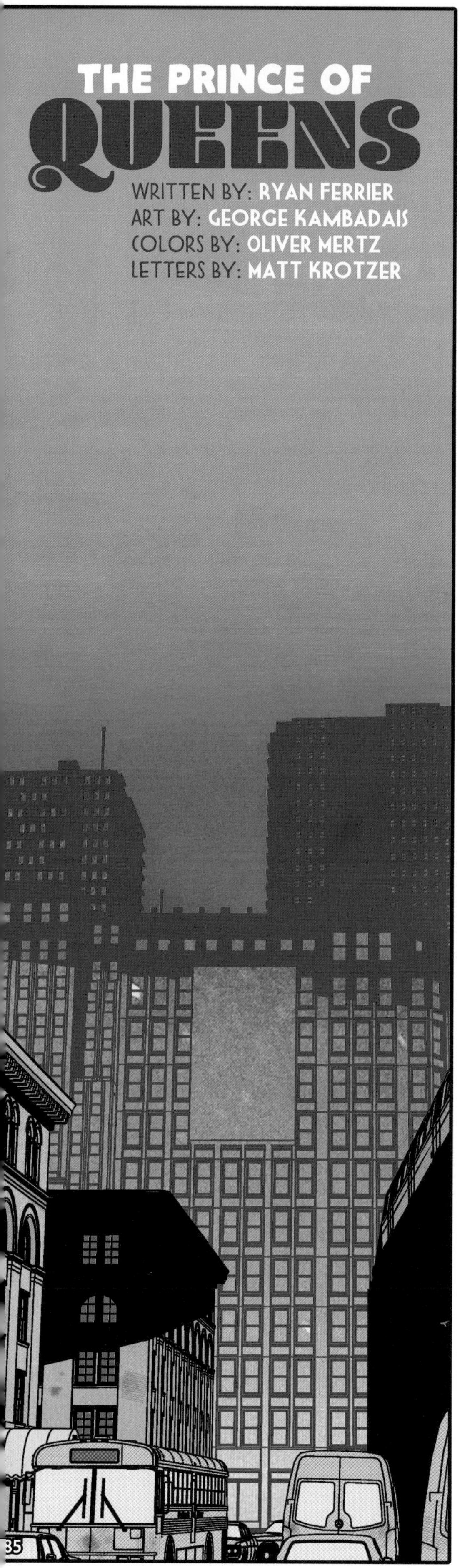
THE PRINCE OF
QUEENS
WRITTEN BY: RYAN FERRIER
ART BY: GEORGE KAMBADAIS
COLORS BY: OLIVER MERTZ
LETTERS BY: MATT KROTZER

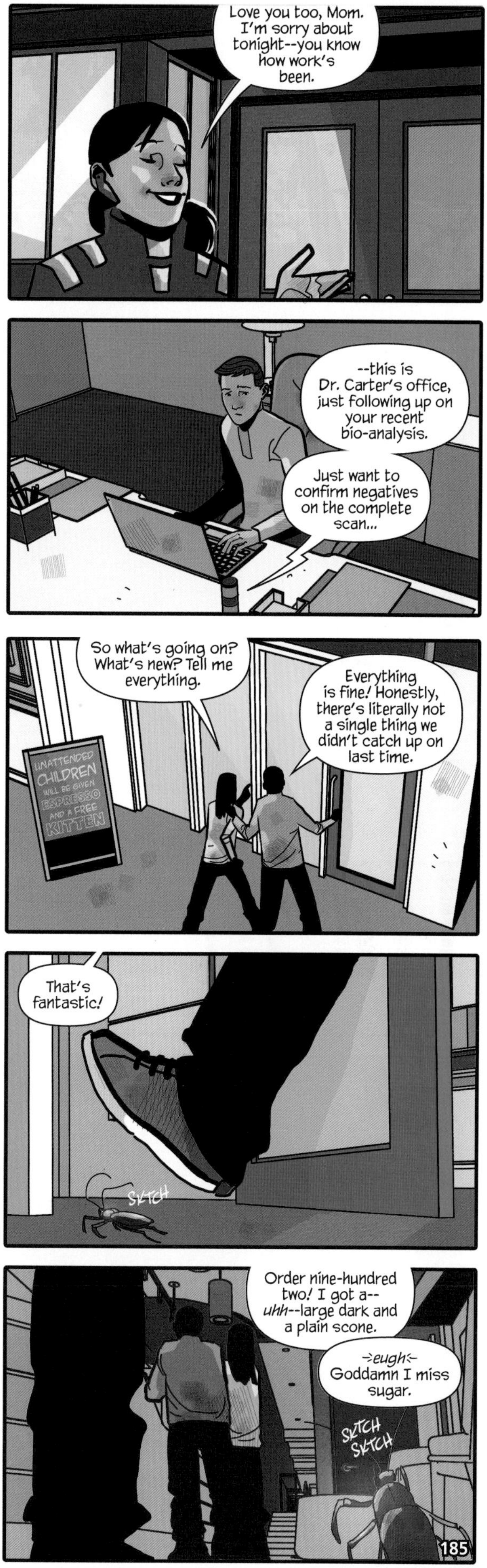
Love you too, Mom. I'm sorry about tonight--you know how work's been.
--this is Dr. Carter's office, just following up on your recent bio-analysis.
Just want to confirm negatives on the complete scan...
So what's going on? What's new? Tell me everything.
Everything is fine! Honestly, there's literally not a single thing we didn't catch up on last time.
UNATTENDED CHILDREN WILL BE GIVEN ESPRESSO AND A FREE KITTEN
That's fantastic!
SKTCH
Order nine-hundred two! I got a--*uhh*--large dark and a plain scone.
eugh Goddamn I miss sugar.
SKTCH SKTCH

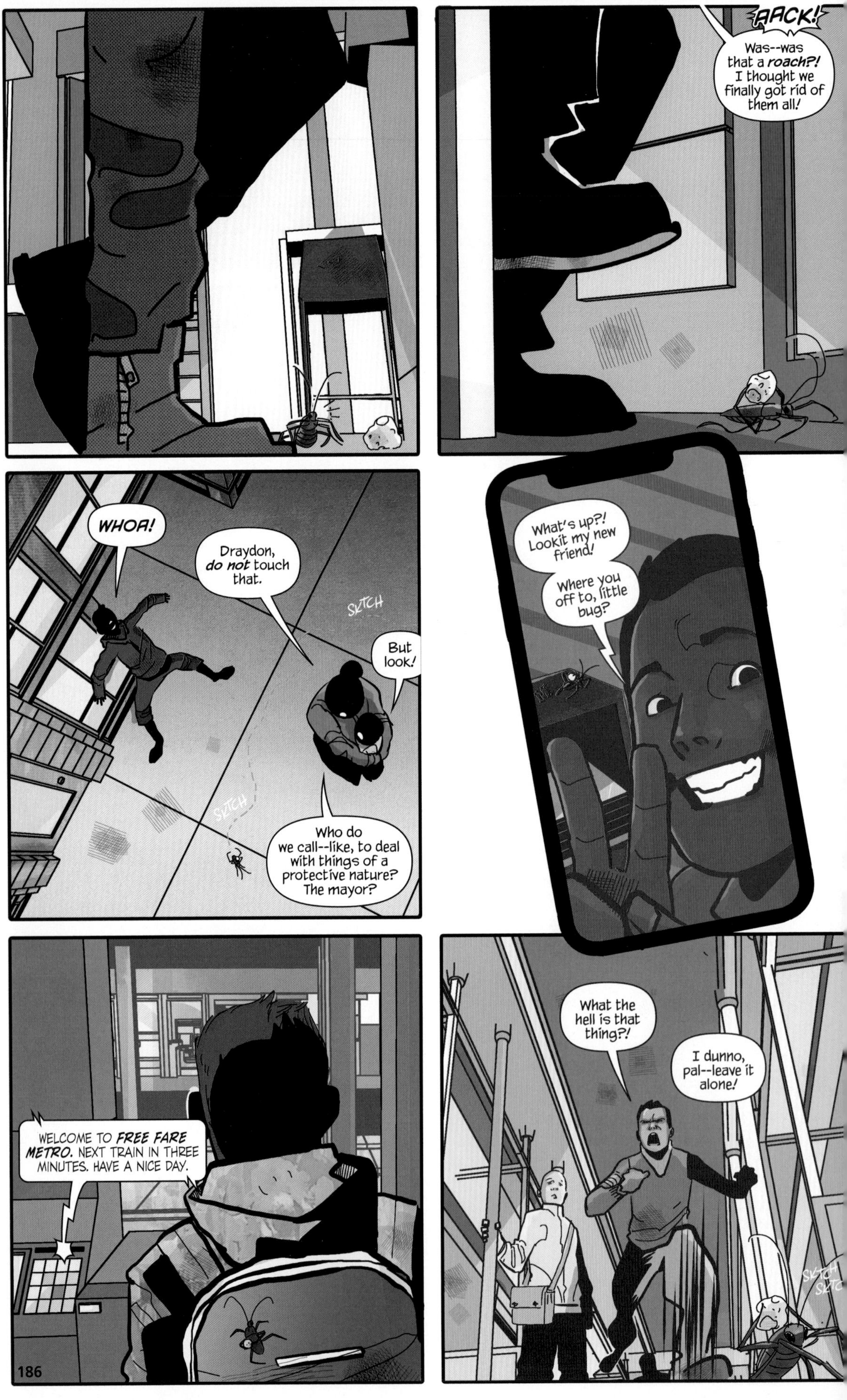
AACK!
Was--was that a *roach?!* I thought we finally got rid of them all!
WHOA!
Draydon, *do not* touch that.
SKTCH
But look!
SKTCH
Who do we call--like, to deal with things of a protective nature? The mayor?
What's up?! Lookit my new friend!
Where you off to, little bug?
WELCOME TO *FREE FARE METRO.* NEXT TRAIN IN THREE MINUTES. HAVE A NICE DAY.
What the hell is that thing?!
I dunno, pal--leave it alone!
SKTCH SKTC

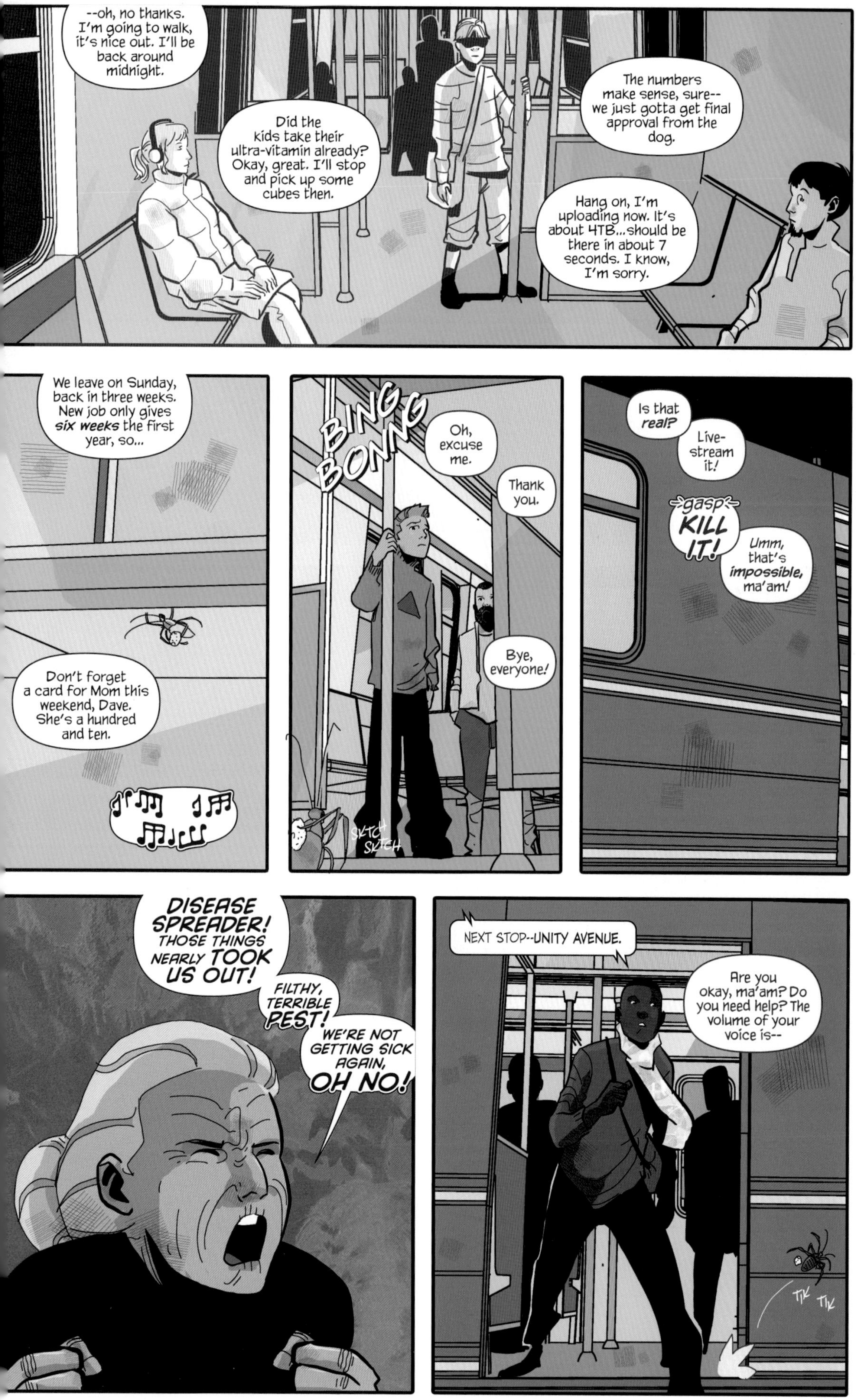
--oh, no thanks. I'm going to walk, it's nice out. I'll be back around midnight.
Did the kids take their ultra-vitamin already? Okay, great. I'll stop and pick up some cubes then.
The numbers make sense, sure--we just gotta get final approval from the dog.
Hang on, I'm uploading now. It's about 4TB...should be there in about 7 seconds. I know, I'm sorry.
We leave on Sunday, back in three weeks. New job only gives *six weeks* the first year, so...
Don't forget a card for Mom this weekend, Dave. She's a hundred and ten.
BING BONNG
Oh, excuse me.
Thank you.
Bye, everyone!
SKTCH SKTCH
Is that *real?*
Live-stream it!
gasp
KILL IT!
Umm, that's *impossible,* ma'am!
DISEASE SPREADER! THOSE THINGS NEARLY TOOK US OUT!
FILTHY, TERRIBLE PEST!
WE'RE NOT GETTING SICK AGAIN, OH NO!
NEXT STOP--UNITY AVENUE.
Are you okay, ma'am? Do you need help? The volume of your voice is--
TIK TIK

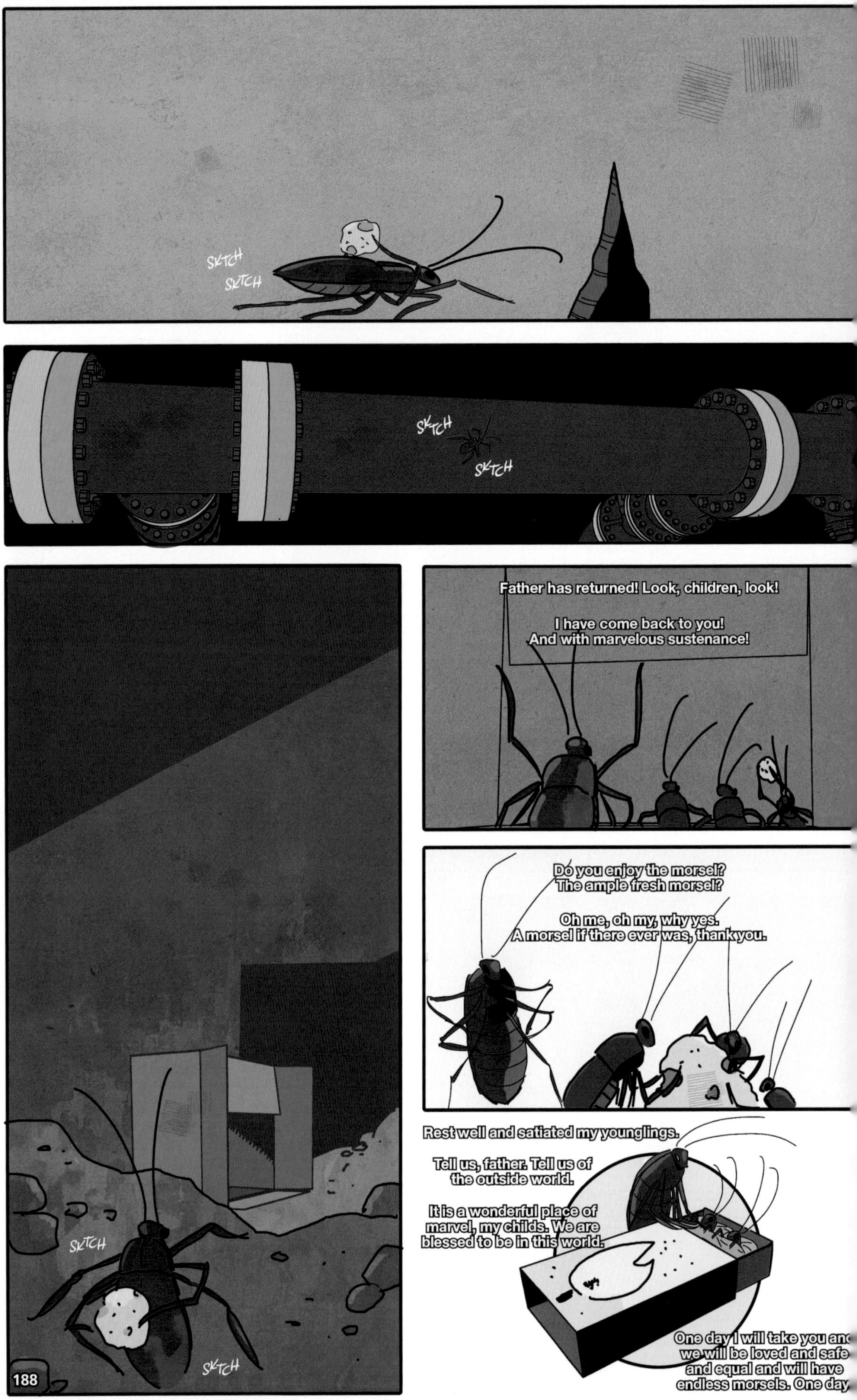
SKTCH
SKTCH
SKTCH
SKTCH
SKTCH
SKTCH
Father has returned! Look, children, look!
I have come back to you! And with marvelous sustenance!
Do you enjoy the morsel? The ample fresh morsel?
Oh me, oh my, why yes. A morsel if there ever was, thank you.
Rest well and satiated my younglings.
Tell us, father. Tell us of the outside world.
It is a wonderful place of marvel, my childs. We are blessed to be in this world.
One day I will take you an
we will be loved and safe
and equal and will have
endless morsels. One day

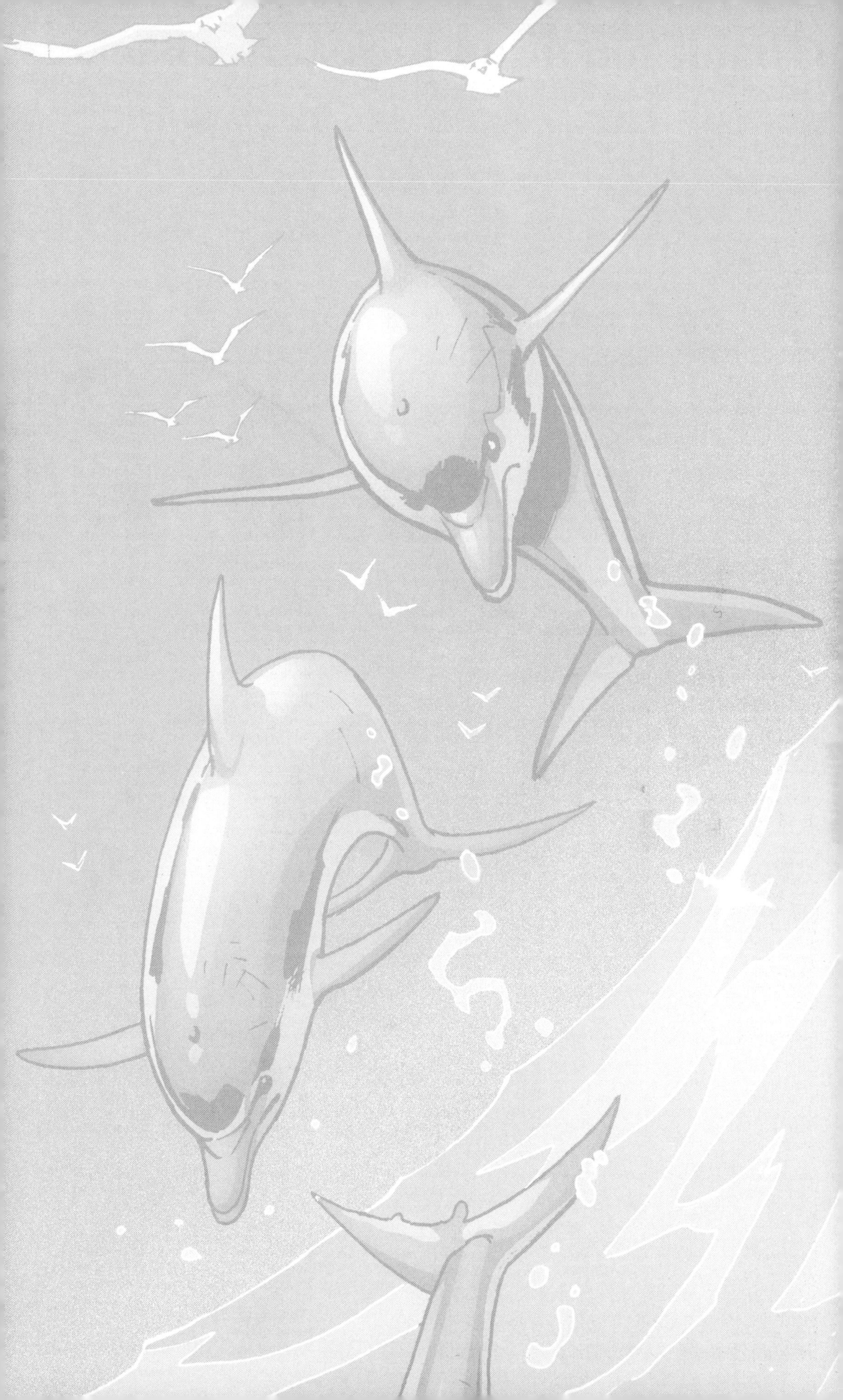

Thank You to our Kickstarter Backers!

2923 Comics
Matthew Abbott
R. Mark Adams
Andy Adams
Clay Adams
Folarin Akinmade
William V. Albert
Edgar V Alcazar III
Bruce Alcorn
The Accidental Aliens
Lucian Allen
Nick Allen
Reid Allison
Will Allred
Amber
Anaxphone
Freyja K. Andersdottir
Jiba Molei Anderson
Rodney Anderson Jr.
William A. Anderson
Stephen P. Anderson
Anonymous
Flavio Palandri Antonelli
Chen Arbel Arenfrid
Artfull_distractions@etsy
Joseph ash
Daniel Ashwell
James Asmus
Lesley Atlansky
Jay Aven
Alex B
Carmen B
Eli B.
Tom B.
Maureen Babb
Tiffany Babb
Elfego Baca
Patrick Bächli
Jeff Baker
Andrew & Jeni Balch
James Ballard
Christopher J Banser
Chris Baratz
Maxy Barnard
Bryan Barnes
Ned Barnett
M. E. Bartley
Andrew Barton
Michael Bates
Joe Bates
Baron Batman
Brett Battels
Sunny Mann BCUKCMD
beardedzilla
Kurt Belcher
Pete Bellisle
Alex Bendig
Brett Bennett
Scott A. Bennett
Hugh Berglind
Zeb Berryman
Matthew Bess
James E. Best III
Kevin Bhasi
Glen Bignell
Justin Birch
Ryan Bis
Carl W Bishop
Doug Bissell
Alan Blank
Sigtýr Blöndal
bn00880
Adam K. Bogert
Shelly Bond
Drew Bond
Patrick Boner
Jasmin Bonilla
Eric Bonin
John H. Bookwalter Jr.
Jason Boone
Jeff Rider & Carla Borsoi

Derek Boudreaux
Bobbi Boyd
john brainard
Josh Brandt
Gary Brantner of
    Rentnarb Studios Comics
J. Brickey
Glen Brixey
David Brooke
JT Brooks
Ash Brown
Jeremy Brown
Curtis Brown
Bruce
Chris Buchner
WPJ Buckley
Dan Buksa
Dena Burnett
Adam Burns
Jeremy Busse-Jones
Joel A. S. Butler
Kate C
Sophia C.
Nolan C.
Chris Call
Alex, Clarissa and
    Levi Campbell
Fraser Campbell
Mike "rentfn" Campbell
Mario Candelaria
Nathen Capaul
Jose Cardenas
Katie Cardwell
Roderick "Ranma711"
    Cardwell
Stephanie Carey
Ryan Carey
Milan Caro
Carol
Jon Carpenter
Conor.H.Carton
Casey
Paul Cassella
Erin Casteel
Ethan Castillo
Arthur Castro
Dominic Caswell
JC Cat
Cdfisher09
cfp33pfc
Nina Silver Ch.
Joshua Chafin
R. Chantrill
Anthony Chanza
Zach Chapman
Nicholaus Chatelain
Toren Chenault
Chuck Childers
Greg Childs
Jey Chiralo
Sunyoung Chong
Peter Christensen
Lor Christine
Alex Chung
Ian Chung
Mike Clark
Richard P Clark
Perry Clark
John A Claus
Donald E. Claxon
Shane Clements
Michael Clinton
Justin du Coeur
Adam Cogan
Colbourn Family
Clifton Coleman
Erin Collins
Justin Colucci
The Comics Pals
Andy Conduit-Turner
Jeff Constable

Alec Conte
Brandon Cox
Jason Crase
CRASH COMICS
criz
Salvatore Cucinotta
Leron Culbreath
Beth Culp
Ryan Cummins
Malcolm & Parker Curtis
Heather Curtis
D_Seer
Marcin W. Dąbrowski
Don Dada
Mohammad Dania
Dan-o
Danté!
Dauchon
David
David@DrivingCreators
Paul T. Davies
William P Davis
Scott Davis
Stuart Day
Daniel de Kadt
Beserat Debebe
Jude Deluca
Tom Depoorter
Ethan Deree
Joel Derig
Eastin DeVerna
Armando DiCianno
Susie Dicker
Garrick Dietze
Angela Diorio
Umar Ditta
Ebeth Doc
Dom!
domiriel
Natalie Doonanco
Edward Douglas
Josh Drescher
Jonathan Dresner
DS
Jon Duckworth
O.C. Dudley
James H. Duke IV
Jeff Durkee
Razaq Durodoye
Greg Dye
Brian Dysart
Kevin E
Jeremy E.
Matt E.
Brandon Eaker
Robert Early
Bret Eayrs
Dave Ebersole
Jeanette Eckert
Trevor Edwards
Laurie Edwards
Jarek Ejsymont
Ahmed Elsayed
Emily!
Eric Sean Emmons
Cpt Emoji
Kenny Endlich
EngineeringBob
Brian Erbe
Todd Erwin
Juan Espinosa
Charlie Etheridge-Nunn
Joey Fanoele
Roberto Faria
Dwayne Farver
Michael C. Fedoris
Ben Ferrari
Adam Ferris
Jonny Fewkes
Carmen Finnigan
Alex Fitch

Mr. Fitz
Tom Fitzpatrick
Patrick Fjeld
Jason A. Fleece
Christopher Fleming
Bo Floyd
Thea Flurry
Jack Flynn
Robbie Foggo
Sam Fokker
Jeremy Forbes
Curt Fortenbery
Tom Foster
Brant Fowler
Abram Fox
Jordan Fox
Gid Freeman
Tracy 'Rayhne' Fretwell
Friar Alex
Jason 'XenoPhage' Frisvold
Matthew Fyfe
Marc Gaffen
The Gaffin Family
Mike Garley
Garonenur
Jimmy Gaspero
Miguel Gastelum
    (Bigsiemigs)
Ryan & Caroline Gaterell
Oliver Gerlach
Domenica Giaime
Andreas Giannoukakis
Matt Gilligan
Larry Gilman
Shaun Gilroy
Geoffrey Gimse
Leon Glaser
Joe Glass
GMarkC
Abi Godsell
Emmet & Jesse Golden-Marx
Cindy Gonzalez
Todd Good
The Gorge Podcast:
    with Ben and Sara
Natalie Grebe
Peter Green
Diana Greenhalgh
Mariah Griffin
Marva Grossman
Erik Groth
Dakota R. Groves
Kisa Gryphon
Akira Guirales
Greg Gustin
Lloyd Gyan
Matty H
Toni H
Karin Haberlin
Stuart Hadley
Anne Hagstrom
Erik Håkansson
Thomas Hall
Kevin Halstead
Stanley Hamilton
Shaun Hamilton
Michael Hansen
Russell Harbison
Brendan Harder
D.C. Harlow
Tristan Harness
William T Harris III
Scott Harris-King
Bob and Shari Harrison
Brentt Harshman
Janet Harvey
Amanda Harvey
Joe Hatton
HeadBangCBFC
Stephen Heger
Mik Hendrix

Eric Henrickson
Jimmy Henriksson
Fred Herman
Kendrick Hernandez
R. Hernandez
K.-H. Herrmann
Patrick Hess
Cristofer "FifthDream" Hess
Jen Hickman
Heather Hill
Tracy Hirano
Emily Hodder
Corey Hodgdon
Irmgard Hoff
Dan Hoizner
Will Holden
Fredrik Holmqvist
DC Hopkins
Jonathon Horner
Fermin Serena Hortas
Jakob Hosmer
Jacob Howell
Heather Hubbard
Xavier Hugonet
Brian Huisman
Christian Humes
Seth Hunt
I Am Hexed Comic
DB Irwin
Matthew Isaac
luke iseman
Farah Ismail
Ivy
Osyp Iwanuch
J&D
John Jack
Tyler James
Rachel James
Iconnu James
@JamesFerguson
Jennifer & Jamie
Jaminx
Robert Jeffrey II
Bernie Jessome
JimS
JKB
jlk
Kurt Johansen
Daryl Johnson
Clifford Jones
Rhea Jones
Travis Jones
David and Stephanie Jones
Tim Jordan
Kevin Joseph
Jp
Brookie Judge
Randy Jung
Paul Kaefer
Daniel Kalban
Liana Kangas
Bella & Katie
Jason Keener
Kris Keiningham
Ian Kellar
Joe Kern
Barbara Randall Kesel
Ketki-Tanmay
Kev Ketner
Anand Khatri
The Daemon Kia
Raena King
Michael R. Kingston
Johan Kjellsson
Adam Klawitter
Nathaniel Knapp
Matt and Camille Knepper
Jeremy Knope
Bill Kohn
Yun Koo
Lukasz Kowalczuk

Christopher Kranz
Bill Kraut
Ben Krieger
Justin Kruger
Steven Kuerbitz
Bart-Jan Kuiper
Vincent Kukua
Matt Kund
Yo Kuri
Trina Kurilla
Jeremy S. Kuris
KylaTea
Kynerae
Marcos L
Marko Lacheta
Corky LaVallee
Max Lazary
Matt Lazorwitz
Sam Learmonth
Andy Leavy
The Lee Family
Linus Lee
Apryl Lee
@lepineisme
Noah Lesgold
William Leung
Marc Levine
Alex Lewis
Sarah Liberman
Daniel Lin
Kelly Little
Llamaentity
Jesse LoBalbo
Mark Locy
Jay Lofstead
Marc Lombardi
Michael Long
Lou
Richard Lowe
James Lucas
Jarred Luján
Hayley M
Rob MacAndrew
Freddy MacKay
Colin Maclaughlin
Maddox
Zoe Maffitt
Andrew Magazzu
maileguy
Makenzye
Jabrayil Malikov
Kate Malloy
Carol Mammano
Jim Manchester
Shaun Manning
Butch Mapa
MardiGraz718
Shawn Marier
Kevin J. "Womzilla"
Maroney
Dr. Justin Martin
(R-Squared Comicz)
Norbert Martin
Randall Brent Martin II
Stephanie Martin
Matt Miner aka
Johnny Rotten
Matthew
Todd Matthy
Thomas Mauer
Bryan Mauney
Deborah Maybury
Moana McAdams/
   Burning Spear Comix
Ty McC (Old Man Sparck)
Seth McCombs
Wesley McCraw
Juliet McCurry
Paul McErlean
Glen McFerren, M.D.
Gerry McGrory
John McGuire
Fred McNamara
Evan Meadow
Eric Meadows

Tim 'Aardvark' Meakins
Jude Melancon
Ken "Merlyn" Mencher
Jonathan Mendonca
Belmondo Mertz
Dr. Melvin "Steve"
   Mesophagus
Larry Mettam
Kate Meyers
MFCOMMAND
MH
Mike Seibert Radio
   Podcast
M.Nat.
Tim Midura
John Mierau
Harpreet Miglani
Milk & Honey Comics
Miracle Man
Mirimele
Chris Mole
Ian Mondrick
Patrick Moniz
Caleb Monroe
Remi Monroe
Olivia Montoya
Jeremiah Monzon
Tucker Moody
Serpent Moon
Tory Morgan
Richard H Morgan
Shannon Morgan
Fionna Morningstar
Scott "politescott" Morrison
James Morrissey
Brooks Moses
Charles Moulton
Ryan Mount
Trevor Mueller
Robert A. Multari
James Mummert
Jonathan Mungeam
J.R. Murdock
Michael Murphy-Burton
Tim Mushel
LeAnna Nash
Hal J Neat
Alexandru Nedel
Neil Moherman Comics
Sean Neprud
James Nettum
Jessica New
Randall Nichols
Dianne Nicholson
John Nielsen
Marieke Nijkamp
Niki
Russell and Karen Nohelty
Nathan Nolan
Casey Nordell
Meredith Nudo
Parker O.
Steve O'Connor
George O'Connor
Mike O'D
Colin Oaten
Alannah Oldfield
oldirtyaustin
Ambly Ornis
John Osborne
Walter Ostlie
John J Ostrosky Jr
Léon Othenin-Girard
Steve Otrupcak
Outland Entertainment
Øydis
Michelle P
Alex P.
Ignasi P.
PJR
Andrew Pam
Ashley M. Papineau
Genevieve Paquin-Saikali
Purple Parfait
Richard Parker

Casey Parkhurst
Jeffrey Parkin
Landen Parkin
Casey Parsons
John Fletcher Pasquini
Ernesto Pavan
Robert Peacock
PedroAsani
Courtney Penn
Wilee Penner
David Pepose
Jamie Perez
Patch Perryman
Einar Petersen
Eraklis Petmezas
Ben Petrila
Chris Pfeifer
Steve Pheley
David Phelps
Lil Phil
Gary Phillips
Jim Phillips
Marco Antonio Piana
Nick Piers
Mercury - Stitch - Pisco
Carolyn Poddig
Martijn Poels
JP Polewczak
Nicholas Poonamallee
Marie & George Popichak
Comic Book Poser
James Post
Jillian Powell
Damon Priest
S L Puma
Mary G. Puppo
Ryan Q
Zack Q.
K. Qing
Jack Quader
Jason Song Quinn
Jorge Quintana
Oliver. R
d e raga
Alan Ralph
Cat Rambo
G. Ranaweera
Randall
Karthik & Ranjani
Joe Ranoia
Mike Rapin
Eric Ratcliffe
the Raymonds
Crazy Matt Reed
Kyle Reid
Carolyn Reid
Derek Reinhard
Remnant
Esther Rhatigan
John Rice
Andrew Richards
Gary Rickelman
Dan Rivera
Jade Robeck
Anika Robinson
Scott Robowski
Jose Rodriguez
Randiman Rogers
Jonathan Romo
Faith Roncoroni
Rene Rosa
Josh Rose
Adam Rose
Jason Rose
Zach Rosenberg
Frances Rowat
Wendy E Rowe
Jeremy Rowland
Scott Rowland
Rusty Rowley
Nick Rumaczyk
Cristov Russell
Katherine S
Sabrina-Delphine S.
Catherine S.

Maher Saadeldin
   (CrimsonMaher)
Jason Saito
Aaron Sammut
Will Sanborn
Chris Sanchez
Sanders Family
Joshua "Bürdmän" Sanders
Niraj Sanghvi
Fabrice Sapolsky
Rahadyan Sastrowardoyo
Jaymes Sattler
Tim Sauke
Regine Sawyer
Scott Schaper
Xander Schrijen
Jake Schroeder =)
Wendy L Schultz
Evan Schultz
Carrie Schurman
Roy Scopazzi
Seamas
Hannah Searle
Donald Yasuo Sekimura
Colin Seymour
Shahazadei
Caitlin Shaw
Shervyn
Anna Tiferet Sikorska
Simon
Bobby Singer
James Sinor
Nick Sladden
Judith the Tank Slayer
Gavin Smith
Jed Brooks Smith
Peter Smyk
Dedren Snead
Dave Snowdon
Diana Soderling
John Sollitto
Kadee Spangler
spiritbane
Michael Stagno
Starfang
R. Dylan Stewart
Charlie Stickney
Anne Stinson
KET Strait
Immortal Studios
Sebastian Suarez
Erin Subramanian
summervillain
Matthew Summo
Karen Lytle Sumpter
Sham "Dantallian" Suri
Kyle Swaffar
Switch
Jesse James Tapia II
David A. Tauster
Tyler Taute
Rico Taveras
floriano taviani
Team Metalshark Bro
Erika Terriquez
@TheCruZader
Reggie Themistocle
Eric Thomas
Cece & Thor Thomas
Toi Thomas
Mark Thompson
Timber
The Tobias Family
Anodyne Tolson
Michael Tomasulo
topnwe
Tora
Pascal Tremblay
Alex Trembley
Al Truistic
Mochi and Tucker
Aaron Turko
Nigel Twumasi
Charles Ullman
Vince Underwood

Sleepington Unicorn
Benjamin Urch
Zathras do Urden
Vadjong
Kalev Vaigro
Cato Vandrare
Amanda Vernon
Elias Villa
John A. Vincent IV
Andrew Vine
Hauke von Bremen
Jared Voss
Gaëtan Voyer-Perrautl
Paul W.
David F. Walker
Alan Waltrip
Kevin Ward
Blaze Ward
Matthew Roger Noah Ward
Christopher Ware
Everett A Warren
Trey Washington
Paweł Wasilewski
Vernon Welles
Craig Welsh
Lee Werrin
Colin Westerfield
Mandy Wetherhold
Michael James Wheeler
Christopher Wheeling
Daniel Whiteman
Zachary Whittaker
Michael Wick
T.J Wiley
Daniel Williams
Lily Williams
Matthew Williams
Elaine Wilson
Akil Wilson
Paul Wilson
Susan Wilson
Wingless Comics
Joe Allen Winn III
Javier Cruz Winnik
Jacob Wisner
CM Wolf
Andrew P. Wolk
Cindy Womack
Wade Woodson
Wuppy
S. Wyatt
Sean Wynn
Raymond Yamamoto
Yankeevic
Ian Yarington
Ellie Yee
Boyan Yordanov
Yancy Young
Paula Z
Sarah Ziemer
Aviv Leo Zippin

Retailer Backers

Challengers Games
   and Comics
Columbus Comics
Excalibur Comics
Olympic Cards
   and Comics
One Stop Comic
   Shop
Rick's Comic City
Royal Collectibles
Urban Legends
   Comic Shop